Your
Florida
Garden

Your Florida Garden

Fifth Edition

John V. Watkins and Herbert S. Wolfe

UNIVERSITY OF FLORIDA PRESS

Gainesville • 1968

A University of Florida Press Book

Library of Congress Catalog Card No.: 68-23403

PRINTED BY STORTER PRINTING COMPANY, INC.
GAINESVILLE, FLORIDA
BOUND BY UNIVERSAL-DIXIE BINDERY, INC.
JACKSONVILLE, FLORIDA

Preface

G ardening in Florida is not like that of other states—nor, in many ways, is gardening in northern Florida the same as in southern Florida. For this reason the garden guides written for northern conditions are a hindrance rather than a help to Florida gardeners. There has been no book to which we could refer the innumerable inquiries about what and when and how to plant and care for gardens in Florida as a whole, although there have been some admirable guides to garden practice in parts of Florida. In particular, available books have failed to stress the fact that the gardening year starts in autumn in Florida, instead of in spring as it does farther north.

The present book has been written in the attempt to fill what was felt to be a serious need for a book on ornamental gardening in Florida. One of the authors has had twenty-seven years of experience in gardening in the northern part of the state, while the other had eight years of garden experience in the extreme southern area and has had fifteen years of northern Florida activity. Both have traveled all over the state many times, observing gardening. We hope earnestly that these results of our experience and observation will make gardening in Florida easier and more satisfying to many other gardeners.

JOHN V. WATKINS
HERBERT S. WOLFE

August 7, 1954
Gainesville, Florida

Preface to the Fifth Edition

It is fourteen years since this book first appeared, and gardening is not static. For this fifth edition the text has been extensively revised to bring it up to date. Many new species have been added, and bromeliads are now discussed in the chapter on orchids. A small section has been included on gardening for retired people—a need which has become increasingly apparent. We hope that the book will be more useful than before.

February, 1968   J.V.W.
Gainesville, Florida   H.S.W.

Table of Contents

Tables and Charts

Figures

Introduction

OVER MUCH OF THE UNITED STATES gardens in growth and bloom are limited to the summer months, and for the remainder of the year they are tucked beneath a blanket of snow—their plants, so gay in summer, dead or inactive. There is no snow covering in many other areas, but in them soil and air are so cold that plants make little or no growth and garden surfaces consequently are sear and brown for several months.

Not so in Florida, where plants of one kind or another are not limited in growth to the summer season. Gardening can and should be an all-year-round undertaking. There must be, of course, no cessation of care and labor, but plants selected to fit the seasons can be grown and brought into bloom and the garden can be kept green throughout the year.

To those who have learned the details of gardening in cold climates, gardenmaking in Florida may be confusing. Much will have to be learned and often unlearned if success is to follow effort. For them, *Your Florida Garden,* written by two authors familiar with plants and gardenmaking in the state, is a book comprehensive in its coverage, dependable in its details. To it, as well, those initiated in the intricacies of Florida gardening may

turn with confidence for additional and sometimes sorely needed
help. A wealth of knowledge is found within its covers, and its
pages furnish information for all who would have fine gardens.
It is recommended to all who are interested in making their home
surroundings and the state of Florida more beautiful.

H. HAROLD HUME
Provost Emeritus for Agriculture
University of Florida

Gainesville, Florida
November 4, 1954

Strength may wield the ponderous spade,
May turn the clod and wheel the compost home;
But elegance, chief grace the garden shows,
And most attractive, is the fair result of
Thought, the creature of a polished mind.

—COWPER

Planning the Garden

A GARDEN CAN AND SHOULD BE beautiful, but it will not become so without careful planning based upon sound principles of garden design. The term "garden" is here used as a synonym for the home grounds around a private dwelling, although certain portions of those grounds may be developed as special kinds of gardens also.

Garden planning reaches its highest development in landscape architecture, which was ably defined by one of its greatest exponents, the late Charles W. Eliot, as "an art whose most important function is to create and preserve beauty in the surroundings of human habitations." While this book does not pretend to be a treatise on landscape architecture, the principles of garden planning are those set forth by the masters of that art, and the creation and preservation of beauty are the aims also of all garden planning. The authors' desire is to enable the average owner of a small home to do, satisfactorily, his own garden planning, and certainly to maintain the garden properly. Should the garden plan be of such magnitude that the services of a trained landscape architect or qualified landscape nurseryman are needed, it is hoped that this book will still make for better understanding between homeowner and professional designer.

Little interest was taken in beautification of small home grounds in America until the latter half of the nineteenth century. Highly developed garden art was to be seen in the large estates of the wealthy; and distinctive garden styles were found at the plantation homes of the Old South, about the ancient dwellings of dons in St. Augustine, at the colonial mansions of Williamsburg, and in the California missions. These gardens were strongly reminiscent of the land from which their designers had come and were often very ornate, but were little suited to the needs of the owner of a small home. Only during the present century has there been keen interest in the beautification of the grounds of the average home.

The basic principles of garden design are the same in all sections of the country, for all sizes of property, and for all exposures. The way in which these principles are carried out will vary widely from one area to another, because of differences in plant materials, in styles of architecture, and in size and shape of ground area, but the fundamental concepts of good garden planning remain unchanged. Two aspects of this art that deserve special consideration are Garden Composition and Garden Areas.

GARDEN COMPOSITION

A well-planned garden is like a beautiful painting in that the effect on the beholder is largely the result of careful composition, even though the viewer is unaware of it. The principles of garden design rest, therefore, on the well-established principles of good artistic composition, and a brief discussion of composition should be helpful in understanding how to create a beautiful garden picture.

Composition may be defined as "the orderly arrangement of parts into a harmonious whole," and in the composition of the garden, we are concerned with the orderly arrangement of buildings and plants so as to produce harmony. In this orderly arrangement we give particular importance to three factors or forms of order—balance, repetition, and sequence.

Balance is attained when the interest is equal on both sides of an axial line, or when it is felt that the amount of interest of plant material on one side is about equal to that on the other (fig. 1). The axis is usually an imaginary line only, of which we are made conscious by creation of a point of focalization in the composition. This balance may be symmetrical if the materials on one side are exactly duplicated in kind, shape, and size on the other side. We call it asymmetrical if the masses of material on the two sides are similar in amount or interest although different in kind and shape. Asymmetrical balance is also called occult balance, because the untrained observer is not able to perceive why there is a feeling of restfulness although he senses it.

To create a balanced garden composition is to develop a garden that will be greatly admired even though visitors may not know *why* they like it. Occult balance may be illustrated by a garden scene in which a flowering dogwood on one side of the picture is balanced in interest by a large group of Fielders White azaleas or Alba plena camellias on the other side. It is easy enough to see that flowering dogwood trees of equal size on each side of the axis balance each other, but it is usually necessary to point out to the novice in garden design that the dogwood and azaleas balance also, just as a tall slender boy may balance a short fat boy on a teeter-totter.

Repetition means that the same part of the picture is repeated, so that our attention is drawn to this element. Pickets in a picket fence illustrate repetitive order, as do the plants in a hedge of aralia or arbor-vitae. Repetition of this sort assures harmony, but only at the expense of monotony. On the other hand, unrestrained variety in planting lacks orderliness and needs repetition. An example is the widespread use of variegated crotons in southern Florida. Mixed crotons, no two alike, give much warm color and avoid monotony; but there is no feeling of repose in this type of planting without any pattern— it does not make a good composition. Monotony may be avoided by rhythm, or the occasional alternation of two or more plant forms, such as the use of snow-white spirea at studied intervals in a border of deep-colored azaleas.

Sequence means a succession of repeated plant forms, plant

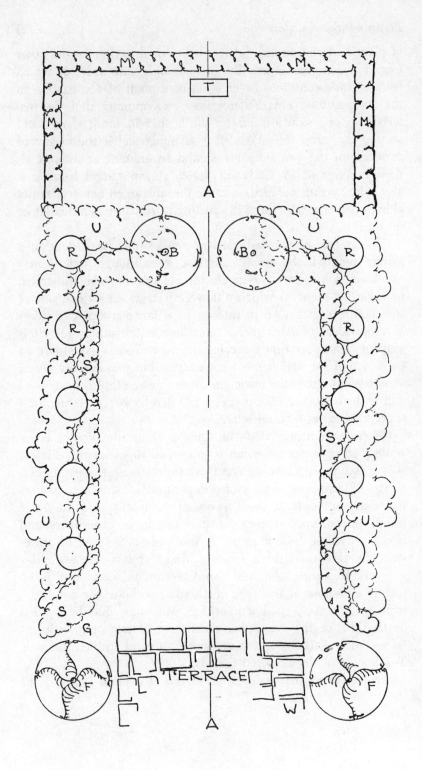

FIGURE 1 (*opposite*)

A SYMMETRICAL PLAN ILLUSTRATING PRINCIPLES OF GARDEN ART IN WHICH OVEREMPHASIS IS EMPLOYED TO ASSURE UNDERSTANDING OF PRINCIPLES. PLOT SIZE—38′ x 70′.

A AXIS. — The line around which parts are arranged in orderly fashion. This line leads the eye to T, the terminus or center of interest. Axes are ignored in many present-day gardens.

B BALANCE. — Matched flowering trees stand at equal distances from the center line to give symmetrical balance, to frame, and to help lead the eye to the center of interest T. In occult balance, one tree might be replaced by a strong group of flowering shrubbery.

F FRAMING. — Palms frame the garden composition at the sides with their trunks, overhead with their fronds, underfoot with their shadows. When the house is viewed from the far end of the garden, these palms frame the terrace W, and the glass-walled Florida room.

G GROUND COVER. — Well-tended grass is the perfect foil for plants in the garden composition.

M MONOTONY. — Clipped hedges of a single species illustrate repetition, which in this example results in monotony, a wearisome sameness.

R REPETITION. — This is an art form that is needed to assure harmony and unity U. Here, flowering shrubs, possibly with white blossoms, help hold the plan together as the eye moves from one to another.

R RHYTHM. — Movement marked by regular recurrence is represented by the same symbol. There is no conflict of interest, no spotty effect, in this simple arrangement.

S SEQUENCE. — A series with continuity. Flowering shrubs, arranged by color, make for continuity from one color group to the next.

S SIMPLICITY. — An essential in all compositions, is difficult to achieve.

T TERMINUS. — An axis or a view line ends at the center of interest. This is frequently lacking in gardens.

U UNITY. — Harmony, a totality of related parts, is illustrated in this planting plan.

W WEIGHT. — The flagged terrace just outside the Florida room has sufficient weight to support the scheme and relates the house with its garden.

groups, or color masses so that the interest of the observer is carried in orderly progression from one to the next.

In selecting plant materials for the garden composition, consideration must be given not only to size, shape, and color, but also to texture. Texture ranges from coarse to fine and refers to the size and arrangement of leaves and twigs. Oleander leaves are large and stiffly held on thick branches, making coarse texture. Casuarina (or Australian-pine), equally as common and as easily grown, has slender, almost leafless, green branchlets clustered closely together, and so has fine texture. Too abrupt transition from coarse to fine texture must be as carefully avoided as too abrupt a change from tall to short plants.

The house is a central feature of the garden composition, and its location and orientation deserve more planning than is often given. We may buy a lot because of its fine shade trees, because it is near friends, because it is on the shore of a lake, or for some other excellent reason; but too seldom do we consider the way the street runs and how the house must face. This should be an important consideration to discerning homeowners. In Florida, some will want their homes to face north, so that azaleas, camellias, and dwarf hollies can be employed for the foundation planting along the front. Others will wish to have the house face east to meet the rising sun. Still others will be concerned that the house be oriented so that the prevailing evening breeze from the southeast may enter the bedrooms. Some will want the living-room windows to look out over a body of water, regardless of the compass direction. Perhaps, if one could have trees for shade on the south and west, a lot on which the house faces north would be the most desirable choice in this land of intense sunlight. However, the question of orientation is one for each family to solve to its own satisfaction. With attic fans or air conditioning so easily installed, the direction of the prevailing breeze is less important than formerly.

Many modern Florida homes are comparatively small, compact houses, more or less centered on level, rectangular lots. With such homes it is unquestionably best to use simple, restrained plantings. Very long sheared hedges, ornate geometric flower beds, and clipped evergreens are seldom appropriate in Florida. In the case of the popular rambling ranch houses, the garden composition should be naturalistic, with no symmetry in the composition of plant materials (fig. 2). Rarely is the small home in Florida formal enough in architecture to require a formal layout of the grounds.

The architectural style of the dwelling house will influence garden composition, the kinds of plants, and their arrangement. It may influence the materials used in garden construction, for it is considered good design sometimes to project the lines of the house into the garden. If the house is of masonry, major walls may extend to enclose patios, service areas, or game lawns. In such cases the material, texture, and color of the house itself are repeated harmoniously in the garden. Detached garages, swimming pool cabañas, and other structures also give opportunity for such repetition.

Each garden picture of importance is viewed from a door or window that frames it. For this reason the location and size of such openings should be carefully considered in their relation to the garden plan. There should be a focal point to catch the eye as one looks out from the door or window, thus establishing an axis or line of view around which the garden composition is developed. For this focal point one may employ a small flowering tree, a showy shrub, a well-designed birdbath, an ornamental gate, or a sundial. A vista of this sort should always be stopped by some such backdrop as a shrub border or a wall, except where an opening in the backdrop gives opportunity to use a view of distant hills or of water as the focal point.

Good garden design does not end, however, with satisfactory composition of the picture. The garden plan must be useful and functional as well as lovely. Useless ornamentation in the garden, like the gingerbread of houses built in the eighteen-nineties, is considered bad taste, and today every shrub or bed of annuals must be planned with an eye to its purpose in the whole garden plan. Graceful curves and pleasing color combinations are wanted still, but simplicity is the keynote of modern garden design.

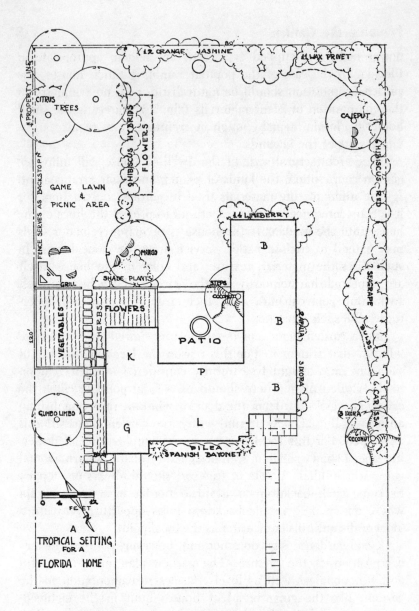

FIGURE 2

A TROPICAL SETTING FOR A FLORIDA HOME

Here, tropical plants are suggested so that the spirit of the landscape will be reminiscent of hot countries. Plant materials have been kept to a minimum as dictated by contemporary practice; yet there are enough plants to frame the house, supply good transition, insure privacy of the out-of-door living area, and to furnish fruits, flowers, and vegetables for the table.

Garden areas

Well-designed home grounds today usually consist of three subdivisions or unit areas, all of which are considered indispensable for the most agreeable and efficient use of the garden by homeowners. These three are: the public area, the private area, and the service area. The relative size of these areas will vary with the particular family, and in planning them, the needs and interests of the whole family must be considered carefully. Usually, the private area will be largest and the service area smallest, but some homeowners may feel it more important to set off the fine house front by a deep lawn than to have a large private area. In a rural district or suburban home, where a vegetable garden may be preferred to a recreation space, the service area may need to exceed the others in space allocation.

The public area consists of the ground between dwelling and sidewalk, and is usually as small as ordinances allow. This setting for the house should be planted very simply with no fussiness or ostentation so that a dignified picture may be presented. The function of the public area is primarily to show the house to best advantage to passers-by. Usually the only woody plants needed are a few trees or palms for framing, background, and shadows, and a restrained foundation planting of shrubs for transition from lawn to house, with possibly a vine for wall decoration. These plants, permanent elements of the garden picture, may well be the most choice and costly plants in the whole design. It is these plants that make the first impression on your guests, as well as the only impression that others receive, and you can well afford to expend thought on their selection and time and care on their maintenance.

The composition of the plants used to decorate the street façade is framed above by the heads of trees, at the sides by their trunks, and at the bottom by their shadows. Usually, shade trees are best placed behind and on either side of the house. Sometimes, informal groups of small broad-leaved trees or palms may stand in the front lawn to subdue large wall spaces and focus attention on the front door, but only when the latter is

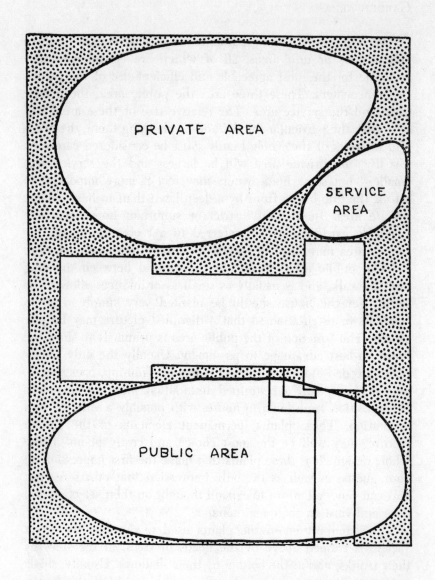

FIGURE 3
UNIT AREAS OF A TYPICAL FLORIDA PROPERTY

unusually well designed should this be done. All trees that stand alone are accent points, and very few of these are needed. If the house has good architectural lines, trees between it and the street are likely to detract rather than add to the composition.

The lawn contributes a great deal to the beauty of the public area and should be as nearly perfect as it is possible to make and maintain it. The function of the lawn is to form a pleasantly unobtrusive foreground for the house and its frame. It should therefore be free from beds of bright flowers, reflecting globes, and pink flamingos. In most parts of Florida, the front lawn can be level or gently sloping. If the slope is considerable, it is best to use retaining walls of stone or brick to keep a fairly level lawn in areas of sandy soil, since such easily eroded soil is not suited to terracing.

Entrance walks, good designers insist, should be straight unless there is a definite need for a curve. Undulating paths are popular with speculative builders, but although a great many are seen, this does not indicate that they are in the best of taste. Entrance walks should be constructed of materials that have character, durability, and a close kinship with the architecture of the house. Ordinarily, front walks should be about 5 ft. in width so that two people may walk side by side in comfort.

Bits of broken sidewalk laid insecurely upon the grass are hazards to safety and should never be employed. Visitors will concentrate upon the insecure footing and will be unable to enjoy the approach to the house because of the irregularities of the small, random pieces of concrete. Brick is a popular material that meets almost all our requirements for an entrance walk. Its color, interest, neatness, drainage, and durability are all excellent, and if it is laid in concrete, maintenance and replacement will be unnecessary even in Florida's light sands.

Flagstones are widely used and are usually in good taste. The individual pieces should be large and thick, and the outer edges should be set in straight lines with generous interstices for planting grass. Key Largo limestone and travertine are popular indigenous paving stones. Pine straw, appropriate with an informal cottage in a woodsy setting, is attractive when the

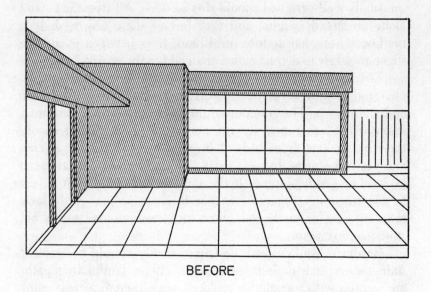

BEFORE

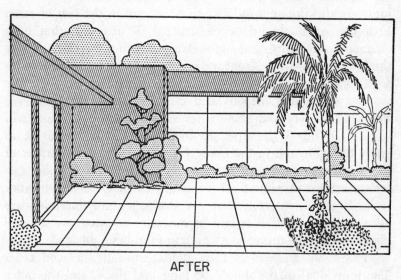

AFTER

FIGURE 4
EFFECT OF PLANTING UPON HOME ATTRACTIVENESS

Trees and shrubs, properly placed, can make a home more attractive and more livable.

edges are carefully kept in even lines by weekly attention with the rake. Concrete is a harsh substance that does not lend itself well to landscape use without special planning; it may be adapted by adding a pigment to give warmth and by casting it into generous-sized flagstones.

Many present-day small homes have carports or garages built directly into the front, and in the event that the lot is narrow, the driveway can well be used as the formal approach to the front door. A broad walk of flagstones or brick can branch off just in front of the planting by the corner of the garage or carport (fig. 3). Very often the paving of the carport driveway is the only smooth masonry upon which small children can ride wheeled toys, and each day this is a much needed play area.

Some people like curved driveways because they allow off-street parking and permit fewest possible steps from car to door. In some neighborhoods there is simply not enough street parking for the many cars owned by the families in the block.

For broad lots with deep set-backs, curved driveways of tinted concrete or asphalt are acceptable, provided parking aprons are beside the house, well back of the façade. It is the opinion of your authors that curved driveways are unsuitable with small houses on 100-ft. lots. Automobiles, whether they be shining current models or rusted jalopies, are inappropriate front-yard accessories. There, they hide from view the front door and its plantings, the very elements thought to be most important in landscape planning.

An important feature of the public area is the base planting, or foundation planting, as it is usually called. This is the grouping of plants which relates the house to the ground and to other parts of the landscape plan. Interest should be focused upon the building and not upon the plants themselves. Variegated species or those bearing intensely colored blossoms are therefore not usually employed in good base-planting compositions.

For houses that stand on piers, a continuous planting of hardy evergreen shrubs is almost essential. As daylight beneath a building may be disturbing, homes on piers are much improved by solid plantings of dwarf broad-leaved evergreens. Careful selection of species and unremitting aftercare are essential lest this type of planting get entirely out of hand. How often have you seen a tiny, white cottage hidden behind a 10-ft. hedge of wax privet? These hardy, cosmopolitan, broad-leaved evergreens were set by some well-meaning nurseryman as a part of the base-planting scheme, but the owner failed to do his part with pruning shears and nursery spade. As a result, the plants grew far out of scale for the little house.

Florida homes are often built on concrete slabs only two steps above ground level. With this type of construction, a restrained use of plant material is certainly in the best taste. Only a few plants are needed to make a pleasant transition from ground to house or to point up architectural details.

The arrangement of plants near a doorway is sometimes called the portal planting. Specimens chosen for this important position should be a low, rounded form, of fine texture, and deep and rich in tone, not boldly variegated, lest they detract attention from the door.

Selection of plants to be used near your home is worthy of your most serious consideration. Plants of open habit, those that are untidy and coarse, and those that grow rapidly or are bare all winter are not recommended for planting around Florida homes. It is better to select evergreens (broad-leaved or coniferous) of fine texture that are slow growing, resistant to disease and insects, and capable of withstanding sun and drought as well as shade and drip from the eaves. These plants, by adding interest, actually change the façade they are chosen to decorate.

As has been suggested above, the architectural style of the house influences strongly the choice of plant materials and their placement. For more than 200 years countless variations have been built, but in general, those houses with doors in the middle and broad windows spaced evenly in the walls of clapboard or brick are of Georgian influence. With a home of this type, most people admire plantings that display complete symmetrical balance—matched evergreens on both sides of the entrance, groups of hardy, dwarf evergreens or ground cover under the windows, and tall specimens at both ends of the building to give height and solidity. The back of the house usually is not symmetrical and here a more informal planting is in order.

While some of us admire symmetry in our houses, there are many others who prefer to own homes that do not demonstrate equilateral balance on both sides of the front door. These charming dwellings may be one or two stories in height, with the entrance off-center and window spacing that is quite unsymmetrical. Typical characteristics are brick or concrete-block construction; a balcony on two-story types; white roof; wrought-iron work, often painted white; a terrace of brick or tile across the front; and, frequently, a partly enclosed court in the rear. With such a house there must be no symmetry in foundation plantings, and rounded, informal masses of plants should be used rather than upright ones.

In tourist sections, tropical settings are desirable, and so palms, yuccas, crotons, hibiscus, and flowering tropical vines are widely employed. In Florida, palm shadows cast upon walls or turf contribute to the feeling of the tropics. Cacti, euphorbias, and century plants are much used with houses of contemporary design.

The second unit of the ideal suburban property is the private area or outdoor living room. This is usually the largest part of residential properties and the one that assumes the closest relationship with the family and its guests. This subdivision has grown out of the old "backyard," which all too often was a catchall for poultry houses, vegetable plots, fuel piles, incinerators, garbage cans, and other utilitarian but hardly ornamental items of household equipment. In its modern development with attractive borders and open central area, an outdoor living room is especially useful in Florida, where it is possible to spend so much of the time in comfort outdoors.

The needs, hobbies, and interests of the family must be carefully considered. These should be listed in detail so that the plan will contain areas that can be enjoyed by all members of the family group. Some will want a quiet, shady retreat for reading; others will prefer an open lawn for badminton or cro-

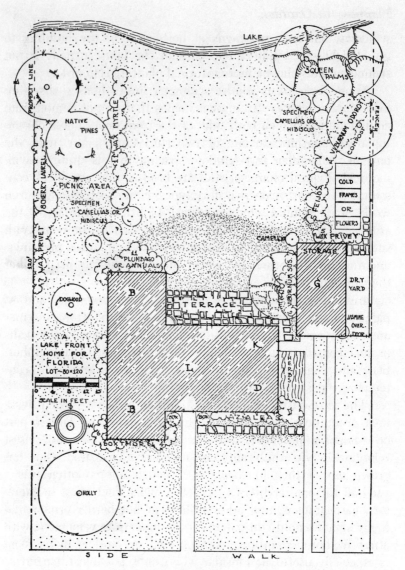

FIGURE 5
A LAKE FRONT HOME FOR FLORIDA

In central Florida, waterfront properties are favored homesites. This planting plan depicts a medium-sized lot (80 x 120 feet) situated between an east-west street and a lake. The land falls gently to the shore, making an interesting lawn as the foreground for a water view. Plants hardy in Central Florida, resistant to insects and diseases, and easy to maintain are indicated in this example.

quet, and perhaps a woodsy spot for an outdoor fireplace. Small children will need play equipment and perhaps a small enclosed area where pets may be kept.

Because of our enjoyable clear weather during the winter months, the outdoor living room might well have a southern or southwestern exposure so that it will receive the maximum amount of sunshine during the afternoon. Garden designers conceive of the outdoor living room as a continuation of the house, a charming extra room out-of-doors. Sliding glass doors opening from the living room or Florida room make an attractive way of entrance. Flagstones set into the ground act as a stepping place just outside the glass doors. The architecture of the house, the space available, and the wishes of the family will influence the treatment of the private area and its enclosing element. A side of the house with proper base plantings will serve as one boundary, possibly the garage or an ell of the house will become another, and the two remaining sides may be walled or planted with appropriate evergreen shrubs to make this a place of seclusion.

If a wall is decided upon, it should be of the same color and material as the house and should be high enough to assure privacy. Such an intimate walled garden may become a patio. In Chapter Two, patio gardens in Florida are discussed in detail.

For the boundary of the outdoor living room, the most popular device is the shrubbery border. From the English concept of landscaping, which preserves and interprets the natural character of the countryside, we have adapted this casual arrangement of plant material in its natural forms, derived from rural hedgerows. Happily, this simple style blends well with most types of small homes. Requiring a minimum of grading and the fewest possible accessories, executed with broad-leaved evergreen shrubs and flowering trees of informal growth habits, and most important of all, easily maintained by the owner himself, this style has been accepted wholeheartedly by suburban America.

As the painter frames his picture, so the garden planner groups annuals, perennials, or bulbs in the shrubbery bays to form separate minor compositions. Sequence, repetition, and variety are fulfilled in such arrangements. Perhaps five or seven plants of feijoa might merge into a group of three wax privets, which in turn would have as neighbors a colony of six oleanders. An interesting sky line is assured by using a group of palms for a flowering tree as an integral part of the shrub border. In this type of planting, the welfare of the individual gives way to the effect of the whole. Planting distances may be about 5 ft. for most broad-leaved evergreen shrubs, which, of course, will be grouped for transition of interest from one species to the next.

One function of enclosure is to exclude inharmonious scenes. On the other hand, sometimes a sense of freedom may be heightened by taking advantage of interesting scenes that lie beyond. In Florida, this often occurs when the private area overlooks an orange grove on rolling acres, a fresh-water lake, or a tidewater lagoon (fig. 5 and picture section).

Maintenance is just as important in this type of garden as in one of geometrically formal design. Even though a replica of a free landscape may be expertly planned and adequately executed, if it is allowed to grow untended, its grace and beauty will be lost.

The terrace as it is used in America today probably had its beginnings in rural England, where it has long been a part of the kitchen or vegetable garden. During the daytime this unit was used for household tasks, but on summer evenings, as the gathering place for the family, it became the center of rural domestic life. Usually a small tree protected a part of the terrace, the floor of which was covered with flagstones, brick, or gravel. Very often flowering vines adorned a part of the house wall. Designers use these devices in present-day versions of the terrace for small homes.

The terrace should be within the outdoor living area, adjacent to the living room or Florida room. It should be at the rear of the house, where there is sufficient seclusion from the gaze of neighbors and passers-by. When located just to the rear of the living room and reached perhaps through sliding glass doors, a terrace assumes an intimate relationship to the house and, at the same time, becomes the central point of introduction to the entire private area. In this position, harmony is achieved, and the terrace is very useful to the family. Florida houses that are built on concrete slabs only two or three steps above the grade present ideal transition from indoors to the terrace.

The longer dimension should be at right angles to the open central lawn of the private area, and should be built one step above the grass. In Florida, where rains are frequent and heavy, an impervious terrace floor is best. Flags of Key Largo limestone or coquina rock, brick set in concrete, or heart-cypress blocks set vertically into the ground are excellent paving materials. Grass, in narrow strips between paving stones, is always very desirable. A species of *Zoisia* will serve this purpose admirably. Gravel, pine straw, turf, and similar spongy materials are too retentive of moisture and are likely to be wet underfoot much of the summer.

The size of the terrace will be influenced by the architecture and size of the house, and by the size of the family and its activities. As a card table with four chairs might be considered minimum furnishing, with two more chairs for entertaining, a good size for the terrace of a small house might be 12 x 18 ft. A rectangular form is more pleasing than an exact square, and, as was mentioned previously, the longer dimension should be at a right angle to the major axis of the private area. To complement contemporary architecture, irregular free-form shapes are frequently seen.

Planting-holes, 18 x 24 in., can be left in the paving next to the wall of the house for dwarf, hardy, evergreen shrubs, perennials, and ground covers, as well as for dwarf palms or espaliered shrubs. Careful selection of plant material here is very important for good transition between terrace and garden.

By thoughtful planning and careful maintenance, homeowners can control, to some degree, the climate within their gardens. To do this, Floridians must work with Nature, using her vagaries of climate to every advantage in this planning. When you build a garden that is refreshingly cooler in summer, and warmer in winter than your neighbor's, you will have created a desirable microclimate.

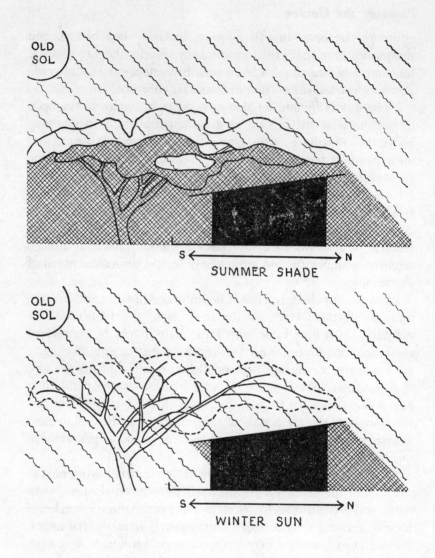

FIGURE 6
SUMMER SHADE AND WINTER SUN

A spreading deciduous tree, such as *Albizia* or *Delonix,* may furnish shade in the summer, but allow the sun to shine through in winter. Careful placement of specially chosen trees and shrubs is the first step in creating a desirable microclimate.

Since the beginning of time, trees have been planted for shade, and here in Florida shade patterns on segments of lawn are almost indispensable. Shadows upon your roof aid air conditioning and temper air drawn inside by attic fans.

Tall, hardy shrubs, needed to create privacy in the outdoor living area, also help to screen out sun, noise, dust, and wind. Living green walls are protection against winter winds, too.

Grass is not only the most beautiful and practical but also the coolest covering for the earth surrounding your house. Turf reflects less heat and glare than does masonry, and so does not raise air and house temperatures as much.

Pools, fountains, and cascades help to lend the illusion of coolness in hot-country patios and gardens, and although these water features are unreservedly commended for their beauty and gaiety, they lower temperatures very little. Actually, water in the garden increases humidity there, and humidity is Florida's greatest climatic torment. There is no way to reduce humidity outdoors. Gardeners cannot alter the climate as dramatically as engineers condition air inside, and so it is that many Floridians seek the comfort of air conditioning when it is hot and muggy and insects are about.

Of late years the hobby garden has come into being. Commuting gardeners develop keen hobby interests in a certain plant, such as camellia, azalea, holly, daylily, or hibiscus, and feature this favorite genus in the makeup of their gardens, particularly in the outdoor living area. At present, such hobby gardens are much in evidence and apparently will continue to have a wide appeal among men gardeners (fig. 5).

The service area, smallest subdivision of the well-designed suburban plot, should be incorporated with the kitchen entrance, the driveway, and the carport or garage. If a washer is housed in the utility room in the carport, it is essential that the drying lines be nearby. These should be of all-metal construction, aligned with the rear wall of the dwelling, and adequately screened from view. Aluminum clothes dryers, resembling giant umbrellas, supply maximum footage of line in minimum space.

The service area can be screened from the outdoor living

room and the street by a well-designed fence, a carefully tended hedge, or an informal shrubbery border. This last treatment is usually the least feasible because of the space that it must occupy. Plant materials used to enclose this diminutive area must be strict in habit so that they will occupy a minimum of space. They must be evergreen for permanent screening and resistant to pests so that maintenance will not be excessive. Aralia is useful in southern Florida; fern-leaf bamboo and upright types of evergreen privet may be used in colder sections. A louvered fence or one of lattice, chain link, or wooden saplings covered with a hardy evergreen vine may screen the service area. Fences are most economical of space and require little maintenance. With masonry construction, a wall which repeats the material and color of the dwelling is usually in good taste. A service area wall of whitewashed brick with a Crimson Lake bougain-villea falling over it is a sight long to be remembered.

Because of heavy traffic in the small space of the service area, flagstones or paving are recommended. Turf or ground covers are apt to be worn through in a short time in the utility yard. Pine straw can be used if the architecture of the house, the locale, and the exposure permit.

The service area can also serve as a pleasant play yard for small children. If this is to be one of its functions, a substantial but attractive fence is needed. A gate that reflects the spirit of the house and garden should be an integral part of this en-closure. A sandbox, swing, and other play equipment may be placed so that activities can be supervised from a kitchen window. Light shade from a small deciduous tree or a palm will be wel-come. More often a play space for children will be part of the private area (fig. 3).

The disposal problem may be solved by "dispose-all" sinks or by sunken containers whose heavy iron lids open by pressure on a pedal. These underground receptacles are by all odds the neatest, most sanitary, and least objectionable of all outdoor dis-posal containers. Fuel-oil tanks are usually the most prominent features of back yards. As most of these are set on high scaffolds, they should be within the enclosed service area, possibly further screened by a hardy but slow growing vine. Tanks for liquid gases or oils, fortunately, are buried underground, and their low filler caps are not objectionable.

The service area is also the place for growing vegetables and cut flowers, since these beds must sometimes look unattractive in order to serve their function. In the service area we ask only for neatness and not beauty (fig. 3).

Swimming pools, major features of many Florida homes, and "rock-'n'-sand" gardens are considered specialized architectural structures outside the purview of this book.

An overall plan, with attention to the principles of composition and to the functions of the three unit areas, will facilitate the development of the most satisfactory garden possible in a short time. This plan must reflect the needs and tastes of your family group, and it may be developed by following these steps.

You will need a pad of graph paper printed with eight divisions to the inch, a 100-ft. tape, and two friends to help with the measuring. As they measure distances from walls to lot lines and call out the figures, you put the lines on the graph paper to the correct scale. Do the same for drives, walks, terraces, trees, and other existing features. At this point you should have a plot plan that resembles fig. 18. If there is room for additional trees, draw in a few in strategic places, but don't overdo this or your garden will be too shady in future years. Now you are ready to design shrubbery borders that will give your property privacy and correct subdivision for different activities. Next, the foundation planting is drawn in to scale. The text of Chapter Seven will help you here. Finally, beds of annuals in shrubbery bays and plants for terraces, patio, and Florida room may be listed and indicated on the graph paper work sheet. It may be desirable to trace this working plan neatly on tracing paper and have this blueprinted as a permanent record.

2

Patios and Florida Rooms

THE WORD "PATIO" IS SPANISH and means literally "court-yard." The Romans and Greeks also had words for it, for the enclosed court, open to the sky and surrounded on all sides by the house, has been a feature of home life along the arid shores of the Mediterranean as far back as there is any history. The enclosing walls gave protection against the hot, dry winds, and the open courtyard gave light and fresh air to the rooms surrounding it, all of which opened onto it. Along one or more sides ran covered passageways, to enable one to pass around the patio from one room to another without having to endure the usual bright sun or the rare rain.

In the semidesert climate of southern Spain the patio was usually the only garden area, and the shade of its walls was welcome in that land of intense insolation and drying winds. Often the well in the center of the patio was the only source of water for the establishment, and a few potted plants and palms were all that could be watered easily. Because of the scarcity of water and the arid climate, plants in the patios of old Spain did not grow with the luxuriance they achieve in Florida patios. Paving was standard practice, since lawns were unknown, and glazed tiles, brick, cobblestone, and decorative mosaic were all used.

All these features are found in patio gardens of Florida, where Spanish types of architecture have long been in favor.

Becoming naturally a part of rambling L-shaped or H-shaped houses, the modern room-sized patio is popular as a part of our design for outdoor living, particularly for the housewife who wishes to reduce gardening to the minimum and yet have an outdoor garden. Always the patio is designed as part of the private area, not of the public area viewed from the street.

Mediterranean influence is still plain in the modern Florida patio, although the great dissimilarity of Florida's climate has naturally brought about many deviations from the Old World type. The house and garage usually form the enclosing walls on three sides, and doors from all rooms may open directly into the patio or into the corridor if one is present. The fourth side of the patio in Florida is often left open for a water view or for easy access to the garden. Sometimes rolling screens of structural glass may close this open side during cold weather. When the enclosing sides are formed by a rambling ranch-type house, the fourth side may be formed by a wooden fence with a wide, double gate, derived from the western corral. Windows and doors may or may not be grilled in the modern patio, but they should look across the court to pleasing compositions.

Paving materials popular in Florida patios include corraline Key Largo limestone, brick, glazed tile, terrazzo, simulated coral-rock, or some combination of these. Sometimes grass is used to cover the entire area, but because of heavy traffic in a small space, its best use is in chinks between paving blocks.

A flowing well or fountain is authentic as the central feature, but sometimes a specimen sea-grape or a palm tree becomes the dominant point of interest. Artesian water, available in some coastal areas, can be employed with telling effect in the central water feature, or city water may be circulated by a hidden electric pump so that it bubbles up in a central pool or fountain, flows down a tiled gutter to a sump, and is returned through a closed system for recirculation.

Shade is very desirable in a patio, and this need is best served by a tree that offers foliage as a sector of living roof to cool part of the patio and the house, yet allows a sunny corner for chilly days. Palms are traditional and very decorative, but they do not cast dense shade. If this be a requirement, a small tree such as loquat, sea-grape, or Brazilian-pepper might be a good selection.

Restraint may not be possible to achieve in patio plantings in Florida because of the luxuriance of growth in our humid climate, yet the character of a patio requires restraint. Plants should be used for wall decoration, for fragrance, for partial shade, and for color interest, but they must not encroach too greatly upon the space designed for human occupancy. Plants that will hug the walls and not sprawl about are best to use. Espaliered shrubs, although unknown in colonial Spain, may serve usefully for wall decoration. Flowering vines on trellises or held to the wall by fastenings of some sort are very popular.

Patio plants should have certain definite characteristics if they are to be successful year in and year out in Florida. They should have the subtropical feeling of the Mediterranean; endurance of restricted growing space; tolerance of dry soils, full sun, high temperatures, and drip from eaves; and resistance to pests. In addition, patio plants should be ones that do not quickly get too large and coarse for their stations.

Potted plants are traditional in patios to add color interest. They may be dwarf palms in urns, seasonal bulbs, annuals for winter color, gay foliaged herbaceous perennials, or succulents with interesting leaf forms. Wall brackets of wrought iron are often installed in groups, and in them are hung pots of blooming orchids, anthuriums, or bromeliads.

Orchids suitable for patio adornment are preferably not the huge hybrid cattleyas but rather the small-flowered spray orchids. These late winter and early spring bloomers are not particularly hard to grow in pots or wooden rafts of tree fern or osmundine, or naturalized on a patio tree. Careful potting after blooming, judicious watering, and control of scale insects should keep spray orchids in condition to produce large numbers of blossoms each winter. Genera especially suitable for patio use include *Coelogyne, Cyrtopodium, Dendrobium, Epidendrum, Oncidium,* and *Phalaenopsis.* (These and other orchids are discussed in Chapter Thirteen.)

PLANTS FOR THE FLORIDA ROOM

In our determination to integrate our Florida homes with the out-of-doors, we accent outdoor living rooms and patios, and use plants freely indoors. An early advocate of this idea was the well-known architectural writer Professor Talbot Hamlin, who wrote years ago: "Living greenery is often woven into the design of the building itself, . . . not to hide, but to enhance, . . . [to] become a part of a good building's architectural design, substituting reality for representation." A Florida room makes this free use of plants indoors very practical. This light and airy retreat, so well-known and so universally desired, is a comparatively large room on the garden side of the house with one or more glass walls. These may be jalousied or constructed of plate glass with sliding doors. Wide eaves shade the glass during summer months, and make it possible to have full ventilation day in and day out.

Flooring must withstand moisture, considerable traffic, and bright light. First choice with most Floridians is terrazzo in cool colors that harmonize with the décor. Useful and comparatively inexpensive is colored concrete, fashioned to the owner's taste by adding tinting powder as the slab is being finished. Other flooring materials include coralline Key Largo limestone, Crab Orchard stone, brick, ceramic tile, and vinyl and asphalt tiles. Unlike patio or terrace paving, the finished floor is set into concrete and not on the earth. For this reason and because of greatly reduced light, grass or other living ground cover cannot be used in interstices.

Plant bins, or planters as they are usually called, are integral furnishings of Florida rooms. Sometimes these run through plate glass walls to relate Florida rooms to the out-of-doors; sometimes these planters occupy substantial portions of the wall space. As room dividers, plant bins are pleasing arrangements. If provision cannot be made for built-in masonry planters, mobile ones of redwood or metal may be had in infinite variety. These movable types are ordinarily supplied with drip pans to catch irrigation water that runs through the growing medium.

If a vining plant is chosen for a mobile planter, vertical support, called a totem pole, is provided.

Sunlight is needed by all plants for the manufacture of food, yet some species require much less light than others. For indoor planters we must depend upon those species that will thrive at lower intensities. When possible, arrange planters near windows or glass walls, and group lamps and furniture against solid walls. Necessity may dictate that a special planter be designed with built-in fluorescent tubes above it as the sole source of light. Such an arrangement can be dramatic and dependable as a conversation piece, but to your authors, plant groups in natural light are more desirable.

Planters need not be expensive, but they must be carefully designed so that they look good in the building they are to complement and so that their occupants will thrive. Masonry holds first place in favor, with concrete blocks, brick, and Crab Orchard stone being the most popular materials of construction. To attain certain effects, ceramic tile may face vertical planter walls. (See the picture section.)

Outside planters are built without bottoms so that water will drain away freely, but indoors plant bins are on concrete slabs. Indoor planters that stand against outside walls should be fitted with several pieces of ½-in. copper tubing that lead through house walls to carry drainage water outside. Against inside walls, bins will be without drainage, and these must be carefully sealed at the bottom so that moisture will not spoil the floor.

After masonry construction has dried thoroughly, insides and bottoms must be waterproofed by painting with two coats of asphaltum. Bottoms and drainage tubes must be carefully sealed with plastic roofing cement so that water does not seep out onto the floor. As mentioned above, movable planters of redwood or metal are usually fitted with drip pans.

When you are ready to fill plant bins, install several inches of coarse gravel in the bottom, and top this with an inch or so of smaller stone. This will assure prompt drainage and good aeration of the growing medium.

Growing media will be selected according to need. If established foliage plants are to be kept in their containers and plunged to their rims (this is the best way), German peat moss is the best filler. The advantages of keeping your plants in their pots are that you can replace any that do not look good, and you can make new arrangements at will. German peat moss is powder-dry when you buy it, so thorough soaking is essential prior to any horticultural use. Level the substance a few inches below the rim of the planter. At once, pots can be buried in this moist element, then soaked for good contact.

If plants are to be knocked out of their containers and grown permanently in bins, the growing medium can be made by composting two parts of hammock soil with one part of rotted cow manure or sludge. Other satisfactory mixtures are garden topsoil and peat, or perlite and peat, in equal parts. A cupful of commercial fertilizer that contains minor elements should be mixed with each bushel. After planting, the growing medium should be firmed to stand about an inch below the container's edge.

Thorough soaking once a week will usually keep the bin contents sufficiently moist. During winter when heat is used, watering must be more frequent for indoor bins and for interior sections of through-the-wall planters. Once a day, plants indoors should be lightly fogged with water from an atomizer. A flit gun or the applicator sold with household insecticides or window cleaners will serve nicely.

Monthly applications of a high-analysis fertilizer dissolved according to printed directions should be made, and setting potted plants in the rain occasionally is an old-fashioned custom soundly based upon good reasoning. Dust is washed from the leaves, and accumulated soluble salts are leached from the soil.

Smooth-leaved foliage plants look smart when they are groomed with polish. Several oily preparations are for sale at your garden center, or, if you prefer, you can use skim milk. Carefully mop upper leaf surfaces with a soft cloth soaked with polish, but do not coat leaf bottoms with the oily film.

Periodic inspection is needed so that mites, thrips, mealybugs, and scales will be identified and controlled before they become numerous. (See Chapter Seventeen on pests.)

Even under the best conditions, plants indoors will eventually need to be taken outside for rehabilitation. Then, the planters can be re-set, possibly with other species to gain totally different effects.

Below are listed some dependable foliage plants; however, our list is far from complete, as Florida is particularly rich in plants that will grow indoors.

Aglaonema spp. AGLAONEMA. Malaya. Aglaonemas of 40 species, native to the Old World tropics, are represented in Florida by several forms. *A. costatum* is one of our very best foliage plants for reduced light; *A. commutatum* vaguely resembles dumb cane and endures drought and darkness; *A. modestum* is the popular Chinese evergreen. All are commended for Florida room plantings, either in their regular containers or set out permanently in planting bins.

Anthurium spp. ANTHURIUM. Tropical America. Although this genus of American aroids contains 500 species, only two or three and their hybrids are widely grown as indoor plants. Even these, under the best conditions, suffer because humidity may not be high enough. The spectacular colored spathes of *A. andraeanum* are favorites wherever seen, and they are well worth the effort that is required to produce them. Possibly anthuriums are best kept in their individual containers of osmundine or shavings and manure, and moved in and out of the Florida room as the condition of the plants dictates. Most spectacular foliage is borne by well-known, easily grown *A. crystallinum*. This can be planted in a bin with other species, and should endure there for some time as it is more tolerant of low humidity than other anthuriums. Watch for mites on anthurium foliage.

Aspidistra elatior. CAST-IRON PLANT. China. For places that have low light intensity, this old parlor favorite excels. Again in fashion now, aspidistra may be depended upon for that sunless corner of a planter indoors or outside. Sunlight cannot be tolerated, but otherwise the plant is not particular as to its environment.

Aucuba japonica var. 'Variegata.' GOLD-DUST TREE. Eastern

Asia. A tough, cold-tolerant, shade-enduring shrub that resembles a serrate-leafed, gold-dotted croton, this hardy plant grows in shaded outdoor sections of through-the-wall planters in northern Florida. Its boldly variegated foliage suggests its use for accent. Not widely available in our state, gold-dust tree could be ordered from nurseries farther north.

Brassaia actinophylla. SCHEFFLERA or QUEENSLAND UMBRELLA-TREE. Australia. (See the picture section.) One of the leaders in popularity for planters, both indoors and out, is this robust, tropical tree from down under. Tall trunks bear compound leaves of great size in graceful array. Tolerating drought and reduced light, and resisting pests, schefflera is rightly outstanding for tropical plantings. Seedlings are to be found in all nurseries, garden centers, and chain stores.

Chamaedorea elegans. HOUSEHOLD PALM. Central America. (See p. 119 and picture section.) One of the truly dwarf palms that grows well in planters that get little or no direct sun and no chill, this little gem from our own tropics cannot be too highly recommended. Other species of the same genus are popular, too.

Chrysalidocarpus lutescens. CANE PALM. Madagascar. (See p. 119 and picture section.) No palm is more admired for household use than this beautiful, plumy, cluster palm from the Old World. Notable as a single specimen in a redwood planter or decorative urn, cane palm also serves well as a part of a mixed planting in a large bin. It is not tolerant of cold or salt and is very subject to attack by mites, thrips, and mealy-bugs.

Cissus spp. CISSUS. Tropics of both hemispheres. Some 200 species make up this genus of graceful, tendril-bearing vines that gives us kangaroo-ivy (*C. antartica*), grape-ivy (*C. rhombifolia*), and others that so willingly spill over the edges of bins to soften the harsh top lines. Tolerant of shade and usual indoor growing conditions, cissus vines may be attacked by mites, thrips, and mealy-bugs.

Cordyline terminalis. TI. Eastern Asia. Showy, persistent leaves of many colors and shapes are held by distinct, clasping petioles. Cultivars are numerous, their names unfortunately confused. Often miscalled dracenas, cordylines must be classed with Florida's most popular patio plants. They are very sensitive to cold.

Crassula spp. CRASSULA. South Africa. Over 250 species of these attractive succulents are known to science; of these, Floridians may use half a dozen for shady planters. The main thing in crassula culture is to avoid over-watering. Alone or in mixed plantings indoors, these little thick-leaved shrubs are most attractive.

Dieffenbachia spp. DIEFFENBACHIA. American Tropics. (See p. 193 and picture section.) Without superiors as plants for your Florida room, the several forms of dieffenbachia, widely available at garden centers, are commended without reservation. These bold, tropical plants grow well without direct sun, and moderate moisture and humidity fill their needs. Mealy-bugs must be controlled.

Dracaena spp. DRACENA. West Africa. (See picture section.) Widely variable in leaf form, size, and color, dracenas for many planter uses can be found at garden centers. Moist soil and rather abundant light are requirements for success. A leaf-spot disease and mites may give trouble.

Ficus spp. RUBBER-TREE or FIG. Southeastern Asia. (See pp. 103 and 163.) Though these are tropical trees of gigantic size, some evergreen figs are among the most popular urn subjects because of their bold leaves and their great tolerance of shade and drought. Popular in the Victorian era as the front parlor India rubber-plant, today, with contemporary architecture, tropical figs are wanted for freestanding urns and for mixed planters as well. Well liked are *Ficus elastica,* with its shiny green leaves, and its varieties: Decora with broad, rich foliage, Doescheri with variegated leaves, and Belgica with reddish new growth. Fiddle-leaf fig (*Ficus lyrata*) is much seen in illustrations in home and garden magazines, and it is, as a result, in great favor for large urns. *Ficus benjamina* and other landscape trees can be used in large containers in your Florida room as well.

Hedera spp. IVY. Europe and Northwestern Africa. (See

pp. 163 and 262 and picture section.) For softening the upper edges of plant bins and to cover the earth in them, nothing can surpass the true ivies. Growing in low light intensity and moderate moisture indoors and out, ivies in two species and many varieties can be had in small pot-plant sizes. The unusual bigeneric hybrid, fatshedera, grows with a thick, upright stem and large, star-pointed, attractive green leaves. Hardy to cold, fatshedera is well liked for shaded outdoor planters.

Monstera spp. MONSTERA. Tropical America. (See p. 165 and picture section.) Ceriman (*M. deliciosa*), with huge dissected leaves, is without peer as a planter specimen. A section of tree fern trunk or palm stem as a totem pole should be inserted for the huge, jointed stem to cling to as it grows upward. A juvenile form, with smaller, less deeply dissected leaves, is frequently seen in mixed planters. Swiss-cheese plant (*M. friedrichstahli*) has thin, light green, oval leaves with elliptical holes ranged on both sides of the midrib. This exotic climber also needs a totem pole for support.

Peperomia spp. PEPEROMIA. Tropical America. (See picture section.) For edgings outdoors in southern Florida and for covering the earth in planters, these diminutive succulents serve well. Reduced light, moist soil, and freedom from frost are necessary. There are more than 500 species in the genus, but Floridians grow only a dozen or so varieties. Some of these have foliage variously mottled with cream or puckered and folded into attractive patterns.

Philodendron spp. PHILODENDRON. Tropical America. (See p. 165 and picture section.) Without question, the leading genus for your Florida room is *Philodendron*. This highly variable group of plants, containing more than 200 species and countless varieties, brings new glamour to the interiors of our Florida homes. In frost-free sections philodendrons thrive outdoors; inside our houses they endure conditions that would be fatal to less tolerant plants. This diverse genus contains rampant vines that will cling to rough walls or totem poles, and self-headers that will remain rosette-like for several years. Leaf forms, colors, sizes, and rapidity of growth are infinite in their array. Surely, a philodendron can be found to fill almost every indoor planting need. Tiny potted plants are for sale in your dime store, but if you seek a sturdy, established specimen for a specific need, you may find it at your garden center.

Polyscias spp. ARALIA. South Sea Islands. (See p. 155 and picture section.) Southern Florida's most popular hedge plant may be taken inside for planter use. This ubiquitous shrub, available in so many leaf forms, endures conditions indoors quite well and can be depended upon for several years if the location is not too dark. Eventually lower leaves will fall, the stem will elongate, and the result will be a tall, leggy individual that you will want to replace with something more compact.

Sansevieria spp. SANSEVIERIA. Tropical Africa. (See p. 200.) If there is a group of plants to rival old-fashioned aspidistra in durability, it is this genus of 50 species. Stiff, erect, succulent leaves grow from horizontal underground stems to give a bold effect. The popular little bird's-nest sansevierias form compact rosettes of broad foliage about 8 in. high. Leaf forms vary, and coloring in different arrangements is characteristic of these foolproof house plants. Much used out-of-doors in tropical lands, sansevierias may grow in planters, or they may stand dramatically alone in their own containers indoors in colder climates. If the design of the foliage meets your need, sansevierias should find a place in your Florida room.

Scindapsus spp. HUNTERS-ROBE. Old World Tropics. (See p. 166.) In southern Florida these tropical lianas are trained on palm trees for the curiosity of their huge blotched leaves. In Florida-room planters they serve well too, when vines with mottled foliage are needed. Totem poles should be furnished for these climbers to cling to. Several forms are for sale.

Setcreasea, Tradescantia, Zebrina, and related genera are ever popular tender succulents from our own tropics, much used as ground covers, patio plants, edgings, and for Florida-room planters. Here belong the ubiquitous wandering Jew (p. 266), oyster-plant (p. 199), seersucker plant, dichorisandra, and more. Alone in small containers, or to cover the earth and droop over the edges of planters, these tender herbs are ever useful. Cuttings, so easily rooted anywhere, are frequently available from friends.

Spathiphyllum spp. SPATHIPHYLLUM. Tropical America. For the amateur who wants aroids that give the general effect of a white anthurium, without its temperamental qualities, these little thin-leafed perennials are most highly commended. Almost sure to behave well in a moderately bright spot in a Florida room, spathiphyllum grows well either alone in an urn or in a made-up planter. For this one, you will have to inquire at your garden center for an established plant. Be on the lookout for mites and mealy-bugs, and take steps to eradicate them at very first signs.

WINDOW BOXES

Window-box gardening is an extremely simple and satisfactory way of adding an interesting composition to a cottage wall, and for apartment dwellers it may be the only type of gardening possible.

Proper construction of a box for window or porch is very important. A box of heart cypress or redwood which has received two coats of asphalt paint or copper naphthenate on the inside as a preservative will last for many years. It is well to strengthen the interior corners with galvanized steel angle braces, as wet soil is quite heavy. For good drainage, half-inch holes should be drilled at intervals of a foot along the center of the bottom, and then the bottom should be covered with an inch of gravel to assure free movement of water without letting the soil wash through. Durable yet decorative brackets of wood or wrought iron should be used to support window boxes. Patented steel or aluminum boxes may be purchased, in sizes and shapes to suit your need, in garden centers, chain stores, and from mail-order houses.

Soil for window boxes, flower pots, or tubs should be high in organic matter. A very satisfactory mix can be made by composting two parts of hammock soil with one part rotted cow manure or sludge. Another satisfactory mixture can be made from equal

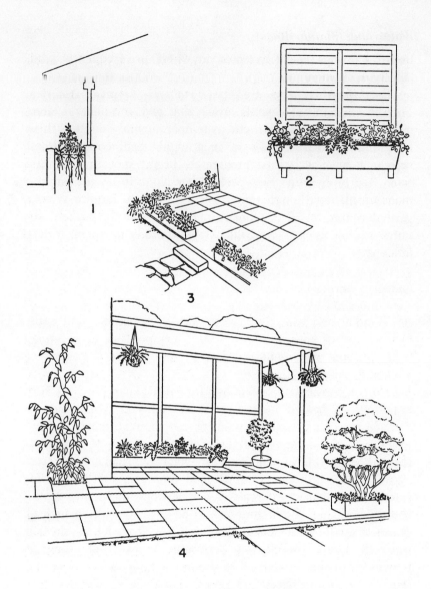

FIGURE 7
PLANTERS AND OUTDOOR BOXES

1. Outdoor planters are built without bottoms.
2. Window boxes add interest to jalousied windows.
3. Terraces may be brightened by low planters.
4. Plants in containers are popular garden accessories.

parts of garden topsoil and peat. A cupful of commercial garden fertilizer that contains minor elements should be mixed with each bushel of composted soil. After planting, the soil should be firmed so that it stands about an inch below the edge of the container.

Thorough soaking once a week will usually keep a shaded porch or window box sufficiently moist. Boxes receiving direct sun must be watered more frequently. Monthly applications of liquid fertilizer discussed on page 29 will keep plants in vigorous condition.

To plant in shaded windows and in pots on porches, consider species recommended for Florida rooms (pp. 30-35). Of course, most of those plants cannot endure freezing. Ferns, particularly leather-leaf and maiden-hair, are all-time favorites for containers not exposed to sun, and their botanical kin, the selaginellas (p. 264), make attractive, lacy foliage plants as well. Begonias of all kinds are leaders in popularity, and some ground covers discussed in Chapter 12 are widely used as pot plants in sheltered places. Among bulbous plants, amaryllis, Amazon-lily, blood-lily, hurricane-lily, ranunculus, and caladium make fine pot plants for shady porches.

Sun-tolerant plants are also needed for window boxes and porches, and many annual flowers thrive in sunny boxes, among them ageratum, lobelia, nasturtium, balcony petunia, portulaca, sweet alyssum, torenia, and verbena. Geranium and weeping lantana are dependable materials for perennial use in sunny boxes, and many bulbous plants that thrive in the sun can be flowered satisfactorily in porch or window boxes. Among these are calla, Dutch iris, Easter lily, freesia, montbretia, narcissus, Roman hyacinth, snowflake, star-of-Bethlehem, and zephyr-lily.

3

Soil, Fertilizer, Water, and Temperature

THE ART OF GARDEN DESIGN concerns only the appearance of plant materials in relation to each other and to the buildings in the landscape picture, but the gardener must know more than design if his garden is to be successful. He must know what will be the effect on his plants, and on their appearance in the future, of the conditions under which he tries to grow them. The Florida gardener, therefore, must know how to create the most favorable environment for his plants. That means that he must study the soil conditions, moisture conditions, and temperature conditions found in his particular section of Florida.

Soil

It is perfectly possible to grow fine plants in the absence of soil, but it is very expensive to do so, and few gardens are planted in anything else. Soil is a term, however, that covers very many kinds of media for the growth of plant roots. Soils may be heavy clay or light sand or medium loam. They may be wholly of mineral origin (inorganic) or chiefly derived from decay of plants (organic). They may be fertile or sterile; well drained or poorly drained; and acid, neutral, or basic in reaction.

Florida has many soil types on which gardens may be planted. Most of the state is a coastal plain, rising to low hills in the backbone of the peninsula and in the northwestern part of the state. Few of these soil types are of great natural fertility, but most of them are capable of being made fertile. In the hills of northwestern Florida the soil is usually a red clay, in the peninsula it is a sand, and in extreme southern Dade County it is again a red clay, thinly scattered over a porous limestone. There are extensive areas of peat or muck and of marl, but few homes are located on such soils, however important they are to commercial vegetable and flower production. Good loam soils are very scarce in Florida, and whether sand or clay, the soils of Florida have been leached of plant nutrients for centuries.

Sandy soils constitute the bulk of Florida gardens, and these provide little more than anchorage for roots. If they are elevated enough to provide good drainage, they dry out rapidly; if low enough to have abundant moisture, they become flooded in rainy seasons. Organic matter has been lost as fast as it was added because of the combination of high temperature, high rainfall, and abundant aeration, and the thin sand offers little encouragement to growth of most garden plants. Deficient plant nutrients can be supplied from the fertilizer sack, but they will be lost quickly in turn. Our first step in improvement of soil conditions, therefore, must be to add organic matter.

Organic matter means the material of plant or animal origin that is added to the soil. The dark residue that decomposes slowly, after the bulk of the added material has been decomposed rapidly, is called humus and is one of the important components of a fertile soil. Perhaps this is a good place to point out that a fertile soil is one which produces abundant plant growth, and that fertility can only be measured by the way plants grow. There is a tendency sometimes to consider that an analysis of the plant nutrient content by a chemist will show how fertile a soil is, but such analysis covers only one of several factors that influence fertility. Soil acidity, organic matter, and drainage are other important factors.

Organic matter has several important values for sandy soils. One of the most important is the increase it makes in the ability of the soil to hold water. It acts like a sponge. It also prevents rapid leaching from the soil of the plant nutrients added as fertilizers, so that they remain available to plant roots for a much longer time Finally, it produces plant nutrients by its slow decomposition. No other treatment can do so much to make a sandy soil better for garden use as the addition of organic matter in large amounts.

There are many sources of organic matter. The Pilgrim colonists in 1621 learned from the Indians to put a fish in the bottom of each hill of corn, and fish residues are still among our best organic materials for fertilizers. Animal manures—cow, horse, sheep, or poultry—are widely used by gardeners, and would be much more used if they were more readily available. They have certain disadvantages besides scarcity, such as high cost, unpleasant odor, and content of weed seed, but when applied liberally to garden soil and mixed well with the top foot, they give splendid results. Animal manures are simply partially decomposed plant materials, and they are deficient in phosphorus and potash. Further decomposition of manure through composting should precede its garden use, in most cases.

Plant residues of various sorts may be used, either immediately or after composting. The term green manure is applied to plants grown on a plot of ground so that they may be plowed under for soil improvement just as animal manures are. Peat and leaf mold from the woods are splendid materials for improvement of sandy soils, but are often expensive or scarce. The largest potentially available source of organic matter for gardens is the compost pile of the gardener, but making this involves considerable effort on his part. All plant residues from the garden—weeds, replaced plants, fallen leaves—and kitchen wastes of fruits, vegetables, or meats can be composted to make a product as effective as animal manure but without its odor. Naturally the compost pile belongs in the service area.

A compost pile may be started at any time of the year, and added to as materials are available. It is necessary to keep the sides of the pile nearly vertical so that the top may remain almost flat. Thus it is usually necessary to have some sort of container for the pile. This may be a square or rectangular pen of boards or concrete blocks, or it may be a circle of woven wire fencing supported by a few stakes. It is better to make two small compost piles in succession than to start a large one that may take more than a year to complete. An enclosure 5 ft. square is a good size to start with, and it should be about 4 ft. high. Larger enclosures will simply require proportionally larger amounts of chemicals; for example, a pen 7 ft. square would need twice as much as one 5 ft. square.

Make a layer of material to be composted about a foot deep, wetting it down well with a hose if it consists of dry weeds and leaves. Then sprinkle evenly over the surface 12 lbs. of commercial fertilizer analyzing 6-6-6. This will be roughly 6 qts. of fertilizer. Then begin accumulating a second layer, and when it is a foot thick, apply another 12 lbs. of fertilizer. Repeat this process until the pile is 4 ft. high, and then start a new one. Do not allow the pile to dry out at any time, but keep it moist by use of a hose if rains are infrequent. After about six months the compost should be well decomposed and ready to be spaded into the garden soil.

Clay soils also benefit from addition of organic matter, but to less extent and for a different reason than sandy soils. Clay holds water only too well, and in consequence is often poorly drained. Organic matter improves the drainage and the penetration of air into clay soils, for plant roots need oxygen just as surely as animals do. A few plants can obtain oxygen rapidly enough from the small amount dissolved in water to enable them to grow in saturated soil, but most garden plants need well-aerated soils. Sandy soils are very well aerated if they are well drained, but clay soils often need aeration, even when they are elevated enough so that there is no problem of high water table.

As has been indicated above, supplying organic matter to soils in Florida is not something that is done once for all time; it must be done almost annually. The rapid action of soil organisms in a climate where the ground rarely freezes causes the organic matter added in one year to be gone for the most part by the next year. So each year the gardener must be prepared to add more humus to the garden soil. If there is a season when the garden, especially that part devoted to beds of annual flowers or vegetables, is not going to be in use for this purpose, the opportunity should not be lost to plant a green manure crop, such as cowpeas or crotalaria, to be spaded under. The ground given over to trees and shrubs cannot have organic matter mixed with the soil once the plants are in place, but mulching—discussed a little later in the chapter—will supply some constant addition of organic matter to the soil surface. Lawns that are not robbed of the clippings when mowed have therein a constant renewal of organic matter, but more may sometimes be added profitably in the form of peat, muck, or compost.

The reaction of the soil, meaning its acidity or lack of acidity, is another matter which the gardener needs to understand. Chemists express soil reaction by use of a scale running from 0 to 14, with 7 as the mid-point. This is called a pH scale; pH 7 means that a soil is neutral, being neither acid nor basic. Numbers below 7 indicate increasing acidity, and numbers above 7 show increasing basicity. The chemist has occasion to use solutions running the full length of the scale, but Florida soils cover only a small portion of it. Our sandy soils are naturally rather acid (pH 4 to 6), but they are easily changed to neutral or even slightly basic reaction (pH 8) by small amounts of lime. Sometimes a virgin soil, especially a flatwoods soil, is too strongly acid (pH 4) for most plants to thrive, but more often the problem in Florida gardens is with soils not acid enough. Most garden plants thrive at reactions ranging from neutral (pH 7) to slightly acid (pH 6) in sandy soils well supplied with organic matter. Several popular shrubs, however, including azalea, camellia, and gardenia, are unable to obtain enough of certain mineral elements, such as iron and manganese, from sandy soils which are not fairly acid (around pH 5). Clay soils yield these elements more readily at less acid reactions (pH 6 to 7) than sandy soils. Marl soils and shell sands are almost pure limestone and cannot be made acid, having always a basic reaction (pH 8 or above), and acid-requiring plants are not adapted to them.

A common source of annoyance to home gardeners is the lime spilled around the foundation when the house was built. If acid-requiring shrubs are planted as foundation plants without the soil having been dug out and replaced, they are quite likely to look yellow and sickly soon. Long continued use of water from limestone strata, from which nearly all Florida water supplies come, may change the reaction of greenhouse soil from acid to neutral, but in the open ground rains usually wash out this small amount of lime. Continued use of some types of fertilizers may cause loss of acidity, too. Whenever soil is too little acid for very sensitive plants, it may be made more acid again by application of alum or sulfur, or by lifting the shrubs and replacing the whole bed to a depth of 9 in. with acid soil. Use of organic matter in liberal amounts when making up shrubbery beds helps prevent rapid change in the reaction of sandy soils, and the constant production of weak acids from the decomposition of the organic matter is an important factor in keeping soils properly acid. In the rather infrequent case of soils too acid for good plant growth, the situation is easily and permanently corrected by application of small quantities of ground limestone. It is not so easy to make neutral soils acid. Sulfur is the material commonly used to increase soil acidity, but it acts slowly. An average sandy garden soil in Florida will be made properly acid (if it is not sufficiently so) by addition of 3 oz. of sulfur dust for each square yard treated, which will take one or two months for maximum effect. Clay soils require about double the above dose. The acidifying material should be evenly mixed in the top few inches if possible.

Fertilizer

Florida soils usually need large amounts of fertilizers. The predominant sandy soil never had much in the way of mineral elements for plant growth, and that little was long ago leached out. Florida's red clay soils are almost as deficient as her sands. Plants cannot grow without small amounts of certain minerals in the soil, but these minerals are not to be considered as food, in spite of the popular error of calling them "plant foods." They make up only about 5 per cent of the dry weight of plants. The true foods of plants are the same as those of animals—including humans—and consist chiefly of carbohydrates, proteins, and fats. Plants make their own foods, with certain exceptions unimportant to gardening, and also all the food of animals, which need the mineral elements as much as plants but count on getting them from plants in their food. The great bulk of plant food comes from the air and water alone, and the mineral nutrients are only raw materials that enter into some of the important plant and animal products. Many soils of the United States have such adequate supplies of mineral nutrients that none needs to be supplied by the gardener, but since Florida soils are almost wholly lacking in these nutrient elements, we must supply relatively large amounts. They may be supplied in the form of organic matter, but this is both expensive and troublesome if we try to supply all mineral needs in this way. The cheapest and easiest way is to buy commercial fertilizer mixtures.

Some gardeners have developed curious ideas about fertilizers, believing them to be harmful, and have theorized that only organic materials should be used to supply needed nutrients. Such gardeners simply do not understand the facts of plant life. Garden plants are unable to absorb through their roots any of the organic compounds in which nutrient elements may exist in plant or animal residues—and some elements never form any organic compounds anyhow. Organic matter must be decomposed by soil organisms until mineral elements are in the same chemical form in which they exist in the fertilizer sack before plants can take in the nutrients. Organic fertilizers have their place in providing a slow, steady rate of supply of certain nutrient elements, notably nitrogen, but plants are not more vigorous or productive if organic fertilizers are used than with proper applications of the inorganic fertilizers commonly employed. As a matter of fact, commercial fertilizer mixtures usually contain some organic materials, but these add greatly to the cost, if used in large amounts, without giving any compensation in plant growth. Organic matter is of great importance to Florida gardeners, but as a soil conditioner primarily, rather than as the source of nutrient elements.

There are over a dozen mineral elements that have been shown by scientists to be necessary for plant growth, but three are of chief concern to the gardener because they are deficient in all Florida soils except mucks. These are nitrogen, phosphorus, and potassium. They are called major nutrient elements because of the large amounts needed for plant growth. Mucks have plenty of nitrogen but lack nearly everything else. Nitrogen is not only the most expensive element in the fertilizer mixture but it is also more readily leached from sandy soils by rain than the other two. Organic matter in soil slows down the rate of leaching of nitrogen and supplies some by its decomposition, so that fertilizer applications are of more lasting benefit on soils with good organic matter content.

Nitrogen should be applied more frequently during rainy summer weather than phosphorus and potash. Many forms of nitrogen are commonly used as fertilizers, both organic and inorganic. Common organic materials are the seed meals (cottonseed, castor bean, etc.), slaughterhouse residues (dried blood, tankage, fish scrap), sewage sludge, and certain manures from fish-eating birds (guanos). These supply nitrogen slowly and are not soluble in water, so that large applications cannot injure roots. Common inorganic materials are nitrate of soda, sulfate of ammonia, ammonium nitrate, and urea. These are quickly available and are immediately dissolved in water, so that an overdose may severely injure roots. Long continued use of nitrate of soda tends to reduce soil acidity, while urea and ammonium sulfate tend to increase acidity of soils when used in large amounts over many years. Probably few gardeners encounter this type of soil reaction change. Deficiency of nitrogen shows up more quickly in plant growth than do deficiencies of other major elements, with yellowing of foliage the characteristic symptom. Plants making large amounts of leafy growth need abundant supplies of nitrogen.

Nitrogen moves down through the soil quite readily to a depth of many feet—indeed, to far below the root zone if rainfall is heavy. Potassium moves much less readily, even in a sandy soil, and phosphorus is fixed in insoluble form fairly near the surface. In making up plant beds, it is desirable to apply the phosphorus and potash on the surface before spading or plowing the soil, so that it is turned under to a depth of 6 or 8 in., since this places it at good depth for utilization by plant roots. In practice, it is usually not expedient for the small-garden owner to have several different fertilizer mixtures; therefore the one mixture he uses should be broadcast before turning the soil. After the plants start growth, he can apply, at periodic intervals, some readily available nitrogen, such as nitrate of soda, to keep up the supply in the soil for plants that grow rapidly and constantly.

Fertilizer mixtures commonly used in Florida are marked 6-6-6, 8-8-8, or some similar combination. These numbers indicate respectively the percentage composition of nitrogen (as N), phosphorus (as P_2O_5), and potassium (as K_2O). The latter two elements are often applied together without nitrogen in preparation for planting. Formerly these three elements were considered to be the only ones ever needed in garden fertilizers, but we have learned that such elements as iron, zinc, copper, magnesium, manganese, molybdenum, and boron may occasionally be so lacking in garden soils as to prevent normal plant growth. In commercial fruit and vegetable production these so-called minor or trace elements are very often needed for satisfactory crops, both in Florida and elsewhere; the home gardener is much less likely to encounter deficiencies. Largely this is because the home-garden soil usually has large amounts of organic matter added to it, and these elements—needed only in very small amounts—occur in the organic matter in sufficient quantity. Deficiency of iron for acid-loving plants, as discussed above, is the most common minor element trouble found in Florida. Where other nutrient deficiencies show up, they may be corrected either by applying fertilizer mixtures containing all the minor elements or by using fritted or chelated sources of the minor elements only. It is doubtful wisdom to add minor elements in either of these ways if there is no evidence from plant foliage that they are not being supplied by the soil.

Fertilizing garden plants involves knowledge not only of what to apply, but also of when and how to apply it. Woody plants normally make one or more flushes of growth a year, with a period between flushes when little or no visible growth is going on. Since the greatest demand for nutrient elements by ornamental woody plants is in connection with these growth flushes, it is considered important to have ample supplies of fertilizer available for plant use whenever a flush is made. Deciduous trees and shrubs usually make a flush only in spring, and it is usually sufficient to fertilize for this flush only, although on light, sandy soils a single application may not last as long as the period of active growth does. Evergreen trees and shrubs usually make either two or three growth flushes each year, and fertilizer should be applied so as to be available for each of these. Herbaceous plants usually grow continuously throughout the period of favorable temperatures and need a small but constant supply of available fertilizer during the whole growing season.

The availability of fertilizer depends on several factors, but the time of application in order to have it properly available is related to the form of nitrogen used. If the nitrogen is all in the form of organic materials—whether manures, compost, or commercial organic fertilizers—application must be made several weeks before the growth flush is expected. If fertilizer contains quickly available, inorganic nitrogen, it may be applied when buds are seen to swell for the flush. There is usually so little rain in Florida during the late winter that fertilizer may be applied well in advance of growth flushes without much likelihood of loss by leaching before the plants can use it. Where flushes are made in spring, summer, and fall, fertilizer may be applied in February, June, and September. Fertilizer for herbaceous plants is better applied monthly, beginning with the first indications of spring growth, until fall slowing of growth is evident or until the plants stop growth for any other reason. Special procedures for certain groups of plants are detailed in the cultural discussions of later chapters.

The quantity of fertilizer to use will depend largely upon the size of the plants concerned, and no general statements can be made. Hence this matter is left for treatment in the chapters on culture of various plant groups. The method of application usually is to spread the fertilizer broadcast over the ground. In the case of herbaceous plants, the material is spread evenly over the whole area of the bed. The same is true of shrubs in beds or borders. Trees and large specimen shrubs are usually fertilized individually, the material being spread evenly from near the trunk out to a little beyond the drip of the outer twigs. Trees or large shrubs in lawn areas may suffer from competition by the sod if fertilizer is broadcast, especially in clay soils, and fertilizer is then placed in holes below the sod. This method is explained in detail in Chapter Five.

WATER

Water constitutes about 85 per cent of the weight of plants, on the average, but there would be little watering problem if plants needed to be supplied only with this amount. There must also be a certain amount of water in the soil for plants to be able to obtain mineral nutrients for growth, but the biggest water problem arises from the free-spending habit of garden plants as regards water. Plants constantly give off water to the atmosphere, not because they like to, but because they cannot help it. There is no way for green plants to take in the carbon dioxide needed for making sugars and the oxygen needed for respiration without having to lose water. Our problem as gardeners is to try to see that the plant never finds itself unable to replace the water it has lost, so that it wilts and perhaps never recovers.

Florida has plenty of rainfall to take care of plant needs if it were only distributed evenly. Usually we have between 50 and 60 in. of rain annually, and an inch per week would be nearly ideal. But we have hardly an inch in some months and up to 20 in. in others. In general, the summer months are too wet and the winter months too dry, and even in summer we may have several weeks of drought sometimes. So the gardener must be prepared to supplement rainfall anywhere in Florida. Plants need more water in summer than in winter, but ours are mainly evergreen gardens whose plants need water at all seasons.

It often seems paradoxical to beginning gardeners that garden soils must not only be well watered but also well drained. Too much water in the soil, that is, a waterlogged soil, is as unfavorable for garden plants in general as an excessively dry soil, because the roots are deprived of oxygen. So we must be sure that our gardens are planted where there is good drainage, and we try to prevent too rapid loss of water from the soil by using organic matter, as discussed above. Watering too heavily may also leach away mineral nutrients from the root zone of the soil. The gardener must learn moderation in this matter, as in others.

The ideal in garden watering is a permanent underground piping system, with spray heads at proper intervals, so that opening one valve waters a large area of lawn or garden. This is expensive to install and therefore is not commonly used. The next best plan is to have hydrants so arranged that a 50-ft. length of hose will reach any portion of the garden from some one of them. Quickly detachable couplings greatly simplify the labor of shifting the hose from one faucet to another. A hose of good quality seems expensive compared to a cheap one, but its purchase will prove more economical in the long run, since a hose costing twice as much is likely to last three or four times as long.

For watering large areas, some type of revolving sprinkler is needed that can be left to run for long periods. A brief period of watering is of little value unless it is very limited in area also, since soil should be wet to a depth of a foot whenever water is applied. A thorough soaking once a week, rather than a wetting of the top inch daily, is the aim of good watering practice. It is important that the sprinkling device distribute water fairly evenly but within this limitation one may spend from one to fifty dollars for a sprinkler. For narrow beds of flowers or small groups of shrubs one may also supply water by means of a porous canvas or perforated plastic hose, which does an excellent job of wetting the soil. Such devices are not suited to extensive lawns or large garden areas, where sprinklers are needed. Nozzles are valuable for spot watering of a few plants, especially newly set shrubs, cuttings, or annuals. The thumb used as a water-breaker is unexcelled for brief periods of watering, but it quickly becomes weary while the nozzle does not.

Contrary to common opinion, watering plants in full sunshine is not harmful to them. If it were, few plants would be growing in Florida, where "sun showers" are common. There is less evaporation of water from leaves and soil when it is applied in the evening, so that watering is slightly more efficient when done near sunset. But there is no injury to garden plants from watering at midday.

Mulching plants in Florida is primarily of value in connection with watering. No other practice is so helpful in conserving soil moisture, except perhaps the mixing of organic matter with the soil, and this is possible only when preparing new plantings. A heavy mulch on the soil surface prevents rapid drying out of the top inch or so, and makes a given application of water last longer for plant use. There are other values in mulching, such as the control of root-knot and the prevention of high temperatures in the top layer of soil in summer, but these are secondary in Florida gardening to moisture conservation. An organic mulch is nearly always used, and may consist of fallen leaves, grass and weeds that have been mowed, or peat humus and leaf mold. Pine needles and oak leaves are commonly used materials. A further advantage of an organic mulch is that its decomposition adds humus to the soil and helps maintain a slightly acid soil reaction. To be really effective a mulch should be several inches thick, and should be renewed annually to replace loss by decay and weathering.

TEMPERATURE

The single factor that limits plant growth most definitely is temperature, and minimum winter temperature at that. Plants may not grow thriftily because of inadequate fertilization and infrequent watering, but they die quickly when the temperature gets too low. Despite much wishful thinking to the contrary, no part of Florida is really tropical—free from occasional freezing temperatures—except the Florida Keys. Mainland Florida is subtropical. Northern Florida is cool subtropical, and southern Florida is warm subtropical. Sometimes there are winters with no freezing cold as far north as Jacksonville, except in certain localized areas, but such winters are infrequent and are sooner or later followed by severe cold. Even the warmest parts of the peninsula experience temperatures as low as 25°F. every few years, if not oftener. The newcomer arrives just ahead of a mild winter and proceeds to show the old-timer that tropical plants can be grown outdoors in Gainesville or Ocala, in spite of popular opinion to the contrary. He may get his picture in the newspaper, proving the error of the opinions of the older gardener. But next winter he learns the hard way.

There is no evidence that the climate is changing appreciably, either. The record of Florida freezes goes back to 1766, only because we have no weather records of earlier times. Severe freezes were recorded in 1835, 1886, 1894-1895, 1899, 1917, 1928, 1934, 1940, 1943, 1947, 1957-1958, and 1962. Sometimes two bad freezes occur in the same winter and then unusual havoc results. The well-known "big freeze" of 1894-1895 is a classic example although not at all an isolated one. Orange trees and ornamental garden plants were injured by a freeze early in December, but many of them were making fine recovery from this attack in the pleasant weather following. Then in early February a second freeze came and found the actively growing plants in much more tender condition than in December, killing them to the ground where the previous cold had only injured the smaller branches. Either freeze by itself would have done easily reparable damage, but the double freeze drove the citrus industry nearly a hundred miles farther south permanently.

Winter temperatures in Florida are, of course, far more mild than those found farther north. Even southern California is not so warm in winter as is southern Florida. The southerly latitude, low elevation, and proximity to the Gulf of Mexico and Atlantic Ocean give a truly subtropical climate to all parts of Florida, although the minimum temperatures from north to south may differ by 15° or 20°, and from central to coastal areas by 10°. Many plants native to tropical regions are successfully

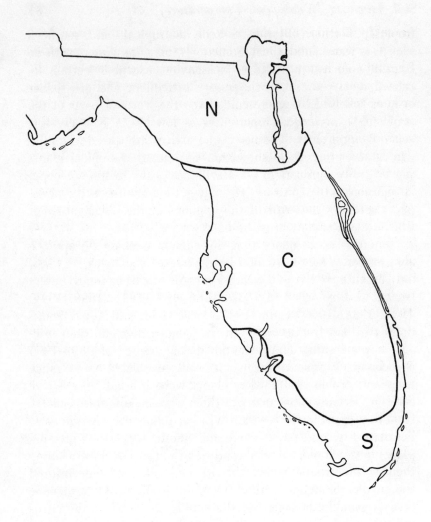

FIGURE 8
CLIMATIC ZONES OF FLORIDA
N—northern
C—central
S—southern

grown in Florida, but they are all likely to suffer some cold injury at times, and the gardener should keep this in mind. Naturally, such injury will be least frequent and least severe in areas that have the highest minimal temperatures in cold spells. Crotons and hibiscus may be grown with success in Palm Beach or Miami Beach, but they cannot be expected to be permanent in Jacksonville or Tallahassee.

The first line of defense in guarding against cold injury is to plant only those trees and shrubs that are completely hardy in a given locality. As an example, we recall the boast of a man who gardens in northern Florida that all of his plants will stand a flat zero. Observations of cold-injured gardens over many years led him to design his garden strictly for hardiness. Temperatures near zero would do little more than damage flower buds. Camellias furnish early winter blossoms, hardy Kurume azaleas follow through with a burst of spring color, and hardy, pest-resisting daylilies are depended upon to carry color interest well into hot weather. Trees for background, framing, and shade are hardy natives—oaks, magnolias, dogwoods, and hollies. In summer this is an all-green garden, and no season finds it out of form. There are plenty of fine materials available for gardens in all parts of the state without trying to bring in plants adapted to warmer winters than our area knows. This does not mean that the gardener may never grow plants known to be tender, but only that such plants should not form the framework of the garden. Let them be planted where they are ornamental when in bloom or foliage, yet do not leave a serious hole in the garden composition when cold inevitably kills them to the ground.

In passing, a word may be in order on using plants adapted only to more cold than Florida gardens experience. The lilacs and peonies and forsythias of northern gardens need a period of continued cold for many weeks to start spring growth. Our Florida climate does not give them this needed chilling except in rare winters and then only in the northern part of the state. We get around this difficulty with tulips by chilling the bulbs in the refrigerator for several weeks, but we cannot take up and chill similarly the trees and shrubs needing it. So we are de-

prived of the pleasure of growing the great majority of the
perennials of northern gardens, although there are so many
other splendid plants available for Florida gardens that we seldom grieve over this. Sometimes shrubs from northern nurseries,
which have been chilled sufficiently before shipping, are planted
in Florida and bloom once. Seldom do they start a second spring.

The second line of defense against cold injury is to have
plants with tissues as fully matured as possible when freezing
temperatures occur. Even the hardiest northern species are easily hurt by cold in midsummer, as laboratory tests show, but
long before winter comes, they have ceased active growth and
matured all tissues. Even in the North, trees are sometimes injured by unusually early frosts or by frosts at normal times
following conditions that have kept plants in active growth unusually late. The problem in Florida is that so many plants from
warmer regions are not impelled to stop growing, thus to mature
their tissues during our mild autumn and winter. Even that
normally dependable shrub, wax privet, may be much hurt by
cold when a freeze follows soon after a warm autumn.

Three factors are particularly involved in keeping plant tissues in active tender growth and retarding maturity. They are
warmth, moisture, and nitrogen. There is little the gardener can
do about excessive warmth in fall and winter—for the problem
of cold injury is as serious late in a very mild winter as early.
Moisture is more often under control, since the late fall and
winter months are usually so dry that without irrigation there
is little tendency to continue growth. Yet here again the problem
is complicated by warmth, for our gardens are largely evergreen
and require much water to stay alive in warm weather. All the
gardener can do is to maintain moderate soil moisture so as to
avoid stimulating growth or plant injury from drought.

There remains nitrogen, which is most subject to control of
any factor. An application of nitrogen will not start a dormant
plant into growth, but an actively growing plant that has used
up its available nitrogen supply will tend to mature its tissues
somewhat. The gardener must avoid heavy applications of nitrogen in late summer or early fall, for this tends to produce soft

growth that does not mature readily. If summer application of nitrogen has stimulated a vigorous flush that is still active in early October, an application of potassium may help to balance the nutrients and enable the plant to mature its tissues normally. Use of mixed fertilizers such as 6-6-6 at proper rates will avoid these problems.

Pruning evergreen shrubs in fall or winter is likely to induce a flush of growth from buds that would otherwise have remained dormant. This new growth would be readily hurt by cold.

The degree of maturity of the twigs of our trees and shrubs, as well as their general health, contributes to their hardiness to cold. Anything which makes for an unhealthy plant makes for easier injury by cold—deficiency of mineral nutrients, lack of water, infestation by insects or fungi, etc. The most vigorous plant is the hardiest of its kind, provided it is as well matured as possible when cold arrives. It is well to remember, also, that application of oil sprays to foliage in late fall or early winter makes the leaves more subject to cold injury than if no oil had been used.

In gardens planted with well-adapted plants that have been well cared for, frost has no terrors; but many gardens are not so designed. Some plants need protection if they are to endure the colder winters. Usually this involves trying in some way to put a blanket around the plant, or else supplying heat. Some gardeners forget that landscape plants generate too little heat to be measured by ordinary means. The object of any plant covering is to slow down the rate at which the heat already in the plant, and in the ground, is lost by radiation or convection.

On a still, clear night in winter, heat is radiated out into space by soil and plants, and their temperature steadily falls. If it reaches the freezing point or below, there is usually frost on boards or straw, or even on the bare ground, and leaves may be frosted. The air temperature may be well above 32°F., but the leaf or soil may still have frost if it is losing heat rapidly by radiation. Thermometers have to be put under a shelter if they are to record the true air temperature. Formation of visible frost is evidence that the object on which it forms has reached a

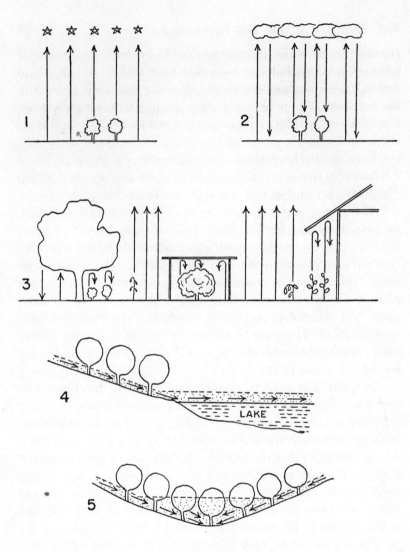

FIGURE 9

PROTECTING PLANTS FROM COLD

1. Heat is lost at night by plants and soil through radiation if the sky is clear.
2. On a cloudy night heat radiated from plants and ground is reflected back again.
3. A covering over plants acts as a reflector to prevent heat loss.
4. Cold air draining down a slope to a lake spreads out in a thin layer over the lake and causes no injury to the trees.
5. Cold air draining into a small valley tends to fill it, making a deep layer which kills some trees on the slopes.

freezing temperature. If there is a covering above the plant that reflects back heat radiated by it and by soil under it, plant and soil will remain above freezing while frost forms around them. Such a covering may be wood, cloth, or paper, but it should not touch the plant. If it is above all parts of the plant, there is no virtue in having it surround the plant. A spreading evergreen tree may effectively protect plants beneath it (fig. 9).

When a freeze occurs in Florida, cold air from the North moves in and pushes out warmer air. This cold air is already below freezing, and it absorbs the heat from plants with which it comes in contact, chilling them below freezing also. A covering is of no avail under these conditions unless it keeps the moving cold air from coming in contact with plants. Tight boxes or cloth covers retard the rate of cooling of plant tissues if they extend clear to the ground. Sometimes trunks of trees are wrapped with insulating material or covered to the height of several feet by a mound of soil. These are more effective for the trunk they cover than are boxes because they insulate better, but they abandon the top of the plant to the cold. Even the best insulator becomes ineffective if the cold continues long enough, but freezes in Florida rarely last more than two or three nights at most.

Heating the air around valuable plants is sometimes attempted, especially in orchards or groves. Only the heat produced is helpful and not the smoke, in spite of popular misconception. Heating is effective in proportion to the quietness of the air. In a severe freeze with steady wind, heating is a waste of money unless there are windbreaks in the lee of which the air is relatively still. During a cold, windy night, a light bulb under an airtight cover may give a small plant the effect of a small, heated greenhouse, and oil or gas heaters are very effective under a shade house that has been tightly covered with plastic sheeting.

As cold winds of freezes nearly always blow from the northwest in Florida, tender plants often have their best chance of survival close to the south side of the house in a freeze. On a frosty night, however, such plants are likely to be as badly hurt as in any other location if there is nothing over them. Gardens with a lake or river northwest of them are also likely to be warmer on a freezing night, perhaps by only one or two degrees, than gardens not so favorably located. On a still, frosty night this would make little or no difference, but a garden located on a gentle slope would be warmer than one on the level ground. Cold air is heavier than warm air, and will flow downhill if there is no obstruction, much as if it were water. A slope down to a lake offers plenty of area over which the cold air may flow away; but a hollow surrounded by sloping ground will be unusually cold, because it will quickly fill up with cold air that flows down into it (fig. 9).

Small plants not over 6 or 8 in. high may be covered with newspapers, troughs, or mulch. Spanish-moss makes a very effective cover for annuals of small size, as it is easy to handle, does not injure plants over which it is placed, and is a fair insulator. Pine straw is used to cover strawberry beds, and paper cups are used to cover small vegetable or flower seedlings. What is said above about coverings applies to these also.

Water gives up a good deal of heat in cooling, and especially in changing from water to ice. Sometimes gardeners leave a hose spraying plants in hope of preventing cold injury. If the water is warmer than the air, this may be effective for light frosts. In heavy freezes, the water usually soon turns to ice on the plant, and the weight of ice may cause severe injury by breaking branches. If ice forms, it will not get below 32°F. nor will the plant tissues enclosed in the ice, so long as the water is kept running, but this means constantly adding more weight of ice. To be effective, the spray must be kept running until the ice has melted. Usually it is a remedy worse than the disease to put the sprayer on plants in a freeze. However, a sprinkler under a plastic covering will keep the temperature up to 10° above that outside. Flooding vegetable fields with relatively warm water is often effective as cold protection, but this is not a method for use in the garden.

In spite of all the gardener can do, there will be times when plants are hurt by cold, and treatment must be given the injured plants. Frozen leaves and shoots may yet thaw out without injury if they are shaded from the morning sun. The well-known pref-

erence of azaleas for north-facing locations is chiefly due to shade
from morning sun while the plants are still frozen following a
cold night. Frost cankers on the south side of tree trunks with
high heads are the result of sunshine on frozen bark in the
morning, and are prevented usually if the exposed area is shaded
with paper, cloth, or boards before the sun is well up after a
freezing night. Applying water to thaw frozen plant tissues is
usually about the worst possible treatment. They should be allowed to thaw naturally in the shade.

If tissues are dead on thawing, the question arises whether
or not to prune. Primarily this is a matter of esthetics for the
home gardener, whereas for the commercial fruit grower it is
one of economics. The gardener is concerned with the appearance of the garden, and since the dead branches and foliage are
unattractive, they might as well be removed as soon as possible.
The orchardist may have to prune twice if he tries to distinguish
sound from injured tissues soon after a freeze, so he prefers to
wait until vigorous growth during the next spring or summer
indicates clearly where to cut. If the gardener is uncertain of
the extent of cold injury, this may be his wisest course also, but
usually he can tell what shoots have been killed and how far
killing has proceeded by examination of the bark. Bark which is
brown clear to the wood is dead, while live bark is green or
white next the wood. Cutting into the bark at intervals from
twig tips toward the ground will usually disclose a point on the
stem below which the bark is alive and above which it is dead,
and the pruning cut should be made a little below this line of
demarcation. Dead tissues do not cause harm to adjacent living
tissues, however, and the only harm from delaying pruning of
dead shoots is to the eye. The idea of circulation of frozen sap
causing injury is without factual basis.

The climatic conditions in one garden are not always exactly
the same as in one nearby because of differences in trees, shrubs,
and soil covering. These small variations within a given climatic
area are responsible for the differing microclimates of gardens—
the climates of small areas. This has already been discussed on
page 19.

4

Propagation of Garden Plants

IT IS NOT REALLY NECESSARY for the gardener to know how to propagate the plants he grows, for he can always buy them from a garden center, florist, or nurseryman. The gardener who cannot propagate his own plants, however, loses one of the deepest satisfactions of gardening and usually loses money, too; for it is very often less expensive to produce one's own plants than to buy them.

Fundamentally there are only two types of propagation—by seeds or by vegetative parts of plants. While there are a few interesting exceptions to the rule in each case, it may be stated as a general rule that seedlings will show some degree of variation from the parent plant, but plants propagated by vegetative parts will reproduce the parent exactly. In cases where the variation among seedlings is very small, as with wild species or with flowers and vegetables that have been selected for uniformity by plant breeders, it is usually much simpler and easier to grow plants for the garden from seeds. When there is much variability among seedlings and horticultural varieties of the species have been selected, it is usually impossible to reproduce these variations by seed, and some vegetative part must be used for propagation. There are also, of course, some garden plants which do not produce any seeds, in which case there is no choice possible.

Plants may be reproduced from several vegetative parts—stems, roots, and leaves. The methods of obtaining new plants

60

from these parts are varied; and the more difficult aspect of plant propagation is not to know what part of the plant to use, but how to treat the propagating material so as to obtain the best results. These various methods will be discussed under the names commonly applied to them by horticulturists—cuttage, layerage, division, separation, and graftage.

SEEDAGE

Small seeds of ornamental plants are usually sown more satisfactorily in some type of easily moved container than in open ground, although large seeds are often better sown in garden beds, especially if no transplanting is involved. The most commonly used container is the *flat,* a shallow box provided with bottom holes to permit free drainage of water. Four inches is ample depth for the flat, and it is better to have two small flats than one large one of unwieldy size. Of course, clay pots may be used also. There are three conditions necessary for seed germination, provided the seeds are alive and their embryos ready to grow: proper warmth, sufficient moisture, and adequate oxygen supply. Free drainage of seed boxes is necessary to assure sufficient supply of oxygen from the air. Coarse gravel, bits of broken pots, or fresh pine straw should cover the drainage holes to prevent their clogging with soil or the loss of soil by washing out.

Seeds will germinate admirably in sterile sand, or even in wet newspapers, but we are interested in healthy and vigorous seedlings, which need a supply of plant nutrients. Usually it is most satisfactory to germinate seeds in good potting soil, high in organic matter. This soil should be treated to kill harmful soil organisms, especially the fungi which cause damping-off of seedlings and the microscopic worms which cause root-knot. Moist soil may be cooked in an oven at 160°F. for two hours, if rather small amounts are needed. Soil may also be drenched with 1 tbsp. each of Terraclor and Captan in 1 gal. of water, or ½ tsp. of Morsodren in 3 gal., 1 pt. of this solution to be applied to each square foot of soil surface. This controls damping-off, but

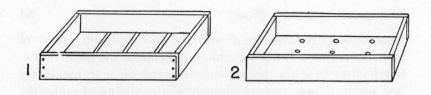

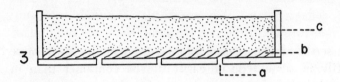

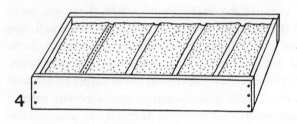

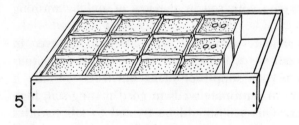

FIGURE 10
PLANTING SEEDS

1. Seed flat showing spacing of bottom boards for drainage.
2. Seed flat showing holes bored in bottom for drainage.
3. Section through seed flat ready for planting: (a) drainage hole; (b) pine straw, pebbles, or crocks; (c) fertile, sterile soil.
4. Seeds sown in rows in flat.
5. Seed flat with soil in plant bands for sowing large seeds.

not root-knot, whereas the cooking controls both of these and most weed seeds, too. Such soil fumigants as Vapam, Mylone, and methyl bromide also control effectively nematodes, fungi, and weeds. A two-week waiting period is usually needed before seeds are planted. These fumigants are widely used in preparing seed beds and for sterilizing garden areas. (See pp. 340-41.) Chopped sphagnum moss and vermiculite are often used as media for seedage because they are sterile yet supply good conditions of moisture and oxygen. Like sand, they supply no plant nutrients, and seedlings should be given weekly applications of soluble fertilizer, according to the manufacturer's directions.

The flat or pot should be filled with soil to ½ in. from the top. Press the soil down firmly with a piece of wood, and flood it with water. When this has drained through, plant the seeds in rows. The general rule is to plant a seed its own thickness deep, that is, covered by its own thickness of soil. Very tiny seeds are usually not covered at all. Larger seeds may be pushed down under the surface while smaller seeds are more easily covered by sifting dry soil over them. Then the pot or flat should be covered with a piece of glass, or a sheet of newspaper laid flat on the soil surface. Both prevent drying out of the soil surface, but the newspaper has the advantage for small seeds in that watering may be done without removing it, thus avoiding possible washing out of such seeds. As soon as seeds begin to sprout, however, the glass or paper must be removed. As ants often carry off seeds, the containers should be made inaccessible to them. Light is not needed for germination of most kinds of seeds and even prevents it in some, but young seedlings need it at once.

Seedlings of most kinds should be transplanted while they are still small to containers that will allow more space (a) for top development, so that the plants will be stocky instead of slender and spindling, and (b) for root development, so that later transfer to the garden or to larger pots will not find the roots badly tangled together. Usually seedlings are transplanted most easily when the first pair of true leaves (not the cotyledons or seed leaves) is fully developed. Small pots and bottomless square bands of paper or wood (plant bands) are used widely

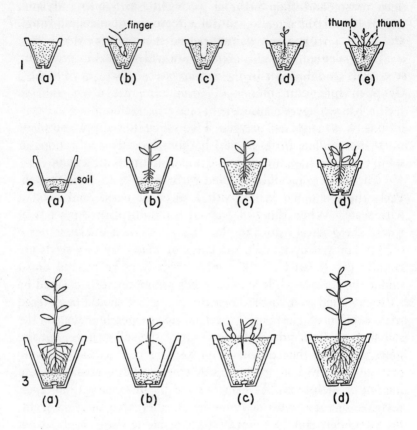

FIGURE 11
POTTING SEEDLINGS AND CUTTINGS

1. Potting seedlings: (a) crocks or pebbles in bottom of pot and three-fourths filled with soil; (b) hole made in soil; (c) pot ready for seedling; (d) seedling in place, ready for soil; (e) soil pressed firmly around seedling roots.

2. Potting cuttings: (a) pot with crocks in bottom and partly filled with soil; (b) rooted cutting in place; (c) soil filled in around cutting to top of pot; (d) soil pressed down around cutting, leaving ½ in. above soil for holding water.

3. Repotting plants: (a) pot with crocks and enough soil to bring plant to right height; (b) shoulders of old soil mass rounded off; (c) soil filled in around root ball; (d) final soil level ½ in. below pot rim.

for transplanting. The new transplants need partial shade for a week or so, and then may be gradually shifted to full sun. Watering must be attended to daily. Usually a light application of soluble fertilizer weekly will give good results. When the seedling roots show at the bottom of the containers, it is time to set the seedlings out in the 'garden, or in the case of woody plants, to shift to larger containers. Always provide for good soil drainage in whatever container the plant is grown.

Nearly all seeds will germinate at temperatures close to 65°F., but this is too low for best germination of most seeds of tropical origin and too high for best results with most seeds native to the temperate zone. Seeds of cool season annuals, planted in August or September, will benefit if the containers are placed in as cool a spot as possible, such as on the north side of the house or under the shade of a tree.

CUTTAGE

By cuttage is understood the propagation of plants by cuttings, or portions cut off from the parent plant and placed under favorable conditions for development of roots or shoots, or both. Some plants may be grown from root cuttings and some from leaf cuttings, but in the case of the majority of ornamental plants that are grown by cuttage, stem cuttings are used. A very important factor in propagation by stem cuttings is the age of the portion of stem used, since the necessary treatment will vary with the maturity of the stem tissue. Primarily this is a matter of food storage, which increases with maturity. Three classes of stem cuttings are used in Florida—softwood, firmwood, and hardwood. Some species may be propagated by any of these types of stem cuttings, but in most cases only one is commonly or easily employed (fig. 12).

Softwood cuttings are made from portions of stem (nearly always the terminal portions) that are composed of immature tissues. Tender shoots of herbaceous plants, even though such plants never become woody, and all immature shoots of woody plants are included. These cuttings always are leafy and, since

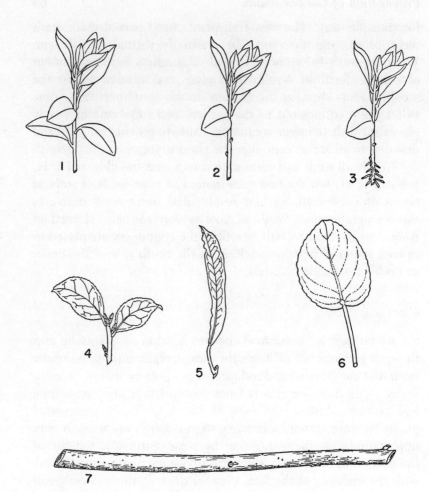

FIGURE 12
TYPES OF CUTTINGS

1. Softwood azalea shoot as cut from bush.
2. Same cutting ready for insertion in rooting medium.
3. Same cutting with roots developed, ready for potting.
4. Firmwood camellia cutting.
5. Leaf-bud cutting of croton.
6. Leaf cutting of African-violet.
7. Hardwood hibiscus cutting.

they are taken from actively growing plants, are usually made during the growing season. The usual degree of maturity preferred in softwood cuttings is such that when the shoot is bent at a sharp angle, the stem breaks cleanly instead of being crushed without breaking (too young), or breaking with woody fibers still continuous (too old). Leaf-bud cuttings are of softwood type.

Firmwood cuttings are made from leafy shoots that have matured fully and are awaiting the beginning of another growth flush. Both narrow-leaved (coniferous) and broad-leaved evergreens are often propagated by firmwood cuttings made during the dormant period; and while terminal portions of twigs are usually employed, it is often possible to make several cuttings from long shoots. Firmwood cuttings are also known as semi-ripe or semi-hardwood cuttings.

Hardwood cuttings are cut from twigs which not only have matured fully but have dropped their leaves for the winter. They are made chiefly from deciduous trees and shrubs, but in a few instances the older, leafless portions of canes of evergreen species are used. Because hardwood cuttings have no leaves, they may be handled quite differently from the leafy softwood and firmwood cuttings.

Softwood cuttings

Softwood cuttings are more extensively employed by gardeners for propagating ornamental plants in Florida than the other two types. Usually the half-hardening of the spring flush of growth gives a satisfactory stage of shoot maturity. The shoots should have reached their maximum expansion, but should not yet have become woody. The warmth and humidity of summer are helpful in supplying a congenial atmosphere, and most cuttings should be well rooted in a month or six weeks. The exact time for taking cuttings to obtain maximum success will vary somewhat with the kind of plant, the earliness or lateness of the particular season, and the technique of the propagation; but with a large number of broad-leaved evergreens, the period from mid-April to mid-June is good for striking softwood cuttings.

Four inches of stem is a good length to take for each cutting,

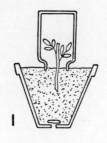

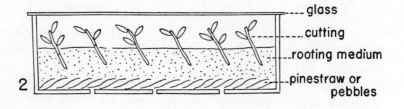

glass
cutting
rooting medium
pinestraw or pebbles

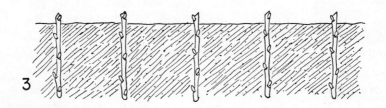

FIGURE 13
ROOTING STEM CUTTINGS

1. Single cutting in pot under glass jar.
2. Cutting box with bottom drainage holes and pane of glass over top.
3. Hardwood cuttings in garden bed during winter.

although it can be shorter or longer. Two or three leaves nearest the tip should be left in place, for softwood cuttings have little stored food to be used in developing roots and will root faster when they have functioning leaves to supply this food and also growth-regulating substances. Lower leaves should be trimmed off close to the stem with a sharp knife. If the leaves are quite large, as in crotons and copperleafs, one may reduce their size in order to utilize available space in the cutting bench economically; but so far as the cuttings are concerned, they will strike root most quickly when leaves are intact. Cuttings must not be allowed to wilt, and should be placed in plastic bags during the period of transfer from the plant to the cutting bench. Only vigorous plants, with leaves free from insects and diseases, should be used for cuttings.

The trimmed cuttings are now ready for insertion in the rooting medium. Some gardeners like to dip the lower ends into a hormone powder, first dipping in water so that the powder will adhere, and shaking off excess powder by tapping the cuttings lightly against the edge of the can. Make a furrow or a series of holes a few inches deep in the rooting medium, and insert the cuttings so that all of the stem below the leaves is below the surface. Cuttings should be slanted so that leaves lie flat, or nearly so, on the surface of the medium, for this will greatly reduce transpiration and lessen chances of wilting. Then press the medium firmly about the stems, smooth over the surface, and flood the medium with water. (Vermiculite must *not* be pressed into place, if it is the medium.)

Leafy cuttings must be exposed to light so that the leaves can make food; yet they are unable to take in more than minute amounts of water, since they have no roots, and so must be prevented from losing water by transpiration. Some easily rooted species—like coleus—need only be put in moist ground that is not exposed to full sun, but most ornamental plants will be successfully increased by softwood cuttings only if some special provision is made to reduce light and increase humidity. Some sort of box is usually needed to hold the rooting medium. Such a box should be covered with material that transmits some light but retains moisture so that the air around the leaves is nearly saturated. Glass is often used, especially where large numbers of cuttings are being rooted, but plastic is preferred by the homeowner with a few cuttings. In any case cuttings should be shaded so that light intensity is greatly reduced from full sunlight, to keep down the air temperature around the cuttings.

A cutting bench or box should preferably be of pecky cypress or redwood, because the conditions maintained in it rot most other woods in a short time. For repeated use, the wood should be painted annually with a preservative material that is not toxic to plants, such as a copper naphthenate solution. It is very important to provide adequate openings in the bottom of the container for drainage and aeration. The sides of the frame should be at least 8 in. deep, so that with 5 in. depth of rooting medium, there is still room for the leaves of the cuttings. These leaves must be moistened daily to maintain the necessary high humidity, and to this end it is convenient if the plastic or glass cover is in a hinged sash. For a very few cuttings, one may use a small pot covered by an inverted glass jar (fig. 13).

Another way to maintain high humidity about leafy cuttings follows: After the cuttings have been inserted in the box of suitable rooting medium, bend four coat hangers to form curved ribs above the slips to support a roof. Over these structural members stretch moist cheesecloth, and then a sheet of vinyl plastic such as is used for shower curtains and freezer bags. The edges of the plastic sheet are tucked under the flat all around to prevent the escape of moisture. While this clear film allows an exchange of air, water vapor will not be lost, and most kinds of cuttings can be forgotten until they are well rooted.

One may also place damp sphagnum moss in the bottom of a bag in which carrots are sold, stick various kinds of cuttings in the moss, and secure the top with staples. Such easy-to-root cuttings as aralia and oleander, thus sealed in a congenial moist chamber, will root on a window sill without muss and bother in three weeks.

The rooting medium is a very important item in the striking of most softwood cuttings. It must be retentive of moisture, yet freely permeable to air, and free from toxic chemical compounds or disease organisms. Fine sand holds moisture so well that insufficient oxygen reaches the sub-surface parts of the cutting where roots are to emerge. Garden soil is likely to contain harmful fungi and bacteria. Coarse, sharp sand has long been considered a reliable rooting medium, but it is not the best for all kinds of plants. Some ornamentals root splendidly in acid peat, and many more root successfully in a mixture of equal volumes of coarse sand and acid peat. Peat is more satisfactory during the spring than in midsummer, when it may cause too much moisture to be retained and permit diseases to attack the cuttings. Other popular rooting media, vermiculite and perlite, are for sale at your garden center. Vermiculite must not be packed, and perlite works best when mixed with peat.

Leaves manufacture more food in full sun than in shade, and if leafy cuttings could be protected from excessive transpiration and also from high temperature, there would be advantages to exposing them to full sun while rooting. It is well known that it is necessary only to have plenty of oxygen and very high humidity around the base of cuttings for roots to develop, and solid rooting media are merely convenient ways of providing these conditions. Popular now is the use of constant or intermittent mist for rooting cuttings during warm weather. No solid rooting medium is needed, but it is convenient to employ one to hold the cuttings in place. The kind of medium does not seem important, provided it is well aerated and drains freely, and is contained in a box which permits free drainage. Turkey grit, coarse sand, old pine sawdust, and mixtures of any of these with peat or vermiculite have all given satisfaction. Wind protection is needed to keep the spray from being blown away from the cuttings. Special nozzles that assure a misty spray without danger of clogging (which would be fatal to cuttings in a short time on a hot day) are now available at hardware and seed stores. Outdoor installations give excellent results so long as temperatures stay in the growing range; they do not function well in winter. A special feature of mist propagation is the leaching of nutrient elements from the leaves of cuttings. Removal of cuttings from the mist as soon as they have sufficient roots to be potted up, and application of quickly available sources of nitrogen and potash to the potted cuttings are important. Usually the spray nozzles can be shut off from 6 P.M. to 8 A.M., thus saving water and decreasing nutrient leaching from cuttings. Rooting is not usually more rapid under mist than in the conventional propagating beds, but larger and more tender cuttings can be used, and sometimes these root more quickly than more mature cuttings.

Leaf-bud cuttings.—A leaf-bud cutting is simply a softwood cutting in which a single leaf with its axillary bud and a small shield of stem tissue is rooted, instead of a piece of whole stem with several leaves and buds. When propagating material is very scarce, the leaf-bud cutting method affords a means of obtaining more than one plant from a single normal cutting. The leaf-bud cutting is placed in the rooting medium with the leaf lying flat and the base of the petiole pressed just deeply enough into the medium for the bud and shield to be covered. Otherwise it is handled exactly like any other softwood cutting. Plants will be smaller when potted up than if standard softwood cuttings had been struck, but there will be more of them (fig. 12).

Many chemical compounds are known that bring about specific growth responses when applied to plants. They are usually called plant hormones. The hormones of most interest in propagation are those which cause roots to develop more quickly and abundantly on cuttings. These are available under numerous trade names at seed stores, and if used carefully according to the manufacturer's directions, they may be helpful in amateur propagation. Some plants root so readily that there is no need for hormone treatment. Others will not root even with it, for species that do not form roots under the usual cutting techniques will not be induced to do so by use of hormones. Their greatest usefulness is with cuttings that root slowly and sparsely at best, and that root more heavily in much less time when the hormone preparation is applied before they are put in the rooting medium. Hormones are not substitutes for suitable media or for proper care in handling cuttings. Most hormones for root-inducing are now supplied in powder form, and after the cuttings are inserted in the medium, the hormone gradually dissolves and enters the basal end of the cutting. Obviously cuttings must be placed in openings in the medium, and not pushed into it, if the hormone powder is to be effective.

Firmwood cuttings

Firmwood cuttings of many evergreen species may be rooted successfully during the dormant period. Coniferous types, such as juniper, podocarpus, and retinospora, and broad-leaved types, such as camellia, privet, and viburnum, are handled in this way. The techniques employed are very similar to those for softwood cuttings, but rooting is usually slower, in part because of the lower temperature and in part because of the more mature tissues used. Leaves are fully developed and so do not wilt so easily as in softwood cuttings, but this means only that failure to keep the humidity high enough around the leaves is not so readily observed. Light and high humidity are as nesessary as ever (fig. 12).

Hardwood cuttings

Hardwood cuttings are made mostly from twigs of dormant deciduous shrubs and trees in autumn, using fully matured, leafless material. Figs and bunch grapes have been propagated in this way for many centuries. Among ornamentals may be mentioned spirea, crape-myrtle, rose stocks, and wisteria. Basal portions of mature shoots of some evergreens—oleander, abelia, privet—from which the leaves have fallen are physiologically similar to deciduous hardwood cuttings and are classed with them (fig. 12).

Hardwood cuttings are made from 8 to 12 in. long and are lined out in a row in the garden, basal end down, with only the uppermost buds of each cutting left above ground. They should be well watered to insure close contact between soil and cuttings. No further attention is usually needed, except to maintain moderate soil moisture, until the rooted cuttings are dug as garden plants the next autumn (fig. 13).

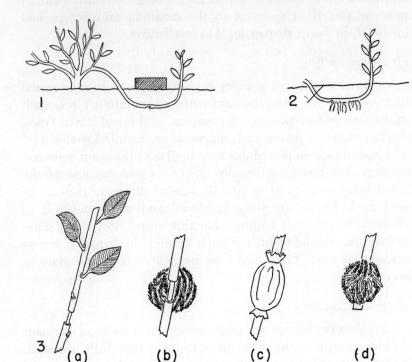

FIGURE 14
LAYERAGE

1. Simple layering of low branch. Note cut in bottom of layered part, to stimulate root formation.
2. Rooted layer cut free from parent plant and ready for transplanting.
3. Marcottage or air-layering: (a) branch with ring of bark removed and leaves removed for a few inches on each side; (b) handful of damp sphagnum moss placed around girdled stem; (c) covering of plastic film or aluminum foil to hold moss in place and prevent loss or gain of water by it; (d) rooted marcot cut free from parent plant below roots, ready for potting (leaves are still present).

Leaf cuttings

Some few herbaceous perennials are readily propagated by using a leaf only, called a leaf cutting. Leaves of many plants will form roots, but few will also develop buds. Leaf cuttings are successful only with certain succulent plants that will form both roots and buds from leaf tissue. Because of their succulent nature, these leaves need less protection from loss of moisture than softwood cuttings do; they may usually be rooted by placing the petiole of the leaf in a rooting medium kept moist (African-violet, gloxinia), or by placing a portion of the leaf flat on the moist medium (begonia, kalanchoë, peperomia), without requiring a glass covering. Sansevieria leaves are cut into 3-in. lengths and inserted half their length in the rooting medium (fig. 12).

Root cuttings

Portions of roots of many species will develop adventitious buds as well as roots, and so may be used to increase plants, although there are few species which cannot be propagated more readily in some other manner. Plumbago, breynia, guava, and wisteria often are increased thus. Pieces of root of lead-pencil size are cut into 3-in. lengths and placed in a rooting medium as if they were hardwood cuttings, except that they may be inserted either vertically or horizontally and do not need to have any tissue exposed. If placed vertically, the end that was nearest the crown must be on top.

LAYERAGE

Layerage is propagation by laying a branch in or on a rooting medium, so that roots develop from it. The rooted portion is then severed from the parent plant and becomes independent. Many plants layer naturally, branches that touch the ground forming roots, while others must be wounded where their branches are in contact with soil before roots will develop. Any plant that can be propagated by cuttings can also be layered, but because layering is much more troublesome for quantity oper-

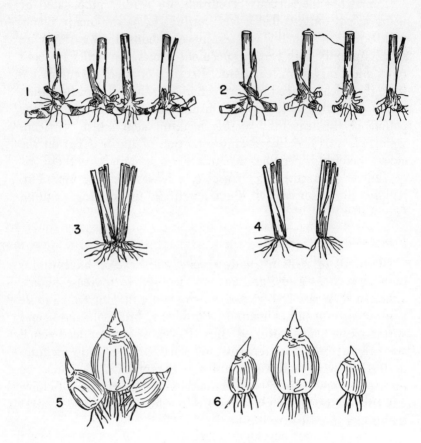

FIGURE 15
DIVISION AND SEPARATION

1,2. Division of canna rhizome into four separate plants.
3,4. Division of daylily plant into two separate plants.
5,6. Separation of two daughter bulbs of narcissus from mother bulb.

ations, it is usually used only for plants that do not easily strike root as cuttings. However, when only one or two plants are wanted, there may be less trouble in layering them than in taking care of cuttings. There are several types of layerage, but the two most commonly used are simple layering and air-layering.

Simple layering is used when a branch is conveniently near the soil, so that it can easily be bent down for part of it to be covered, usually at a point a foot or less back from the tip. The covered area is wounded by slicing away a little bark or by cutting a tongue in the wood by a slanting cut, and the branch then held in place by a brick or a wire staple. Special care must be taken to keep the soil moist, or roots will not develop. Layering is usually started at the beginning of the growing season, so that roots may be well developed by the end of summer.

Air-layering consists in bringing the rooting medium to branches far from the ground, so that roots may form up in the air. Formerly this was done by the use of split pots full of soil, but the modern method is to use sphagnum moss as the rooting medium and to enclose it in a watertight covering of plastic film or aluminum foil. This obviates all need for watering during the rooting period. A ring of bark is removed from the point where roots are wanted, a handful of damp sphagnum moss is carefully tied around this place, and the wrapper is applied so that it is tight around the stem above and below the moss. Usually best results are obtained by starting the operation when the spring flush of growth is well under way. When examination of the ball shows good root development, the branch is severed below the rooting zone, the wrapper is carefully removed, and the new plant is potted. It will require shade for several weeks until the root system becomes better developed. Marcottage and "mossing-off" are other names for this type of propagation.

DIVISION

Propagation by division means that a plant that has branched underground, so that several aerial stems with somewhat independent root systems have arisen, is divided by cutting or tearing apart into several independent plants. This method of multiplication is commonly used for many herbaceous perennials that have underground stems or rhizomes, such as canna, violet, and Shasta daisy, and for cluster-type palms and bamboos. In the case of banana and pineapple, the suckers that arise laterally are cut off to form new plants even before any roots have developed, but most clumps of perennials form divisions that are already well rooted. Daylily is a well-known example. In general, flowering perennials are best divided after their season of flowering, with the winter dormant period as second choice. For bamboos and palms, the beginning of the summer rainy season is favored for division. Small palms, like the lady palm, may be lifted and broken or cut into segments, but large palms, such as *Caryota mitis,* must be divided by carefully removing suckers while they are still small, as is done for bananas. All divisions should be potted or planted in good soil and watered carefully until they become well established.

SEPARATION

Separation is the term used for propagation by means of plant parts that naturally become separated from the parent plant without man's aid. Bulbs, corms, tubers, and tuberous roots that reproduce the plant are examples of such plant parts. Sweet-potato roots might be classed here, but not dahlia roots, since these must have some stem tissue attached, and this requires division of the stem. Propagation by separation involves no leafy or tender tissues, whereas division usually does involve them. When old plants have died to the ground, they are carefully dug to obtain their bulbs or tubers, and these are planted where desired or stored until one is ready to plant them.

GRAFTAGE

Graftage is the type of propagation in which part of one plant is made to grow on another plant. Often we employ it in order to obtain a more satisfactory root system than a cutting or layer would develop, but in other cases it may be the only convenient vegetative method of propagation. Nearly all fruit trees and many ornamental woody plants are propagated by graftage. It is very rarely used for herbaceous plants. Graftage includes two main methods—budding and grafting. Both require more skill than the other vegetative methods of propagation.

Budding

Budding consists of inserting a bud, together with a small amount of adjacent stem tissue, under the bark of a portion of the stem of another plant. To this end the bark of the latter plant, called the rootstock, must slip. This means that the cambium layer between bark and wood must be actively dividing. For that reason budding can be done only during the growing season. Not many ornamentals are budded—chiefly roses, citrus fruits, and sometimes mangos.

The usual form of budding for these plants is shield budding, with a T-shaped incision in the bark of the stock. An oval shield of stem tissue, including in its center an axillary bud, is sliced from one of the last matured shoots of the plant we wish to multiply, and the leaf adjoining the bud is cut off to leave a short portion of petiole to act as a handle. The flaps of the T-incision are raised, the bud shield is slid into place, and the incision closed by wrapping the stem tightly with a rubber band, a strip of plastic, or a piece of adhesive tape. This should be wrapped with overlapping edges from below the incision to above it, so that a watertight covering is made, to prevent drying out of the bud or stock and to hold the bud tissue tightly against the stock. In a couple of weeks the wrapping can be removed and the bud exposed. When it is firmly united, the stock is cut off at an angle just above the bud, to encourage its growth. The young bud sprout will easily be broken loose if it is not carefully tied to a small stake the first season. In the northern half of the state, budding is often done just at the end of the growing season, and buds do not start until the beginning of the next growing season. In such dormant budding the stock is not cut back until spring.

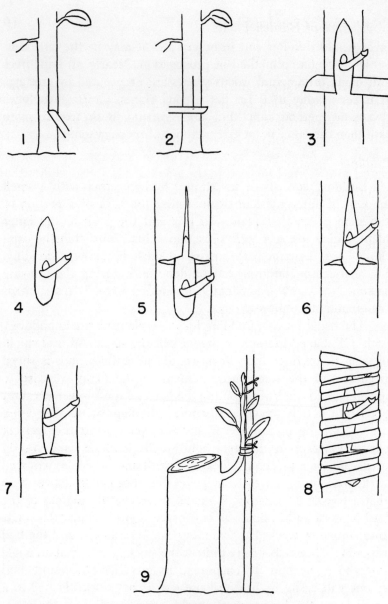

FIGURE 16
BUDDING WOODY PLANTS

1. Vertical cut, and 2. horizontal cut through bark of understock plant.
3. Cutting bud from parent plant. 4. The excised bud ready for insertion.
5,6,7. Steps in inserting bud under bark of stock through the T-incision.
8. Bud wrapped with strip of rubber or plastic to hold it tightly in place.
9. Sprouted bud tied to stake to assure good form. Stock has been cut off at a slant, just above bud, before sprouting began.

Grafting

Grafting, as distinguished from budding, consists of the insertion of a portion of stem, called the scion, into the stem or root tissue of the stock plant. A scion need have only a single bud, although usually it has several, and the whole diameter of the stem is employed. In most forms of grafting, the scion is placed in a vertical incision in the wood of the stock, so that the cambium layers coincide at one or both sides of the stock. The careful matching of cambium of scion and stock is of utmost importance and needs careful attention if the two portions of stem are not of equal diameter or of equal bark thickness. Grafting is done mostly during the dormant period. Among ornamentals commonly grafted are privet, gardenia, camellia, hibiscus, mango, and Oriental magnolia.

The simple cleft graft is most often used. The stock plant is cut off near the ground and the stump split down the center with a heavy knife. This cleft is opened by a small wedge wide enough so that the scion can be inserted. The scion is cut at the lower end to a wedge shape, and pushed into position so that the cambium layers are in contact. If the stock is large enough, a scion may be inserted on each side of the cleft. Then the wedges are removed, the stock bound tightly with heavy string to keep the scions firmly in place, and the cut surface coated with melted paraffin or tree-wound paint. When the stock plants are growing in the garden, the whole graft—scion and stock—is covered with sand to keep it from drying out and from cold injury. When rootstocks are in containers, they are readily moved to prevent drying and frost. Scions are usually taken from the terminal part of well-matured twigs, but several scions may be made from vigorous twigs, each scion being 4 to 6 in. long.

Deciduous species are grafted with leafless scions, but broad-leaved evergreens should be worked with leafy scions. As in softwood cuttings, the presence of leaves speeds the production of new plants. All of the graft should be coated with melted paraffin to prevent drying and protected further by an inverted glass jar, partially shaded by cloth. When scions grow to the

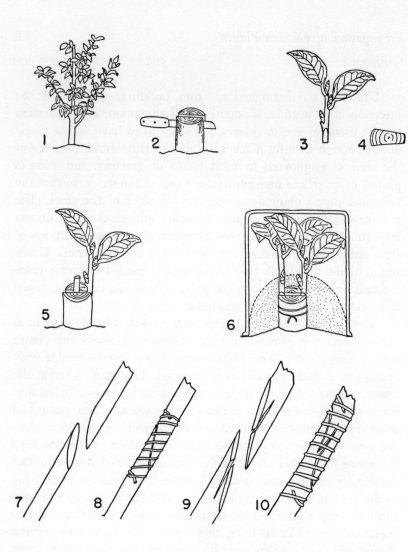

FIGURE 17
GRAFTING WOODY PLANTS

1. Stock plant of camellia ready for grafting.
2. Stock plant cut off 4 in. above ground and cleft by grafting knife.
3. Camellia scion cut for cleft grafting.
4. Cross section of scion.
5. Scion inserted on one side of cleft, held open by small wedge.
6. Completed graft, the small wedge removed, the stock tied tightly with cord, sand covering stock, and glass jar over all.
7,8. Splice-grafted scion and stock before and after binding with rubber bands or cord.
9,10. Whip-grafted scion and stock.

glass, remove the jars and stake and shade the new shoots until they mature to sturdy wood (fig. 17).

Cleft grafts may be made high up on stems, as is done in top-working some fruit trees, but there is little occasion for doing this with ornamental plants.

A modified form of cleft graft is the side graft, in which the stock incision is made from the side without cutting off the top. Side grafting is done only with young, rapidly growing stocks, and employs similarly the tips of the most recently matured shoots as scions. The incision is made downward at a steep angle so as not to go past the center of the stem, and the graft is wrapped like a bud with a rubber band or plastic strip. If leaves are left on, as with roses, gardenias, and hibiscus, the grafted plants must be kept under glass. When the scion has united firmly, the stock is cut off just above the graft.

Splice grafting is one of the easiest types of graftage to perform, although it is not suited to many plants. It requires that scion and stock be of the same thickness where they are to be joined. A long slanting cut is made across each, so that when they are put together they seem to be continuous, and the two parts are tied firmly together in this position. Hibiscus is often propagated by splice grafting. A modification of this method, called whip grafting, increases the area of cambium contact by cutting a tongue in both scion and stock after making the usual slanting cut for splice grafting. In addition to providing more contact surface, the whip graft also prevents stock and scion from slipping while they are being tied. Splice and whip grafting are mostly suited only to stems of small size, while cleft grafting is adapted to large stocks (fig. 17).

5

Trees

TREES ARE ESSENTIAL to the successful development of any landscape plan, and one of the first steps in a home beautification project is to select the kinds of trees and their best locations. Early attention is especially important to the possibility of utilizing existing trees on the lot where the house is to be built. Too often the lot is cleared of all trees before thought is given to landscape needs. Trees relate the house and garden to the ground and also to the sky, and scale relations must be carefully considered. One must think in terms of mature tree size rather than in terms of the size of nursery stock when choosing trees for home grounds. Many tropical species grow very rapidly and ultimately reach huge size, banyans and ear-trees being well-known examples. Such trees are not suited for small residential properties and should be used only on campuses, in parks, and in arboreta.

Shade is very important in Florida gardens because of the large number of intensely sunny days in this state each year. Broad-leaved evergreens, such as live oak, mango, and magnolia, may be chosen if year-round shade is wanted, while deciduous species, such as flowering dogwood, mimosa, and royal poinciana, are better in places where summer shade but winter sun is desired (fig. 6).

Framing is an important function of trees in landscape design. Trees set toward the property line on both sides of the

84

public area, rather forward of the house, enframe the dwelling and the front yard, giving a finish and completeness that can be attained in no other way. For this usage, small, erect types should be chosen in most cases. Two or three larger trees—preferably broad-leaved evergreens—set near the rear property line will form a background that provides solidarity and definition (fig. 18).

Selection of these for home plantings should take into consideration their hardiness to cold, adaptability to soil conditions, length of life, freedom from pests, and resistance to strong winds. Attractive foliage is the prime requisite in a shade tree, but much of the color of the garden picture can come from selection of trees combining masses of beautiful flowers with handsome foliage. In some notable instances, the striking effect of a tree may be due to colorful fruits rather than flowers.

The glamour of exotic species should not blind us to the beauty and value of our native trees. From the more than 300 species indigenous to this state, one may select suitable trees for almost any garden need. Few natives are as spectacular as some of the exotics, but they make up in dependability what they lack in show. Trees already growing on property to be landscaped should be left in place, so far as possible, if they are healthy and shapely specimens of desirable species. They will provide immediately in the landscape picture what will take many years to produce from new plantings. If the existing trees, however, are short-lived kinds that grow rapidly and have little decorative value, they should be removed before the house is built. Later on, nursery trees of desirable kinds can be set out where they are needed.

TREE PLANTING AND CARE

Trees for planting are usually available from three sources —digging wild plants, buying nursery stock, and raising trees from seeds or cuttings. Many trees in Florida gardens have come from the woods, although it is obvious that only native species can be thus obtained. It is quite possible to find and transplant

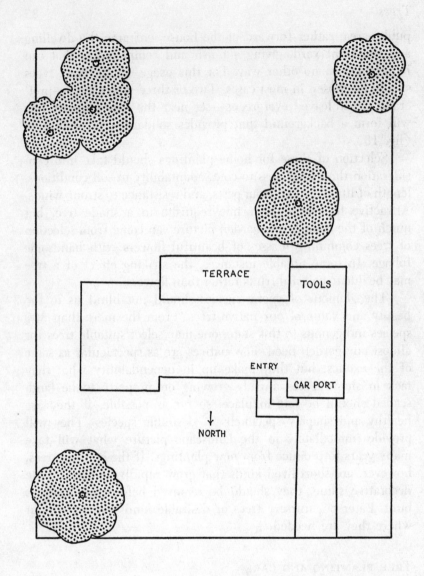

TERRACE

TOOLS

ENTRY

CAR PORT

↓
NORTH

FIGURE 18
PLACEMENT OF TREES
Well-placed trees are essential for a successful landscape development.

fine specimens from woodlands, but it is not so easy as it sounds. Wild trees grow under conditions of intense competition usually, and so have sparse root systems thinly spread over a wide area. It is very hard to obtain more than a small fraction of this root system, and very severe cutting back of the top is usually necessary to compensate for loss of roots. Very small trees are easier to transplant successfully from the woods than larger ones. Apart from the danger of getting the wrong species by mistake, there is also the matter of trespass to remember. Digging trees from land belonging to someone else without his permission may lead to arrest and prosecution. There is also some expense involved in driving some distance to a woodland for a tree—a matter often overlooked in thinking of wild trees as cost-free.

Nursery trees offer many advantages to the homeowner, even for native species, and are usually his principal dependence for exotics. Reputable nurseries offer trees of assured kinds that have been transplanted, root-pruned, cultivated, fertilized, sprayed for pests, and irrigated. They have compact root systems and need minimum pruning, so that they will usually reach a given size much sooner than trees dug in the woods. As a rule, it is more satisfactory and probably no more expensive to buy nursery stock.

Nearly any tree can be raised by the homeowner from seed or cutting. The chief objection is the length of time involved. Usually it will take from five to ten years longer to produce a tree of a given size in this way than if it is bought from a nursery. If time is not important in filling in some details of the landscape picture, the gardener may derive much satisfaction from producing his own trees. Indeed, many excellent species of trees are not in sufficiently wide use to be carried by most nurseries, and they are available to the average gardener only if he raises them.

Trees are most successfully transplanted when conditions favor a minimum loss of moisture from their leaves and branches. Deciduous trees are best moved in December and January, while they are completely bare of leaves. Soil temperatures in Florida remain well above freezing all winter, and root development

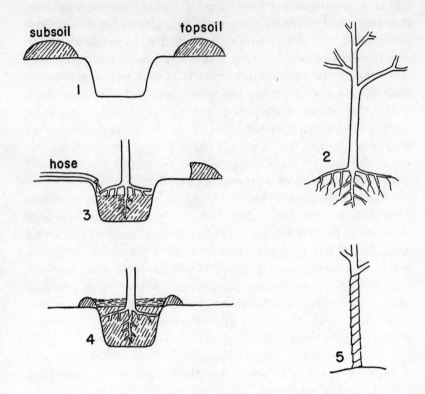

FIGURE 19

TRANSPLANTING DECIDUOUS TREES

1. Hole prepared for tree, subsoil laid aside for discard.
2. Tree ready for planting.
3. Tree in place and hole half filled with topsoil.
4. Planting completed, with basin to hold water and thick layer of mulch.
5. Tree trunk wrapped with strips of burlap or kraft paper to prevent sunburn, desiccation, and borer attack.

can proceed while the top is dormant. Trees transplanted in December have several months to develop new rootlets before the new growth appears on the branches. Evergreen trees may also be moved during the winter months in many cases, since cool weather greatly retards transpiration from their foliage. With some species, however, the danger of cold injury to a flush of growth induced by pruning at transplanting makes it preferable to delay moving them until the danger of frost is past. Orange trees in southern Florida are usually set out during the early winter, but in the northern part of the state the best time is in March or April.

Planting holes should be prepared at least a month ahead of the time when trees are to be transplanted. These holes should be of generous size, about 1 ft. in depth and 1 to 2 ft. in diameter. The excavated dirt should be put aside and the hole filled with as good topsoil as can be obtained, after first putting a shovelful of compost or manure and a handful or two of commercial fertilizer (6-6-6) in the bottom. A depression should be left at the top to hold a little water, and the soil in the hole kept slightly moist.

When planting time comes, whether the trees are from a nursery or from the woods, it is important not to let the roots dry out at any time. Dig out the hole again, and set the tree so that it will be neither more nor less deep in the ground than it had been grown before. Cut back any straggling roots so that all can be spread out, without cramping, as they have been growing. Then slowly shovel the soil back, washing it around the fine roots with a gentle stream of water from the hose. When the hole is full, make a basin around the margin of the hole to facilitate watering, and fill this basin with grass or leaves. This basin should be filled with water once a week until the rainy season begins (fig. 19).

The newly planted tree must have its foliage reduced, if evergreen, in proportion to the loss of roots in transplanting. Lateral branches should be headed back for half of their length, and limbs on the lower part of the trunk may need removal completely if it is desired to have the head several feet high.

Shade trees are often moved with a large central leader, and care must be taken not to head this back so as to leave a large wound which does not heal readily. Pruning to a lateral bud with a slanting cut helps to avoid this difficulty. Trees with several feet of trunk are likely to suffer from the loss of the shade from other adjacent trees in the nursery row and from the pruning of their own branches. The chance of survival will be greatly increased by wrapping the trunks and the larger branches with burlap, paper, Spanish-moss, or similar material. Any such wrapping will protect the trunk from sunscald during frosts and from borers later in the season, and water-absorbent materials can be kept moist all winter to prevent drying out of the bark. With the advent of the spring flush of growth, the wrap is no longer needed and may be allowed to weather away, or by summer it may safely be taken off entirely to improve appearances. If the top was cut back very heavily and the first year's growth does not shade the trunk completely, a paper wrap may be desirable as a guard against borers during warm weather and frost cankers for the second winter.

Spacing of trees is important, if they are to develop into shapely specimens. Small trees, such as flowering dogwood and orchid-tree, have ample room if spaced 25 ft. apart, magnolias and tropical-almond need 50 ft., and live oaks need 70 ft. of living space.

No fertilizing of new trees will be needed during their first year if the planting hole was made up properly. Beginning with the second spring, regular fertilizer applications should be made. The usual practice with shade trees is to fertilize only in early spring, applying 1 lb. of fertilizer (6-6-6, for example) for each inch of trunk diameter.* This is often broadcast under the tree with excellent results, but in the case of trees surrounded by a thick turf—especially on heavy soils—the tree roots may get little of the nutrients. In such cases, the fertilizer is best applied in holes made by a crowbar or similar tool to a depth of a foot and spaced 3 or 4 ft. apart. The area fertilized should extend from a little beyond the drip of the branches half way back to

* A pint of fertilizer of such analysis weighs about a pound.

the trunk. Holes should never be made close together in successive years.

Little pruning of lawn trees is usually needed. Occasionally it is necessary to remove crowding, crossing, or interfering branches and those killed by cold or broken by winds. In rare cases, a weak crotch resulting from two leaders growing side by side may threaten a later split of half the top. Such crotches are easily avoided by heading back one of two competing leaders in young trees. Pruning of ornamental trees is best done just at the beginning of the spring flush of growth, since wounds heal most rapidly then. Hand pruning shears, long-handled lopping shears, and pruning saws are desirable for tree maintenance, although the average gardener will get along with hand shears and a carpenter's saw. Branches over ½ in. in diameter should not be cut with hand shears. All pruning cuts should be made close to a lateral bud or twig, if removing only part of a branch, or close to the parent branch or trunk when removing all of a lateral branch. Leaving a stub is sure to prevent healing and bring an invasion of rot. Branches too large to be supported by one hand while sawing them off at the base should be cut twice. The first cut is started on the underside about a foot out from the trunk, and after cutting one-fourth through, the cut is completed from above. Then the remaining foot is cut off flush with the trunk. This method prevents tearing away some of the wood and bark of the trunk by the fall of the branch, thus avoiding a wound which heals with difficulty. If the cut surface is more than 2 in. across, it is advisable to treat it with a commercial tree-wound dressing or even with house paint. This will prevent checking of the wood exposed and will help to keep out insect and fungus pests until the wound heals over.

Spanish-moss hanging from old oak trees gives a certain ante-bellum impression, but it is not good for the health of lawn trees. This fast growing pest does not take any nourishment from trees, but it shades out the inner branches, causing death of many small twigs, and tends to force growth outward. It should be pulled off the trees each year or killed by spraying. Lead arsenate, at the rate of 1 lb. in 100 gal. of water or one tsp. per gal. of water, has killed Spanish-moss without injury to the foliage of a great many evergreen trees and shrubs, but the dead moss takes months to disintegrate and drop off the twigs.

TREES RECOMMENDED FOR FLORIDA GARDENS

Few trees are equally suitable in all parts of Florida, and so it is helpful in describing them to indicate the portion of the state to which they are adapted. It is convenient to divide the state into three sections for this purpose—northern, central, and southern. Northern Florida (N) is the area lying north of a line drawn across the state through Ocala and Bunnell. Southern Florida (S) is chiefly the coastal strip southward from Stuart on the east coast and Bradenton on the west coast, although parts of the Ridge section around Avon Park with good air drainage are about as warm as the coast. Central Florida (C) covers the region between these other two areas. (See fig. 8.)

After each species is given its common name (if any), its native home, its area of adaptation, and the usual height attained in Florida. Most trees are propagated only by seed, but in a few cases some vegetative method is used, and in such cases this is mentioned in describing the species.

Many other species of trees are growing in Florida besides the ones listed here, which have been selected as having been widely planted and as being above average in desirability. Many more are worthy of trial on a wider basis.

Acacia auriculaeformis. ACACIA. Australia. (S). 20-30 ft. A rapidly growing evergreen tree with flattened branchlets (phyllodes) instead of leaves, and abundance of small, yellow flowers. It is rather easily broken up in hurricanes, but recovers quickly, and has no other bad traits. Several other species of *Acacia* are offered occasionally by nurseries, all with yellow flowers and all quite tender to cold.

Achras zapota. SAPODILLA. Central America. (S). 20-40 ft. This handsome evergreen tree tends to be somewhat upright in habit. It has tough wood and leathery leaves clustered at the twig tips. The fruit, like an apple in size, is an unattractive brown color, but is very pleasant to eat. Storm-fast and pest-free, the sapodilla is warmly recommended where showy flowers are not needed. Some nurseries carry grafted trees with unusually large fruits. The tree is quite tolerant of salt spray, so is adapted to coastal planting.

Albizia julibrissin. MIMOSA-TREE. Eastern Asia. (N). 20-30 ft. Also known as the silk-tree, the mimosa-tree is common from Virginia to central Florida. A deciduous tree of low, spreading habit, it is a showy sight from late April to early July for its abundant pink blossom heads, like powder puffs, and its fern-like foliage. It needs full sun for best development, and tolerates salt spray quite well. The dry seed pods are not very attractive in late summer and fall. Mimosa wilt, a fungus disease carried in the soil, is virulent over much of the lower South, including parts of Florida. There is no cure, but resistant trees grown from root cuttings may be obtained from some nurseries. The larger, faster growing, tropical relative, the womanstongue tree (*A. lebbek*) so abundant in southern Florida, is not recommended for garden planting.

Araucaria spp. Tropics of both hemispheres. (C,S). 50-70 ft. Because of their strongly geometric forms and closely packed, scale-like leaves, araucaria trees are among the most striking trees in Florida landscape plantings. Norfolk-Island-pine, *A. excelsa,* serves as a strong single accent to enhance the feeling of the tropics outdoors, and is a very popular urn subject as well. Bunya-bunya, *A. bidwilli,* more hardy and with much larger, broader leaves, is planted outdoors in protected places in northern Florida where there is sufficient space for a spreading, symmetrical tree. There are other species in this genus also, some or all of which may be called "monkey-puzzle trees."

Bauhinia spp. ORCHID-TREE. China to India. (C,S). 15-25 ft. These are the most conspicuous flowering trees in central Florida, deservedly popular for the profusion of orchid-like flowers borne during the cool months. All display twin-lobed leaves that make identification easy. *B. purpurea,* first to bloom in the fall while the leaves are still on the trees, has flowers of many tones and shapes and petals that never overlap. *B. varie-*

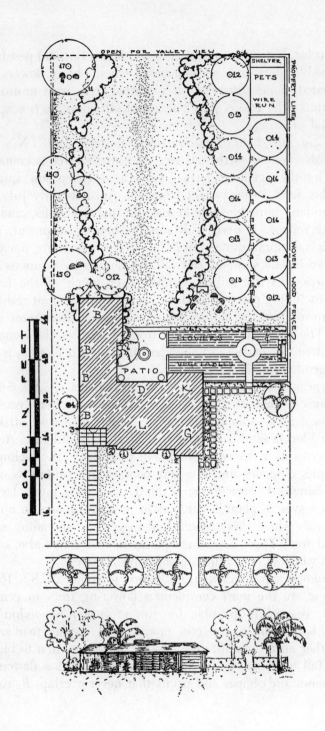

OPEN FOR VALLEY VIEW

SHELTER

PETS

WIRE RUN

PROPERTY LINE

WOVEN WOOD FENCE

WOVEN WIRE FENCE

EXISTING FRUIT TREES

FLOWERS

VEGETABLES

SEAT

PATIO

B

B

B

B

D

K

L

G

SCALE IN FEET

FIGURE 20 (*opposite*)

<small>A LANDSCAPE PLAN FOR NORTHWESTERN FLORIDA</small>

Here is a planting plan developed for a masonry house in the northwestern part of the state, which stands on a rather large lot and therefore lends itself well to the development of a fruit garden in the spacious out-of-door living area to the rear of the dwelling. While the street façade is simply treated, the backyard arrangement is one which would appeal most strongly to amateur horticulturists, as a considerable amount of time could be spent in the care of the trees and vines.

<small>PLANT MATERIALS (100 x 216 ft. lot)</small>

Key no.	Suggested plant material
1	Spanish bayonet
2	Bear-grass
3	Firethorn, espaliered
4	Gardenia
5	Cabbage palm
6	Pindo palm
7	Sasanqua
8	Japonica
9	Wax privet
10	Sweet viburnum
11	Cherry-laurel
12	Loquat
13	Oriental persimmon
14	Peach
15	Magnolia
16	Plum
17	Pecan

gata blooms next (January to April), bearing flowers with broad, overlapping petals during or after leaf-fall. *B. monandra,* the summer-bloomer, bears large, pink flowers with overlapping petals throughout the warm months. These flowers possess one stamen only. Most spectacular is the Hong Kong orchid-tree, *B. blakeana,* which produces its reddish-purple, 6-in., fragrant flowers from October to March. This rare tree, which never sets seeds, is increased by graftage or marcottage and is available in nurseries in southern Florida. Other bauhinias—trees, shrubs, and vines—are worth trying in warm locations.

Bischofia javanica. BISCHOFIA or TOOG. Southeastern Asia. (C,S). 30-40 ft. This handsome, fast growing evergreen tree is unusual for its trifoliate leaves. It has no attractive flowers, but makes a fine, round-headed shade tree with considerable ability to endure wind. Like many large evergreen trees, this one competes severely with grass and may better have a ground cover than a lawn under its spread. Recovery from freezing injury is rapid. No seeds are known to be produced in Florida, but propagation by cutting is easy with mature twigs 6 in. long.

Bombax ellipticum. SHAVING-BRUSH-TREE. Mexico and Central America. (S). 15-20 ft. This little tree with large, palmately compound leaves of five to seven leaflets is the most common shaving-brush-tree in Florida, and is usually labelled *Pachira fastuosa.* It is deciduous in winter, and before the leaves appear in spring it produces its showy flowers. The pink to purple petals are 4 to 5 in. long, and the great pompon of stamens has filaments ranging from white to rose-pink. The new leaves are also purplish-red when they appear, and the fruits are pods, some 5 in. long, filled with small seeds like peas imbedded in cotton. Flowers open at night and remain attractive only one day. Propagation is by seeds.

Bombax malabaricum. RED-COTTON-TREE. India. (S). 30-60 ft. No tree makes a more conspicuous show than this large deciduous species when it covers its bare branch-tips with large, flaming red, tulip-like blossoms in midwinter. Other characteristics are a stout, buttressed trunk and thick branches armed with heavy, short spines, and compound leaves of five leaflets.

Brassaia actinophylla. SCHEFFLERA or QUEENSLAND UM-BRELLA-TREE. Australia. (C, S). 20-40 ft. This robust, tropical tree is planted in warm locations for the curiosity of its huge compound leaves and the spectacular red inflorescences standing above the foliage. Its adaptation to many environments allows schefflera to grow both indoors and outside as a planter subject, shrub, or tree. Increase is easily accomplished by seedage, cuttage, or marcottage.

Bucida buceras. BLACK-OLIVE. Southern Florida. (S). 25-40 ft. This native tree has no attractive flowers or fruits, but it is much planted in coastal regions because it is so resistant to wind. It is evergreen, with small leaves clustered near the twig tips, and makes a dense, rounded head. A slow grower, black-olive takes many years to reach medium size.

Bursera simaruba. GUMBO-LIMBO. Southern Florida. (S). 30-50 ft. Another tree without flowers or fruits of attractiveness, the gumbo-limbo is popular for its curious, bright reddish bark and gnarled limbs. It is a large tree of rapid growth, and the thin, smooth bark of the branches looks as if it had been freshly shellacked. While easily grown from seed, it may be more rapidly propagated by large branch cuttings.

Callistemon spp. BOTTLE-BRUSH. Australia. (C,S). 20 ft. In warm sections of the Florida peninsula, no flowering trees are more appealing than the colorful bottle-brushes. One or more species and hybrid forms are used effectively as free-standing specimens because of their graceful habit and bright, hanging inflorescences. Propagation is by seeds or marcots.

Cassia spp. CASSIA or SENNA. India. (S). 20-30 ft. Several species of cassias are among the showiest flowering trees in Florida. All are deciduous in winter, and the long pods are not attractive then, nor is the tree a shapely one. The branches are surprisingly resistant to windstorms. Most widely planted is *C. fistula,* the golden-shower, which reaches a height of 30 ft. It has great masses of bright yellow flowers from April to June, followed by long, slender, cylindrical pods filled at maturity with a thick, black paste in which the seeds are imbedded. This paste is the cassia of pharmacy. *C. grandis,* the pink-shower, is an equally large tree with an abundance of rose-pink flowers borne in early spring before the leaves appear. C. *nodosa,* the pink-and-white-shower, is a smaller tree with spreading habit, which bears quantities of blossom clusters all along its branches. The pink flowers fade out soon, so that both pink and whitish blossoms are seen in the clusters. Very similar is C. *javanica,* the apple-blossom cassia, which is distinguished by a spiny trunk. Both bloom in late spring with the leaves. Many other cassias are available for trial, and some will doubtless prove fine additions to our ornamental trees.

Castanospermum australe. MORETON BAY-CHESTNUT. Australia. (S). 40-50 ft. This large evergreen tree has pinnately compound leaves 1½ ft. long, and produces showy clusters of yellow flowers in spring. The seeds are the size of chestnuts and are edible when roasted. It has not been so widely planted as it deserves to be.

Casuarina equisetifolia. AUSTRALIAN-PINE. Australia. (S). 50-70 ft. While rather tender to cold, this tall, slender tree with gray-green "needles" is remarkably tolerant of salt spray and brackish water. It is used extensively in warm coastal areas for high screens, windbreaks, and clipped hedges of any height from 3 to 20 ft. It seems to thrive on all types of soil. A sister species of darker green color and more dense growth habit, C. *cunninghamiana,* is hardy enough to be planted throughout the central area and even in Gainesville, although it is often hurt by cold there. A third casuarina, C. *lepidophloia,* is less lofty and much more densely dark green. It is extensively used in southern Florida as a windbreak, but has the bad habit of suckering abundantly from the roots. Since this species does not produce seed in Florida, as the others do, these root-sprouts form the only mode of propagation. They make much extra work for the gardener, however, who cannot control them with a powerful mower as the grove owner can. This species may be grafted on seedlings of C. *equisetifolia,* thus avoiding this tendency to sucker. For some obscure reason the name Brazilian-oak has attached itself to this species, whereas the others are always called Australian-pine, although they are not related at all to either oaks or pines.

Catesbaea spinosa. LILY-THORN. Southern Florida. (S). 10-15 ft. A small, shrubby evergreen tree, the lily-thorn has slender, wiry branches with small leaves and many long, slender thorns. Its attractive feature is the profusion of creamy-white flowers borne in late winter. Where a very small-scale flowering tree is wanted, this may serve nicely.

Cercis canadensis. REDBUD. Eastern United States. (N,C). 20-30 ft. This native Florida tree makes a brave show in early spring with its tiny, rose-pink flowers borne all along the twigs and branches before the leaves appear. Well-grown specimens make a spreading canopy of shade in summer, small enough for a very small garden. In winter the bare branches hung with dirty-looking, little pods are not so ornamental. Nurseries offer a white-flowered form and a similar Chinese species, *C. chinensis,* with purplish-pink blooms. Grafted specimens are available, but most trees are grown from seed. Good soil drainage is important.

Chamaecyparis thyoides. WHITE-CEDAR. Northern Florida. (N,C). 40-80 ft. Attractive ascending growth, complete hardiness, resistance to wind, and adaptation to wet soils are some of the characteristics which make this native evergreen one of the very best for accent use in Florida landscapes.

Chionanthus virginica. FRINGE-TREE. Eastern United States. (N). 20-30 ft. Like the redbud, this tree is both native to Florida and deciduous. Its interest lies in the clusters of greenish-white flowers with slender petals giving a fringe effect, which are produced along with the leaves in early spring. The tree is slow growing and thrives only on fairly good soil, but is a fine garden ornament where well adapted.

Chrysophyllum olivaeforme. SATIN-LEAF. Southern Florida. (S). 10-20 ft. This is a very small, slender tree with no beautiful flowers but with very attractive foliage. The leaves are somewhat leathery, 4 to 5 in. long, glossy dark green above and lustrous coppery beneath. It is very tender and slow growing, yet old trees fruit so abundantly that volunteer seedlings are sometimes pests.

Cinnamomum camphora. CAMPHOR. Eastern Asia. (N).

25-40 ft. Originally introduced into Florida as a source of camphor, this handsome, hardy evergreen tree has become very popular in northern Florida as a garden specimen. On soils of moderate fertility that do not become too dry during spring droughts, the camphor tree makes a satisfactory round-headed shade tree. It is rather difficult to maintain lawn grass under that shade, so that a ground cover may be needed. Seedlings do not transplant readily from open ground, but should be started in containers. Camphor is rather subject to attack by spider mites, which change the dark green leaves to a rusty bronze color. The cassia-bark tree, *C. cassia,* is a sister species from China, which makes a similarly handsome evergreen tree for southern Florida.

Citrus spp. While the various citrus trees are primarily of interest as orchard trees, some forms are highly esteemed for landscape use. They vary greatly in cold endurance. Kumquats (properly *Fortunella,* not *Citrus*), calamondins, and satsumas may be grown anywhere in the state. Limes are satisfactory only in the warm parts of central and southern Florida. Oranges, grapefruit, and tangelos can be grown in a few well-protected locations in the northern area, and anywhere in the areas south of that. They range in size from 10 ft. kumquats—hardly more than shrubs in usage—to over 40-ft. height for grapefruit. All are alike, however, in being rather more subject to pests than the other trees recommended for home gardens. This means that they will not be very ornamental if they are not well cared for, both in pest control and in fertilizing, since fruit is carried away in quantity and makes a permanent drain on soil nutrients. Nearly any citrus tree worth growing as a garden specimen is worth buying as a budded nursery plant, so that its fruit character is definitely known. For good fruit production it is better either to keep trees mulched heavily or to keep a clean, cultivated circle around them of at least half the top diameter, since this permits more ready application of fertilizers and reduces competition by grass. However, mature kumquats and calamondins that are being grown only as ornamentals may be allowed to have turf close around them. Citrus trees are usually fertilized three times a year, in February, June, and October. The last application should be made after the trees have entered dormancy, especially in northern Florida.

Coccoloba spp. American Tropics. (S). 15-40 ft. Most important and most commonly seen in Florida landscapes is seagrape, *C. uvifera.* It is distinguished by large, broadly rounded leaves with red veins. Both the new growth and old leaves develop attractive red color. It is notably tolerant of salt spray and is popular in seaside plantings, where its stout twigs and dense growth habit make it effective as a background or windbreak. It hardly exceeds 25 ft. Pigeon-plum, *C. laurifolia,* is a native 40-ft. tree with oval 4-in. leaves and smaller fruits than sea-grape. It is a desirable landscape tree for seaside locations also. Big-leaf sea-grape, *C. grandifolia,* has the largest leaves (yard-broad) of any woody plant seen in Florida. This tropical relative of our native species is grown for the curiosity of its huge, disc-form leaves.

Cochlospermum vitifolium. COCHLOSPERMUM. Middle America. (S). 25-40 ft. This slender deciduous tree makes a fine sight in early spring when the leafless branches put forth terminal clusters of bright yellow, funnel-shaped flowers, some 4 in. across, looking like large wild roses. Later the large, five-lobed leaves appear. It needs full sun and begins blooming while quite small. Propagation is by seeds or by softwood cuttings. The wood of this tree is soft and brittle.

Cordia sebestena. GEIGER-TREE. Florida Keys. (S). 15-20 ft. In areas that are warm enough, this small tree offers a note of garden color during most of the year. Small clusters of orange-red flowers appear at the branch tips, looking somewhat like geranium flower heads. Besides being very tender, this tree does not tolerate poor drainage but does endure salt spray well and grows well on limestone soil.

Cornus florida. FLOWERING DOGWOOD. Eastern United States. (N, C). 20-30 ft. The flowering dogwood is one of the delights of springtime in the hardwood hammocks of the northern half of the state as well as in the gardens of that area. It does not tolerate waterlogged soil. The conspicuous white bracts surround a cluster of inconspicuous true flowers. From these

develop clusters of scarlet fruits which, together with the red
tints attained by the old leaves, make this tree colorful again in
autumn. Even after the leaves have all fallen, the tree is still
unusually attractive among deciduous species because of the succession of whorls of branches, giving a somewhat pagoda-like
effect. The only pest usually of any importance is a trunk borer
that may enter the bark of recently transplanted trees or those
injured by frost, bruising, or high water. Unfortunately, the
pink-flowered form of the species, so often seen in the North,
does not bloom well except in northwestern Florida.

Cunninghamia lanceolata. CHINA-FIR. China. (N). 40-60
ft. This conifer is sometimes planted in northern Florida in
place of the less hardy araucarias. Disease-resistance, hardiness,
and long life are reflected in the popularity that China-fir en-
joys in the upper counties.

Cupressus lusitanica. PORTUGUESE CYPRESS. Middle America. (N,C). 30-40 ft. This handsome, evergreen, true cypress
is not to be confused with the deciduous bald-cypress of the
southern states which produces cypress lumber. Somewhat like
the native red-cedar in habit, the cypress makes a large, rounded
head of grayish-green foliage, more compact than red-cedar, with
the twigs branched in all directions but with similar scale-like
leaves. It needs plenty of space for development, so is satisfactory only as a specimen plant. The tall, spire-like Italian cypress
(*C. sempervirens*), which may reach 50 or 60 ft. with a
maximum diameter of only 3 or 4 ft., is rarely planted now,
although it was popular many years ago. Both are grown readily
from seed.

Dalbergia sissoo. SISSOO. India. (C,S), 30-45 ft. This
shapely tree bears pinnate leaves of three to five roundish leaflets
alternately on zigzag rachises. Inconspicuous blossoms are followed by little pods about 4 in. long. Because of its neat, attractive habit, light foliage, and resistance to drought, this is a
good framing or avenue tree for central Florida. In a few areas
sissoo has escaped from cultivation.

Delonix regia. ROYAL POINCIANA. Madagascar. (S). 20-30
ft. This large deciduous tree, often spreading twice its height,

is rather unattractive during the winter, when its sprawling habit is accentuated by large, black pods that look like old-fashioned razor strops. But when the lovely, fern-like foliage clothes the branches and the great trusses of orange-red flowers appear in May and June, this is admitted to be one of the most gorgeous of all flowering trees. Culture is easy if attempted only in the warmest locations. There is considerable variation in color of seedlings, from true orange to scarlet red, but so far none of these seedling forms has been propagated vegetatively. In the West Indies, this popular tree is usually called "flamboyant," which is to say "the flaming."

Eriobotrya japonica. LOQUAT. China. (N,C,S). 15-25 ft. This evergreen tree is attractive at all times, but especially so when covered with clusters of yellow fruit from January until March or April. The flowers are not showy but are wonderfully fragrant, so that a loquat tree in bloom fills the garden with a spicy fragrance. While the tree is hardy everywhere in the state, blossoms and young fruit are often killed by cold in northern Florida, so that fruiting is more dependable in the southern area. Fire-blight, which kills back branches, may take the whole tree if prompt pruning is not done with sterilized shears.

Erythrina variegata. CORAL-TREE. India. (S). 20-30 ft. This small, round-headed tree is notable for the masses of coral-red flowers borne in February and March. The leaves are trifoliate, and the trunk and branches are armed with prickles. The tree would be much more widely grown were it not for an insect that lays eggs in the tips of flowering twigs. The larvae tunnel out and kill the tips so that no flowers are produced. Another coral-tree popular in southern Florida is the shrubby *E. crista-galli.*

Ficus spp. RUBBER-TREE or FIG. Mostly Southeastern Asia. (S). 25-80 ft. The ornamental tree species of the great genus *Ficus* are all tropical evergreens. Because they generally grow to great size, they are not recommended for home landscaping, although several are valued in roadside or park plantings. Many species have the curious, undesirable habit of putting down from their branches aerial roots that develop into trunks after becoming established in the ground. The banyan tree is properly

F. benghalensis, but the name is usually applied in Florida to any species that produces multiple trunks. The bo-tree (*F. religiosa*) from India, the laurel fig (*F. retusa*) of India and Burma, and the weeping fig (*F. benjamina*) of India make handsome small-leaved, round-headed trees. India-rubber plant (*F. elastica*) in several types and fiddle-leaf fig (*F. lyrata*) are popular urn-subjects for indoor decoration. Both become huge trees outdoors in southern Florida. All species of *Ficus* grow readily from cuttings and air-layers.

Grevillea robusta. SILK-OAK. Australia. (C,S). 40-70 ft. The silk-oak is admired for its fern-like, evergreen foliage and its trusses of golden-yellow flowers in spring. The habit is columnar, so that a tall tree does not spread widely. It thrives especially in the Ridge section of central Florida. Here, too, and southward is sometimes seen red-flowered *G. banksi,* a much smaller tree.

Ilex opaca. AMERICAN HOLLY. Eastern United States. (N). 25-40 ft. One of our finest native trees for garden use, the holly is well known and justly popular. Several horticultural varieties, differing in leaf and fruit characters, are offered by nurseries. Varieties with quite spiny leaves, like the traditional Christmas holly pictures, are Croonenburg, Howard, Lake City, Savannah, and Taber. East Palatka is a fine garden variety with only a little spine at the leaf tip. Holly succeeds only on a somewhat acid soil of fair fertility that is well drained but not droughty. Berries are borne only on pistillate (female) trees, and unless a staminate (male) tree is known to be growing in the neighborhood, one should be planted. It is possible to get a set of fruit by using a hormone spray at blossoming, but few gardeners are prepared to spray their holly trees for fruiting. Since seedlings are unreliable for fruiting, holly is usually propagated by softwood cuttings.

A form of the American holly, dune holly (*I. opaca* var. *arenicola*), differs chiefly in its ability to thrive on sand dunes and its occurrence mostly south of the range of American holly. For the Ridge section it provides a good substitute for the better known species, which it often equals in size under garden conditions, although rarely 20 ft. high in its native haunts. Only one variety, Fort McCoy, has so far been propagated.

Two other native Florida hollies are grown sometimes as small trees and sometimes as shrubs. These are dahoon, *I. cassine*, and yaupon, *I. vomitoria*. The latter is not of value as a tree and will be discussed in Chapter Seven, but the dahoon holly makes a very nice small tree, adapted to all parts of Florida. It is tolerant of low, poorly drained soil but also grows well on high, well-drained ground if watered well for a few years until a deep root system develops. Leaves are spineless, but fruit clusters are as showy as the larger fruits of American holly. The variety Glen-cassine has been propagated.

Ilex cornuta. Chinese holly. China. (N,C). 10-20 ft. In foliage, this rather unfamiliar holly often more nearly resembles the traditional English holly than our American species. It is a small, shrubby tree of dense foliage with glossy, dark green leaves, which may have many or few marginal spines. 'Burford,' the best-known variety, has only a single spine at the leaf tip, while 'Rotunda,' a low growing variety, has the margin full of spines. Berries are larger and not so numerous as in American holly, but make a beautiful show. American holly males do not pollinate Chinese holly trees, and usually staminate trees of this latter species are needed for fruiting. 'Burford' may fruit sparingly by itself.

Ilex rotunda. Round holly. Japan. (N,C). 15-25 ft. This is another small, evergreen holly of easy culture that is deservedly popular in Florida. It is of more rapid growth than our other hollies and has somewhat drooping branches. The red berries are small but are borne in dense clusters that extend well back on the branches. Cultural conditions are the same as those for American holly, but the latter does not pollinate the round holly, which must have a male tree of its own kind. The variety 'Lord' is the only named form with berries offered by nurseries, while 'Romal' is a male variety to go with it.

Jacaranda acutifolia. Jacaranda. Argentina. (C,S). 25-40 ft. The large panicles of blue flowers that cover this tree in April, May, or June make it one of the most spectacular of our ornamental trees. It is rather unattractive in late winter, being deciduous, but has graceful, feathery foliage the rest of the year. The tree thrives under usual garden care and makes a light shade.

Koelreuteria formosana. GOLDEN-RAIN-TREE. Formosa. (N, C). 20-30 ft. This tree is not always shapely, but it is well worth growing because it furnishes garden color when few trees provide it. Great masses of bright yellow flowers appear at the branch tips in October, followed about a month later by equally showy clusters of bright red, papery pods. The large, compound leaves have a fern-like appearance. The tree often has a rounded head that makes good shade without preventing grass growth.

Lagerstroemia speciosa. QUEEN CRAPE-MYRTLE. Southeastern Asia. (S). 20-30 ft. This tree is very showy when in bloom during late spring and early summer. Large terminal panicles, like those of the mango, are produced at the end of the spring growth, and these contain hundreds of pink flowers about 3 in. in diameter. The growth habit is rather upright, with large, rough leaves that are shed in late winter. Size of tree, leaves, panicles, and flowers are all much greater than in the common crape-myrtle, *L. indica,* which is usually a shrub although often seen as a tree. Queen crape-myrtle may be propagated by softwood cuttings or by root suckers that may result from injury to roots. Seeds are rarely formed in Florida.

Litchi chinensis. LYCHEE. China. (C,S). 20-30 ft. This handsome evergreen tree is quite showy in June when the bright red fruits are mature. These persist for several weeks, although the high price now paid for them does not encourage gardeners to leave them unpicked. A little less hardy to cold in Florida than the orange, the lychee thrives under similar cultural conditions otherwise. Heavy mulching is of special benefit to it. Only the Chen (Brewster) variety is commonly grown, and it is propagated by air-layering.

Magnolia grandiflora. SOUTHERN MAGNOLIA. Eastern United States. (N,C). 40-60 ft. This stately evergreen tree is one of the several native species that stand comparison well with any exotics. Handsome at all seasons, it is especially lovely in late spring when bearing the large, fragrant, creamy-white blossoms. Native to fertile hardwood hammocks, magnolias thrive under

garden care, responding better to mulching than to clean cultivation. Transplanting is more satisfactory in spring than in fall.
Grafted specimens are offered by nurseries, but seedlings are
also commonly planted.

The Oriental magnolias, *M. liliflora* and its better known
hybrid, *M. soulangeana,* and the starry magnolia, *M. stellata,*
are rarely seen as trees in Florida, being usually shrubby here.
They are described in Chapter Seven.

Malus angustifolia. SOUTHERN CRAB-APPLE. Southeastern
United States. (N). 25 ft. For delightful apple blossoms, Floridians have here their own native apple tree. Although it is
attacked by many pests, the beauty of its flowers makes it very
worthwhile to care for one of these little deciduous trees if you
live within their range, the upper tier of Florida counties.

Mangifera indica. MANGO. India. (S). 20-40 ft. The mango
tree not only bears one of the world's finest fruits (at least in
the best varieties) but is a handsome evergreen tree as well.
Few shade trees are more satisfactory in southern Florida, except
for the occasional need for pest control. The fruit of seedling
trees is usually so poor in quality that there is no excuse for
planting anything except a budded or grafted tree of known
character. Growth is rapid under good garden care, as recommended for orange trees. Mature trees seem to thrive in sod if
care is taken to provide ample supplies of nitrogen.

Melaleuca leucadendra. CAJEPUT. Australia. (C,S). 25-40
ft. The soft, thick, papery, whitish bark, the slender, upright
habit, the small, narrow leaves, and the yellow-white blossom
clusters make this distinctive tree a favorite lawn and street specimen. It has become naturalized in some swampy areas, but also
thrives in deep, sandy soils. The flowers are beloved of bees, but
the honey is of poor quality, and as a small amount seriously
lowers the grade of a good honey, extensive plantings should not
be made in areas producing commercial honey. The tiny seeds
must be planted with care not to cover them too deeply. The
tree is tolerant of salt spray and strong wind.

Pachira spp. SHAVING-BRUSH-TREE. Tropical America (S).
15-25 ft. Three species of *Pachira* are infrequently seen in

southern Florida, all with petals 8 to 12 in. long and with large, chestnut-like seeds imbedded in a soft pulp. Like species of *Bombax* and *Ceiba*, to which they are related, these trees have large, palmately compound leaves, deciduous in winter. All have gigantic clusters of stamens, from white to purplish in color, like oversized shaving brushes. *P. insignis* from Brazil is the only species with showy petals, purplish-red, and has very fragrant flowers. *P. aquatica* has pale greenish-yellow petals, and *P. macrocarpa* has petals brownish outside and light pink within. All are propagated by seed.

Pandanus utilis. COMMON SCREW-PINE. Madagascar. (S). 10-20 ft. This curious, sparsely branched tree is conspicuous both for its pineapple-like leaves, 3 ft. long, borne in a spiral or screw around the stubby branches, and for the sturdy brace-roots that arise from the trunk for several feet above the ground. Small plants that have not developed stems look very much like pineapple plants. The aggregate fruits are 6 or 8 in. in diameter and conspicuous on the tree, although useless. The Veitch screw-pine or ribbon-plant, *P. veitchi,* is similar in habit but has longer leaves, banded with white. It is often grown as a pot plant for foliage effects while young. Screw-pines like full sun and tolerate salt spray. Propagation is by division of young suckers, or by seed if available. (*P. veitchi* does not fruit.)

Parkinsonia aculeata. JERUSALEM-THORN. Tropical America. (N,C,S). 15-25 ft. The lacy foliage, pendulous habit, clusters of yellow blossoms, and green bark of this graceful, small tree make it unusual as well as attractive. Blooming period is April to June. Only light shade is produced in summer and none at all in winter, as the tree is deciduous. It is also thorny. Seedlings are best grown in containers, since they do not transplant well from open ground. This tree is suited to seaside exposures.

Peltophorum inerme. PELTOPHORUM. Philippine Islands. (C,S). 25-40 ft. This beautiful evergreen tree bears in summer great upright spikes of showy, golden-yellow flowers. The foliage is feathery, dark green, and makes a dense shade.

Pinus spp. Several pines native to Florida make very satisfactory garden specimens, especially when they are already on the property when the house is built. They are especially suitable for casting the light, shifting shade under which azaleas and camellias thrive. Handsome pine trees are often badly injured by the carelessness of construction crews. It is a good precaution, before clearing the site, to select the trees desired permanently and to build sturdy cribs of 2 x 4 lumber around them. This will make it impossible for the contractor to pile building materials against the trunks or gouge the bark in turning trucks. Longleaf (*P. palustris*) and slash (*P. elliotti*) pines are especially worth saving in northern and central Florida, while Southern slash pine (*P. elliotti* var. *densa*) is a fine tree in extreme southern areas. In the sand-dune areas, the sand pine (*P. clausa*), also called scrub pine, is desirable; and possibly most beautiful of all is northern Florida's spruce pine, *P. glabra.*

Plumeria spp. FRANGIPANI. Tropical America. (S). 10-15 ft. Several species of frangipani are common in all tropical countries, grown for their delightfully fragrant flowers. They are all short, stocky trees of spreading habit with thick, stubby branches of soft wood, milky sap, and large, leathery leaves. The species most often seen in Florida gardens are *P. rubra,* with broad leaves and purplish-red flowers, and *P. alba,* with narrow leaves rolled at the margins and white flowers. Leaves are clustered near the branch tips and flowers are borne terminally all through late spring and summer.

Quercus virginiana. LIVE OAK. Southeastern United States. (N,C,S). 50-75 ft. There are nearly 30 species of oak, evergreen or deciduous, in Florida, and these range in size from the dwarf running oak to majestic patriarchs. All are completely adapted to our climate and resistant to pests. Several species have been planted widely as street, roadside, and shade trees, but not all are of equal merit. The live oak is by far the most desirable because it has a much longer useful life than other native species. Water oak (*Q. nigra*) is often planted because it grows rapidly, but at 50 years of age it has reached senility. Many a Florida city has had to cut down huge street trees of only half-a-century growth because they were riddled with decay and menacing lives and property in every storm. The laurel oak (*Q.*

laurifolia) is a better tree, being more nearly evergreen and not reaching senility until 75 or 80 years. For city streets that is still much too short a useful life. The live oak should still be sturdy of limb at the second-century mark, and while it grows less rapidly than the other species, it makes a handsome, small tree in 20 years or less. Besides being wind-resistant, live oak tolerates salt spray. Young trees will respond to good cultural treatment, and will be more shapely if Spanish-moss is removed annually. Mature trees usually have a greater spread than height, and do not permit lawn grasses to grow under them.

Ravenala madagascariensis. TRAVELERS-TREE. Madagascar. (S). 25 ft. Here is one of southern Florida's most striking trees, because its head is a large, symmetrical fan of banana-like leaves. Travelers-trees are much planted as freestanding specimens and as accent points in outdoor living rooms. There is no truth in the oft-heard idea that the foliage fan must face a certain point of the compass.

Schinus terebinthifolius. BRAZILIAN PEPPER-TREE. Brazil. (C,S). 20-30 ft. This tree of rapid growth bears in winter clusters of small, red berries which, added to its crisp, evergreen foliage, make it very decorative. Leafy twigs with fruit clusters are popular also for Christmas decoration. In northern Florida the species is not hardy, but it comes up quickly from the roots after being frozen, and so persists as a shrubby tree which fruits nearly every year. Further south it is a good shade tree. Seedling trees may be either male or female, and softwood cuttings are used to assure trees with fruit.

Spathodea campanulata. AFRICAN TULIP-TREE. Tropical Africa. (S). 25-40 ft. All through the winter and until late in spring, this tall evergreen tree is showy with clusters of bright red flowers. It is rather easily hurt by cold and by wind storms, but recovers rapidly from both. The habit is upright rather than spreading, so that it is suited to small gardens.

Swietenia mahagoni. MAHOGANY. Southern Florida. (S). 25-40 ft. This native tree, which yields one of the world's finest cabinet woods, is also a handsome shade tree for the warmer parts of southern Florida. Young trees are likely to be killed even in these areas unless given some protection, but mature trees are hardy there. The fine, feathery foliage does not cast a very dense shade, so that lawns grow well under it, and the tree is tolerant of salt spray. Sometimes it is defoliated by a tent cater-pillar, but prompt control measures will check this pest.

Tabebuia spp. Tropical America. (S). Although growth hab-its in this genus of 100 species vary tremendously, all produce trumpet-shaped blossoms and cylindrical pods that are typical of the bignonia family. Most widely planted in Florida is the silver-trumpet-tree, *T. argentea,* whose picturesquely contorted gray branches and bright yellow, springtime flowers make it a door-yard favorite in protected locations. It rarely reaches 25 ft. *T. pentaphylla* is a taller (to 40 ft.), more symmetrical tree with compound leaves which are shed just before the attractive pink blossoms appear in spring. It is an outstanding avenue tree. Other species and hybrids are planted in the warmest parts of the peninsula.

Tamarindus indica. TAMARIND. Tropical Africa. (S). 20-40 ft. Better known for its nutritious pods, the tamarind is also an attractive, round-headed lawn tree, which casts a fairly light shade. The feathery foliage is evergreen, and the tough twigs and branches endure wind and salt spray alike. The flowers, which appear from May to July, are pleasantly colored but not at all showy. In late spring the brown pods mature, having a thin, brit-tle shell surrounding a dark brown paste in which large, flat seeds are imbedded. The paste, which is acidulous and used in cooling drinks, has commercial value for making meat sauces.

Terminalia catappa. TROPICAL-ALMOND. (S). Southeastern Asia. 25-50 ft. Few trees in southern Florida show any autumn coloring of foliage, and that is one important reason for the pop-ularity of this species. It is deciduous, and before the leaves fall in late winter, they turn red, making quite a show of color. The flowers and fruit are inconspicuous, but the tree itself is distinc-tive, even apart from its color, because of the whorled, horizontal branches, the smooth, brownish-gray bark, and the large leaves clustered near the twig tips. The common name is misleading, for while there is a tiny bit of edible kernel in the leathery fruit, it is not sufficient reward for the great effort needed to discover it. The tree is popular for street or avenue planting and endures salt spray well. A related species, *T. muelleri,* is also a handsome tree, much smaller in size, which is adapted to the same area. It has attractive, small clusters of tiny, white flowers, somewhat like lilies-of-the-valley, but does not develop red color in the leaves.

Ulmus spp. ELM. Old and New Worlds. (N,C). The graceful American elm, beloved in northern cities, does not thrive in our state, although some species native to Florida are occasionally seen in landscape plantings. By far the most popular species here, however, is the Siberian elm, *U. pumila.* This fast growing, small, deciduous tree is quite well adapted to our conditions and widely available. It is likely to be confused with the Chinese elm, *U. parvifolia,* which is more weeping in habit and has smaller leaves. Some forms are almost evergreen in mild winters in central Florida.

Vitex agnus-castus. CHASTE-TREE. Europe. (N). 10-20 ft. This shrubby tree is popular in dooryard plantings for the spikes of fragrant, lilac-colored blossoms borne in summer. Deciduous during the winter, the lacy, digitate leaves are attractive in summer also. A variety of *V. trifolia,* with white-margined leaves, is popular as a shrub or clipped hedge, as well as in tree form in southern Florida. Propagation is by softwood cuttings in summer.

TREES FOR SPECIAL USES

Avenue plantings

Bischofia	Magnolia
Bombax	Mangifera
Bucida	Melaleuca
Casuarina	Peltophorum
Cornus	Quercus
Delonix	Swietenia
Ilex	Tamarindus
Jacaranda	Terminalia

Flowering specimens

Acacia	Delonix
Albizia	Eriobotrya
Bauhinia	Erythrina
Bombax	Jacaranda
Cassia	Koelreuteria
Castanospermum	Lagerstroemia
Catesbaea	Magnolia
Cercis	Parkinsonia
Chionanthus	Peltophorum
Citrus	Plumeria
Cordia	Tabebuia
Cornus	Vitex

Seaside plantings

Achras	Ficus
Bursera	Grevillea
Casuarina	Melaleuca
Coccoloba	Swietenia
Cordia	Tamarindus
Eriobotrya	Terminalia

6

Palms

Nowhere else in the continental United States is it possible to grow the wide variety of palms that can be successfully cultivated in our state. Mainly tropical in distribution, these graceful trees do much to make Florida's landscape distinctively different. Many native and exotic species, varying from dwarfs of a few feet to magnificent trees which attain a height of 100 ft., are widely employed with telling effect in this subtropical tourist land.

Palms may be used in many ways in landscape plantings. Species in varying heights can be planted in attractive groups; they may be used as enframement and background for the home, but the most notable way that palms can be employed is as avenue trees. Tall, clean-growing, single-trunked specimens, planted at 25- to 30-ft. intervals on both sides of an avenue, make a picture that is not soon forgotten. Yet palms are not wholly satisfactory for ordinary street usage because they cast so little shade.

Temperature is the chief factor that limits the distribution of palms. Along the coast from Jupiter to Bradenton, it is possible to grow all but the most tender of tropical palms. As one progresses northward and inland the list becomes notably shorter, until finally, upon reaching the Georgia line, only about half a dozen species are fully reliable in all winters. Palms should be permanent elements in landscaping, and once chosen to serve a definite purpose in a planting, they must be hardy in all weather.

Transplanting

Palms may be transplanted at any time of the year, but the beginning of the rainy season is most favorable. Root development is most rapid then and the plant rallies from the transplanting operation most quickly. Several weeks before moving palms, planting holes should be prepared as described in the preceding chapter. Palms are transplanted in all sizes from small seedlings to finished landscape specimens; size is limited only by the mechanical equipment that is at hand to transport them. The size of the root ball is much smaller, in proportion, than that habitually taken with a typical woody tree. In fact, sometimes roots are trimmed with a sharp axe to within a foot or two of the trunk, since branch roots farther back function, and new roots develop from the crown each year. It is well known that palm roots will emerge higher and higher above the crown, and therefore it is common practice to set palm trees slightly deeper than they grew. It is easy to plant too deeply, but too shallow planting is *more* dangerous and must be studiously avoided.

When the palm is in place, the fertile soil that was taken from the enriched hole should be replaced and water allowed to flow in from the hose to eliminate air pockets and to make a good contact between roots and particles of soil. The job should be finished by tramping to firm the soil and then building a saucer around the tree to hold water. Once each week that it does not rain, this depression should be filled with water.

Because of drastic reduction of roots, it is accepted practice to remove leaves when transplanting large palms. The uppermost leaf stems are tied around the bud as protection. Every effort must be made not to harm this vital structure, for palms have only a single growing point and die if it is destroyed. When a large palm is being dug, it must be guyed so that it does not fall hard and harm the bud.

Palms over 8 ft. in trunk height should be firmly braced after transplanting. Three 2 x 4's spiked to the trunk at one end and then firmly secured to "dead men" in the ground are the most satisfactory braces. If these timbers remain in place for about 18 months, a sturdy root system will have been built to hold the palm against strong winds. Choice exotics may be braced each autumn as routine protection. Wounds in palm trunks never heal, so as few holes as possible should be made in the trunks.

AFTERCARE

Young palms grow rapidly to mature landscape sizes when they are encouraged by proper cultivation and fertilization. It is a good plan to keep a circle of clean earth around young trees in lawns for the first few years. A 5- to 7-ft. ring should be cultivated frequently with a scuffle hoe; a hose should be allowed to run slowly for several hours once a week during dry spells; and fertilizer should be applied several times during each growing season. Palms that have been neglected can usually be reconditioned by filling rotted cow manure into post holes that are dug at intervals around the trunk. Unlike woody trees, a neglected palm will never show an increase in the diameter of the trunk existing at the time it is rejuvenated. The trunk formed above this point will expand to much greater thickness when vigorous growth is renewed.

Most palms are rather resistant to diseases, insects, and drought. Once they become established, the lawn can be allowed to grow up around the trunk, and little routine maintenance is required. All brown leaves and flower and fruit clusters should be removed with a sharp pruning saw as soon as they become unattractive with age.

PROPAGATION

Palms are increased by seeds and by division. As soon as they are ripe, seeds should be sown in beds, pots, or boxes of fertile soil. Cover the seeds to a depth approximating their diameters and cover the whole with one thickness of burlap. This material will conserve moisture and discourage birds and rodents. In winter seed beds must have full sun, but during warmer months they must be protected by cheesecloth or slat shade. When rains begin, the burlap should be renewed so that seeds will not be washed out of the soil.

Palm seeds vary greatly in the length of time required for germination. Some will sprout in a few weeks, while others will require as much as one or two years to come up. It is quite evident, therefore, that close attention is needed until seedlings are well under way.

Seedlings may be potted shortly after germination; they must be potted before the roots attain much length. They may be set individually in clay flowerpots, paper plant bands, wooden boxes, or discarded motor-oil cans. The soil used in these containers should be a fertile organic mixture of slightly acid reaction.

Coconuts are set in rows and buried only one-half their thickness, the upper portions being fully exposed. Germination should be complete in about five months.

Division is the method of vegetative propagation in which a plant is divided into several units (p. 77). Species of *Phoenix, Chrysalidocarpus, Rhapis,* and *Caryota* may be so multiplied when well-rooted offsets are found. If the specimen is in a container, it can be turned out and cut into units with shears or an axe. If it is a lawn specimen, sturdy offsets several years old can be severed from the old tree with a large chisel or a heavy crowbar. These offsets may be potted or set directly in the garden where they are to grow.

PALMS RECOMMENDED FOR FLORIDA

Acrocomia totai. GRU-GRU. Argentina. (C,S). 45 ft. This handsome, pinnate-leaved palm grows well in Florida and would be even more widely planted if it were not for the vicious, long, black spines that beset its trunk thickly. If these are cut off above head height, gru-gru makes a fine specimen or group planting. One or two other species of *Acrocomia* are occasionally seen in Florida, all similarly armed.

Archontophoenix spp. KING PALM. Australia. (S). Two species of these slender palms with ringed trunks are often seen in Florida—the Alexandra king palm (*A. alexandrae*) and the piccabeen king palm (*A. cunninghamiana*). Both look somewhat like slender royal palms and may reach a height of over 50 ft. They are usually planted as lawn specimens, and are distinguished most readily by the color of the lower leaf surface, which is bright green in the piccabeen and gray-green in the Alexandra.

Arecastrum romanzoffianum. QUEEN PALM. Brazil. (C,S). 40 ft. This very popular palm in central Florida is usually better known by its former name, *Cocos plumosa.* Wherever oranges can be grown successfully, the graceful, plumy queen palm is highly recommended for avenue planting, as a lawn specimen, or as a background subject. It serves as a fair substitute for the royal palm in areas too cold for that tender species.

Arenga pinnata. SUGAR PALM. East Indies. (S). 40 ft. Limited chiefly by its great tenderness to cold, sugar palm makes a striking specimen because of its tremendous pinnate leaves. The name is given it because of the high concentration of sugar in the sap, which flows freely when the flower cluster is cut. In India and Java this is an important source of sugar.

Butia capitata. PINDO PALM. Paraguay. (N,C,S). 20 ft. This hardy, slow growing palm, formerly called *Cocos australis,* is well adapted to Florida's soils and climate. Stiff, recurved pinnate leaves of bluish-green color are borne on stout trunks with persistent leaf bases. Orange-yellow fruits, the size of large olives, are juicy and pleasantly flavored. Slow growth and spreading habit make the pindo palm poorly suited for planting along streets or walks. It requires plenty of space as a lawn specimen. This hardiest pinnate-leaved palm is very effective in groups or specimen plantings, and is especially recommended for parks and campuses. It is tolerant of salt spray. Seeds require many months for germination.

Caryota spp. FISH-TAIL PALM. Southeastern Asia. (S). Two

palms with peculiar fish-tailed leaflets are common in southern Florida. Although they are easily distinguished, neither has been commonly known by a distinctive name. The larger species, C. *urens,* has a single sturdy trunk which may reach a height of 40 ft. Its size and age are limited by the fact that when it finally begins to bloom, the blossom clusters are borne lower and lower on the trunk each year, and when they reach the bottom, the palm dies. It makes a handsome lawn specimen until then. The other species, C. *mitis,* always suckers from the base to produce several stems, no one of which reaches over 25 ft. In addition to its popularity as a lawn specimen, this palm is often grown in urns for lobby, Florida room, or patio decoration.

Chamaedorea elegans. HOUSEHOLD PALM. Central America. (S). This tiny, pinnate-leaved palm with very slender, ringed trunk is unusual among palms for the development of typical leaves of mature form on seedlings only a few months old, and for flowering in small pots. Tolerant of shade and drought, these dainty dwarf palms are unusually suitable for container culture in patios and on terraces, where not exposed to full sun, and as pot plants in screened porches or even in living rooms. Seeds form readily following hand pollination, as there are male and female plants, and germinate in a few months.

Chamaerops humilis. EUROPEAN FAN PALM. Southern Europe. (N,C,S). 10 ft. This dwarf, hardy, slow growing palm, the only one native to Europe, is the hardiest to cold of all palms. The trunk is short and the fan-shaped leaves are borne thickly in a bushy head. Often several trunks arise. Useful as a lawn specimen or for low groups, this little palm is highly recommended.

Chrysalidocarpus lutescens. CANE PALM. Madagascar. (S). 20 ft. As an urn subject or patio plant, this little palm with clustered yellow stems is very popular. It was formerly known as *Areca lutescens* and many still think of it by this name. Because it requires moist, fertile soil and freedom from frost and salt spray, cane palm is limited in its distribution in Florida. Where conditions are favorable, it is warmly recommended for outdoor specimen planting as well as pot culture indoors.

Coccothrinax argentata. SILVER PALM. Southern Florida. (S). 20 ft. This slender, fine-scale palm is native to the Florida Keys and the adjacent mainland on well-drained soils. Occasionally used as a lawn specimen in that area, silver palm is distinctive for the silvery undersurface of its small, fan-shaped leaves.

Cocos nucifera. COCONUT PALM. Southeastern Asia. (S). 75 ft. This graceful palm is not at all suited to avenues because its slender trunk never grows straight, but as a specimen tree in parkways or lawns, or in a background group, it is very satisfactory. The tremendous leaves give a tropical feeling, and the clusters of huge fruits add interest. The heavy nuts can be a serious hazard, however, and should be cut off before they fall, when coconut palms are planted beside a walk. These palms are tolerant of salt spray and brackish water but do not require salt in the soil as is sometimes wrongly supposed. In the warmest coastal areas the coconut palm cannot be surpassed as an ornamental.

Cycas spp. CYCAD. The cycads are not even closely related to palms, but because they have a palm-like appearance and are often called "palms," it seems logical to include them here for convenience. Actually they are ancient plants intermediate between ferns and pines. The fern cycas or fern "palm" (*C. circinalis*), native to the East Indies, is the better species for Florida, where it thrives in warm locations. Leaves 6 to 8 ft. long and soft-feathery in texture are borne on a trunk which may become 15 or 20 ft. high. The more common sago cycas, or sago "palm" (*C. revoluta*), is hardy to cold anywhere in Florida, being native to Japan. Very slow growing, it is more like a shrub, rarely exceeding 6 ft. in height. The stiff, glossy green leaves are 2 to 3 ft. long and would make the sago cycas a highly satisfactory ornamental if they were not so frequently disfigured by a leaf-spotting disease. Both cycads grow better in partial shade than in full sun.

Dictyosperma album. PRINCESS PALM. Mauritius. (S). 30 ft. This is another slender-trunked palm, looking like a miniature royal, which thrives in nearly frost-free areas of Florida, where it is chiefly used as a lawn specimen. There is a variety *album* with darker green leaves and reddish veins.

Howeia spp. SENTRY PALM. Lord Howe Island. (S). 20 ft. From a tiny island in the Indian Ocean come two species of sentry palms that have long been popular in the florist trade (usually called *Kentias*) for tubbed specimen plants. In addition to this use in lobbies, dining rooms, and patios, these slender, pinnate-leaved palms make attractive lawn specimens in the warmest areas of Florida. Belmore sentry palm (*H. belmoreana*) has leaves with short petioles and upward arching pinnae, while the faster growing Forster sentry palm (*H. forsteriana*) has long petioles and pinnae which spread horizontally for half their length before drooping.

Latania loddigesi. SILVER LATANIA PALM. Mauritius. (S). 20 ft. This slow growing, tender palm has large, fan-shaped leaves with a silver bloom on the surface and reddish petiole margins, making it a very distinctive specimen plant.

Licuala grandis. LICUALA PALM. New Britain Island. (S). This dwarf, fan-leaved palm from Melanesia is unusually attractive for planting in patios, terraces, and Florida rooms, where it can have partial shade. It thrives in rich organic compost, kept moist. This rare species is worthy of wider use as a tubbed or lawn specimen.

Livistona chinensis. CHINESE FAN PALM. China. (C,S). 25 ft. Widely planted in Florida as a lawn specimen, this graceful palm is well adapted to soil conditions here. It grows fairly rapidly and when mature may endure winters in northern Florida. Much less common is the taller (75 ft.) Australian fan palm, *L. australis,* which is also attractive.

Mascarena verschaffelti. SPINDLE PALM. Mauritius. (S). 25 ft. This pinnate-leaved palm of fairly rapid growth is distinctive for the prominent bulge in the trunk giving it a spindle shape. It makes a handsome lawn specimen. Formerly the genus was known as *Hyophorbe.*

Paurotis wrighti. SAW-CABBAGE PALM. Caribbean area. (S, C). 20 ft. In high favor for landscape work, this dwarf, fine-scale, native palm with clustered trunks is found as a specimen in some of southern Florida's most beautiful gardens. It is easy of culture, and tolerant both of salt drift and poor drainage. The petioles are lined with heavy curved spines.

Phoenix spp. DATE PALM. Many species of date palms thrive in Florida. All are pinnate-leaved and have trunks covered with old leaf bases. The unmodified name, date palm, belongs to *P. dactylifera,* the source of edible dates, which has been in cultivation for thousands of years. Other species bear a distinguishing adjective. The date palm is hardy from Jacksonville south, but is not especially ornamental and rarely matures edible dates here, so that it is seldom planted. The Canary Island date palm, *P. canariensis,* is hardy almost anywhere in the state and thrives on all soils. Because of its massive trunk, its huge, drooping leaves, and its susceptibility to attack by the palm leaf skeletonizer, it is not recommended as a dooryard tree. Until it attains some size, which takes many years, its fronds interfere with traffic too often for recommendation as a street tree, although it is a striking avenue palm when parkways are wide enough (30 ft.) to accommodate it. For parks and municipal properties its monumental size is well adapted. It may reach 40 ft. in height The pygmy date palm, *P. roebeleni,* seldom exceeds 8 ft. in height. The most popular dwarf palm, this tiny brother of the preceding giant is a native of Southeastern Asia, and not surprisingly is limited to warm locations in Florida. As a pot plant, patio subject, or component of a landscape planting, pygmy date is worthy of the high esteem in which it is held for its delicate, feathery foliage. A partially shaded location and fairly fertile soil are preferred. Senegal date palm, *P. reclinata,* grows in clumps of slender, leaning trunks up to 20 ft. high, and finds wide usage as a patio or lawn specimen. It is tolerant of salt spray, but not hardy in unprotected northern areas. Cliff date palm, *P. rupicola,* is similar in size and climatic adaptation, but forms a single curved trunk instead of a clump. It also makes a good specimen plant of fine scale for small gardens.

Pritchardia pacifica. FIJI FAN PALM. Fiji Islands. (S). 30 ft. This graceful, distinctive, fan-leaved palm is limited in its Florida planting by unusual tenderness to cold. It is easily hurt by wind, also, so that it should be planted as a lawn specimen where it will have good wind protection.

Pseudophoenix sargenti. SARGENT CHERRY PALM. West Indies. (S). 25 ft. This small, handsome palm greatly resembles a small royal palm until the bright red fruits appear. The wild specimens have nearly all been carried away from the two or three Keys where they had become naturalized, but seedlings have been grown in nurseries. Slow growing, the cherry palm is well adapted to southern Florida.

Ptychosperma spp. Australasian Tropics. (S). Two very different palms with very slender trunks represent this genus in Florida. Solitaire palm, *P. elegans,* has a single trunk up to 25 ft. high but not over 4 in. in diameter, with a feather duster crown. Macarthur palm, *P. macarthuri,* forms a cluster of shorter trunks. Both have prominent green crown shafts, formed by the clasping bases of the lowest leaves, and clusters of red fruits from the bottom of the collar. Small size and fine scale make both good for patios, framing, and as tubbed specimens.

Rhapidophyllum hystrix. NEEDLE PALM. Florida. (N,C). 5 ft. This tiny indigene is notable for dwarf habit, cold hardiness, shade tolerance, and the peculiar sharp, black spines borne on the leaf sheaths. Trunks run horizontally just below the surface of the earth. With permission of the owner, dig needle palms from northern Florida hammocks, or grow them from seeds. Partial shade and fairly moist soil are preferred.

Rhapis spp. LADY PALM. China. (N,C,S). Two species of the dwarf, slender lady palms are common in Florida. Both have fan leaves and sucker abundantly to form clusters of thin stems. The broad-leaved lady palm, *R. excelsa,* may reach 15 ft. in height, while the slender lady palm, *R. humilis,* hardly exceeds 5 ft. Both require shaded locations and are very popular as tub specimens as well as in palm groups.

Roystonea spp. ROYAL PALM. All royal palms have clean, erect, cement-gray trunks, topped by a glossy green collar several feet high, from which the large pinnate leaves spread out. They are deservedly popular as avenue trees, and have a stately habit as lawn specimens. In southern Florida, especially along the coasts, they thrive splendidly, and are probably more planted than any other palm. The most common species is Cuban royal, R. *regia,* which may reach 50 ft. and has a slight bulge in the stem, giving it the shape of a cigar. Taller growing is the less widely planted Florida royal, R. *elata,* which is native to wet hammocks in the Everglades. The best-known examples are the lofty specimens around the Hialeah racetrack. Still taller, often exceeding 100 ft., is Carib royal from the West Indies, C. *oleracea.* It is the only royal with no swelling of the trunk. Puerto Rican royal, R. *borinquena,* is much like the Cuban, although not quite so tall. The last two thrive where the Cuban royal grows well also. All royal palms make very rapid growth when supplied abundantly with water and fertilizer, and all endure wind and salt spray well.

Sabal palmetto. CABBAGE PALMETTO. Southeastern United States. (N,C,S). 80 ft. The hardiest of our native palms, this well-known species is Florida's official state tree and is abundant in all except the extreme western parts of the state. Thriving on a wide variety of soil types, and tolerant of both salt spray and brackish water, the cabbage palmetto is popular in group plantings, for avenue rows, and as a lawn specimen. Two introduced species of the same genus are sometimes seen in Florida, differing from the native palm chiefly in having thicker trunks of less height and grayish-green leaves of even larger size. The Puerto Rican hat palm, S. *causiarum,* may reach 40 ft., while the Hispaniolan palmetto, S. *umbraculifera,* attains 60 ft. Both are suited for the same landscape uses as the cabbage palmetto, but are not fully hardy in the northern section of the state.

Serenoa repens. SAW PALMETTO. Southeastern United States. (N,C,S). 4 ft. The spiny-petioled saw palmettos are only troublesome weeds to cattlemen and farmers, but they do have landscape values. When one is building on land whereon they are growing, clumps may often be left to good advantage, since they blend in well in both foundation plantings and informal shrubbery borders. Normally the trunks creep along the ground, so that the height of the plant is the leaf length. Rarely specimens are found with erect trunks, and such palms make attractive, fine-scale specimens, but they are not easily transplanted.

Thrinax spp. THATCH PALM. Southern Florida. (S). 30 ft. Two native fan-leaved species of thatch palm are sometimes seen in southern Florida gardens. The brittle thatch palm, *T. microcarpa,* has a rather thick trunk, often nearly a foot in diameter, with leaves grayish-green above and silvery below; the Jamaica thatch palm, *T. parviflora,* never has a trunk more than 6 in. thick and has leaves yellowish-green above and light green below.

Trachycarpus fortunei. WINDMILL PALM. China and Japan. (N,C). 20 ft. This hardy, slow growing, fan-leaved palm is a good lawn specimen for small gardens in the northern half of the state. The erect trunk is densely clothed with black, hair-like fiber, even after the leaf stalks have dropped off.

Veitchia merrilli. MANILA PALM. Philippines. (S). 25 ft. This medium-small palm is very ornamental because of bright red clusters of fruit in addition to its handsome feathery foliage. It resembles somewhat a small royal palm, and has proved well adapted to the limestone soils of the Miami area and the Keys.

Washingtonia spp. WASHINGTON PALM. California and and Mexico. (N,C,S). There are only two species of Washington palms, and while both are native only in western deserts, they both thrive mightily in Florida's humid climate. The commonly planted species is *W. robusta,* the Mexican Washington palm, which often reaches upward of 80 ft. in height. The California Washington palm, *W. filifera,* differs chiefly in having a shorter, stouter trunk rarely exceeding 50 ft. Being of rather rapid growth, these palms become very tall too soon for good lawn specimens, although very attractive while young. They find an admirable use in avenue plantings, where they are picturesque and effective. The old leaves are normally retained for years, making a brown "Mother Hubbard" often hanging to the ground from where the living leaves spread out. Most gardeners prefer to cut off these dead leaves promptly, as high as they can be reached by ladder and pole pruner, because they increase the fire hazard and serve as breeding places for rodents.

7

Shrubs and Vines

SHRUBS, TREES, AND LAWN are primary elements in any landscape development, and shrubs are in some ways the most important of the three. At least we may develop the shrubbery portions of the plan, and see them fulfilling their role, while the trees are still of negligible size and the lawn is newly sprigged. Unlike the case of trees, it is seldom that wild shrubs existing on a building site can be utilized where they stand. Where more than a dozen native species of trees, including several of the best in the world, are available for landscape use in Florida, there are not half that number of really worthy native shrubs, although a few of these are outstanding in merit. We rely heavily on exotic shrubs in Florida landscaping.

Shrubs have a variety of important functions in landscaping. Perhaps the most common usage is in foundation planting, which relates the house to the ground. Tall shrubs at the corners and low shrubs under the windows are called for, and a large number of different plants are available for these needs in all sections of the state. The border of shrubs at the garden boundaries not only assures privacy and provides definite limits to the landscape picture, but it also furnishes a background of green against which lower growing flowering plants show up effectively. Shrubs are the materials universally used for hedges to separate areas within gardens, or for relatively low screens to cut off undesired views or unwelcome winds. Specimen shrubs find wide usage as focal points at the ends of garden vistas or as accent to break the monotony of shrubbery walls.

Florida has many colorful woody vines available for landscape use. Here, the many species of vines are used for softening architectural lines and hiding architectural faults, for adding brilliant splashes of color, for screens and shade when grown on supporting frames, and for ground covers in areas where grasses will not grow. Many beautiful evergreen vines are colorful during the tourist season; others are cherished for cool, year-round green color. A few deciduous kinds are admired because they change with the seasons. Some vines cling to masonry, others twine about trees or wires, and still others are sprawlers that must be tied in place.

The line of demarcation between shrubs and vines is not always clear. Sometimes, for example, bougainvillea and wisteria serve as shrubs when they are sheared as standards; yet in the same garden they may grow freely as vines. Similarly it is possible to grow many trees as shrubs by constant pruning, and it is not easy to say whether one deals with a tree or a shrub in these cases. In this book, plants of variable habit under domestication have been classified according to their most common use, as trees, shrubs, or vines.

GROWING SHRUBS AND VINES

Proper spacing of shrubs is important to their development as shapely plants. A general rule is to set plants in the shrub border (unless they are to form a tight hedge) at a distance apart equal to two-thirds of the height they are expected to reach ultimately. In foundation plantings the semidwarf species such as boxthorn, lime-berry, and Kurume azaleas may be spaced 2 ft. apart. More robust growing shrubs should never be closer than 3 ft. apart, and if there is no objection to a somewhat spotty effect for the first season, a spacing interval of 4 ft. may give even more satisfaction in the end. Choice specimen plants require even more free space for development than do foundation shrubs. These latter should be set out at least 2 ft. from

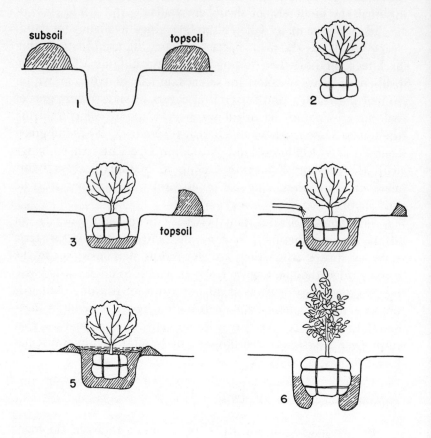

FIGURE 21
TRANSPLANTING EVERGREEN SHRUBS

1. Hole ready for planting, with subsoil laid aside for discard.
2. Balled evergreen shrub ready for planting.
3. Plant in place, adjusted to correct depth by placing topsoil underneath.
4. Topsoil filled in nearly to top of hole, and settled by water.
5. Completed planting with mulched basin to hold water.
6. Hole prepared with center pedestal of unexcavated soil to prevent settling of heavy camellia plant.

the foundation wall of the house. For ventilators, carry the planting out into small promontories, to allow for the circulation of air and the entry of workmen when necessary.

Preparation of holes or beds for shrubs and vines should be made well in advance of planting time. Special care is usually needed in preparing for base plantings, because almost always the soil next to the foundation contains considerable amounts of concrete and mortar, both on the surface and mixed in the top foot. Most foundation shrubs cannot tolerate the presence of these lime-bearing materials. It is not sufficient merely to rake away and carry off the larger fragments. The only satisfactory plan is to remove the soil to a depth of a foot and to replace it with a fertile soil of acid reaction, such as may be made by mixing good topsoil with an equal amount of peat or compost. It may be an added measure of insurance against mineral deficiencies to fortify this mixture with a sprinkling (1 qt. to a wheelbarrowful) of commercial fertilizer containing a mixture of trace nutrient elements. Shrubbery beds along property lines benefit from similar treatment. After beds have been prepared, they should be well soaked to settle the soil. Any grasses or other weeds that appear should be removed promptly, and the beds should be kept slightly moist constantly.

Most evergreen shrubs are transplanted to gardens from tin cans, and little or no disturbance of the root system occurs. Others, field grown, are forced to have compact root systems by periodic root pruning. These, then, are carefully dug and the roots held tightly in place by burlap. Canned and B&B plants are transplanted without reducing the foliage area. Shrubs which are dug with bare roots, on the other hand, lose most absorbing roots in the process, and they must have a proportional amount of the leaves and tender shoots cut off so that they do not wilt and die. Deciduous shrubs lose all their leaves anyhow in the late fall, and may best be transplanted then, since new roots will have some months to develop before new leaves appear. Evergreen shrubs are transplanted best during early winter also, even though canned or balled, since the cool weather makes for minimum moisture loss from leaves. However, evergreens with intact root systems can be moved at any season of the year when they are not in a tender flush of growth. If evergreen shrubs must be cut back to compensate for considerable root loss, it is better to delay transplanting until near the end of the season of possible frost. Such plants are stimulated to start their buds into growth during any warm winter weather, and the soft, new shoots are easy prey to any frost.

When planting time comes, shrubs should be set about on the beds and arranged to give the best landscape effect as well as to allow proper spacing. Marks should be made around each root mass or container, the plants set aside, and the soil dug out as indicated for each plant. It is important that shrubs should not be set deeper than they have been growing. If they are container-grown or bare-root, it is easy enough to see the soil line; but if they are balled in burlap, the cloth usually is wrapped around the trunk so that no soil line is visible. Lest the plant suffer by being set too deep, it is best to cut away the burlap collar until the soil surface of the ball is visible next to the trunk. Heavy shrubs may sink somewhat into the soil of the planting hole if it has not previously been well firmed under them. Often this settling process takes place over a period of weeks and is not noticed until the plant begins to turn yellow (fig. 21).

After shrubs have been set at the proper depth, holes are backfilled and the soil firmed around the roots or root ball with the feet. Specimen plants should have a ridge of soil around the hole, making a shallow basin. Either bed or basin should then be mulched heavily with grass, leaves, peat, or compost. The entire shrubbery bed should then be well soaked, and this irrigation repeated weekly until rains make it unnecessary.

Shrubs can give a continuously pleasing effect only if good conditions of growth are maintained for them. Lawn grass should not be allowed to encroach on shrubbery beds, not only because an unkempt effect is produced thus, but also because of danger of injury to the plants by the lawn mower and because grasses compete for soil moisture and nutrients. Frequent, systematic edging is necessary during the summer months to keep grass beyond the drip of outer branches. Clean cultivation may be used for specimen shrubs, with lawn encircling them, but shrubbery beds thrive better under mulch. Shrubs should never be allowed to suffer from drought. It should be borne in mind that most plants flower more freely when grown in sunny locations than in partial shade.

Fertilizer need not be applied during the first season to shrubs planted as above. During the late winter of each year an application of commercial fertilizer, acid in reaction, should be made. Usually fertilizer is broadcast directly on the mulch and washed in with the hose. Quite large shrubs growing in sod may benefit from having fertilizer placed in punch-bar holes, as described previously for trees. Again at the beginning of the rainy season it is well to make a second yearly application of fertilizer to ornamental shrubs. Such analyses as 8-8-8 or 6-6-6 are satisfactory for any shrubs. From 2 to 4 pts. of a balanced fertilizer such as 6-6-6 should be applied for 100 sq. ft. of shrubbery bed. Specimen plants of large size should be fertilized more heavily. As a suggestion, height may be multiplied by width, and 1 pt. of fertilizer applied for each 10 sq. ft. Special fertilizer mixtures are often advertised for use on camellias and azaleas, which are so notably sensitive about soil acidity. These mixtures are also excellent for gardenias, hollies, hibiscus, and other choice landscape shrubs. However, any good garden fertilizer will prove quite satisfactory if it has an acid-forming tendency, and your dealer can give assurance about this.

Soil preparation, planting, and aftercare of woody vines should be the same as for shrubs. Fertilizer application will usually be smaller than for shrubs because most vines develop far-ranging root systems which extend for many feet. Your only guide to fertilization amounts is the apparent health of the vines.

Most ornamental shrubs grow very rapidly in Florida's humid, subtropical climate, and they usually need frequent, systematic pruning to keep them in scale. Informal, naturalistic pruning is preferred generally today, rather than shearing to geometrical forms, although hedges and portal plants are often sheared. Shoots of unusual vigor should be headed back with hand pruning shears to a point well below the contour of the

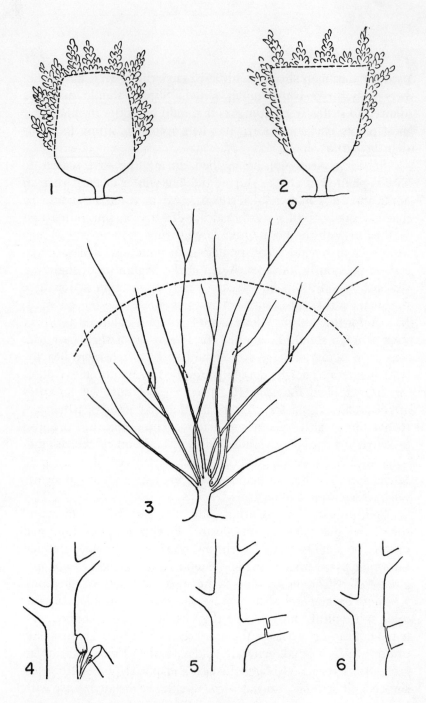

PRUNING WOODY PLANTS

1,2.   Pruning formal or hedge shrubs—1 is right, 2 is wrong way.
3.   Pruning informal shrubs by thinning.
4,5,6.   Cutting off large limb. 4 shows how limb splits away if only one cut is made. 5 and 6 show proper series of cuts to avoid splitting. Make cut first from below in 5, and then from a little further out until limb falls clear. Then cut off stub close to the trunk as in 6.

bush. Latent buds lower on the pruned stem will develop into several shoots of normal size in place of the one rampant shoot. Fine, twiggy growths should be reduced in amount without regular pattern and in moderation, so that the shrub will not have an artificial, barbered look. The aim of informal pruning is to maintain a normal habit of growth within certain limits of size. Pinching—the removal of tender shoot tips with thumb and forefinger—should be practiced all through the growing season on each flush of growth, to encourage development of well-branched, compact shrubs.

The time when shrubs should be pruned will depend upon growth and blooming habits largely. In general it may be said that species blooming in winter and spring should be pruned immediately after flowering is ended. Such shrubs usually form their flower buds in early summer, and blossoms will be sacrificed if they are pruned after this time. Examples of such spring-bloomers are azaleas, camellias, spireas, hydrangeas, bougainvilleas, and flowering-quince. Shrubs that bloom in summer and fall usually develop flowers on the current season's growth, and should be pruned before the spring flush of growth begins. This group includes abelia, oleander, thryallis, plumbago, hibiscus, yellow-elder, and many other species. The crape-myrtle belongs to this group, but since it sheds its leaves in the fall, it is standard practice to prune it as soon as it is leafless. Many species with recurrent blooming need to have old inflorescences pruned away as soon as blooms fade, and often need some vegetative pruning for vigorous new growth.

Coniferous (or narrow-leaved) evergreens and broad-leaved evergreens grown for foliage rather than bloom should be headed back informally all through the growing season, whenever shoots grow out of bounds. Such periodic pruning will keep cherry-laurel, wax privet, wax-myrtle, podocarpus, and junipers shapely and compact.

Hedges need frequent shearing from early spring to late summer to keep them neat and attractive. Hedge shears are accompanied by directions for use, which state that trimming must be done while the new growth is tender and succulent, lest the shear blades be forced out of alignment. This warning of the manufacturer is also good horticultural advice, because clipped hedges will be kept in best possible condition when sheared in this way. A precaution that must always be kept in mind in trimming hedges is that the sides must never slope so that the top of the hedge is wider than the bottom. Sides must be vertical or slope slightly inward toward the top if the lower portion is to remain healthy, as an overhanging top shades the lower portion, causing it to die back.

Some vines need no pruning, while others need regular attention. Those which grow very rampantly may benefit from root pruning to decrease vigor. Those that tend to sucker freely should have these suckers thinned to prevent crowding. Old, weak canes should be removed in favor of younger, more vigorous ones. Shoots of strong vigor should be headed back by pruning or pinching to induce lateral branching. Time of pruning depends on blooming period, as for shrubs.

SHRUBS RECOMMENDED FOR FLORIDA GARDENS

Abelia grandiflora. GLOSSY ABELIA. China. (N). This medium-sized shrub has small, shiny leaves, bright crimson twigs, and clusters of small, white flowers from late spring until fall. It makes its best growth on heavier soils in northwestern Florida, where it is highly regarded for hedge use, foundation planting, or specimens. Cuttings of mature twigs in winter are rooted for propagation. Abelia prefers full sun and needs good soil moisture.

Acalypha wilkesiana. COPPER-LEAF. Polynesia. (S). This rampant growing shrub with large, reddish leaves is well known in southern Florida, where it is usually employed too freely. As foundation material it is too coarse in texture, and it usually gets out of scale quickly. Certainly it gives too strong a color accent. Copper-leaf grows readily from cuttings, and succeeds in any situation which is not too shady. It is too garish for hedge use.

Agave americana. CENTURY PLANT. Tropical America. (N,

C,S). While agaves are herbaceous perennials in that they develop no woody stems, they are more like shrubs in use, size, and hardiness and are included here. They are characterized by rounded masses of stiff, swordshaped leaves, from 4 to 6 ft. long and as many inches wide at the base, always armed with long, sharp terminal thorns. These must be clipped off as soon as each new leaf is fully grown. Some species have leaves with marginal spines also, among them our native century plant. After many years, indefinite in number but only a fraction of a century, a lofty flower spike may be produced, resembling a gigantic candelabrum. When blooming is ended, the plant dies. Suckers from the base are the common means of propagation and should not be detached until well rooted. The most common form of century plant in cultivation is the variety *variegata*, with the leaves twisted, dark green with marginal bands of yellow; but forms with gray-green leaves and other variegated types are seen in Florida also. Sisal agave, *A. sisalana,* from whose leaves sisal hemp is made, is used in southern Florida landscaping. The smooth, green leaves have no marginal prickles, and the flower spike has many of the flowers transformed into miniature suckers called bulbils, by which it is easily propagated. Enduring heat, drought, and salt spray, agaves thrive also in soil of good moisture content, and will grow in full sun or partial shade.

Allamanda cathartica. YELLOW ALLAMANDA. Brazil. (C,S). Free-flowering and colorful, this is a popular tender ornamental. Its natural habit is scrambling, so that it may be pruned to shrub form or trained as a vine. The more common variety is 'Henderson,' with flowers 4 in. or more across, borne all through the growing season, but several other varieties grow in Florida. Oleander allamanda, *A. neriifolia,* is also yellow-flowered, but blooms only in winter and does not tend to vine. Purple allamanda, *A. violacea,* is rare and its common name is often misapplied to a *Cryptostegia.* All allamandas love full sun and not too moist soil, and are propagated by softwood or firmwood cuttings. Only *A. neriifolia* produces seed often.

Ardisia crenata. CORAL ARDISIA or SPICE-BERRY. China. (N,C,S). A small, slow growing shrub with glossy, scalloped, dark green leaves, coral ardisia is notable for the clusters of crimson berries which it bears all winter. This shade-loving plant comes readily from seeds.

Ardisia escallonioides. MARLBERRY. Florida and Mexico. (S). Common in southern Florida, marlberry makes a satisfactory large shrub that tolerates shade and salt spray. Clusters of white flowers, borne at intervals through the year, are followed by clusters of black berries like those of the camphor tree. Seed propagation is easy.

Azalea spp. AZALEA. See Chapter Eight.

Bambusa multiplex. DWARF BAMBOO. China. (C,S). Most bamboos grow rampantly, but this species makes a satisfactory sheared hedge, or can be maintained as a large green mass by shearing. Annual root pruning must be practiced to prevent the roots from spreading widely and competing with nearby plants. It is propagated by division of old clumps.

Beaucarnea recurvata. PONY-TAIL. Mexico. (C,S). 15-20 ft. This is one of Florida's most dramatic plants because of the way the trunk expands into a great bulge at the soil line. Nursery-grown seedlings may be set in well-drained sites not subject to low temperatures.

Berberis spp. BARBERRY. Asia. (N). For partially shaded and north-side locations on superior soils, barberries are recommended for the Panhandle. Best grower is wintergreen barberry, *B. julianae,* a handsome, hardy evergreen with compact, weeping, thorny branches. Japanese barberry, *B. thunbergi,* is grown mostly as the red-leaved form 'Atropurpurea' by western Floridians. Its tiny, armed branches, holding small red leaves closely, form a fine-scale foundation plant suited to use with white masonry. Increase is by cuttings.

Bixa orellana. ANNATTO. American Tropics. (S). Known also as "lipstick bush," this large shrub is quite showy both for its large terminal panicles of rose-pink blossoms in late summer and fall, and for the clusters of spiny red fruits that follow. The pods contain small seeds coated with a scarlet pigment, the annatto dye used to color foods—or lips. A sunny location is preferred. Propagation is by seeds.

Breynia nivosa. SNOW-BUSH. South Pacific Islands. (C,S). Ornamental for its multicolored leaves, this small shrub is popular for hedges and accents. The common form has small leaves mottled green and white, but the variety *roseopicta* has pink and red mottling also. Root and leafy tip cuttings are used for propagation.

Brunfelsia americana. LADY-OF-THE-NIGHT. West Indies. (S). Notable for its fragrance at night, this large shrub bears in summer an abundance of long, slender, trumpet-shaped flowers that are white at first and turn yellow in a few days. Rarely seen in Florida gardens are related species, notably *B. calycina* in several botanical varieties, that have blue or purple flowers, fading gradually to white, borne chiefly during the winter and spring. All brunfelsias need half shade and a fairly heavy soil free from root-knot nematodes. They are propagated by seed or softwood cuttings.

Buddleja spp. BUTTERFLY-BUSH. These are outsized, evergreen shrubs that bear blossoms which are Florida's nearest approach to lilacs. *B. lindleyana* from China is quite hardy and bears violet flowers all summer. *B. officinalis,* also Chinese, is fairly hardy, but has spikes of lilac-pink in winter. *B. asiatica* from southern Asia with white flowers and *B. madagascarensis* from Madagascar with orange-yellow flowers both bloom in winter also, but are not hardy in northern Florida.

Buxus microphylla. JAPANESE BOXWOOD. Japan. (N,C). Used chiefly for low, formal hedges and edgings to walks, boxwood is satisfactory in northern Florida. Very slow growing and small-leaved, it shears well and is easily kept low. Root-knot nematodes are troublesome on sandy soils. Boxwood is propagated by softwood cuttings.

Calliandra haematocephala. POWDER-PUFF. Tropical regions. (C,S). One of central Florida's most popular evergreen shrubs, this large, sprawling plant is beloved for the showy red pompons that are held above the silky foliage much of the year. Amateurs increase powder-puffs by air-layering.

Callicarpa americana. BEAUTY-BERRY. Southeastern United States. (N). This native of hardwood forests makes a brave show in autumn when the leaves fall to reveal the clusters of violet berries at nodes along the stems. It is propagated by seeds or cuttings. There is a white-fruited form also.

Callistemon rigidus. BOTTLE-BRUSH. Australia. (N,C,S). Brilliant red flower clusters at the branch tips, the size and shape of brushes for bottles, and stiff, narrow leaves characterize this shrub. Slow growing and hardy, this plant serves best as an accent in sunny spots. Propagation is by seeds or softwood cuttings. Plants should be grown in containers, as they are very hard to transplant from open ground.

Camellia spp. CAMELLIA. See Chapter Eight.

Carissa grandiflora. COMMON CARISSA or NATAL-PLUM. East Africa. (C,S). Utilized as a defensive hedge, as a specimen plant, or espaliered along a wall, the shining evergreen leaves, large, white flowers, and bright red fruits of the carissa make it a notable ornamental shrub. The twigs are armed with large, forked thorns. The oval fruits look somewhat like European plums, but are not so pleasant to eat out of hand, although they make delicious jelly. Of compact growth habit and slow growing, carissa thrives in full sun and endures salt spray. A sister species, the karanda (*C. carandas*), is popular in the Palm Beach area as a sheared hedge. With small flowers and black fruits, karanda is less showy than common carissa, but is vigorous and salt tolerant. Both are easily propagated by seeds or by layering, and are somewhat tender above Orlando and Tampa. Selection and vegetative propagation have been used to perpetuate certain forms for special landscaping uses.

Cassia spp. CASSIA or SENNA. The genus *Cassia* is a very large one with many species of ornamental value, both trees and shrubs. The latter all have yellow flowers and are mostly suited only to southern Florida. *C. alata,* the candle-bush, is a large, spreading shrub from Argentina, very tender to frost, producing large spikes of golden-yellow flowers from November to January. Like crape-myrtle, it is most satisfactory if pruned back hard after blooming. *C. bicapsularis* is unusual in its ability to thrive in northern Florida also, although it will be killed to the ground there in most winters. The foliage of this large shrub from the

American tropics is glossy green, and the masses of yellow flowers appear in October and November, continuing until February in southern Florida but being cut short by frost in the northern area. *C. corymbosa,* native to Argentina, is another large shrub with attractive foliage, which covers itself with yellow in fall and then repeats the process in late spring. *C. didymobotrya,* from tropical Africa, blooms during the winter and spring, with erect racemes of yellow a foot long. *C. surratensis,* native to India, blooms in the autumn. All cassias flower more freely in full sun, and need annual pruning to keep them from becoming straggly. Seeds are produced abundantly and provide easy propagation.

Casuarina spp. Often grown as sheared hedges, the casuarinas are still more common as trees, and are described as such in Chapter Five.

Cephalotaxus harringtonia. PLUM-YEW. Japan. (N). Looking like a dwarf podocarpus, plum-yew is a useful shrub for the same purpose as boxwood—a slow growing, low, formal hedge or edging. It can be kept at a height of 12 in. or allowed to reach twice that height, and thrives in sun or shade. Propagation is by softwood cuttings in spring.

Chaenomeles lagenaria. FLOWERING-QUINCE. Japan. (N). One of our few deciduous flowering shrubs, flowering-quince is really satisfactory only in the heavy soils of western Florida. Its dark red flowers make a brilliant show in late winter. It may be increased by either hardwood or softwood cuttings. San José scale is a serious pest.

Chamaecyparis ericoides. HEATH RETINOSPORA. (N). Often listed by nurseries as *Retinospora ericoides,* heath retinospora finds considerable use as a columnar specimen, especially for portal planting. The tiny needle-leaves are green in summer but turn a rusty bronze during the winter. The only real virtue of this conifer is its cylindrical habit of growth.

Chrysobalanus icaco. COCO-PLUM. Southern Florida. (S). In coastal sections of extreme southern Florida, coco-plum occurs wild as a shrub or even a small tree. In landscape arrangements this salt-tolerant, privet-like evergreen is kept to shrub size by frequent pruning. Collect wild plants with permission of the landowner, or root cuttings under mist.

Clerodendrum speciosissimum. JAVA GLORY-BOWER. Java. (S). This shrub of medium size bears large clusters of scarlet flowers during most of the year. A sister species, *C. thomsoniae,* may also be trained to shrub form, although more common as a vine. Full sun is best, and old flower clusters should be pruned off. Softwood cuttings are used for increase.

Cleyera japonica. CLEYERA. Eastern Asia. (N,C,S). Related to the camellia, this slow growing, compact evergreen shrub has glossy, dark green leaves with reddish petioles and upright habit. The small clusters of fragrant, creamy-white, little flowers and the small, dark red, puffy berries are attractive but not showy. Few pests trouble this handsome hardy shrub, which tolerates both sun and shade and endures poor drainage fairly well. It is propagated by seeds or softwood cuttings. There is some question whether the genus name should be *Cleyera* or *Ternstroemia.*

Clusia rosea. CLUSIA. Tropical America. (S). Native·to the West Indies, where it may be a 50-ft. tree, but probably never native to Florida, clusia is often grown as a large shrub in warm areas. The broadly rounded, leathery leaves resemble greatly thickened and broadened magnolia leaves. In summer pink-and-white flowers, 2 to 3 in. across, appear near the twig tips, followed by round, greenish-white fruits some 3 in. in diameter. These turn black at ripeness and split open, revealing the seeds surrounded by a resinous, black material once used to caulk the seams of boats and giving rise to one common name, "pitch-apple." The clone 'Variegata' is popular for its attractive marbled foliage.

Cocculus laurifolius. COCCULUS. Southeastern Asia. (N,C, S). Naturally scrambling in habit, this species is easily trained in shrub form, where its drooping branches covered with long evergreen leaves make it an attractive foliage plant for foundation work, screens, and borders. Softwood cuttings root easily in summer under mist.

Codiaeum variegatum. CROTON. Malaysia. (S). An endless

variety of the colorful and variable forms of this shrub are seen in every possible landscape usage in southern Florida. Often they are used to excess, since their bright foliage colors should properly be employed only as accents or highlights in green compositions. Crotons are propagated easily by softwood cuttings in summer.

Coffea arabica. COFFEE. Ethiopia. (S). Suited only to the warmest locations, coffee shrubs are highly ornamental as well as interesting for their production of beans for home roasting and grinding. Glossy evergreen leaves are attractive at all times, and periodically the branches are covered for a few days with white blossoms, followed some months later by small red fruits. Dwarf varieties need no pruning, and more vigorous varieties are easily kept to desired size. Propagation is by seed.

Conocarpus erectus. SILVER BUTTON-BUSH. Southern Florida. (S). Along tidal watercourses of the lower peninsula, striking silver-leaved individuals may be discovered growing in stands of typical green-leaved *Conocarpus.* Garden planners use such bright plants as focal points in borders of all green shrubs. Being notably salt-tolerant, this good native plant is most useful in seaside landscapes. Strike cuttings under mist.

Cryptostegia grandiflora. PALAY RUBBER-VINE. Africa. (S). Often mistaken for and miscalled "purple allamanda," the rubber-vines are easily trained to shrub form and make very attractive hedges or specimen plants. They are quite tender, but tolerate salt spray well. The purple flowers are borne in profusion all summer, and show up well against the glossy, dark green leaves. Propagation is by seeds or cuttings.

Cuphea hyssopifolia. CUPHEA. Tropical America. (C,S). Diminutive by all standards, this tiny, fine-scale shrub is unexcelled for edgings, planters, and foundation plantings. Various clones display tiny flowers in tones of red, pink, lavender, and in white. Nematode-free soil and protection from freezes are recommended.

Dombeya wallichi. PINK-BALL. Madagascar. (S). Large, hairy, heart-shaped leaves characterize this large, bushy shrub whose twigs are terminated in midwinter by huge clusters of pink flowers on long stems. Old flower clusters should be pruned off as they fade. It is easily propagated by softwood cuttings.

Duranta repens. GOLDEN-DEWDROP. Caribbean area. (C,S). This large, fast growing shrub is popular as a border or background plant, but is too vigorous and tall for use in foundation plantings. Terminal clusters of light blue flowers in summer are followed in autumn by yellow berries which hang throughout the winter. Foliage is not noteworthy, and canes are thorny. When frozen down, new canes make vigorous growth to bloom again the next season. Propagation is by seeds or cuttings of firm wood.

Elaeagnus pungens. SILVERTHORN. China. (N,C,S). Several horticultural forms are offered of this satisfactory species. Scrambling in natural habit, it is easily trained in shrub form by cutting out the long, succulent shoots that rise from the foliage mass in spring and summer. It shears well for hedges and foundation shrubs or other formal shapes. Leaves are glossy green above, but silvery beneath with bronzed, scurfy scales on the young shoots. Thriving in sun or shade, it is quite cold hardy and endures salt spray. It is propagated by seeds or softwood cuttings. A sister species, the lingaro (*E. philippensis*), has narrower leaves, silvery beneath, borne on long, arching branches. Suited only to southern and central Florida, this tropical shrub is an excellent source of jelly from its small, pink fruits.

Enallagma cucurbitina. BLACK-CALABASH. Southern Florida. (S). For its large, lustrous leaves that are almost black and its tolerance of shade and of thin alkaline sand, this large native shrub is frequently indicated for shrubbery borders by landscape planners. By systematic pruning it is maintained as a compact shrub. Increase is by cuttage or seedage.

Eranthemum nervosum. ERANTHEMUM. India. (S). This tender, almost herbaceous shrub grows to the height of 4 ft. and has coarse, glabrous, opposite leaves about the size and shape of magnolia leaves but not so leathery. In winter, spikes of deep blue, trumpet-shaped flowers are borne abundantly at the branch tips and from the uppermost leaf axils. Eranthemum grows well in half shade, and needs annual pruning because of its rank growth if given ample moisture and nutrients. It is propagated by softwood cuttings. Sometimes it is called "blue sage," but this name belongs to *Salvia* species.

Ervatamia coronaria. CRAPE-JASMINE. India. (S). With its opposite, glossy, evergreen leaves and fragrant, white flowers, crape-jasmine is often confused with cape-jasmine. The milky juice easily distinguishes the former, which also has larger, glossier leaves, smaller flowers, less hardiness to cold, and greater tolerance of nematodes in sandy soil than has gardenia. Usually the double-flowered form is grown, and the scent is more marked at night. The petals are ruffled or craped, giving rise to the name crape-jasmine. A sunny location is best for this fine, large shrub, which is best used in borders. Propagation is by softwood cuttings.

Eugenia uniflora. PITANGA or SURINAM-CHERRY. Brazil. (C,S). This beautiful evergreen shrub is very popular in the southern half of the state as a hedge plant because it shears well. In border plantings, and often in hedges also, it bears in late spring quantities of delicious red or black fruits that are also decorative. The glossy foliage tolerates salt spray. The related brush-cherry (*E. paniculata*) from Australia is frequently seen in the same areas as a sheared accent plant in foundation plantings. Less common, but highly recommended for southern Florida, is a native species with beautiful foliage, the red-stopper (*E. confusa*). It thrives in shade, and its glossy leaves are also salt spray tolerant. The box-leaf eugenia, *E. myrtoides,* is another native species well worth cultivating more widely. It has small leaves, densely borne on the branches. All eugenias are easily grown from seeds.

Euphorbia pulcherrima. POINSETTIA. Central America. (N, C,S). Easily hurt by cold, poinsettia is planted all over the state for Christmas color. Both the bright color of the blooms and the temporary character of the plant in the northern half of the state suggest that it might best be planted with hardy evergreen shrubbery as background. Here the color will show to advantage; yet when the plants are killed by cold, their absence will not be noticed. Single red types are most common, but double and triple forms make full blooms at no extra cost or care. For those who admire them, there are poinsettias with white or pink bracts. Leafless stems may be cut into 12-in. lengths in late winter and placed in the soil where flowering plants are wanted, leaving only one or two buds above ground. Growth is very rapid, and it is recommended that shoot tips be pinched back in late summer to make the plants branch and become more compact. Poinsettias thrive only in full sun.

Several other euphorbias are much used in landscaping in extreme southern Florida. Crown-of-thorns, *E. mili*, and its hybrids are planted as ground covers in "rock-'n'-sand" gardens, as planter subjects, and as pot plants. Noted for its attractive bracts, the armature of its stems, and its ability to thrive in hot, dry locations, this low euphorbe is frequently seen in frostless areas. Milkstripe euphorbia, *E. lactea*, almost leafless and without flowers most of the time, is grown as a defensive hedge, as a freestanding specimen outdoors, and as an urn-subject. Pencil-tree, *E. tirucalli*, also practically leafless and flowerless, is grown as an oceanfront defensive hedge because it thrives in front-dune locations. Occasionally pencil-tree is seen as a freestanding specimen or urn-subject in home grounds near the tip of the peninsula.

Eurya japonica. EURYA. Eastern Asia. (N). This dwarf, evergreen shrub is excellent for foundation plantings. Slow growing, fine in scale, and compact in habit, eurya is successful in partial shade or on north sides of structures. The small leaves are rugose and dark green. Flowers are inconspicuous. Propagation is by seed or softwood cuttings.

Feijoa sellowiana. FEIJOA. Brazil. (N,C,S). Originally introduced as a fruit plant, feijoa has proved to be far more satisfactory as a landscape shrub. Leaves are gray-green above with grayish-white undersurfaces, and on new growth the color is lighter green. Feijoa is used for hedges, foundation plantings, and borders. Individually the flowers are quite showy, but they make no mass effect of color. This shrub thrives in sun or shade and stands salt spray well. Seedlings are easily grown, but feijoa is notably resistant to propagation by cuttage.

Flacourtia indica. GOVERNOR-PLUM. Southeastern Asia. (S). This large, thorny, evergreen shrub is suitable for informal borders or defensive hedges. New shoots are bright red for a time, adding color, and the maroon fruits, nearly an inch across, make excellent jelly. Some forms are very good to eat out of hand. There are other species of *Flacourtia* in cultivation also, with similar characters in general. All have separate male and female plants, so that softwood cuttings are used to propagate plants bearing fruit.

Gardenia jasminoides. GARDENIA or CAPE-JASMINE. China. (N,C,S). Many gardeners are not aware that the florists' gardenias, often available all winter, and the cape-jasmines that bloom in their gardens in late spring are horticultural forms of the same species. Gardenias thrive in deep, fertile soil, slightly acid in reaction, with good moisture supply. Root-knot, caused by microscopic worms in the soil, is a major hazard for gardenias on sandy soil. Heavy mulching helps control this pest, and complete control is obtained by soil sterilization. In southern Florida purchase plants grafted on the related G. *thunbergia,* which is highly resistant to attack. White-fly is everywhere a troublesome pest. Full sun is liked, but gardenias thrive also in light, shifting shade from pines or tall palms. A lake front location is fine if the water level is constant, but inundation kills the plants. When a potted gardenia is received at Easter or on Mother's Day, it should be placed in a cool, moist location, for the dry atmosphere of heated houses is not conducive to its continued welfare. Dropping of flower buds is the first response to an uncongenial environment. Several times daily the foliage should be lightly sprayed with the mist from a hand atomizer. After blossoming, the plant may be knocked out of the container and planted in the garden. Gardenias are propagated by softwood cuttings in northern Florida and by grafting on G. *thunbergia* in southern Florida.

Genipa clusiaefolia. SEVEN-YEAR-APPLE. Southern Florida. (S). Shrubby growth, large, glossy, evergreen leaves, and marked tolerance of salt and lime combine to make this native of seaside hammocks an excellent choice for waterfront landscaping in southern counties. Propagation is by seeds from the 3-in. woody fruits.

Hamelia patens. SCARLET-BUSH. Tropical America. (S). Native to the hammocks of extreme southern Florida, this large shrub has attractive evergreen foliage and bears terminal clusters of bright scarlet flowers an inch long but very slender. In winter the leaves often become red unless there is frost, in which case they are shed, and the bush is leafless for a short time. Tender to cold and to salt spray, the scarlet-bush offers bright color during most of the year in adapted locations. The flowers are soon followed by small, black berries, whose seeds provide easy multiplication. Softwood cuttings can be struck also.

Hibiscus acetocella. RED-LEAF HIBISCUS. South Africa. (C, S). Stems, leaves, and flowers of this rankly vigorous shrub are all magenta-red. The leaves are maple-like, and the flowers, 3 in. across with a dark eye, are borne in the autumn. Like those of several other *Hibiscus* species, flowers open in the morning and close by midday. Often confused with roselle (*H. sabdariffa*), red-leaf hibiscus has only its unusual color to recommend it. Propagation by seeds or cuttings is easy.

Hibiscus rosa-sinensis. HIBISCUS. See Chapter Eight.

Hibiscus syriacus. SHRUBBY ALTHEA or ROSE-OF-SHARON. China. (N). This hardy, upright, deciduous shrub is widely grown in the South, growing and flowering better on heavy soils than on sandy ones. Many horticultural forms have been selected, with single or double flowers in white, pink, rose, lavender, red, and purple. The blooming period is from May to September. Altheas are easily propagated by hardwood or softwood cuttings.

Hydrangea macrophylla. HYDRANGEA. Japan. (N,C). Briefly deciduous in winter, this half-woody shrub bears huge trusses of white, pink, or blue in late spring, against a background of dense green foliage. In Florida this species thrives only in shaded locations, such as the north side of a house. Varieties with white flowers are constant, but others are pink or blue depending on soil reaction. If the soil is acid, flowers are blue; if alkaline, flowers are pink. Gardeners may alter the acidity to obtain either color at will. Propagation is by softwood cuttings in summer.

Oakleaf hydrangea (*H. quercifolia*) is native to northern Florida and is sparingly cultivated there. Characterized by deeply lobed leaves, this deciduous spreading shrub bears in early summer large panicles of white flowers which become purplish with age. It thrives in sun or shade on well-drained soil.

Ilex spp. HOLLY. (N,C). Several evergreen hollies of shrubby habit are among our best landscape material. The native yaupon (*I. vomitoria*) is unsurpassed as a sheared hedge or clipped accent plant, having small, glossy green leaves. Informal hedges are also attractive and are colorful with their tiny, red berries in winter. Like all hollies, yaupon must be grown from cuttings or grafted to be sure of fruiting plants. It is very tolerant of salt spray. Japanese holly (*I. crenata*) is a dwarf species with small leaves and black fruits. Its slow growth and small size make it well suited to use in foundation plantings, but it is thrifty only in nematode-free, shaded locations such as the north side of a house. It also is grown from cuttings. Chinese holly (*I. cornuta*), especially varieties 'Burford' and 'National,' makes a beautiful shrub of large size with very glossy green leaves and large, red berries. All hollies prefer slightly acid soil of good drainage.

Illicium spp. ANISE-TREE. (N,C). Possessed of attractive evergreen foliage which gives off a strong, pleasing aromatic odor when crushed, anise-trees deserve more use in shrub borders. They can be kept to desired height by pruning, and thrive in slightly acid soil and in rather heavy shade. Florida anise-tree (*I. floridanum*) has attractive, dark red flowers like many-rayed stars, about 1½ in. across, in March and April, while Japanese anise-tree (*I. anisatum*) has greenish-yellow flowers 1 in. across. Both species grow thriftily with little care and with few pests. They are propagated by cuttage, or seeds when available.

Ixora coccinea. IXORA or FLAME-OF-THE-WOODS. Southeastern Asia. (S). Several species and many hybrids of *Ixora* are cultivated in Florida, but this one is most common. Compact habit, evergreen foliage, and abundance of bright red, pink, terra-cotta, or orange flowers make ixoras favored shrubs for specimens, hedges, or foundation plantings. On calcareous soils they are likely to show evidence of nutritional deficiencies if they are not set in carefully prepared acid soil. Softwood cuttings are used to propagate these shrubs.

Jasminum spp. JASMINE. (N,C,S). Many species of true jasmine flourish in Florida, besides the numerous unrelated ornamentals with fragrant flowers that are called some kind of jasmine also. The yellow-flowered species of *Jasminum* are all shrubs, while all the white-flowered species are vining in habit. Some of these are easily trained to shrub form and are described here, while the others are discussed among the vines. All true jasmines may be propagated by softwood cuttings, and layer naturally where canes touch the ground. Most widely grown is primrose jasmine (*J. mesnyi*), which makes a rounded mass of green up to 10 ft. high. Flowering occurs in late winter and is more abundant in the northern area, particularly following cold winters. Italian jasmine (*J. humile*) makes an even larger but less dense mass, and showy jasmine (*J. floridum*) reaches a height of only 4 ft., with open habit. These three all have yellow flowers and compound leaves, and are hardy everywhere in Florida.

Five species with white flowers are commonly grown as low to medium shrubs, although they will become scramblers if allowed to do so. All but one have intensely fragrant flowers, all but one are evergreen, and all but one have more than six corolla lobes. Poets' jasmine (*J. officinale*) is the only one with compound leaves, having five to seven leaflets, and is the only deciduous species and the only one hardy in northern Florida. It has flowers about 1 in. across with only five lobes. Catalonian jasmine (*J. officinale* var. *grandiflorum*) is very similar except for flowers about 1½ in. wide. Downy jasmine (*J. multiflorum*) is the species most common in Florida, and is distinguished by its velvety leaves and nearly odorless flowers. Although often killed to the ground in northern Florida, it usually blooms again the next summer. Star jasmine, often listed as *J. gracillimum*, is only a variant form of downy jasmine with larger, fragrant, but less abundant flowers. Arabian jasmine (*J. sambac*) responds to cold similarly to downy jasmine, and is especially distinguished by tufts of yellow hairs in the axils of the large veins on the lower leaf surface. Two varieties are grown, 'Maid of Orleans' with semidouble flowers and 'Grand Duke' with fully double ones. In both the corolla lobes are short and broad. Wax jasmine (*J. volubile*), native to Africa, has long been called Australian jasmine and listed as *J. gracile,* or erroneously as *J. simplicifolium.* It has flowers less than an inch wide with very short calyx lobes, and occasionally bears small black fruits. It blooms most heavily in spring, but is sparing of bloom unless grown in full sun. *J. nitidum* has no common name, but has also had much confusion as to its scientific name, being listed often as *J. amplexicaule* and erroneously as *J. ilicifolium.* Native to the Admiralty Islands north of New Guinea, it has waxy leaves and flowers which are rose-pink in bud and open to a width of 1 to 2 in. The corolla tube is long, and the long slender corolla and calyx lobes stand out at right angles to it. In northern Florida this plant recovers from freezes a little less readily than downy jasmine.

Juniperus spp. Juniper. (N). This dependable genus of coniferous shrubs contains several beautiful species that thrive in northern Florida. One of the best low ground covers is shore juniper (*J. conferta*). Very popular as a spreading shrub of medium size is Pfitzer juniper (*J. chinensis* var. *pfitzeriana*). One of the best tall evergreens for sheared accents is the so-called Japanese juniper (*J. chinensis* var. *columnaris*). All junipers thrive in full sun and are tolerant of dry conditions, and shore juniper endures salt spray also. Propagation is by firmwood cuttings.

Kopsia arborea. See *Ochrosia elliptica.*

Lagerstroemia indica. Crape-myrtle. Southeastern Asia. (N,C,S). While well suited to the northern area, this old southern favorite grows in the warmest areas also. Flowering is usually continuous all summer long, especially if old bloom clusters are cut off to prevent seeding. Plants tend to get "leggy" if they are not headed back severely each year as soon as the leaves fall. Several flower colors are available from white through pinks to deep rose. Propagation may be by either hardwood or softwood cuttings, except for the white variety, which comes best from root cuttings.

Lantana camara. LANTANA. Caribbean area. (C,S). So well adapted that it has escaped from cultivation in some places to become a weed, lantana is a coarse, odoriferous shrub that grows rampantly in dry, sunny locations. Flowers are two-toned in white, yellow, pink, and red and purple combinations. It is killed by frost but recovers quickly. Usually better shrubs are available for any given use, but sometimes it may suit a difficult, sunny spot as nothing else seems to do. The trailing or weeping lantana (*L. montevidensis*) is a more desirable plant, which makes a good ground cover or low, broad hedge. The small flowers are usually lilac-colored but sometimes white. Lantanas are propagated by seeds or softwood cuttings.

Ligustrum japonicum. WAX PRIVET. Okinawa. (N,C,S). One of the most widely used shrubs in our state, wax privet is good for hedges, borders, foundation planting, or specimens. It is host to the white-fly, which does it little harm but may multiply to injure other shrubs. In sandy soil wax privet is often injured by root-knot nematodes, to escape which it is often grafted on a resistant species (*L. quihoui*). The tree privet (*L. lucidum*) quickly grows to tree size and should not be used in plantings unless a tree is wanted. Nurseries still confuse the scientific names, which botanists realized long ago had been exchanged somehow. Several other species and horticultural forms are occasionally found in Florida gardens, the nomenclature often being mixed up. In northwestern Florida the small-leaved, tardily deciduous, Amur privet (*L. amurense*) serves well as a sheared hedge or for other topiary effects. All privets are easily propagated by either softwood or firmwood cuttings or by seeds.

Loropetalum chinense. LOROPETALUM. China. (N,C). This compact shrub, with its outward pointing branches and rough, evergreen leaves, is recommended for foundation plantings in sections where winter temperatures regularly drop below freezing. High, shifting shade and north-side locations with well-drained soil are suggested. Cuttage is used for increase.

Magnolia soulangeana. ORIENTAL MAGNOLIA. China. (N). Becoming small trees in the North, the deciduous Oriental magnolias are shrubby in habit in Florida. The large pink to purple flowers are borne during late fall and winter while the plants are leafless. Several color forms are available, but the most common has petals pale pinkish-purple outside and white inside. One parent of the *M. soulangeana* group, *M. liliflora,* has narrower, dark purple petals. Softwood cuttings are used for propagation.

Malpighia coccigera. HOLLY MALPIGHIA. West Indies. (S). This dwarf evergreen shrub has small, holly-like leaves, dainty, pale pink blossoms in spring and summer, and small, red cherries in late fall and early winter. Hardly 3 ft. high, this fine-textured shrub thrives well in partial shade, but is very subject to attack by the root-knot nematode. Several named varieties, selected for special growth habits, may be chosen for planters, "rock-'n'-sand" gardens, and urns. Propagation is by seed or cuttings. The larger sister species, *M. glabra,* the Barbados-cherry, has larger three-lobed fruit and leaves without spines. More useful as a fruit, it is less ornamental.

Malvaviscus arboreus. TURKS-CAP. Tropical America. (C, S). This sturdy shrub resembles hibiscus somewhat in foliage, and the flowers look like unopened hibiscus blooms, so that it is sometimes called in error "sleeping hibiscus." The common form has drooping red flowers, but varieties with white or pink flowers or with variegated leaves are grown by fanciers. The most common use is for hedges, and frequent shearing is needed to keep them neat. Hardwood cuttings may simply be lined out where a hedge is wanted, and they will soon grow to the desired size. Turks-cap endures neglect and unfavorable conditions unusually well, but plants respond to good culture. They are fairly tolerant of salt spray.

Michelia fuscata. BANANA-SHRUB. China. (N). This large, shrubby relative of the magnolias has attractive evergreen foliage and bears in spring brownish-yellow flowers with the odor of ripe bananas. Completely hardy to cold in Florida, banana-shrub serves well where a large, dense mass of green is desired. It is very subject to attack by magnolia scale, but otherwise is fairly free of pests. It is propagated easily by seed.

Murraya paniculata. ORANGE-JASMINE. China. (S). This distant relative of *Citrus* makes a fine medium- to large-sized shrub with compact habit, pinnately compound leaves, small, fragrant, white flowers, and small, red berries. It is well-suited to use as a lawn specimen, accent shrub, or tall, informal screen, and grows better in sun than in shade. Propagation is easily done by seeds and not so easily by softwood cuttings.

Myrica cerifera. WAX-MYRTLE. Southeastern United States. (N,C,S). Few native shrubs are used more widely in Florida gardens than this southern bay-berry, which becomes a small tree in our low hammock areas. Since it is found in every county in the state, plants are usually obtained from the wild, especially from damp flatwoods, and should be severely pruned at digging. Regular summer pruning is needed to keep plants trim looking. Wax-myrtle thrives in either sun or shade and tolerates salt spray and poor drainage. It may be grown from softwood cuttings.

Nandina domestica. NANDINA. China. (N). On the clay soils of northwestern Florida, this small shrub is justly popular for the decorative effect of its clumps of erect, reed-like stems, its large, fern-like leaves, which become red in winter, and its clusters of bright scarlet fruits. On sandy soils of the peninsula, it is progressively less satisfactory as one goes south. It thrives in partial shade on well-drained soils. It is propagated by seeds, which germinate slowly, or by division of the suckers from old clumps.

Nerium oleander. OLEANDER. Mediterranean area. (N,C,S). This cosmopolitan evergreen shrub is too well known to warrant any discussion other than to point out that it is too coarse and fast growing for use in foundation plantings, except for large buildings. Adapted to almost any soil conditions and quite tolerant of salt spray, oleander is valuable for tall screens and windbreaks and is available in a range of flower colors from white to dark red. It sometimes suffers severely from attack by oleander scale and oleander caterpillar. Propagation is by cuttings, either hardwood or softwood. The milky juice of the leaves and shoots is poisonous, and the toxic material is carried on particles in smoke from burning oleander brush, so that some municipalities have passed ordinances prohibiting such burning.

Ochrosia elliptica. OCHROSIA. South Sea Islands. (S). Known also erroneously as *Kopsia arborea,* this handsome, large, evergreen shrub has fruit which somewhat resembles that of carissa. The glossy, leathery leaves are quite salt-resistant, making it a fine seaside shrub, and its handsome foliage is enhanced by the bright red fruits, borne in pairs. These fruits are poisonous, but they are the source of the seeds for propagation.

Osmanthus fragrans. SWEET-OLIVE. Eastern Asia. (N). Known also as tea-olive, this large evergreen shrub is popular for the fragrance of the small, white flowers, borne in clusters from late fall to early spring. Occasionally reaching 20 ft., sweet-olive grows slowly and is usually seen as a shrub under 10 ft. The oval leaves are 3 to 4 in. long with margins entire or finely toothed. Culture is easy. The hollyleaf osmanthus (*O. ilicifolius*) has smaller leaves with two or four large spiny teeth on each side, and bears similar flowers in summer. A hybrid between these two species, Fortune's osmanthus (*O. fortunei*), has larger leaves with many spines. Confusion with hollies may be avoided if it is remembered that osmanthus leaves are opposite, while holly leaves are alternate. All osmanthus are propagated by seeds or softwood cuttings.

Photinia spp. PHOTINIA. China, Japan. (N). These robust Asiatic evergreens are among the most dependable shrubs for northern Florida because they survive all minimum temperatures. Chinese photinia, *P. serrulata,* is a huge shrub of dense habit that bears large, sharply toothed leaves on heavy twigs. Springtime dividend is the bright show of white flowers in 6-in. panicles. Red-leaf photinia, *P. glabra,* is noted for the vivid red of its new leaves early in spring. During the remainder of the year when foliage is green, this is an undistinguished shrub of open habit. An attractive hybrid between these two species displays desirable characteristics of both parents.

Pittosporum tobira. PITTOSPORUM. China, Japan. (N,C,S). This shrub of medium size is much liked for use in foundation plantings or as sheared specimens or clipped hedges, either in the common form with dark green leaves or in the variegated form with leaves light green and white. Thriving alike in sun and shade, pittosporum is valued near the sea because of tolerance of salt spray. Leaves are often disfigured by a leaf-spotting fungus, unfortunately. In northwestern Florida this species is unusually well adapted and regularly sets seeds, which are used for propagation. In peninsular Florida seeds rarely form, and propagation is by cuttings of softwood tips.

Plumbago capensis. PLUMBAGO. South Africa. (C,S). Because of small size, light green foliage, and almost constant production of attractive, light blue flowers, plumbago is one of the most popular shrubs of Florida. In the northern area it is likely to be killed to the ground in cold winters, but it usually recovers soon. Fertile soil in sun or shade, good moisture supply, and annual cutting back in spring are requirements for its success. There is a form with white flowers. Plumbago is propagated by leafy tips under mist, division, root cuttings, or seeds.

Podocarpus macrophylla. YEW PODOCARPUS. China, Japan. (N,C,S). Particularly in the shrubby botanical variety *maki,* yew podocarpus is one of the finest coniferous evergreens for Florida. It is hardy, slow growing, amenable to shearing, free from pests, and tolerant of both sun and shade and of drought. It is unexcelled for sheared hedges, portal specimens, or accent plants, and makes excellent background in shrub borders. Seeds are borne abundantly by female plants, and either sex is readily propagated by softwood cuttings. Fern podocarpus (*P. gracilior*), from South Africa, has very slender leaves and slender, drooping branches. It is tender to cold and is recommended only for gardens in Tampa and southward. A sister species, *P. nagi,* has such broad leaves as to be recognized with difficulty as a relative, and is characterized by a stiff central leader and regular, hatrack type branching.

Poinciana pulcherrima. DWARF POINCIANA. American Tropics. (S). In spite of its deciduous habit and straggling aspect, this shrub is so brilliantly colorful all spring and summer as to merit use in many gardens. It is characterized by pinnately twice compound leaves and a few thorns. The flowers are either red and yellow, or all yellow (var. *flava*). When grown in fertile soil and headed back in winter regularly, it makes a fine specimen. Seeds are used for increase.

Polyscias spp. ARALIA. South Sea Islands. (S). Several species of this tropical genus are widely grown in southern Florida as hedges or screens. Upright in habit and with pinnately compound leaves often mottled green and white, aralias tolerate full sun, poor soil, and salt spray, but grow well in shade also. They are readily propagated by cuttings of mature wood in summer. Plants may reach 20 ft. in height.

Prunus caroliniana. CHERRY-LAUREL. Southeastern United States. (N,C). This handsome, native, evergreen tree is widely grown in shrub form for hedges and sheared specimen plants. It should be called laurel cherry, since it is a true cherry and not a laurel, but the reversed name is very firmly established horticulturally. It is especially useful where considerable height is wanted. Usually small plants are collected in hammock areas, but mature trees produce seeds abundantly if seedage is preferred. Soil must be well drained.

Psychotria undata. WILD-COFFEE. Southern Florida and West Indies. (S). This small- or medium-sized evergreen shrub has glossy green leaves with deeply impressed veins, and bears small clusters of white flowers followed by showy scarlet fruits about ¼ in. long. While leaves and fruits resemble those of true coffee and both are in the same family, the bush is grown purely as an ornamental and not as a coffee substitute. The compact habit and attractive appearance of wild-coffee make it worthy of wider use in nearly frost-free areas. Propagation by seed is very easy, and so is its culture. Native to hammocks of the southernmost area, wild-coffee tolerates shade, but plants are less compact under shade than in sunny locations.

Pyracantha spp. FIRETHORN. China. (N,C). No fruiting shrub is more showy in northern Florida during the autumn and winter months than firethorns, of which several species of confused botanical status are grown commonly. Since they grow rampantly, annual pruning is needed; but it must be carefully done, or there will be no fruits. Flowers are borne on spurs from canes a year or more old, so spring pruning must always leave several canes from the previous year when cutting off at the ground some old branches. Younger canes can be headed back to flowering spurs. Firethorns may be used as specimen plants, either in bush form or espaliered, in foundation plantings for large buildings, or in shrubbery borders. All are evergreen shrubs with thorny branches and clusters of red or yellow berries. Hardy to cold, they are sometimes attacked by fire blight. Propagation is usually by cuttings, either hardwood in winter or softwood in summer, but seedlings are easily grown. However, seedlings are erratic in fruiting behavior.

Rhodomyrtus tomentosa. DOWNY-MYRTLE. Eastern Asia. (S). Woolly foliage, beautiful pink flowers, and jelly fruits on shrubs of compact habit make downy-myrtle one of southern Florida's best plants for foundations of large buildings and for enclosing shrubbery borders. It is so well adapted to conditions in southern Florida that it has escaped from cultivation in some areas.

Russelia equisetiformis. CORAL-PLANT. Tropical America. (C,S). Attractive weeping habit of leafless, rush-like, green branches and bright red, hanging, firecracker-like flowers combine to make coral-plant very popular in warm sections of the peninsula.

Serissa foetida. SERISSA. Japan. (N,C,S). Here is a tiny shrub whose ½ in.-long leaves and small, white blossoms give it very fine texture. Tolerance of sun or shade and of temperatures experienced in northern Florida in winter make this a worthy landscape shrub. Propagation is by cuttage.

Severinia buxifolia. BOXTHORN. Southern China. (C,S). Small, oval, glossy leaves, closely packed on slender, thorny branches, make this a good shrub for sheared hedges. Compact and slow growing, boxthorn is quite tolerant to salt spray and thrives in both sun and shade. The small, white flowers are not at all showy, but the glossy black fruits are attractive all winter. Thorns make the plants unpleasant to handle without heavy gloves, and the foliage is quite subject to sooty-mold resulting from presence of white-flies. From Gainesville south boxthorn is quite satisfactory. Propagation is usually by seed, although cuttings root readily.

Spiraea cantoniensis. REEVES SPIREA. China. (N,C). In both single and double forms, the small, white flowers of Reeves spirea are a prominent feature of early spring in northern and northwestern Florida, the double-flowered form being much the more desirable one. Thunberg spirea, *S. thunbergi,* is a little shrub of weeping habit that bears great quantities of tiny white flowers in late winter. For masses of glistening white in informal shrubbery borders, these hardy deciduous shrubs are unsurpassed. Less common and more limited to the cooler areas are the white-flowered Vanhoutte spirea (*S. vanhouttei*), often called bridal-wreath, and the pink-flowered Anthony Waterer spirea (*S. bumalda*). Older canes must be thinned out to give younger and more vigorous ones a chance to bloom. All spireas are grown from hardwood or softwood cuttings.

Stenolobium stans. YELLOW-ELDER or YELLOW-TRUMPET. Tropical America. (C,S). This large shrub is notable for the profusion of big, yellow flowers during fall and early winter months and again in spring. Sprawling in habit, it needs drastic periodic pruning. Leaves are compound, and the trumpet-flowers are fragrant. It thrives in either sun or shade, and has become somewhat naturalized in parts of southern Florida. It is propagated easily by seed, but softwood cuttings may be used also.

Tetrapanax papyriferus. RICE-PAPER PLANT. Formosa. (C, S). Used in the Orient for making rice paper from its stems, this large, half-woody shrub is sometimes grown in Florida gardens for the bizarre appearance of its large, deeply lobed leaves, which are a foot across and densely white-hairy beneath. Huge, woolly panicles of flowers in the late winter or spring are highly decorative. Frequently killed to the ground in northern Florida, plants recover quickly in spring. Propagation is by suckers that appear in alarming numbers, or by seeds.

Tetrazygia bicolor. TETRAZYGIA. South Florida. (S). In southern Dade County this fine native evergreen may become a small tree, but is more common as a large shrub and may be cultivated as such in gardens. From late winter until well along in summer it bears profuse clusters of yellowish-white flowers. The leaves are distinctive for having three prominent veins running lengthwise. Tetrazygia thrives in sun and shade and endures drought and neglect well. Propagation is by seeds.

Thryallis glauca. THRYALLIS or SHOWER-OF-GOLD. Mexico to Panama. (C,S). This small evergreen shrub is almost constantly covered with small, yellow flowers during the whole growing season. Plants are killed to the ground by temperatures below 28°F., but usually sprout again. Thryallis thrives in sun or shade and is popular for foundation plantings, shrubbery borders, accents, and specimens. It is propagated by seeds, sown while still green, or by tender softwood cuttings in summer.

Thuja orientalis. ARBOR-VITAE or BIOTA. China. (N,C,S). Several horticultural varieties of this well-known coniferous shrub are known by Latin names descriptive of their shape. Their formal shapes are not easy to use in informal landscaping. Tolerant of drought, they are intolerant of shade and salt spray. Unfortunately they are very subject to a fungus blight that causes the interior twigs to turn brown and die. Propagation is by firmwood cuttings.

Thunbergia erecta. KINGS-MANTLE. West Africa. (C,S). Dark green, opposite leaves and dark blue flowers combine to make this handsome shrub of small to medium size popular for foundation work or informal borders. Flowering continues all through the growing season. Plants thrive in light shade, but need good soil that is free of nematodes. Propagation is by seeds or softwood cuttings. There is also a white-flowered form.

Tibouchina semidecandra.. PRINCESS-FLOWER. Brazil. (S). This rampant, soft shrub has velvety leaves with three to five longitudinal veins instead of the usual single midrib. Large purple flowers some 3 in. across are produced freely nearly all year. The foliage turns bronze in color before the old leaves fall. Princess-flower will grow 8 or 10 ft. high, but looks much better if kept cut back for compact growth. Sunny locations in fairly moist and fertile soil are preferred. Propagation is by softwood cuttings.

Triphasia trifolia. LIME-BERRY. Southeastern Asia. (S). This graceful evergreen shrub of dense habit is amenable to shearing and so is suitable for both formal and informal use where small size is indicated. It is most often employed for a hedge, for which purpose its thorns may be an added advantage. On sandy soil the root-knot nematodes often limit growth, so fumigation of soil before planting is recommended. Propagation is by seeds usually, but softwood cuttings may be used.

Viburnum spp. VIBURNUM. China. (N,C). Two beautiful evergreen species of viburnum are common in Florida gardens, where they thrive in both sun and shade. The larger one, *V. odoratissimum,* or sweet viburnum, may become a tree in fertile soil, and in any case is such a large shrub that it is recommended for screens and border plantings only. It is tolerant of salt spray. The other species, *V. suspensum,* or Sandankwa viburnum, is much slower growing and is satisfactory for foundation work if pruned regularly. Both species have attractive clusters of white flowers in spring, but are usually pruned so severely that blossoming is not conspicuous. They are propagated by cuttings, hardwood or softwood, or by layering. In northwestern Florida evergreen *V. tinus* and some of the many deciduous viburnums are sometimes seen in gardens.

Yucca aloifolia. SPANISH-BAYONET. Southeastern United States. (N,C,S). While not typical woody plants and so not true shrubs, yuccas are shrubby in habit and usage and have fibrous stems like palms. Spanish-bayonet and very similar Spanish-dagger (*Y. gloriosa*) have trunks several feet high, clothed with sharp-pointed leaves the size of a bayonet. These points must be removed periodically with pruning shears as the leaves unfurl from the terminal growing point. *Yucca elephantipes* is popular because the flaccid leaves are tipped with blunt horns that are completely harmless. Tall growing species above are useful for oceanfront plantings, foundation groups for ranch houses, and as parts of enclosing shrub barriers. Related beargrass, *Y. smalliana,* is distinguished readily by the long threads hanging from the leaf margins and by its low rosette of leaves. Bear-grass flowers rise to a height of 5 or 6 ft. Yuccas are transplanted from the wild; they are increased by simply planting sections of unrooted stems or by seeds.

Zamia floridana. COONTIE. Florida. (N,C,S). This native cycad develops no aerial trunk, and so makes a low, rounded mass of evergreen, fern-like foliage. Coontie thrives in shade, but also grows well in dry, sunny locations. It is suitable for low, wide borders or edgings, and for foundation planting. Seeds are used for propagation. Florida red scale is a serious pest.

VINES RECOMMENDED FOR FLORIDA GARDENS

Allamanda cathartica. YELLOW ALLAMANDA. Brazil. (C,S). This scrambling vine is more often trained as a shrub, but is effective for covering trellises or pergolas, and is most impressive when planted beside cajeput trees, so that its huge, golden bells are borne in the treetops. 'Henderson' variety, with large, glossy leaves and big, golden-yellow flowers, is most popular and blooms all through the growing season. Either softwood or firmwood cuttings may be rooted.

Antigonon leptopus. CORAL-VINE. Mexico. (N,C,S). The large racemes of rose-pink flowers borne freely all through the growing season make this a popular vine all over Florida. It is a rapidly growing climber, holding on by tendrils, and covers trellises or spreads through trees easily. Old vines should be cut to the ground after blooming ends, as they are unattractive in winter and bloom better on vigorous new shoots. In the northern area, the plants are often killed to the ground in winter anyhow, but recover rapidly in spring. Seeds are produced freely, and volunteer seedlings may appear around old plants.

Bauhinia galpini. South Africa. (C,S). With the typical two-parted leaves of the genus, *B. galpini* is a half-climbing or scrambling shrub with brick-red flowers. It should be trained on a trellis for effective show. Propagation is by seeds.

Beaumontia grandiflora. HERALDS-TRUMPET. Northern India. (C,S). Large, white flowers of overpowering fragrance, and rough, evergreen leaves resembling those of the loquat, characterize this rampant climber. The flowers are much like Easter lilies in size and texture, although the petals are united into a trumpet, and are borne in great numbers in spring. The vine grows well in full sun in rich, well-drained soil with a heavy mulch. A strong supporting frame should be provided for this heavy climber. Heavy annual pruning will increase flower production. Plants are propagated by cuttings, softwood or firmwood, with some difficulty; layering is much easier.

Bougainvillea spp. BOUGAINVILLEA. Brazil. (C,S). These evergreen scramblers are deservedly popular in central and southern Florida, and are sometimes seen in the northern area, although frequently killed to the ground. Two species are widely planted in several varieties, with colored bracts ranging from white through salmon, golden, pink, crimson, brick-red, and magenta to purple. The latter two colors are likely to clash with many garden flowers. Varieties differ in vigor as well as in bract color. Bougainvilleas thrive in full sun in well-drained soil, and may be heavily pruned or allowed to grow freely. Some varieties may be propagated by cuttings, while others must be layered for easy rooting.

Clerodendrum thomsoniae. BLEEDING-HEART GLORY-BOWER. West Africa. (S). The crimson corollas are nearly enclosed in the white, heart-shaped calyces, whence the name "bleeding heart." The vigorous twining vines blossom profusely all summer, and flower clusters last for many days after cutting. Glossy green leaves add to the attractiveness of this glory-bower. A trellis should be provided and a heavy mulch maintained.

Clytostoma callistegioides. PAINTED-TRUMPET. Argentina. (N,C,S). Suited to all sections of our state, this evergreen vine is especially popular in northern Florida because it is one of our hardiest flowering climbers. Attractive lavender flowers streaked with purple inside are produced freely in April and May. Slow growing the first year or two, painted-trumpet soon becomes vigorous and covers fences, arbors, or trellises with a dense mass of hardy, evergreen foliage. It is propagated by layers or by firmwood or softwood cuttings. It is still listed by some nurseries as *Bignonia speciosa.*

Combretum grandiflorum. SHOWY COMBRETUM. West Africa. (S). In winter this rambling vine bears quantities of showy, orange-red, tubular flowers, 2 in. long, in large, one-sided clusters resembling giant red toothbrushes. The slender leaves are up to 6 in. long, and in winter those near the branch tips turn bright red. Flowering is more abundant if trimming and cutting back are done at once after the bloom period ends. Infrequently seen in Florida, this species deserves wider planting. It is propagated by seeds and needs full sun.

Congea tomentosa. WOOLLY CONGEA. Burma. (S). Congea bears large panicles of tiny, white flowers in small clusters, with three showy bracts subtending each cluster. These bracts are about 1 in. long, velvety, and change in color from white to lavender during several weeks, finally becoming dusky gray. The vine itself is a woody climbing shrub, much branched, with coarse, hairy leaves to 6 in. long and very hairy new shoots. It is propagated by seeds.

Cydista aequinoctialis. CYDISTA. West Indies and northern South America. (S). Closely related to painted-trumpet and with similar foliage, this vine is grown for its attractive flowers and for the curiosity of the garlic odor of its crushed leaves. The pink or lavender flowers have veins of rose or purple, and are followed by pods over a foot long. Propagation is by seeds or layers.

Derris scandens. MALAY JEWEL-VINE. Malaya. (S). This vigorous woody climber has pinnately compound leaves with many small leaflets, and bears quantities of small, white, fragrant, pea-like flowers in long racemes all during the summer and autumn. It is propagated easily by seeds or by softwood cuttings.

Doxantha unguis-cati. CATS-CLAW. West Indies to Argentina. (N,C,S). The leaves of this fast growing, evergreen, woody vine are opposite, consisting of two small pointed leaflets with a tough, slender tendril where the third leaflet should be. This tendril ends in three sharp recurved hooks, feeling much like cat claws and enabling the vine to climb easily on any rough surface. The wide, yellow trumpets, some 2 in. long, are produced freely in spring. Cats-claw is very effective for covering walls of houses, garages, or barns, or trunks of tall palms, but often becomes a nuisance in trees. Propagation by seed is very easy, and stems lying on the ground root freely.

Ficus pumila. Creeping fig. Eastern Asia. (N,C,S). Completely lacking in flower color, the creeping fig is the best vine for covering masonry walls with green. It requires annual shearing after it once covers the surface, since lateral branches growing out from the wall develop large leaves and fruits that make an unkempt appearance. Hardy and evergreen, fig vine covers walls rapidly. For tracery effects on white walls, vines should have frequent root pruning or be planted behind metal shields to restrain root growth. Propagation is easily done by firmwood or softwood cuttings.

Gelsemium sempervirens. Carolina yellow-jasmine. Southeastern United States. (N). A familiar sight along roadsides in northern Florida in early spring is the bright yellow of the sweet-scented flowers of this slender native climber. Easily transplanted from the woods as small seedlings or developed from seeds in the garden, the Carolina yellow-jasmine is easily grown in any partially shaded, well-drained location. It is used effectively to cover small arbors or trellises, to train over a garage gable end, or to trail across a doorway. The small, glossy, evergreen leaves do not make a dense covering. Propagation is by seeds, layers, or softwood cuttings.

Hedera spp. Ivy. (N). Both Algerian ivy (*H. canariensis*) and English ivy (*H. helix*) are widely used in the cooler portions of Florida as wall covers. Both thrive only in shade, as on north-facing walls and chimneys or climbing on evergreen trees. Aerial roots produced abundantly from all stems enable the vines to climb easily on rough surfaces. Both species are tolerant of salt spray, and are easily propagated by cuttings.

Hylocereus undatus. Night-blooming cereus. American Tropics. (S). Large, white, many petalled flowers, 6 to 8 in. across, open at night all summer long and perfume the quiet night air around this unusual cactus. The green, leafless stem is three-angled, with sharp thorns along the scalloped ridges, and may grow to more than 20 ft. in length. Helped by brown, twine-like aerial roots, this scrambler is usually seen along low stone walls or trained up low-branching, open-topped trees. The spectacular flowers are followed by large, red, edible fruits. Propagation is by stem cuttings.

Ipomoea horsfalliae var. *briggsi.* HORSFALL MORNING-GLORY. American Tropics. (S). Both the waxy, dark green leaves of several palmate leaflets and the large, magenta-crimson flowers produced in December and January make this a handsome vine. Sometimes there is a second bloom period in early summer. On light, sandy soils root-knot nematodes are pests which heavy mulching and application of nematocides help control. Like other morning-glories, it needs a supporting trellis on which to twine, and is propagated by softwood cuttings, or layers.

Ipomoea tuberosa. WOODEN-ROSE. Tropics. (S). Although covered in the late autumn with bright yellow morning-glories, this species is chiefly of interest for its curious fruits. Persistent, brown, woody sepals and rounded, satiny brown seed pods combine to give the impression of a rose carved from wood, and are currently very popular in dried arrangements. The vine grows rankly and has leaves much like those of the preceding species. Propagation by seed is easy.

Jasminum spp. JASMINE. (S). Two species of jasmine with fragrant white flowers and black fruits are evergreen vines which bloom nearly all year in southern Florida. Azores jasmine, *J. fluminense,* is actually native to Brazil. It is distinguished by trifoliate leaves and is rampantly vigorous. Gold Coast jasmine, *J. dichotamum,* has simple leaves and pink flower buds and is only moderately vigorous. Both species escape easily from cultivation as birds scatter the seeds, but only the Azores jasmine has become a nuisance as a weed. In addition to these vining species, several scrambling species of jasmine can climb, but they are easily and commonly maintained as shrubs and are discussed earlier in this chapter.

Lonicera japonica. JAPANESE HONEYSUCKLE. Eastern Asia. (N,C). Similar in general appearance to the following species, Japanese honeysuckle has fragrant, white flowers, turning yellow, borne in pairs from leaf axils, and black fruits. Rampantly vigorous, the vine tends to get out of hand on fertile soil, and makes a fairly dense foliage cover for fences or trellises. It is propagated by seeds or hardwood cuttings.

Lonicera sempervirens. TRUMPET HONEYSUCKLE. Eastern United States. (N,C). This native, high climbing, evergreen vine with slender, twining stems bears at intervals during the spring and summer terminal spikes of coral-red, tubular flowers, yellow within, which are not fragrant. The dark green foliage is not very dense except when vines grow in fertile soil with good moisture supply. Red fruits usually set in quantity enough to assure seed for propagation.

Monstera deliciosa. CERIMAN. Mexico. (S). The huge incised and perforated leathery leaves of this herbaceous evergreen climber always excite admiration in tourists. It may be grown on a heavy trellis, but is at its best when allowed to climb the trunk of a large tree, to which it clings by heavy aerial roots. It is an aroid, and produces large, white spathes, like oversized callas, followed by edible green fruits the size and shape of an ear of corn, which require a year or more to mature. The leaves are often 30 in. long and 20 in. wide, on leathery petioles a foot or more long. Seeds are rarely produced, so that propagation is usually by cutting the stem into sections, each with a single leaf. (See picture section.)

Petrea volubilis. QUEENS-WREATH. Tropical America. (S). This vigorous evergreen vine has large, sandpaper-harsh leaves from twining woody stems. Over several months in spring and summer it bears a profusion of purplish-blue flowers in long racemes from leaf axils. Petals are deep purple and sepals blue-gray, each flower being about an inch wide. This very showy vine is propagated by softwood cuttings or layers.

Philodendron spp. PHILODENDRON. American Tropics. (S). Many species and countless hybrids of philodendron are seen in the gardens of southern Florida. They are grown for their heavy foliage, being trained on tree trunks, on trellises against patio walls, or on "totem poles" formed by a section of tree-fern trunk set in a large urn of soil. All are propagated by sections of stem with a leaf. (See p. 33 and picture section.)

Podranea ricasoliana. PODRANEA. South Africa. (C,S). Known formerly as *Pandorea,* this attractive climber has pinnately compound leaves with seven to eleven leaflets and loose clusters of bell-shaped, pale-pink flowers, delicately striped with red, some 2 in. long. Root-knot nematode is a pest on sandy soils. Branches that droop to the ground layer naturally for increase, or softwood cuttings may be struck.

Porana paniculata. SNOW-CREEPER. India. (S). During late November and early December, this vigorous evergreen, woody climber is covered with a profusion of tiny, fragrant, white flowers in panicles at the tip of every branchlet. The name "Christmas-vine," which is sometimes used, is singularly inappropriate because by Christmas the vine has always finished blooming, and only the dead remnants of the flowers are visible. The leaves of this twining vine are large, heart-shaped, and downy underneath. Propagation is by softwood cuttings or layering. Annual pruning is needed in order to keep snow-creeper in bounds.

Pyrostegia ignea. FLAME-VINE. Brazil. (C,S). No flowering vine is more often seen in peninsular Florida than flame-vine, whose spectacular show of brilliant orange blossoms brightens the winter landscape. The vigorous evergreen vine clothes water towers and tree stumps or conceals fences, glorifying its drab supports. Indeed, heavy pruning is needed to restrain flame-vine. It is propagated by softwood cuttings or layers.

Quisqualis indica. RANGOON-CREEPER. Burma and Malaya. (C,S). The fragrant flowers of this sturdy twiner are white when they open in the morning but become pink and finally dark red. The large opposite leaves are shed in winter, and the flowers are borne in spikes at the tips of new shoots in late spring and summer. Rapid in growth, this climbing vine gives quick covering of trellises or arbors. It is propagated by seeds or by softwood cuttings.

Scindapsus aureus. HUNTERS-ROBE. Solomon Islands. (S). This climbing aroid with its huge variegated leaves is popular for planting at the bases of palm trees so that the trunks are covered by the foliage of the vine. On big plants the large, pointed leaves may be over 2 ft. long. Hunters-robe climbs by hold-fast aerial roots, and needs a shaded, moist location for success. Propagation is by stem cuttings.

Senecio confusus. MEXICAN FLAME-VINE. Mexico. (C,S). The cheerful orange-red, daisy-type blossoms of this evergreen vine are produced all year long unless it is killed to the ground. Even then, the vine quickly recovers and is soon in bloom again. The flowers are about an inch across and are borne in terminal clusters on new growth. Propagation is by layers, seeds, or softwood cuttings. The plants thrive in nearly any soil, even close to the ocean.

Solandra guttata. CHALICE-VINE. Mexico. (S). This shrubby, tropical climber is grown for the curious, huge, goblet-shaped flowers, often 8 or 9 in. long, borne freely in summer. They are creamy-white at first, then darken to golden-yellow, and are fragrant at night. The heavy evergreen vine requires a strong trellis and plenty of space, as well as abundant moisture and fertilizer. It is propagated by seed or softwood cuttings.

Solanum spp. NIGHTSHADE. (C,S). Three species of this genus, to which potato and eggplant also belong, are attractive vines in warm areas. Jasmine nightshade (*S. jasminoides*) from Brazil is a slender, twining vine of medium size, with small, dark green leaves making dense foliage. From spring until winter it bears at intervals branching clusters of white flowers with bluish tinge about an inch across, followed by small, black berries. Brazilian nightshade (*S. seaforthianum*) is a graceful, delicate vine with rather small, pinnately divided leaves. Drooping clusters of lavender-blue flowers an inch in diameter are borne during the spring months, followed by small, scarlet berries beloved of birds. Costa Rican nightshade (*S. wendlandi*) is a very rampant liana, growing 20 ft. in a single season, with prickles on the thick stem and petioles. From April to October it bears great, flat clusters, a foot across, of blue flowers from 2 to 2½ in. wide, which last a long time. The leaves on older parts are like those of the preceding species, only larger, but on young shoots they are simple and up to 4 in. long. All three species are showy in bloom if provided with a trellis or arbor of suitable size. Costa Rican nightshade is vigorous even on poor sandy soil if well watered and fertilized. All these vines are easily grown from seeds or softwood cuttings; however, Costa Rican nightshade rarely fruits in Florida.

Stephanotis floribunda. STEPHANOTIS. Madagascar. (S). The waxy green leaves, much like those of wax privet, and the fragrant, waxy white flowers make this twiner a very popular vine. Funnel-shaped flowers, about 2 in. long, are borne in small axillary clusters all summer. They are much used by florists in wedding bouquets. Propagation by seed is very easy, or softwood cuttings may be struck.

Stigmaphyllon lingulatum. GOLDEN-CREEPER. American Tropics. (S). One of the showiest of vines is this evergreen climber with long, narrow, dark green leaves, often listed as *S. periplocifolium.* From March to May it is covered with a sheet of glowing golden-yellow flowers borne in large clusters. On moist, mucky soils it flourishes, but on light sands it needs much attention to water and fertilizer, as well as heavy mulching. It grows slowly while small. More common but less showy is the fringed Amazon-vine (*S. ciliatum*) with heart-shaped leaves fringed with hairs. It bears bright yellow flowers profusely all summer. Both species are propagated by layering and softwood cuttings.

Tecomaria capensis. CAPE-HONEYSUCKLE. South Africa. (C,S). Often pruned as a shrub and sometimes trained as a small tree, this relative of the flame-vine makes a good evergreen climber also. Orange-red flowers are borne in terminal clusters during most of the year, and pinnately compound leaves are dense and attractive. It is propagated by seeds or softwood cuttings.

Thunbergia grandiflora. SKY-FLOWER. India. (C,S). This rampant evergreen climber has large, soft, dark green leaves. From early summer until late winter it bears a succession of pendant racemes of large, sky-blue flowers some 3 in. across. There is also a white-flowered form of this species, less commonly seen. For quick covering of arbors and trellises this vine is excellent, but it needs heavy pruning to keep it in bounds. Root-knot is troublesome. Sweet clock-vine (*T. fragrans*), also from India, is a slender vine of moderate vigor that bears in late summer slender-tubed, white flowers about 1½ in. across. Both species are propagated by cuttings or layers.

Trachelospermum jasminoides. CONFEDERATE-JASMINE. China. (N,C,S). Notable for the intense fragrance of its flowers, which are not unlike those of true jasmines, this twining woody vine has small, waxy, dark green leaves. The pure white flowers, about ¾ in. across, are produced in great abundance in April and May. Besides its use for covering fences, arbors, and porches, this vine is a good ground cover, thriving on a wide variety of soils. Slow growing at first, it becomes a climber of moderate vigor. How this plant from southern China came to be associated with the Confederacy is an interesting puzzle. Marcottage for increase is recommended to amateur gardeners.

Wisteria sinensis. CHINESE WISTERIA. China. (N). Since the many other wisterias of northern gardens are not grown in Florida, this species is simply called "wisteria" here. It is a very vigorous twining climber, forming thick woody stems and climbing in a few seasons to the tops of tall pine trees. On a trellis or arbor or trained as a tree, wisteria needs heavy annual pruning. Leafless all winter, it produces long pendant clusters of blue or white pea-shaped flowers in early spring, along with the first leaves. In spite of the heavy cables which its stems form around tree trunks, no cases are known of injury to the trees from girdling by this vine. It has a strong tendency to sucker from the roots, which range far and wide, and vigorous shoots 20 ft. long may appear unexpectedly in unwanted places. It is propagated by seeds, layers, root-sprouts, or hardwood cuttings.

8

Azalea, Camellia, Hibiscus, Rose

Most of the flowering shrubs of Florida do not have horticultural varieties or have only very few. There are four very common shrubs, however, which are grown here in hundreds of varieties—azaleas, camellias, hibiscus, and roses. It is not sufficient to consider whether one of these kinds of shrub can be grown in Florida; we often need to know which varieties are satisfactory, and to know the important characteristics of these varieties. Consequently these important groups of flowering shrubs are given a chapter to themselves.

AZALEAS

Botanically all azaleas are *Rhododendron,* but to gardeners, azaleas and rhododendrons are quite distinct. Except for one species found in extreme northwestern Florida, rhododenrons are not satisfactory garden plants here. Both evergreen and deciduous azaleas are widely seen, but evergreen types greatly predominate. Two groups of evergreen azaleas are well adapted to Florida—the Indian and the Kurume.

Indian azaleas do not come from India, but are derived from several Chinese and Japanese species, much mixed by hybridizing over a century or more. The name "Indian" reminds us

170

that a couple of hundred years ago, all of eastern Asia was "the Indies." No scientific species name can be given these azaleas, since they are of multiple origin, and while *R. indicum* is often seen as the Latin name (usually as *Azalea indica*), these varieties usually have more of *R. simsi* in their ancestry than any one other species.

Indian azaleas are attractive as evergreen shrubs, but their outstanding value is for the brilliant and abundant display of flowers in late winter and spring. The large flowers have a wide range of color—white, salmon-pink, rose-pink, rose-red, orange, orange-red, crimson, rose-purple, and violet-purple. Some varieties bloom early in the winter, some in early spring, and others in between these early and late varieties. There is also a range in varietal habit, from dwarf type to vigorous, large shrubs. Indian azaleas are not recommended south of a line from Bradenton to Stuart.

Kurume azaleas, on the other hand, are entirely derived from *R. obtusum*, a Japanese species, and were introduced as varieties directly from Japan, some decades ago. In general, the leaves and flowers are smaller than those of Indian azaleas, and there are more dwarf forms, although some Kurume varieties are vigorous. The color range is much the same as in Indian azaleas, but whereas the latter are mostly single-flowered, there are many Kurume varieties with double flowers. Kurume azaleas are less likely to respond to warm periods in winter than are Indian azaleas, and so may be grown somewhat further north, but both groups are usually hardy all over Florida. Garden uses of Kurume varieties are the same as for Indian ones, but they do not thrive as far down the peninsula, a line from Brooksville to DeLand marking about their southern limit.

Deciduous azaleas of several species are native to Florida. Florida flame azalea (*R. austrinum*) with yellow or orange flowers, and Piedmont azalea (*R. canescens*) with pink or white blossoms, reach only into northern Florida, but Southern swamp azalea (*R. serrulatum*), with strongly scented, white flowers, is found as far south as Sebring. The first two blossom in great clusters before the new leaves appear, while the last species blooms in summer. All deserve more use in Florida gardens than they have received.

All azaleas need acid soil of good organic content. Shallow rooting habit makes it easy to transplant azaleas, even in full bloom. All azaleas need abundant soil moisture, which is in part assured by heavy organic mulches, and thrive best in light shade on sandy soils, although tolerating full sun on fertile clays. All are satisfactory for use in foundation plantings, in shrubbery borders, or as specimen groups. They are especially effective in bold groups of a single color, or when grouped for color sequence. More than 50 varieties of Indian and 20 varieties of Kurume azaleas are in the nursery trade.

Azaleas produce vigorous shoots in spring that grow out beyond the contour of the plant to produce an undesirable, two-story effect. This condition may be avoided by pinching out shoot tips before new shoots push out too far, repeating the process as often as new growth flushes appear. If shoots are not pinched while tender, they will have to be pruned with shears later to keep growth compact. Flower buds are differentiated in midsummer, and pruning after early July is likely to sacrifice some flowers next spring. Propagation may be done by softwood cuttings, air-layering, or simple layering.

AZALEA VARIETIES RECOMMENDED FOR FLORIDA*

Indian Azaleas—as far south as Bradenton, Lake Placid, and Stuart
  White—Fielders White E, New White E, Indica alba M
  Light pink—Elegans E, Elegans superba M, George Franc E, Macrantha VL
  Deep pink to rose-red—Brilliant E, Pride of Dorking L, Prince of Wales M, Southern Charm M
  Orange-red—Coccinea major E, Glory of Sunninghill M, President Clay E, Prince of Orange M, Sublanceolata L
  Salmon—Duc de Rohan E, Frederick the Great L, Lawsal M
  Lavender-purple—Formosa M, Phoenicea E, Violacea rubra M
  Variegated—Anthenon E, George L. Taber M, Magnifica VL

Kurume Azaleas—as far south as Brooksville, Leesburg, and DeLand
  White—Snow M, Hakata Shiro L, Ramontacea M
  Light pink—Apple Blossom L, Coral Bells M, Fairy E, Hortensia M, Peachblow E
  Deep pink—Morning Glow M, Rose M, Sunstar M
  Red—Benigiri M, Christmas Cheer M, Hexe M, Hinodegiri M

Purple—Amoena *E*, Amoena superba *M*
Salmon—Bridesmaid *E*, Pink Pearl *E*, Salmon Beauty *M*, Salmon Queen *M*
Orange—Flame *M*, Vesuvius *M*

* *E* early, *M* midseason, *L* late, *VL* very late, extending into summer

CAMELLIAS

Several species of camellia are growing in Florida, but the dominating one is *Camellia japonica,* native to China but cultivated intensively in Japan for the past 1,500 years. Long considered an aristocrat among shrubs in the Deep South, this camellia (often called "japonica") has been a part of rural life in northern Florida since ante-bellum days. The compact growing habit, glossy green foliage, and variety of beautiful flowers borne in showy quantities in winter and early spring account in great part for the wide popularity of this handsome shrub. It grows slowly, but lives long and may attain a height of over 20 ft. after many years.

Garden uses of camellias are many; indeed, it is often said that there is hardly a usage to which broad-leaved evergreens are put that camellias cannot serve equally well. No other shrub is more attractive for foliage alone, and only the relatively high cost of plants and the need to spray for certain pests regularly have prevented widespread use of camellias in shrubbery borders. They are effective as foundation and hedge plants, being amenable to pruning to definite form and only slowly increasing in size. The major use, however, is as specimen plants, as camellias have become important "hobby" plants. Many a garden in the Gulf states has a section set aside for a camellia collection, the extent of which is limited only by the purse of the gardener.

The large number of camellia varieties already offered by nurseries is being increased each year, and rather few varieties have been grown for long enough to know what their mature garden habit is. Varieties long in cultivation, however, demonstrate great variability in growth habit.

Even more readily noted are differences in time of blooming, some varieties beginning to bloom in early fall, while others put on their first flowers in early winter, and still others in late winter. There is also tremendous variation in flower type, from single flowers with one row of petals and a central mass of stamens to completely doubled flowers of very formal habit, with all gradations in between. Finally, flower color ranges from white through pink to red, with many variegated combinations of these colors. Over 2,000 varieties have been named and propagated, and many new ones are added to the list each year, not all equally worthy. The long life of cut Japonica camellias is an important characteristic.

Sasanqua camellias (*C. sasanqua*) are native to Japan and are not nearly so long in cultivation in America nor so high in present popularity as are forms of *C. japonica.* Until recently the word "camellia" brought to thought only the Japonica varieties, but now many Sasanqua varieties are found in Florida gardens, too; and while nine people out of ten mean *C. japonica* when they say "camellia," it is no longer a satisfactory usage to limit the word thus. Sasanquas are characterized by much smaller leaves and by flowers of much less color range and shorter life after cutting than Japonicas. Most Sasanqua flowers are single, with fragile, crinkled petals, and are scented. They appear in autumn and early winter, and Sasanquas are more often planted for mass effect than are Japonicas because of their free flowering. They make good flowering hedges and endure sun better than do Japonicas usually.

Other camellia species are rarely seen in Florida. Some fanciers grow *C. reticulata* and its hybrids, but it remains to be seen whether they will become popular. The variety Appleblossom is probably *C. saluenensis,* and the variety Betty McCaskill is *C. maliflora,* both being long in cultivation but not widely known. Forms and hybrids of *C. saluenensis* are being tried, also.

Camellias of all kinds are fully hardy everywhere in Florida, although their flowers may be killed by cold after the buds have swollen for opening. Most varieties do not thrive far south of Tampa, Orlando, and Daytona Beach. Camellias are very sensitive to presence of lime in the soil, especially in sandy soil, and care must be taken to provide an acid soil for them, preferably between pH 5 and 6, and with plenty of peat or other organic material incorporated into the planting sites. They are also easily injured by too deep planting, so that care must be taken to avoid setting plants deeper than they stood in the nursery. Even then the heavy ball of soil around the roots may sink after planting if a large hole filled with highly organic soil has been prepared, unless due care is exercised. For large, heavy balls, it is best to leave a central pedestal when digging the hole, excavating widely all around it, and cut it off at such depth that when the ball rests on it, the plant is at the right depth (fig. 20).

Poor soil drainage results in rotting of roots, and is manifested above ground by a generally unthrifty condition with falling leaves and flower buds, dying twigs, and eventually the death of the whole plant. In peninsular Florida, camellias thrive under broken, shifting shade such as is cast by pines, palms, and small deciduous trees. On the heavier soils of western Florida, they flourish in full sun also. Few shrubs bloom as well in the shade as do camellias. Heavy organic mulch is an important item in their culture. Camellias are usually fertilized in late winter and again in early summer. Principal pests are tea scale and spider mites, both of which attack the leaves of camellias very commonly.

Propagation is by cuttings, air-layering, or grafting on vigorous stocks in late winter, using leafy scions and enclosing the graft by a glass jar (fig. 17).

SOME JAPONICA CAMELLIA VARIETIES RECOMMENDED FOR FLORIDA GENERALLY

Dark Red—Mathotiana Supreme, Mrs. Charles Cobb, Paulette Goddard, Pensacola Red, Prof. C. S. Sargent

Rose-red—Gloire de Nantes, Guilio Nuccio, Mathotiana rosea, Prince Eugene Napoleon, Woodville Red

Deep Pink—Betty Sheffield Pink, Debutante, Drama Girl, Lady Clare, R. L. Wheeler

Light Pink—C. H. Wilson, Magnoliaeflora, Pink Perfection, Tomorrows Dawn, Wildwood

White—Alba plena, Charlie Bettes, Colonial Dame, White Empress, Winter Morn

Variegated—Adolphe Audusson var., Carters Sunburst, Elegans, Herme, Ville de
    Nantes
SASANQUA VARIETIES RECOMMENDED FOR FLORIDA
    Pink—Briar Rose, Cleopatra, Hebe, Rosea
    White—Mine-no-yuke
    White Blushed Rose—Blanchette, Dawn, Narumigata

HIBISCUS

The genus *Hibiscus* has some 200 species, but the use of
hibiscus as a common name is limited almost entirely to *H.
rosa-sinensis,* native to southern China and often specified as
Chinese hibiscus. Tremendously popular in all tropical countries,
where it usually grows with weed-like vigor, hibiscus has been
cultivated in Florida for at least a century and is now a leading
hobby plant with as wide a range of colors and flower forms
as are to be found in any shrub. Colors now available range
from white through all shades of pink, yellow, and red to a
lavender-purple, and flowers often combine several different colors. There are literally thousands of named varieties.

For the most part these beautiful and varied sorts seem to
have been derived chiefly from the one parent species, *H. rosa-
sinensis,* although the origin of yellow color in hibiscus varieties
remains a mystery. Quite a few hybrids have been obtained,
however, by crossing the Chinese hibiscus with the fringed hibiscus (*H. schizopetalus*) from tropical East Africa, grown in a
very limited way for its hanging red flowers with reflexed petals
deeply cut and fringed. The hybrids are usually not separated
from other hibiscus varieties, but they commonly show some
degree of petal fringing and have the petals bent back toward
the stem somewhat. Distinctive dusky tones have come from
crossing Chinese hibiscus with the shrub althea (*H. syriacus*).

Hibiscus plants are shrubs, sometimes reaching 20 ft. in
height but usually pruned by man or Nature to a smaller size.
Graceful habit, glossy evergreen leaves, and showy blossoms in
varied bright colors make hibiscus justly popular for landscape
usage. As with camellias, the cost of fashionable varieties has

limited their use to specimen status. Vigorous varieties of less costliness are excellent hedge and border shrubs and foundation plants for large buildings.

In southern Florida, hibiscus is rarely hurt much by cold, and even in central Florida it is a dependable landscape item. In northern Florida it is definitely transitory, and should be planted in among hardy evergreen shrubs so that during its frequent eclipses from cold its absence will not leave a gap in the garden composition. If roots are heavily mulched, or the base of the shrub is mounded with soil, hibiscus will usually sprout again and be in bloom once more by the end of summer following a severe freeze.

Flowers are produced on new shoots, so that pruning to control size and shape will not affect blooming much. The flowering period lasts as long as new growth flushes are made, so that in extreme southern Florida flowers are borne every month in the year. Heaviest production is naturally during the period of greatest vegetative growth, from May to October. Individual flowers usually open in the morning and close at night, never to open again, but a few varieties last for two days. Blossoms put in the refrigerator in the morning will behave that evening as if it were still morning. Only a very few varieties have fragrant flowers.

Hibiscus is tolerant of varying soil conditions, but does best with moderate fertility and moisture. Chlorosis may appear on calcareous soils, and strapleaf (greatly distorted foliage) may be seen when molybdenum is deficient. Full sun is requisite for good flowering. Root-knot nematode attacks hibiscus, and many varieties are severely affected, while some are only slightly troubled. The former group should be grafted or budded on resistant varieties.

Propagation is often by cuttings, either softwood or firmwood, but air-layering is easily accomplished. Many varieties with lovely flowers grow weakly on their own roots, however, and must be grafted on vigorous stocks.

HIBISCUS VARIETIES RECOMMENDED FOR FLORIDA*

Singles

White—Madonna, Ruth Wilcox,* White Wings*
Pink—Agnes Gault,* Helen Walker,* Mrs. Mary Johnson,* Pink Versicolor*
Red—Brilliant (Single Scarlet),* Katoka Red,* Mollie Cummings, Red Versicolor*
Rose—Commander Earle C. Taylor,* Lois Miller,* Ross Estey*
Orange—Gen. George C. Marshall,* Houdini, September Song*
Yellow—Cadenza,* Delight,* Jim Hendry,* Show Girl*
Multicolor—Dick Pope, Mary Estrella, Rita Barnes, Sophisticate*
Brown—Dr. Gillette,* Fantastic, John F. Kennedy
Lavender—Delicata,* Ines Blue, Kunia Beauty

Doubles

White—Elephant Ear,* Picardy
Pink—Kona, Mary Morgan,* Nannette Peach, Sea Shell*
Rose—Flamingo Plume,* Nina Freeman, Peachblow,* Ruth Stuart Allen*
Red—Celia Lamberti,* John Paul Jones,* Patricia Gautier*
Orange—Dr. Dupuis,* Florida Sands,* Jigora,* Senorita*
Yellow—Everglades Nursery, Hilo Island,* Hiroshima,* Mrs. James E. Hendry, Veronica*
Multicolor—Breathless, Talisman
Brown—Brown Derby, Dusky*
Lavender—Dolores, Marguerite*

*Satisfactory on own roots

ROSES

The rose is the world's most popular flower, and in order to have fresh buds for their homes, Florida gardeners plant millions of rose bushes each year. The majority of these, field-grown in climates quite different from ours, are budded on stocks that are neither long-lived nor productive in Florida. In contrast, when roses are grafted on roots of *Rosa fortuneana* and are faithfully protected from leaf-spotting diseases, they may be very productive for two decades or more.

Roses in the landscape picture may be grown in three ways: (1) as specimen or bedding shrubs, (2) as climbers on trellis or fence, and (3) as a part of the cutting garden. Varieties suited to one of these uses are usually not satisfactory for another.

As permanent shrubs in the landscape plan, certain of the

Tea roses (*Rosa odorata*) can be used. Such varieties as Louis Philippe† with dark red flowers, Duchesse de Brabant with pink blossoms, and Marie van Houtte with white flowers, thrive year after year in the garden. Tea roses have small flowers, small leaves, and short shoot growth, but they have a high degree of resistance to diseases. Grown either as specimens or in shrubbery beds for landscape effect, they are dependable for long life and bloom over many months.

Several species of *Rosa* furnish perennial climbers for Florida. Probably the best adapted to our climate—so well adapted that it was once thought to be native because it had become naturalized in neighboring states—is Cherokee rose (*R. laevigata*) from China. A vigorous evergreen climber with white flowers in spring, this is very thorny and is rather hard to control. For a fence cover or to screen unsightly objects from view it serves well. The yellow and white Banksia roses (*R. banksiae*), also from China, are other evergreen climbers which are long-lived but thornless. Clusters of small yellow or white flowers, single or double, are produced abundantly in late spring. Most famous descendant of Banksia rose is Fortune's rose (*R. fortuneana*). Because of its resistance to soil and air-borne diseases and its marked adaptation to our climate, it is long-lived and very floriferous. This species is the best stock for Florida, as above noted. Belle of Portugal (Belle Portugaise) is a climbing Tea rose (*R. odorata* var. *gigantea*) of great vigor that becomes dormant in winter. Quantities of huge pink flowers are borne in spring for several weeks. Climbing forms of both Louis Philippe and Marie van Houtte are available. Marechal Niel is a Noisette type, hybrid between *R. chinensis* and *R. moschata,* which is an old southern favorite with light yellow blossoms and evergreen leaves. It thrives in more shade than most roses tolerate, and is the only perennial climbing rose which does well in extreme southern Florida. In northwestern Florida some of the Large-flowered Climbers (*R. wichuriana* hybrids) flourish, such as

† Usually classed as a Tea rose, it belongs properly to the closely related species, *R. chinensis.*

Paul's Scarlet and Silver Moon, but they rapidly cease to be desirable as their culture is pushed down the peninsula.

If the landscape design calls for a rose garden, it is good practice to arrange trellises for climbing roses around its boundary to protect the more delicate bush varieties from wind injury. Sometimes a vigorous climber can be used in the narrow space on either side of a garage doorway, and if tied to horizontal wires above, it will add interest to the gable end. Yellow Banksia does well for this use. A pleasing effect can be obtained by training red or deep pink climbers on white walls in espalier fashion.

For cutting purposes, the Hybrid Tea roses are much preferred. As the name suggests, they are the product of a great deal of hybridization among rose species, which has resulted in many beautiful colors and color combinations. They have a habit of recurring bloom, so that flowers are borne over many months, and they make vigorous flushes of growth, providing long stems for cutting; but as a rule they do not survive the Florida summers or are greatly weakened by them. Planted in late fall or early winter, they produce quantities of lovely roses during the winter and spring, but must be replaced next fall.

Among the Hybrid Teas, Red Radiance and Radiance (pink) are unusual for their vigor and resistance to disease, but are not so attractive as many varieties requiring only a little more care.

HYBRID TEA ROSES RECOMMENDED FOR FLORIDA

Red—Crimson Glory, Etoile de Holland, Mirandy, Tropicana
Pink—Charlotte Armstrong, Dainty Bess (single), Editor McFarland, Tiffany
Yellow—Eclipse, Golden Scepter, King's Ransom, Lady Elgin, Mrs. P. S. DuPont
White—K. A. Victoria, White Knight
Bicolor—Comtesse Vandal, Lucky Piece, Pres. Herbert Hoover, Talisman

To these may be added Lady Hillingdon, a yellow Tea rose, and Frau Karl Druschki, a white Hybrid Perpetual, both of which are standard bush roses here.

While the Hybrid Teas are the principal group grown for cutting, there is a group of roses with flowers in clusters, the

Polyanthas (*R. multiflora*), which are also popular for cutting. The bushes are lower and the flowers smaller than is true of the Hybrid Teas, and they are equally short lived in the garden, but they provide quantities of blossoms over a long season, having the same habit of repeated blooming. Older varieties suitable for Florida include Cecile Brunner and Else Poulsen, both pink-flowered. Other desirable Polyanthas include China Doll and The Fairy (both pink), Golden Salmon (deep yellow), and Margo Koster (red). Very popular is a group of Polyanthas of larger size and very free-flowering habit called Floribundas.

FLORIBUNDA VARIETIES RECOMMENDED FOR FLORIDA

Red—El Capitan, Floradora, Fusilier, Red Pinocchio
Pink—Fashion, Pink Chiffon, Pinocchio
Yellow—Allgold, Gold Cup, Goldilocks
White—Ivory Fashion, Saratoga
Bicolor—Circus, Rumba

Another group derived from the Polyanthas are the Miniatures, which are smaller in flowers, foliage, and growth habit, but otherwise very similar. Examples are Red Imp (red), Cinderella and Midget (pink), and Baby Gold Star (yellow).

The Grandiflora class consists of crosses between Polyanthas and Hybrid Teas. They have the height and flower form of Hybrid Teas, with the cluster habit and free flowering of the Polyanthas, and have individual flowers larger than the Floribundas. Queen Elizabeth (pink) was the first variety of this class and is still one of the best. Other good varieties are Carrousel, Montezuma, Roundelay, and Starfire (red), Pink Parfait (pink), Buccaneer (yellow), and Mt. Shasta (white).

Most of the Hybrid Teas and the Polyanthas have developed sports from bush varieties which make unusually long canes, requiring trellis or pillar support. These climbing forms are still as short lived as the normal bush forms, but offer additional material for temporary climbing display.

Roses may be grown anywhere in the state. Requirements for success are few: a location with sunshine for half of the day, preferably the morning; a soil of moderate fertility, well drained,

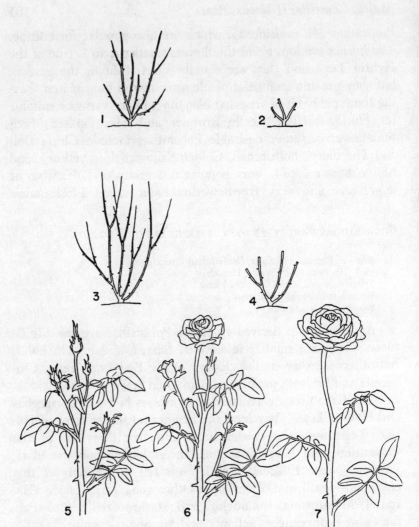

FIGURE 23
PRUNING ROSE BUSHES

1,2. Prune a weak rose bush to two or three best canes about 8 in. long.
3,4. Prune a vigorous bush to four or five strong canes about 1 ft. long.
5,6,7. Pinching out extra buds produces larger roses: 5 shows the stage at which to disbud, 6 shows rose size if not disbudded, 7 shows effect of disbudding.

and free from competition of tree or shrub roots; and careful attention to watering, fertilizing, and pest control. Almost any soil except beach sand can be used, but maintaining good soil moisture is much more difficult on sandy soils than on loams and clays. In preparing rose beds on sandy soil, it is good practice to apply from 4 to 6 in. thickness of decomposed leaves, peat, or old manure over the garden bed. Over the top of this layer spread 4 lbs. of superphosphate per 100 sq. ft., and mix all of this thoroughly to a depth of 12 in.

Planting is best done in November in southern Florida and in December or January in northern Florida. Only strong two-year-old bushes are worth planting. They should be spaced from 24 to 36 in. apart in the beds. Long narrow beds are best, so that no rose bush is more than two rows from the edge, since this makes for greater ease of spraying and picking. At planting time, roses shipped dry-root should be soaked for an hour or more in a tub of water. A hole should be made, 6 or 8 in. deep and a foot in diameter, and a handful of mixed fertilizer placed in the bottom and covered with an inch of soil. Then the bush is set in place, with roots well spread out, and adjusted so that it will stand at the same depth as it did in the nursery. If any roots are so long that they must be doubled up to get them into the hole, they should be cut to proper length; broken roots should be pruned to the break. Fill in the excavated soil, firming it in place, and soak well with water so that no air pockets are left around the roots. Then mulch the surface of the bed 2 in. deep with leaves or grass. Roses on Fortuneana stock are often canned.

Pruning of newly planted bushes is necessary to assure vigorous shoots needed to produce cutting roses, but when planting is done before mid-December, it is better to delay pruning until after buds start growth. Only four or five strong canes are wanted on each bush, and four or five good buds on each of these are all which should develop. Usually canes are left about 12 in. long.

After growth starts, cutting and bedding roses—both of which make recurring flushes of growth and bear flowers on each new flush—should have applications of fertilizer every 2 months to maintain vigorous growth. Apply 2 pts. of 6-6-6 per 100 sq. ft. of bed, or ½ cup per bush to single plants. It is particularly important to fertilize before a new flush of growth (and of bloom) starts.

Providing ample soil moisture is of great importance. At least once a week the soil should be well soaked by running the sprinkler for two hours, unless there has been a good rain. It is better to irrigate in the morning than in the late afternoon, so that the leaves are not wet during the night, a condition conducive to foliage disease.

Several insect pests attack roses, especially thrips in the flower buds, and the grower must be constantly alert to start control measures when needed. The biggest single handicap to rose growing is probably disease of the leaves. While this is more serious in our hot, wet summer than at other seasons, there is no time of year when young shoots are not likely to be infected. Only a regular program of spraying can assure the healthy foliage that permits the plant to make fine roses.

By the end of summer roses that are still vigorous may be pruned back as at planting for fall bloom. Pruning of climbers is mostly the removal of canes which are over two years old and so will not produce flowering shoots. This requires some cane removal each year.

Roses should be cut before buds open widely. Indeed, old-fashioned singles cannot be left until buds reach full size, or cut life is very brief. It is best to cut roses in Florida early in the morning, to avoid the disappointment of finding in the afternoon that what would have been buds in the morning are now full-blown roses. Stems should be cut as short as possible, especially early in the season, for long stems remove many leaves that are needed to make food for the next growth flush. After bushes become large and vigorous, longer stems may be cut without serious harm, but even then there should always be two or three healthy leaves and their buds left on each cane which is cut. Roses should be cut with a sharp knife rather than shears, as the latter tend to crush the water-conducting tubes of the stem. Cuts should be made just above buds that will grow outward and make the bush spread more widely. As soon as possible after buds are cut, stems should be plunged in a vessel of warm water and left in a cool place for a while before making an arrangement. Stem ends gradually become plugged, so half an inch should be cut off each stem every second day to permit water to reach the flowers readily.

9

Herbaceous Perennials

Becuse some annuals do not thrive in the heat and humidity of Florida summers, we are thankful for the group of perennials that thrive in our climate and give so much color to the summer and fall gardens. The well-known perennials of northern gardens are as unsuited to Florida as are their tree and shrub companions, but there are many semitropical, summer-blooming perennials that are dependable elements of the Florida garden through rain, heat, or hurricanes, and most of them survive such cold as Florida winters know. Some of them are evergreen, as daylilies, periwinkles, and violets, having foliage that is a permanent feature of the garden scheme; and most of them need so little attention that spraying, dusting, cultivating, and staking can be forgotten.

Herbaceous perennials are most satisfactory when grown in large groups or drifts in front of a shrubbery border (fig. 23). When planted thus, a root restrainer is recommended. This is simply a piece of metal roofing at least 18 in. wide, set vertically into the ground to its full width in front of the woody plants, so that their roots will be prevented from competing with the less robust herbaceous plants. After the restrainer is in place, the beds for the perennials should be made up just as for planting shrubs. Herbaceous perennials do not need to be replanted annually, but usually after three years the plants need to be lifted, divided, and replanted after the bed has been well enriched. One disadvantage of gardening with perennials is that they require summer maintenance—fertilizing, weeding, and even watering—whereas annuals may be grown in winter and forgotten in summer.

Not all herbaceous perennials are prized for bloom, but some are grown only for their leaves—the foliage plants which are now so popular, with leaves that are conspicuous for size, variegated color, curious shape, or geometrical pattern. Most of these plants are killed to the ground annually except in the warmest areas of the state, but they sprout readily again in spring if the underground parts are heavily mulched after the dead top is cut away. This dormant period is a good time to divide and transplant perennial foliage plants. Their best use is as specimens or as bold clumps before a background of evergreen shrubs, so that they serve to provide interest at strategic points in the garden design.

HERBACEOUS PERENNIALS RECOMMENDED FOR FLORIDA

Alpinia speciosa. SHELL-FLOWER. Southeastern Asia. (C,S). Clumps of upright stalks, 4 to 8 ft. high, from underground rhizomes bear long, heavy leaves with a spicy fragrance when crushed. Drooping clusters of large flowers are borne terminally on the stems all summer and fall. The individual flowers have two pearly white petals and the third yellow mottled with red, the whole looking somewhat like some seashells. Moist, rich soil is preferred, and full sun. The plants sprout quickly in spring after being killed to the ground by frost. They are propagated by division.

Angelonia angustifolia. ANGELONIA. Tropical America. (S). This low herb, a foot or so tall, with narrow, smooth leaves, bears racemes of blue-violet flowers profusely in summer and fall. It is so well adapted to southern Florida that it has become naturalized in places. Propagation is by seed or herbaceous cuttings.

Asclepias tuberosa. BUTTERFLY-WEED. Eastern United States. (N,C,S). A native herb, this plant grows some 4 ft. high

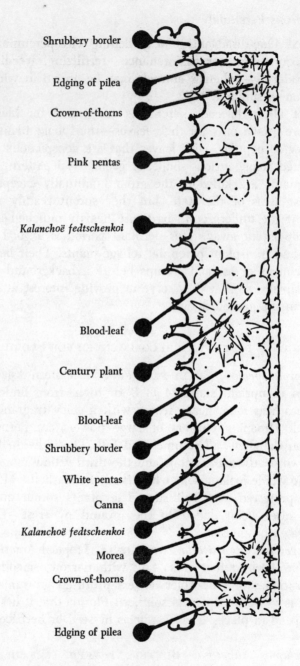

Shrubbery border

Edging of pilea

Crown-of-thorns

Pink pentas

Kalanchoë fedtschenkoi

Blood-leaf

Century plant

Blood-leaf

Shrubbery border

White pentas

Canna

Kalanchoë fedtschenkoi

Morea

Crown-of-thorns

Edging of pilea

FIGURE 24
HERBACEOUS BORDER IN THE TROPICAL MANNER

and produces from June to September large heads of showy flowers with red petals and orange centers. It likes full sun and fairly moist soil, but tolerates a wide range of soil conditions. Propagation is by division or seed.

Aster laevis. SMOOTH ASTER. Eastern United States. (N,C, S). A sturdy branching plant to 3 ft. or so in height, the smooth aster bears blue, daisy-like flowers an inch across in great profusion from March to November in southern Florida. Killed to the ground by winter cold in the northern part of the state, the blooming period is late summer and fall. Full sun and well-drained soil are best. It is propagated by herbaceous cuttings or division.

Begonia spp. BEGONIA. Several species and innumerable hybrid forms of begonia are widely used in Florida as porch and patio plants, and some of them in southern Florida are planted permanently in the garden. These are fibrous-rooted types, with either erect, branching stems or creeping, rhizomatous stems. The tuberous-rooted forms with large, showy flowers are usually disappointing in Florida. Most kinds of begonias need partial shade, protection from wind and cold, and rich, well-drained soil. However, some of the rhizomatous types, such as *B. heracleifolia* and its hybrid offspring *B. ricinifolia,* thrive in full sun on rather infertile soil. The florist begonias used for bedding as annuals, derived from *B. semperflorens,* are grown as perennials only in pots and window boxes. Propagation of begonia depends on type. The Rex type with large, showy leaves is propagated by leaf cuttings, the other rhizomatous types by softwood cuttings, and the florist begonias by seed, herbaceous cuttings, or division.

Beloperone guttata. SHRIMP-PLANT. Mexico. (C,S). The showy, orange-red bracts of the flower spikes of this plant are its striking feature. They are borne on slender jointed stems, freely branching from the base of the plant, which rise to 3 or 4 ft. in height usually. In northern Florida they are often winter-killed to the ground if plants are left outdoors. They bloom all through the growing season and have few if any pests. Propagation is by division, herbaceous cuttings, or seeds.

Bryophyllum. See *Kalanchoë.*

Caladium bicolor. CALADIUM. American Tropics. (S). Hardy in gardens only in southern Florida, caladiums are very popular foliage pot plants elsewhere in the state because of the beautiful color patterns of the large, arrow-shaped leaves in green, white, pink, red, and yellow. There are dozens of named varieties, which grow well in moist, rich soil and tolerate shade. They are propagated by tubers.

Canna generalis. CANNA. Tropical America. (N,C,S). The garden cannas are the result of many years of hybridizing and selection, and there is a wide range of flower colors available from April to August in red, pink, yellow, and white. The sturdy canes with large leaves, which may be green or bronze, rise from underground rhizomes to 4 or 5 ft. in height usually. Cannas have a wide tolerance for soils, if given plenty of light, water, and fertilizer, but like best a fairly rich, moist soil. Division of the rhizomes every three or four years prevents overcrowding. Canna leaf-roller is the principal pest.

Chrysanthemum maximum. SHASTA DAISY. Europe. (N,C, S). A vigorous, coarse-leaved herb with matted underground stems, the Shasta daisy is a true perennial in northern Florida but is grown as an annual in the southern half of the state because of soil-borne diseases. In May and June large, white daisies, 3 or 4 in. across, with yellow centers, are borne on stiff, leafy stems at a height of about 2 ft. Plants thrive in full sun and in moist, well-drained, fertile soil. Propagation is by division for perennials, or by seed sown in late summer or fall for annuals.

Chrysanthemum morifolium. CHRYSANTHEMUM. Eastern Asia. (N,C,S). Florists now have chrysanthemums in bloom every month in the year, but as garden plants in Florida they make a riot of color from October to December. While the plants are true perennials and will live over in northern Florida even though killed to the ground, it is recommended that they be grown as vegetatively propagated annuals to prevent the carryover of diseases that reduce greatly the growth and flowering of plants grown as perennials. The most satisfactory procedure is to buy in June small rooted cuttings of favored varieties from specialists, establish them in pots for a month, and then set them out in a garden bed that has not had chrysanthemums in it for a couple of years. Second choice is to take tip cuttings of vigorous plants in the spring and strike them in a sterile rooting medium. The propagating box should also be sterilized or else be made of new lumber. It is a good idea to dip the cuttings in a solution of wettable Captan or Fermate (a teaspoonful in a quart of water) to decrease the attack of leaves by disease in the cutting box.

Chrysanthemum plants make a branching top and should be spaced 12 to 18 in. apart in the garden row. As soon as the plants have reached a height of 10 in., they should be tied to small stakes about 3 ft. high. Wooden stakes are better than wire because they will not bend in the wind. Tie the plant to the stake loosely every 6 or 8 in. Mulch the plants well, and fertilize every two or three weeks until blossom buds appear. Garden chrysanthemums are small-flowered types and should be trained to develop much-branched tops. Pinch out terminal buds when there are two or three pairs of leaves, to encourage lateral buds to develop, and if shoots from any of these grow long and slender, pinch out their tips also. Pinching after early August will destroy flower buds, however.

Varieties flowering in October and early November escape possible frost injury but are subject to considerable damage from certain insects, notably thrips and mirids, that require timely spraying for control. Varieties maturing in late November and December are less likely to be attacked by insects, especially in northern Florida, but run serious danger of being hurt by cold. Covering the plants with cloth (held well above them) when buds show color will protect them from a light frost, but for a real freeze the only solution is to dig the plants and move them into a warm building. Plants in full bloom can be transplanted into large pots for moving in and out as the weather changes, or they may simply be transplanted into glasshouse beds.

Large-flowered chrysanthemums are often grown by florists

in Florida, but the large amount of hand labor required for tying and disbudding during the summer and the more rigorous spray program needed make them hardly worthwhile to the home gardener. The so-called azaleamums, a type of chrysanthemum very popular in northern gardens, will thrive and flower in Florida, but the blossoms open during early fall when insect attacks are most severe, and attractive flowers are rarely seen. Being low-headed with much branched stems, azaleamums do not need staking.

Coleus blumei. COLEUS. Java. (N,C,S). Valued alike for bedding plants and for window boxes, coleus with its brightly variegated leaves is grown everywhere in Florida as a foliage plant. In the northern half of the state, plants are likely to be killed to the ground outdoors in winter; but in the southern section they grow outdoors all year. They thrive in partial shade and prefer a fairly rich soil with good moisture, but are tolerant of much less ideal conditions if not allowed to suffer from drought. Root-knot is a serious problem on sandy soils, and heavy infestation of mealy-bugs may develop during dry weather. No plant is more easily propagated. Tip cuttings stuck into the garden soil in a shaded spot root in a few weeks if kept watered.

Colocasia, Alocasia, and *Xanthosoma.* ELEPHANT-EARS. Old and New World Tropics. (N,C,S). Huge, arrow-shaped, green, variegated, or maroon leaves are borne from large, underground, tuberous stems. Killed to the ground in most winters, leaves reappear with the advent of warm weather. The common elephant-ear is *Colocasia antiquorum.* Its sister species, *C. esculentum,* is the well-known dasheen, whose tubers are used so widely as food in Asia. Species of *Xanthosoma* and *Alocasia* are cultivated extensively in tropical America for food under such names as yautia, tanier, and malanga. Propagation is by division.

Cortaderia selloana. PAMPAS-GRASS. Argentina. (N,C,S). Forming large clumps 8 or 10 ft. high, with silver or pink feathery plumes rising a few feet more in autumn, this vigorous relative of our native maiden-cane is often grown in Florida as a lawn specimen. It is also an effective screening plant. Full sun and plenty of fertilizer are needed for good growth. It blends well with bamboo, agave, and yucca. In northern Florida the leaves are often killed by cold, but the brown foliage persists until new leaves arise in spring from the rhizome. As only female plants are desired, propagation is by division.

Cyperus alternifolius. UMBRELLA-PLANT. Africa. (N,C,S). Often grown as a foliage plant in porches and patios, this distant relative of the grasses makes its best contribution to the garden picture when grown at the edge of a stream, pool, or lake. The triangular stems are 2 or 3 ft. high, with the spreading crown of narrow leaves looking like bare umbrella ribs. The sister species, *C. papyrus,* is the papyrus plant of the ancients. It bears its plumy crown at a height of 6 to 8 ft. usually, and is grown only in water gardens, where it makes a fine effect. Propagation is by division usually, but the "umbrella" of *C. alternifolius* will develop plantlets from the leaf axils if it is cut off with an inch of stem and placed in moist sand in a cutting bench.

Dieffenbachia spp. DIEFFENBACHIA. American Tropics. (S). Two species of *Dieffenbachia* are often used as foliage plants in porch or patio containers, or even in the garden itself in southern Florida. The erect stems rise to a height of 3 or 4 ft. with large, clasping leaves which are often spotted with white or yellow. Dieffenbachias need considerable shade and rich, fairly moist soil. When a stem loses the lower leaves and becomes a bare cane with a tuft of leaves at the top, this top is rooted by air-layering and becomes a new, low plant. For multiplication, the whole cane is laid horizontally in a cutting bench of sand and covered an inch deep. New shoots and roots will arise here and there, and an old cane may be cut into many new plants.

Gerbera jamesoni. TRANSVAAL-DAISY. South Africa. (N,C, S). This is a flowering perennial with no visible stem. A basal rosette of leaves 6 to 8 in. high bears a daisy-like flower on a stalk often twice that height. Flower colors range from white to red, and blossoms may be single or double. The blooming period is all year unless the plants are killed to the ground by frost; then the underground stems sprout again in spring, and soon the plants are blooming again. Transvaal-daisy needs full

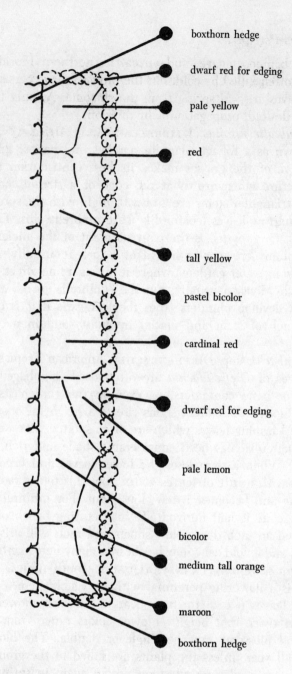

boxthorn hedge

dwarf red for edging

pale yellow

red

tall yellow

pastel bicolor

cardinal red

dwarf red for edging

pale lemon

bicolor

medium tall orange

maroon

boxthorn hedge

FIGURE 25
A DAYLILY BORDER FOR COLOR SEQUENCE

sun and well-drained soil, even enduring considerable drought. It is subject to attack by Southern blight. The clumps of rosettes become too dense after three or four years, and should then be lifted, divided, and replanted.

Hedychium coronarium. GINGER-LILY. Southeastern Asia. (N,C,S). Although killed to the ground in northern Florida winters, ginger-lily makes a rapid and vigorous recovery, and both its luxuriant, green foliage and its showy, fragrant flowers are enjoyed in gardens all over the state. The erect, leafy stems rise from 4 to 6 ft., and are crowned in autumn with spikes of spicy-scented white flowers. Ginger-lily prefers shade and thrives in rich, moist soil, but also grows well in any good garden soil if given adequate watering. It makes a good screen or herbaceous background for annuals. Vigorous in growth, the plants are relatively free of pests. They are propagated by division.

Heliconia caribaea. WILD-PLANTAIN. Tropical America. (S). Closely related to the banana, the wild-plantain has somewhat similar green leaves of more leathery texture which are borne on long, purplish petioles rising directly from the ground without any trunk. Petioles are often 4 to 5 ft. in length and leaf blades equally long. Showy flower clusters are raised to the petiole height, with scarlet or yellow bracts, 6 or 8 in. long, enclosing the flowers. Often grown as bizarre specimen plants, the wild-plantain is a striking foliage plant for tropical gardens, where its culture is like that of banana. It is propagated by division.

Hemerocallis spp. DAYLILY. Eastern Asia. (N,C,S). The daylily is one of the most satisfactory of all herbaceous perennials for Florida, being hardy, colorful, and resistant to many pests. Our garden varieties are mostly the result of much crossbreeding and so are not referable to any species. Many evergreen varieties are available in a variety of shades of yellow and red. Each flower lasts but one day, whence the common and scientific names, but the flower scapes may have new flowers opening daily for weeks in any one variety, and a succession of varieties extends the possible blossoming period from March until June.

The daylily has remarkable adaptability to soil and climate. It is one of the few perennials equally at home in Michigan and in Florida. It thrives alike in the muck of the Everglades, the oolitic rock of the Miami area, the well-drained sand hills of central Florida, and the red clay hills of western Florida. The tenacious, rope-like roots permeate a large amount of soil and store water to help carry plants through dry periods. Full sun is preferred for daylilies, but they thrive in shade, although blooming less profusely, and light, broken shade is desirable to prevent quick fading of color in varieties of deep red or mulberry tones.

As is true of most perennials, daylilies are used most effectively when planted in drifts in front of shrubbery (fig. 25). If colors are grouped separately in these drifts, better effects are likely to be obtained than if colors are mixed, for the daylilies become harmonious color accents against the green shrubbery background. Particularly with the bright yellow varieties it is effective to combine them with shrubs that bloom at the same time in complementary colors such as blue or purple.

Daylilies are propagated by division. After three or four years, clumps usually need to be divided and replanted in enriched beds.

Iresine lindeni. BLOOD-LEAF. Tropical America. (C,S). For bold, maroon-red masses in sun or partial shade, blood-leaf is understandably very popular. Tolerant of sandy soil, hot sun, and high humidity, this vigorous perennial soon grows into symmetrical mounds of striking ruby hue. For planters and as a ground cover, blood-leaf excels. Increase by cuttage is easy.

Iris spp. IRIS. Southeastern United States. (N). The colorful iris varieties of northern gardens are in general unsuited to Florida, but several beautiful species with blue flowers, native to Louisiana and Florida, thrive in the northern half of our state. Since they are found wild only in moist ground, the gardener will succeed best with them if they are planted in a depression filled with muck where the slow drip from a faucet keeps the soil constantly wet. Full sun is needed. Propagation is by division of the rhizomes, best done in June.

Jacobinia spp. JACOBINIA. South America. (N,C,S). These

coarse herbs, up to 8 ft. in height, with large, pointed leaves, bear slender terminal panicles of red, orange, or pink flowers. The blooming season is April to August. Aerial portions are killed to the ground by frost, but new sprouts come out in spring from the base. Jacobinias thrive in sun or shade, and need abundant soil moisture for best growth. They are propagated by softwood or firmwood cuttings, or by division.

Kalanchoë spp. Tropical regions. (S). Long known as bryophyllums and rejoicing in multitudinous common names, these cosmopolitan herbs are often seen in gardens in Florida, chiefly as ground covers and foliage plants. The different kinds vary considerably, but all are grown for the bizarre effect of the opposite succulent leaves and the colorful distinctive blossoms. Many kinds form small plants at points along the leaf margins, and these are used for increase. Most popular is *K. fedtschenkoi,* erroneously called "gray sedum" in extreme southern Florida, where it is one of the most popular ground covers. *K. marmorata* has 6-in. leaves blotched with purple, while *K. verticillata* bears long-linear leaves with purple dots and produces plantlets at leaf ends only.

Mirabilis jalapa. FOUR-O'CLOCK. Tropical America. (N,C,S). An erect, bushy herb reaching a height of 2 or 3 ft. usually, four-o'clocks are popular for the abundance of fragrant, trumpet-shaped flowers in shades of red, yellow, white, or striped. Blooming season is from August to October, and flowers open in late afternoon, closing the next morning. Killed to the ground by frost, four-o'clocks recover quickly in spring. Full sun and well-drained soil are preferred. The large, black seeds offer an easy method of increase.

Moraea iridioides. MOREA. South Africa. (N,C,S). This iris-relative substitutes well for the true irises in Florida's light sandy soils. Flowers are white with yellow and blue markings and are borne in midsummer. Unfortunately, the flowers do not last more than a day. Other species with yellow or lilac flowers deserve wider trial in Florida. Full sun and good drainage are needed for success. Propagation is usually by division, or by separation in species with corms.

Musa spp. BANANA. Southeastern Asia. (N,C,S). Two kinds of edible bananas are grown for fruit and ornament in central and southern Florida, and chiefly for foliage effect in northern Florida, where the plants are usually killed to the ground each winter. Cavendish banana has a trunk not over 6 ft. high, while the common banana has a tall trunk. Actually the only true vegetative stem is the large, subterranean corm from which the leaves arise, their concentric, tubular bases forming the apparent aerial stem. Clumps of banana plants give a striking exotic effect in the garden; a small clump makes a good foundation element in the interior corners of ranch-type houses. Banana plants need abundance of water and should have wind protection to keep the large, tender leaves from tearing. Propagation is by division, using suckers from 2 to 4 ft. in height.

Nierembergia frutescens. TALL CUPFLOWER. Chile. (N,C, S). This much-branched perennial reaches a height of 2 or 3 ft. commonly, and bears a profusion of petunia-like flowers from April to October, or even longer in southern Florida. The usual variety has white flowers tinted with blue, the throat yellow, but other varieties have white or purple flowers. The underground parts persist through the winter after frost has killed the aerial parts. Full sun and fertile, well-drained soil are needed for success. Propagation is by division, softwood cuttings, or seed.

Odontonema stricta. FIRESPIKE. American Tropics. (N,C, S). Rankly vigorous, almost a shrub, this perennial is especially useful for its masses of scarlet flowers borne in dense terminal clusters on plants 5 to 6 ft. high. In large clumps the glossy green leaves are handsome, too. Killed to the ground by frost, firespike soon recovers in spring, and in July and August is ablaze again. It is propagated by softwood cuttings or division.

Pedilanthus tithymaloides. SLIPPER-FLOWER. Tropical America. (S). Characterized by succulent, zigzag stems 4 or 5 ft. high with milky juice, this semishrubby relative of poinsettia has the tiny flowers enclosed in a small, slipper-like bract of red or purple color. The triangular leaves may be all green or blotched with white. The plants endure drought and neglect and have few pests. Propagation is by stem cuttings.

Pentas lanceolata. PENTAS. Tropical Africa. (C,S). This is another semishrubby herb, which grows vigorously in shaded gardens without much attention. The hairy stems are 2 to 3 ft. tall, with large hairy leaves, the midrib and veins slightly sunken below the upper surface. The large, flat clusters of long-tubed, starry flowers in lilac, white, pink, or red colors are borne almost all year long. The cut flowers have good keeping quality. Propagation is by softwood cuttings, which root very easily in a garden bed or even in a vase of water.

Phormium tenax. NEW ZEALAND FLAX. New Zealand. (C, S). For the strong character of the tall, dusky leaves, this perennial is in high favor with garden designers. The sword-shaped, folded, keeled leaves rise 'from fleshy rhizomes. One clone has variegated foliage, and others are noted for leaves with reddish cast. A large clump by doorway, passage, or gate is thought to be pleasing with contemporary architecture.

Physostegia virginiana. FALSE DRAGONHEAD. Eastern North America. (N,C). One of the few herbaceous perennials in Florida native to northern states, this species has slender, leafy stems some 3 ft. high, topped by one or more spikes of white, pink, or lilac flowers. The blooming season is late summer and autumn. Frost kills the aerial stems, but plants sprout again vigorously in spring. Preferring full sun and moist, rich soil, false dragonhead tolerates a wide range of soil conditions. It is propagated by division or seedage.

Rhoeo discolor. OYSTER-PLANT. Tropical America. (C,S). This tender, short-stemmed foliage plant has long, strap-shaped leaves, green above and purplish below. The clusters of tiny, white flowers are enclosed in two boat-shaped, purplish bracts, which somewhat resemble the halves of an oyster shell. Either sun or shade suits this tropical plant. In colder parts of the state it is feasible to dig the plants in the fall and carry them through the winter in pots that can be taken indoors on frosty nights. Propagation is by seed or by division of young offsets arising from the base.

Rudbeckia laciniata var. *hortensia.* GOLDEN-GLOW. Eastern North America. (N). This is a double-flowered form of a northern perennial that will grow in northwestern Florida. The branching, leafy stems are often 4 or 5 ft. tall, and the branches end in large, golden-yellow, daisy-like flowers borne in late summer and autumn. The flowers keep satisfactorily after cutting, or will last for days in the garden. Golden-glow does especially well on the east side of a border or wall, where it has morning sun and afternoon shade. The tops die to the ground each winter. Propagation is by division or softwood cuttings.

Ruellia brittoniana. RUELLIA. Mexico. (N,C,S). An erect, bushy herb, 2 to 3 ft. high with small, tapering leaves, ruellia has long been listed incorrectly as *Strobilanthes isophyllus.* It is notable for the profusion of blue, trumpet-shaped flowers borne in clusters from the leaf axils from May to November. The blossoms fade in bright sunlight, so that plants in partial shade are more attractive, but ruellia thrives in sun or shade and endures almost any hardship. It is killed to the ground by frost but recovers quickly.

Salvia farinacea. BLUE SAGE. Texas. (N,C,S). This native herb is good both for accent color and for cut flowers. The clustered stems are 2 to 3 ft. high, with finely pubescent leaves. Quantities of small, blue flowers with white, hairy calyces are borne in clusters from the branch tips. Full sun and well-drained soil are essential, and response to water and fertilizer will be good. Propagation is by seed or softwood cuttings. The native *S. azurea* is equally lovely and satisfactory to grow.

Salvia splendens. SCARLET SAGE. Brazil. (N,C,S). In northern Florida this is treated as an annual, since plants killed by cold do not usually sprout again in spring; in the warmer areas it is a true perennial. The spikes of large, scarlet flowers are borne from June to November on much-branched, leafy stems reaching 3 or 4 ft. in height. Full sun is needed, and the plants thrive in light sandy soil with water and fertilizer. Scarlet sage is propagated most easily by seed, but may be multiplied by division or softwood cuttings. Seedlings bloom the first year.

Sansevieria trifasciata. SANSEVIERIA. Tropical Africa. (S). Grown everywhere in pots and urns for hotel lobbies, living rooms, and Florida rooms, sansevierias are valued for porch, garden, and patio usage in southern Florida and even for garden plantings. The stemless plants have upright, sword-shaped, succulent leaves which rise 2 or 3 ft. usually, and are banded crosswise with alternate bands of light and dark green. Several species are in cultivation, some for commercial production of fiber. Sansevierias are rugged plants, tolerant of heat, drought, sun, or shade (but not of cold), and thrive with little or no attention, having almost no pests. Propagation is by division or by leaf cuttings, except that marginally banded sorts will not come true from leaf cuttings and must be grown from pieces of the underground stem.

Stokesia laevis. STOKES ASTER. Southeastern United States. (N,C,S). This native Florida herb is one of the best perennials for this state. It grows in clumps, 12 to 18 in. high, from underground stems, and the coarse-leaved aerial stems bear terminally large, daisy-like, blue flowers, 3 or 4 in. across. There are also white, lilac, pink, and yellow forms, but these are not very dependable and are rarely seen. Stokes aster needs full sun and good soil drainage, and while it grows more luxuriantly in fertile soil, it persists and blooms in light sands. Flowers keep well after cutting, and are produced from May to September in abundance. Propagation is by division, and clumps usually need to be divided every three or four years.

Strelitzia reginae. BIRD-OF-PARADISE FLOWER. South Africa. (C,S). Like the travelers-tree, this small relative of the banana has the leaves in two ranks, making a flattened head. Leaf blades rising to a height of 3 or 4 ft. are borne on long petioles from an underground stem. The curious, showy flowers have orange-yellow sepals and blue petals and are lifted above the leaves, looking a little like brilliant birds about to fly away. As tender to cold as the banana, strelitzia does not recover as well when frozen down. Rich, moist soil and full sun are desired. Propagation is by seeds. Another species, *S. nicolai,* develops a trunk and grows to 15 or 20 ft. with white and blue blossoms, equally odd and showy.

Strobilanthes dyerianus. Burma. (C,S). This subshrub is grown as a foliage plant for its large leaves, which are rich purple

below and have a metallic iridescence above, showing blue,
red, and lilac tints, with sunken veins of bronze-green. It is
propagated by softwood cuttings or division.

Verbena hybrida. VERBENA. Tropical America. (N,C,S).
The common garden verbena is the result of hybridizing and
selection, resulting in many color forms—blue, rose, pink, red,
lavender, white, and variegated. It is a low creeping herb, grown
as an annual in the North but as a true perennial in Florida.
The stems and leaves are grayish-green because of pubescence,
and the flowers are borne in great abundance in flattened clusters or heads from June until October. Culture is simple, as
verbena tolerates heat and drought well. Spider mites are troublesome pests. Verbenas afford strong accent notes of color, and are
fine for window boxes, edgings, rock gardens, and ground cover
usage. Propagation is often by cuttage, as seedlings may be of uncertain color. The moss verbena (*V. tenuisecta*), from South
America, with small, blue flowers and finely divided leaves, is
naturalized in Florida.

Vinca rosea. MADAGASCAR PERIWINKLE. Old World Tropics.
(N,C,S). A true perennial in the southern part of the state, this
beautiful herb must be grown as an annual in northern Florida.
It makes an erect stem, 18 to 24 in. high with pubescent, oval
leaves, and is covered almost constantly with cheerful white or
rose-pink flowers an inch across. So well adapted that it readily
escapes from cultivation, Madagascar periwinkle thrives in sun
on any well-drained soil. It is propagated readily by seed or
softwood cuttings. A sister species, the big-leaf periwinkle (*V.
major*) is a hardy, creeping perennial often used in window
boxes, especially in its variegated-leaved form. It should be
grown in shade and is propagated by cuttings or layers. (See
p. 265.)

Viola odorata. SWEET VIOLET. Eurasia. (N,C,S). Several
species of violet are native in Florida, but this exotic species
best repays cultivation, thriving everywhere in the state. Leaves
and flowers arise from underground stems, the flowers being
large, fragrant, and deep violet in color. Violets need shade, good
moisture, and soil with good organic content. They respond to

good fertilization. The blooming season is from December to May unless cold slows growth. Propagation is usually by division, and clumps need dividing and replanting every two or three years, done preferably in September. Spotted leaves should be carefully removed and destroyed, so that the disease causing this condition may be held in check.

10

Annual Flowers

FLOWERING HERBACEOUS ANNUALS are unique among the ornamental plants in Florida gardens, in that the same species and varieties are grown here as are seen in northern gardens. The season at which they are grown may be quite different in the two regions, but because annuals need to be in the garden for only part of the year, it is possible to find a season when the temperature conditions in Florida are suitable for almost any annual. The important thing is to know what growing conditions favor a given annual.

Most annuals may be put in one of two classes—cool season or warm season—but the matter is not quite as simple as that. Our cool season is from October to April, and in northern Florida a cool season annual must be able to endure frost if it is to be planted by seed in the garden. During the warm season— April to October—there is a combination of high temperature and high humidity together with a host of insect and disease pests, which often proves too much for species that enjoy summer heat in the North (fig. 26).

Florida gardens, even in the northern section, are made cheerful by many colorful annuals all winter. In southern Florida even more kinds are grown throughout the winter months. These winter annuals are sown in fall or early winter. Less numerous are the annuals that can tolerate Florida summers. They are sown in spring and early summer usually, since they

204

are tender to cold, but some of them grow well in southern Florida at all seasons of the year.

Annuals have many uses in the garden. One of the most favored landscape usages is to provide color in front of shrubbery borders (fig. 27). Annuals of varying heights may be used effectively in flower borders of some depth, the taller species at the rear and progressively shorter ones in front. Formal beds of annuals are not usually desired in the home garden, although they may be effective in parks and botanic gardens; but beds in the service area are much to be desired, for no other garden plants furnish so many flowers for cutting to supply the home as do annuals. Many low-growing annuals make effective edgings for walks. For window boxes and porch gardening, annuals provide necessary color. Some of the rugged types, which endure heat and drought and reseed themselves year after year, even serve as colorful ground covers on areas that will not support a lawn grass. Phlox, petunia, calliopsis, sweet alyssum, and gaillardia are examples of such annuals.

These same species have special interest for those who have winter homes in Florida but spend the summer in the North and arrive in Florida in late October or November. They may find young plants of these, and other species which volunteer readily, well started in the garden, ready for transplanting to new places for blooming, and thus saving many weeks' time in growing plants from seed. However, the price of such easy gardening is the poorer quality of these volunteers after a few generations of self-perpetuation. Double-flowered forms revert to singles, and the range of flower colors narrows to one or two for a species. Of course, one may buy seedlings from a florist, and the annuals that flower in a couple of months may be planted as seed in November in time for midwinter blooming.

In buying flower seeds, as in most business transactions, one gets about what one pays for, if dealing with reliable merchants. Annual flower seeds are usually offered both as individual named varieties of specified color and character, and as color mixtures. The latter are much cheaper, and they should not be expected to produce flowers of as high quality as the more expensive seeds. Often the mixtures are chiefly made up of a few colors, not always the most pleasing, because these are associated with vigor and abundant seed formation. If one wishes to see what the range of available colors is, these mixed packets of seed serve as a good introduction; but the best plants and finest quality flowers will come from the highest priced seeds of individual colors. In buying seedlings from your florist, nursery, or garden center for transplanting, it is well to ascertain whether

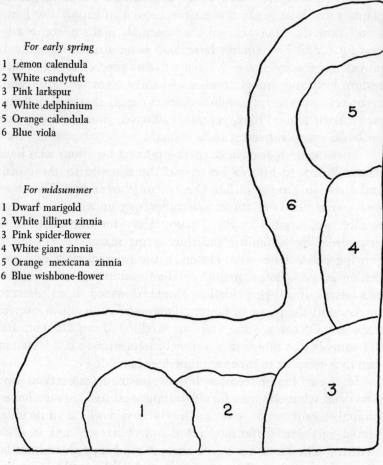

For early spring

1 Lemon calendula
2 White candytuft
3 Pink larkspur
4 White delphinium
5 Orange calendula
6 Blue viola

For midsummer

1 Dwarf marigold
2 White lilliput zinnia
3 Pink spider-flower
4 White giant zinnia
5 Orange mexicana zinnia
6 Blue wishbone-flower

FIGURE 26
BRIGHT ANNUALS FOR EARLY SPRING AND MIDSUMMER

these are mixed colors or are of named varieties, in order that later disappointment may be avoided.

Planting of seeds was treated in Chapter Four. When it is time to set out seedlings in the garden or to transplant rooted cuttings to open beds, it is well to do this on a cloudy afternoon. This will give some hours for development of rootlets to assist in taking in water before the next day's sun begins to demand water from the leaves. If the root system is very sparse, it may be necessary to shade the transplants for a few days. Annuals should be spaced about half as far apart as the height to which they will grow. If the seedlings are tall and slender, unbranched, it is a good idea to pinch out the tip of the plant when transplanting, to induce branching and a bushy habit.

The garden beds in Florida will usually need incorporation of considerable amounts of organic matter to make them good media for growing annuals. Unless the garden area is quite low lying, drainage is likely to be adequate. Fertilizer will be needed to supply plant nutrients, and is better applied frequently (every two weeks) in small amounts than in large quantities at long intervals. Any good garden fertilizer suitable for the area will grow good flowers. It is a good idea to water the newly set seedlings with a dilute solution of high-analysis, soluble fertilizer, to give a quick response. Thereafter fertilizer may be applied in dry form, thinly scattered, or in solution.

Careful attention to watering is needed with annuals, especially in the first few weeks of their garden life, because their roots are shallow. Mulching with organic materials helps conserve moisture, and in summer it reduces surface temperatures of the soil favorably. If bare soil is preferred around the annual plants, more care in cultivation and watering must be given. The chief value of cultivation is to keep weeds down, and hoeing should be exceedingly shallow lest roots of the flowering plants be injured. Troubles caused by soil fungi and nematodes may be avoided by fumigating beds as explained on page 340. Weeds may also be controlled by some fumigants.

Some annuals will need to be tied to light stakes in order to keep the flower clusters off the ground. Close watch must be

kept for incidence of pests, for half of the battle against them
is won if they are detected and remedial measures adopted
promptly on their becoming active in the garden. With many
kinds of annuals the length of the blooming period is much increased if the old flowers are removed as soon as they have
passed their prime. Some kinds even stop blooming rather

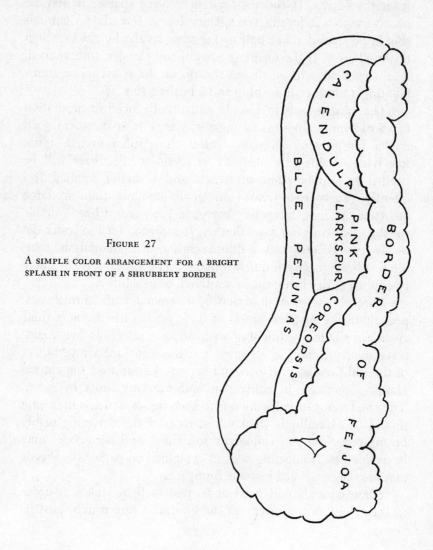

FIGURE 27

A SIMPLE COLOR ARRANGEMENT FOR A BRIGHT
SPLASH IN FRONT OF A SHRUBBERY BORDER

promptly if flowers are allowed to set fruit. All kinds will look more attractive if old blossoms are regularly picked off.

Production of annual flowers for exhibition in flower shows is different in only a few respects from growing them for garden enjoyment. Specimen plants for exhibition should be planted at wider spacing than garden annuals, perhaps 2 ft. apart, so that each plant develops symmetrically. Staking is of greater importance, since straight stems and spikes are desired. Disbudding, or removal of all flower buds except the terminal one, is necessary if the largest possible inflorescences are to be produced in some species. This is true of bachelors-button, calendula, carnation, cosmos, lupine, nasturtium, salpiglossis, scabiosa, and strawflower, for example, but not of delphinium, hollyhock, larkspur, schizanthus, snapdragon, and sweet-pea.

Herbaceous annuals recommended for Florida

AGERATUM. *Ageratum houstonianum.* Mexico. (Tender). For blue flowers in summer, ageratum, or floss-flower, is excellent. Besides both light and dark blue colors, flowers may be had in white, pink, and purple, and the soft, lacy flower clusters are equally desirable for bedding, edgings, and cutting. Dwarf types ranging from 3 to 8 in. high are most satisfactory, but some cutting varieties are 18 in. tall. Either sun or part shade is satisfactory, as is any well-drained soil. Culture is easy and the tiny seeds germinate in about a week. Often seedlings volunteer around old plants, and tip cuttings root easily in early summer. Not hardy to frost, ageratum should be started indoors and bedded out after frost danger is over in northern Florida. Sow seeds from February to April there, but from August to March in southern Florida. About three months are needed from seeding to blooming, and the flowering season lasts three or four months.

ALYSSUM, SWEET. *Lobularia maritima.* Mediterranean area. (Hardy). The varieties of sweet alyssum, with white or lilac flowers, are among the best annuals for edging. The low growing plants, seldom exceeding 8 in. high, thrive in either sun or partial shade. This is one of the few annuals that may be had in bloom every month of the year in Florida, tolerating both frost and heat. Seeds germinate in a week and plants bloom in six to eight weeks from seeding. Flowers are borne profusely for three months from any one set of plants, so that a succession of plantings at intervals of twelve weeks will keep blooming plants always in the garden. The small seeds should not be planted in June and July, but any other months are satisfactory.

ARCTOTIS. *Arctotis* spp. South Africa. (Hardy). Known also as African-daisy, arctotis bears daisy-like flowers 2 to 3 in. in diameter in a wide range of colors. One of the best known types is *A. stoechadifolia,* with silvery white petals and a blue center with a golden yellow zone around it, called the blue-eyed African-daisy. This is an erect plant, up to 3 ft. high, thriving in rather poor sandy soils in full sun. Hybrids of *A. breviscapa* are stemless and greatly resemble gerberas in growth habit and in range of color, having white, yellow, pink, red, mauve, and brown shades. Arctotis flowers are valued for cutting, but should not be used in arrangements for evening because they close at night. Seeds require ten days for germination, and about three months more are needed for first blooming. Flowers are borne constantly for two or three months. Seedlings often volunteer in the garden year after year. Besides being fine for cutting, arctotis makes good borders.

ASTER, CHINA-. *Callistephus chinensis.* China. (Tender). China-asters, which are not at all the same as our native perennial asters, have long been highly prized for cut flowers. A great range of flower forms and colors has been developed, especially in double-flowered varieties, with colors of white, peach, pink, scarlet, purple, and blue in many shades. Flowers are from 3 to 5 in. across, borne on plants 2 to 3 ft. high. China-aster grows in either sun or semishade, but is plagued by a host of insects and diseases that make it more difficult to grow than many other annuals. It should not be grown two years in the same garden plot, and should be kept in vigorous growth by careful attention to water and fertilizer. In northern Florida it is a summer flower and does better with partial shade; in southern Florida it is successful only as a winter and spring flower, and needs full sun.

Seeds germinate in a week, and flowers may be produced in three to four months more, the bloom period lasting about two months.

BACHELORS-BUTTON. *Centaurea cyanus.* Southeastern Europe. (Hardy). The old-fashioned bachelors-button, or cornflower, is available in several colors other than the familiar blue —white, pink, red, and nearly black maroon—all in double-flowered form. There are also dwarf types of plant, only a foot high, besides the usual forms of 24- to 36-in. height. Thriving only in relatively cool weather, bachelors-button gives splendid cut flowers for winter and spring in northern Florida, and is also effective in border plantings. Seeds of separate colors may be planted to make very pleasing color combinations. Plants grow well in either sun or part shade and are in general of easy culture. In the warm weather of late spring both spider-mites and soil diseases cause trouble. The fairly large seeds germinate in about a week, and first blooms may be expected in three months. Keeping old flowers picked is important for long blooming of plants.

BALSAM. *Impatiens balsamina.* Southeastern Asia. (Tender). Easily and quickly grown, balsam is popular for pot plants or window boxes, as well as for garden borders. Double camellia-flowered types are now grown almost exclusively, being available in both standard (2 to 3 ft.) and dwarf (8 in.) plants. The cheerful flowers come in white, pink, scarlet, and lilac colors, with blooms over 2 in. across on the large plants and 1½ in. on the dwarf forms. Balsam prefers moist, rich soil, and at least half the day of sun. Seeds take a week to germinate, and seedlings should be pinched to assure stocky plants. From seed to blossoming is six or eight weeks, and the blooming period is about the same. While balsam is better for summer bloom in northern Florida, it may be grown all year in southern Florida but does better during the winter months. Cuttage is a popular way of increasing balsam plants that are favorites because of especially fine blossoms.

BEGONIA. *Begonia semperflorens.* Brazil. (Tender). Widely grown as perennials or winter bedding plants in southern Flor-

ida, the fibrous-rooted semperflorens begonias are grown elsewhere in the state in pots and window boxes or as summer
bedding plants. Bright, showy flowers in shades of white, pink,
and red are borne profusely on plants hardly a foot high. Begonias thrive in full sun or in half shade, but are very subject to
root-knot. The very fine seeds should be sown in pasteurized
coarse compost, sphagnum, or vermiculite, and the potted seedlings bedded out before they become pot-bound. It takes ten
days for germination of seeds and three or four months for
plants to bloom from seed, but they continue in bloom for many
months. Forms of *B. gracilis* are also in the trade, of similar
habit. Everblooming begonias come with either green or bronzed
foliage. All may be increased by cuttings also.

BELLIS. *Bellis perennis.* Western Europe. (Hardy). A biennial in northern areas, bellis, or English-daisy, is grown widely
as an annual and is satisfactory only as such in Florida, since
it cannot tolerate hot summers. Only the double-flowered type
is cultivated, and this has flowers 2 in. across in white, rose, or
red, borne like gerbera on stemless plants with flower stalks 4 to
6 in. high above the basal rosette of leaves. The flowers are excellent for cutting, and make a handsome edging if plants are
set closely. Bellis grows best in full sun in Florida, where it may
be in bloom all spring. Seeds sprout in a week or less, but it is
five to six months before the plants bloom.

BLUE LACE-FLOWER. *Trachymene caerulea.* Australia. (Tender). Often listed still in seed catalogs under the old genus
name *Didiscus,* blue lace-flower is grown chiefly for cutting,
since the plants are not very handsome. The rounded umbels of
flowers, somewhat like those of its well-known relative, Queen
Anne's lace, are beautiful sky-blue, from 2 to 3 in. across, borne
on long stems. Plants are not very easily grown by amateur
gardeners. Seeds should be planted directly in the garden bed in
a sunny spot, in spring in northern Florida, but in fall in southern sections. Seeds take only a week to germinate, but it requires
three or four months for blooming.

BRACHYCOME. *Brachycome iberidifolia.* Australia. (Hardy).
Known also as Swan River-daisy, this species makes a bushy

little plant less than a foot in height, bearing large quantities of single, daisy-like flowers, some 2 in. across, in blue, white, rose, or violet shades. Suitable for edgings, the blossoms are excellent for cutting, being especially suited to use in miniature arrangements. The plants grow well in either sun or semishade. A week is needed for germination of seeds, and about four months for the first flowers to appear, the blooming period lasting a couple of months. Brachycome is satisfactory only for winter and early sping flowering.

BROWALLIA. *Browallia* spp. Northern South America. (Hardy). Three species of browallia are cultivated for their attractive blue flowers, borne freely. The flowers of *B. viscosa* are large, tubular, deep blue with a white eye, while *B. speciosa* has large violet-blue flowers, and *B. elata* has small blue and white flowers. The plants of all species are short, and if properly pinched to induce early branching, will be less than a foot high. Browallias are popular for bedding and as pot plants. Seeds germinate in ten days, and seedlings bloom in about three months more. Except for inability to endure summer conditions in Florida, culture of browallia is easy. Old plants will make renewed blooming if cut back, and the tips will root as cuttings. Volunteer seedlings often appear around old plants.

CALENDULA. *Calendula officinalis.* Southern Europe. (Hardy). Without doubt this attractive species is one of the most dependable winter-blooming annuals for Florida. Flowers from 3 to 4 in. in diameter, in shades of yellow, orange, apricot, and buff, are borne freely on plants up to 2 ft. high over a period of three months or more. Colorful as border plants in the garden picture, calendula flowers are esteemed also for cutting. Only double-flowered kinds are offered, with both plain and shaggy petals, although in late spring some single flowers may appear. Plants thrive in full sun on any well-drained soil. Seeds take five days to germinate, and about three months from seed to blooming is required. Late summer seedlings should be shaded from midday sun. In northern Florida, calendulas may be hurt by frost, but they recover quickly from anything but a hard freeze.

CALIFORNIA-POPPY. *Eschscholzia californica.* California and Oregon. (Hardy). Because of its easy culture and profusion of satin-petalled flowers, California-poppy is a garden favorite. The original single yellow flowers have been developed by plant breeders so that now there are also semidouble and double flowers in yellow, orange, apricot, gold, rose, scarlet, and purple. Both erect plants, 15 to 18 in. high, and spreading ones, less than 12 in. tall, are offered. Chiefly valued for garden color, California-poppy provides cut flowers which are very satisfactory for daytime use, but which close at night. They should be cut as soon as the buds show color. The plants thrive in full sun in sandy soil. The large seeds may be sown broadcast, germinating in a week, and often volunteer from last year's plants. It is about three months from seed to blooming, so this flower is available only in spring or early summer, since it thrives only in cool weather.

CALLIOPSIS. *Coreopsis tinctoria.* Western United States. (Hardy). Daisy-like flowers with yellow, golden, or crimson petals and a dark red eye are borne profusely on the stiff, wiry stems of calliopsis. Single, semidouble, and double flowers are available, varying in size from 2 in. for singles to 1¼ in. for doubles, and both tall forms (20 to 36 in.) and dwarf (8 to 12 in.) types of plants. Calliopsis is easy to grow anywhere in Florida except in summer, thriving in dry, sunny locations and often becoming naturalized. The flowers make excellent garden color, and they last many days after cutting. Seeds take from one to two weeks for germination, and four months from planting to blooming. The golden-wave, *C. basalis,* is a perennial relative which may be grown as an annual in Florida.

CANDYTUFT. *Iberis* spp. Europe. (Hardy). Two species of candytuft are popular annuals for edging. The rocket candytuft (*I. amara*) produces small spikes of white flowers, looking somewhat like hyacinths, and the globe candytuft (*I. umbellata*) has flattened clusters of white, pink, red, lilac, or purple flowers. Both species make floriferous bushy plants, less than a foot high, and thrive in sun in Florida. Blooming abundantly for a few weeks, candytuft must be planted every two or three weeks to maintain continuous flowering. Primarily valued for edging, like sweet alyssum on a little larger scale, the flower clusters are also good in low arrangements. Seeds germinate in about a week, but require three or four months to bloom. Only in spring can candytuft be flowered here, as it must grow during cool weather.

CARNATION. *Dianthus caryophyllus.* Eurasia. (Hardy). Annual carnations, like florist carnations except in size, have delightful fragrance, variety of lovely colors, and long season of blooming to recommend them. Two groups of annual carnations have been developed by extensive hybridization—the Chabaud type with flowers 2 to 3 in. across, and the Marguerite type with flowers 1½ to 2 in. wide. Both types are double-flowered, in white, yellow, pink, or red shades, spicily fragrant, and borne on plants 15 to 18 in. tall. Seeds sprout in five days and blooming follows four months or more later, often lasting three months. Staking, tying, and disbudding are requisite for large, straight-stemmed flowers. Crown rot is a serious fungus disease of carnation.

CELOSIA. *Celosia argentea* var. *cristata.* Asia. (Tender). Known also as cocks-comb, celosia offers a variety of form and color of flowers for garden color, for unusual cut flowers, or for dried bouquets. Both plumy and crested celosias are grown, with orange, pink, and purple colors available in addition to the familiar yellow and crimson flowers, borne on either dwarf (8 to 10 in.) or tall (2 to 3 ft.) plants. A summer flower in northern Florida, celosia may be grown all year in the southern part of the state. Culture is very easy, except for precautions against root-knot. The tiny seeds take five days to germinate and two months more are needed until blooming, which continues for about three months.

CHINESE FORGET-ME-NOT. *Cynoglossum amabile.* Eastern Asia. (Hardy). A biennial of northern gardens, this easily grown species is an annual in Florida because it cannot tolerate heat. Flower colors are deep and light blue, white, and pink, and the branching plants may be dwarf (under 10 in.) or tall (over 2 ft.). Not hardy enough to endure frost without protection, the plants are even less able to endure summer heat in

Florida. Flower spikes do not hold up well for cutting, so that usage is chiefly for color in borders. Seeds sprout in a week, and blooming from seed takes about three months. Plants should bloom for two or three months continuously.

CHRYSANTHEMUM, ANNUAL. *Chrysanthemum* spp. North Africa. (Tender). Three species of *Chrysanthemum*—*C. carinatum, C. coronarium,* and *C. nivelli*—all true daisies, produce attractive flowers for Florida gardens. They are mostly single-flowered, showing little resemblance to the well-known perennial chrysanthemums. Flowers are about 2 in. across, with white, yellow, rose, scarlet, or purple petals, and dark eyes with surrounding zones of contrasting color. The bushy plants are about 2 ft. tall. Seeds should be sown in late winter in northern Florida for summer bloom, but are best planted in the fall for winter and spring bloom in southern Florida. Sunny locations with well-drained soil are preferred. Seeds take only a week to sprout, but four or five months are needed for blooming from seed.

CLARKIA. *Clarkia elegans.* California. (Hardy). Not often seen in Florida gardens, the colorful and easily grown clarkias deserve wider use for borders and for cutting. Long spikes of double flowers about an inch in diameter, in shades of white, pink, salmon rose, mauve, red, and purple, are borne on plants about 2 ft. high. Probably *C. pulchella* has entered into some garden forms also. Seeds germinate in about a week, but six or seven months elapse before blooming, so that clarkias are spring flowers in Florida, since they thrive only in cool weather. They prefer partial shade to full sun.

CLEOME. *Cleome spinosa.* Tropical America. (Tender). Where height is needed in the background of a flower border, cleome is a good choice. Plants 3 to 4 ft. tall bear large terminal clusters of fragrant flowers with wide-spreading petals and long, arching stamens that look like long spider legs and give rise to "spider-flower" as one name. Pink flowers are most common, but white and golden yellow flowers have arisen as sports. Cleome is easily grown, enjoying full sun and doing well in sandy soils, especially if well mulched. The flowers make a fine effect also in massive plantings in front of evergreen shrubs. From seed to blooming takes six or seven months, so summer flowering requires autumn planting. Seedlings volunteer readily from last year's plants.

Cosmos. *Cosmos* spp. Mexico. (Tender). While not especially attractive as garden plants, cosmos furnishes quantities of large, showy flowers for cutting over a long period. Early cosmos (*C. bipinnatus*) has single, semidouble, or double flowers from 3 to 6 in. across, in white, rose, scarlet, or crimson colors. Late cosmos (*C. sulphureus*) has single or semidouble, orange or yellow flowers, 2 to 3 in. in diameter. In Florida, plants usually grow about 3 ft. high. As common names suggest, the late or Klondyke cosmos flowers in autumn in northern Florida, while early cosmos is a summer bloomer. In southern Florida, late cosmos is grown for winter and spring flowers only. Seeds germinate in about a week, and plants bloom in two to three months. Culture is very easy, but the tall plants need staking to prevent being blown over or broken by wind.

Cypress-vine. *Quamoclit pennata.* Tropical America. (Tender). This is a graceful, small vine, growing to 10 ft. high, which bears in summer and fall large numbers of dainty, trumpet-shaped flowers, from 1 to 1½ in. across, of scarlet or white color. It is excellent for temporary screening of porches or for trellises, as it grows rapidly. Seeds germinate in about a week if soaked overnight in warm water, and flowers are produced within two months of planting, the blooming period lasting several months. Volunteers often appear from old plants. Even in southern Florida, cypress-vine does best in summer.

Dahlia. *Dahlia pinnata.* Mexico. (Tender). Dahlias are perennials, but often bloom the first year from seed, and in Florida they are successful as annuals. Especially popular are dwarf hybrid races, Coltness hybrids having single flowers and Unwin hybrids semidouble flowers, about 3 in. across in both cases on plants not over 3 ft. high. There are also tall, double-flowered varieties, up to 5 ft. high, with cactus or semicactus flowers up to 6 or 8 in. across. Dahlia colors are wide ranging—yellow, orange, salmon, scarlet, lavender, purple, or white. For successful culture, dahlias should have sterilized, fertile soil of good moisture-holding properties, and full sun. It takes only a week or so for seeds to sprout and two to three months for seedlings to bloom, with several months of flowering. In northern Florida dahlias are summer bloomers, but in southern sections they do better for late winter and spring bloom. Unfortunately, these beautiful flowers have a host of pests—nematodes, spider-mites, aphids, and thrips.

DELPHINIUM, ANNUAL. *Delphinium grandiflorum*. China. (Hardy). As is the case with dahlias, some perennial delphiniums flower the first year from seed and so are widely grown in Florida as annuals. All species of the genus *Delphinium* are larkspurs, but the flower trade has long called the Chinese larkspur "delphinium" and the European larkspur "larkspur." Annual delphiniums produce splendid flowers for cutting, the colors being dark blue, light blue, or white, on erect stems about 2 ft. high, and make fine border plants also. Distinctly cool season plants, delphiniums need good soil moisture, sunny location, and soil free of disease. Fresh seed should be assured and planted in late summer and fall for spring bloom, as it takes about five or six months from planting to flowering. In southern Florida seed should be chilled in a refrigerator for a month before planting. Crown rot is a serious fungus disease.

DIANTHUS or PINK. *Dianthus chinensis*. Eastern Asia. (Hardy). The genus *Dianthus* includes both carnations and pinks, but the flower trade reserves dianthus as a common name for pinks. Most of the varieties of annual dianthus are derived from the Chinese pink, but hybrids of this with *D. plumarius* and *D. caryophyllus* have increased the range of varieties offered. Like their sisters, the carnations, dianthus flowers are spicily fragrant and prized for cutting. Both single and double flowers may be grown in a number of gay colors—white, pink, scarlet, and crimson, either self-colored or with contrasting eye. Plants are bushy, not over 18 in. high. Seeds should be sown in place, where they germinate in about a week and produce blooms in about three and a half months. Plants are quite hardy to cold but cannot tolerate summer heat. They bloom continuously for several months in winter and spring.

DIMORPHOTHECA. *Dimorphotheca sinuata.* South Africa. (Hardy). Known sometimes as African-daisy or as Cape-marigold, dimorphotheca produces single, daisy-like flowers, 3 to 4 in. across, in many colors—white, yellow, gold, salmon, apricot, rose, and scarlet. *D. pluvialis* is one parent of hybrid forms. The spreading plants, branching from the base, are less than 2 ft. high. Very hardy to cold, dimorphotheca would be very easy to grow if it were not for soil-borne diseases so prevalent in Florida. The flowers are excellent for cutting, but close at night. This is a fine border or bedding plant also. Seeds germinate in five days, and seedlings need about four or five months to bloom.

GAILLARDIA. *Gaillardia pulchella* var. *picta.* Southern United States. (Hardy). The brilliant, daisy-like flowers of gaillardia, or blanket-flower, are excellent for cutting because of long stems and good keeping quality. Single, semidouble, and double forms are available in yellow, orange, and red shades, the flowers being 2 to 3 in. across. Gaillardia blossoms profusely even in light, droughty sands along the seashore, and volunteers readily. Culture is very easy. The plants endure heat well, producing myriads of summer flowers. Seeds take eight days to sprout, and seedlings bloom in another two or three months, with an equally long blooming period. Portola hybrids are grown in southern Florida as winter and spring flowers.

GILIA. *Gilia capitata.* California to Washington. (Hardy). Sky-blue flowers and lacy, fern-like foliage make gilia excellent for cutting. The tiny flowers, only ½ in. across, are borne in dense, clover-like heads an inch in diameter, and the name "thimble-flower" is sometimes given because of the shape of these heads. Plants grow about 2 ft. high and bloom profusely. The very small seeds germinate in ten days, with four months from seed to bloom. The plants thrive in Florida from early fall to early summer, but are not heat tolerant. A sister species, *G. rubra,* is a native Florida perennial that produces tall spikes of glowing red in summer.

GLOBE-AMARANTH. *Gomphrena globosa.* American Tropics. (Tender). During hot weather this relative of the lowly pigweed produces quantities of harsh, straw-like, white, pink, or red flowers in tight heads like clover, about ¾ in. across. Grown chiefly for cutting, the flowers are popular for dried bouquets as well as for fresh use. The bushy plants rarely exceed 2 ft. in height. Culture is easy except for tenderness to frost, and volunteers occur readily in the garden. Seeds need six days to germinate and six or eight weeks more to bloom, with a blooming period of four or five months.

GODETIA. *Godetia amoena.* Pacific Northwest. (Hardy). Not common in cultivation, godetia, or satin-flower, succeeds in cool weather in Florida. Valued for cutting, the spikes bear single or double flowers, 2 to 3 in. across, in white, pink, lavender, blue, and scarlet. Plants are bushy and stand only 12 to 18 in. high. The tiny seeds germinate in a week in autumn; seedlings bloom after about four months, the bloom period lasting about two months.

GYPSOPHILA. *Gypsophila elegans.* Caucasus. (Hardy). The dainty flowers of annual "gyp," or annual babys-breath, are much admired for adding grace to arrangements of larger blooms. The bell-shaped flowers are only ½ in. across, but are produced in great profusion on bushy plants with slender, wiry branches. Although white is the usual color, varieties blossom in rose or scarlet. Seeds germinate in six days, and flowers may be expected in two or three months from seeding, but the bloom period lasts only two or three weeks. Succession plantings must be made every three weeks through the fall and winter in order to keep blooming plants continuously in the garden. Culture is easy.

HELICHRYSUM. *Helichrysum bracteatum.* Australia. (Tender). The leading everlasting for dried bouquets, helichrysum, or strawflower, is a vigorous annual, easily grown in sunny soil. The double, 2-in. flowers come in a wide range of bright colors —white, yellow, gold, salmon, rose, and crimson shades. Both dwarf (about 1 ft. high) and tall (2 to 3 ft.) forms are available. Flowers may be cut for fresh use, but they are not exceptionally attractive thus, whereas the bright colors are well retained on drying. Stems should be cut when the heads are half open, stripped of leaves, and hung in bundles with the blossoms downward, in a dry, shady place until fully dried. In northern

Florida plants should be set out after danger of frost is over, but in warm locations helichrysum may be planted in early fall. Cuture is very easy, and the plants bloom well right through the summer from spring seeding.

HOLLYHOCK. *Althea rosea.* China. (Hardy). Old-fashioned hollyhocks are biennials which do not thrive in Florida. A strain which flowers the first year from seed is now widely grown in Florida gardens. Single, semidouble, and double flowers from 4 to 5 in. across are borne in terminal spikes on erect stems up to 6 ft. high. Flower colors may be white, yellow, apricot, rose, scarlet, crimson, or wine. Seeds germinate in a week but take five or six months to produce blossoms. The plants are easy to grow during the cool part of the year in any well-drained soil with plenty of sun, but are subject to root-knot and spider-mites. Rarely do plants survive the summer.

HUNNEMANNIA. *Hunnemannia fumariaefolia.* Mexico. (Hardy). Known also as Mexican tulip-poppy, hunnemannia is closely related to California-poppy and has very similar flowers, single or semidouble. The only color is golden yellow, however, and the flowers last several days when cut in the bud. The vigorous plants with finely divided leaves stand 2 ft. or less high and are very easily grown. Sandy soil and full sun are needed. Seedlings should not be transplanted except when grown in pots or bands; usually seed is sown directly in the garden. Seeds sprout in about ten days, but five or six months are needed for blooming. The plants do not endure Florida summers, and are grown for winter and spring bloom.

LARKSPUR, ANNUAL. *Delphinium ajacis.* Southern Europe. (Hardy). With the development of fine varieties with fully double flowers, single-flowered larkspurs are less popular than formerly. Flowers an inch and more in diameter are borne in dense spikes on plants 3 to 5 ft. high, which branch freely from the base, thus assuring a succession of bloom. Many atttractive colors are available—white, lilac, dark blue, pink, and scarlet. No flower is more highly prized for cutting, and none makes a finer effect as a tall border. Distinctly a cool weather plant, larkspur is suitable only for fall planting to give spring blooms.

Seeds germinate in about two weeks, and the first blossoms come three months or more later. If planted too early in the fall while soil temperatures are high, germination may be very poor unless seeds have been chilled for a month in the refrigerator. The plants tolerate some shade, and early season seedlings benefit especially from protection from hot sun.

LINARIA. *Linaria maroccana.* Morocco. (Hardy). The Moroccan linaria, or toadflax, is a dainty flower, greatly resembling a miniature snapdragon. The dwarf bushy plants, less than a foot high, bear quantities of these little flowers, only ½ in. across, during winter and spring. Flower colors are white, yellow, pink, mauve, dark blue, violet, and crimson. Suited only to the cool season, linaria is easily grown even on poor sandy soil, and often volunteers year after year. Seeds germinate in five days, and flowers are first borne in about three months from seed, the blooming period continuing for several months, even through frosts.

LINUM. *Linum grandiflorum* var. *rubra.* North Africa. (Hardy). The genus to which flax belongs has given us the red-flowered, bushy annual often called scarlet flax. The bright scarlet, inch-broad, single flowers are borne profusely on knee-high plants that have lacy foliage. Admirable for color in the border, the flowers are good for cutting but last one day only. Hardy to cold, easily transplanted, and rather free from pests, linum is easily grown. It takes ten days for seeds to germinate and nearly five months more for blooming. Like linaria, linum is a cool-season plant for spring bloom. Blue flax (*L. narbonense*), with sapphire blue flowers, is also offered as a perennial blooming the first year from seed.

LOBELIA. *Lobelia erinus.* South Africa. (Tender). Lobelia is valued for its lovely blue flowers, which may be either light or dark blue, and with or without a white eye. The single, salver-form blossoms, about an inch across, are borne profusely for months. Plants may be tall (18 in.), dwarf (5 in.), or trailing, and thrive in full sun or partial shade. Trailing varieties are very popular for pots and window boxes, while the bushy kinds are valued for edgings and borders. Although lobelia cannot endure frost, neither does it thrive in hot weather, so that it must be grown in Florida far enough south to avoid frost as a winter bloomer, or in the northern part in early spring. The exceedingly fine seeds germinate in ten days, and the flowers appear in another four months.

LUPINE. *Lupinus hartwegi.* Mexico. (Hardy). The long spikes of lupines are prized for cutting, as they last for days. The modern product of the plant breeder's art is a plant 3 to 4 ft. tall, branching from the base so that half a dozen spikes are produced. Flowers are over ½ in. across, in white, light blue, dark blue, pink, or rose-purple. Lupines are very striking border plants also. They prefer a soil of good moisture content and thrive in sun or partial shade. The Texas bluebonnet (*L. subcarnosus*), another annual lupine, with bright blue flowers on plants under a foot high, is also grown somewhat. As lupines like cool weather, they are planted in fall for spring bloom. It takes four days for seed germination and three months from seed to blossoming. Seeds from the spring may be saved for fall planting if kept in a dry place over summer. *L. luteus,* a soil-improvement legume, dependably produces beautiful yellow flowers in springtime, and *L. angustifolius,* the famous "blue lupine," is also excellent for cutting. Both were introduced originally for soil improvement.

MARIGOLD. *Tagetes* spp. Mexico. (Tender). Three species of marigolds are highly valued in Florida gardens, especially for their ability to thrive in summer heat. While all are native to Mexico, the two important species carry misleading names. The African marigold (*T. erecta*) is a tall, erect plant, from 2 to 3 ft. high, with double flowers in chrysanthemum, dahlia, and carnation types, measuring 3 to 4 in. across. The French marigolds (*T. patula*) are smaller plants, from 8 to 18 in. high, with either single or double flowers from 1 to 2 in. across usually. Both of these highly developed species are offered in many varieties, in varying shades of yellow, orange, and red. Much less widely grown is the Mexican marigold (*T. tenuifolia* var. *pumila*), which is usually under 2 ft. tall and bears great quantities of orange-yellow flowers about an inch in diameter. In extreme southern Florida the African marigold may be grown for blooming in both winter and summer, but the French marigolds are satisfactory only for winter and spring. In northern Florida all three species flower through the summer and fall, and are especially enjoyed for late fall color in the garden. Marigolds are splendid cut flowers, especially varieties with odorless foliage. They are equally valued for borders and the dwarf kinds for edgings. Culture is very easy, as heat, drought, and pests are all tolerated well, and plants thrive in sun or partial shade. Seeds germinate in a few days, and plants bloom in two months, the bloom period lasting several months.

MIGNONETTE. *Reseda odorata*. North Africa. (Hardy). This is an old-fashioned flower, which is prized for its delightful fragrance. The low, bushy plants bear dense spikes of small flowers that make fragrant components of borders and bouquets. Red is the most common color, but white and yellow varieties may be had. Mignonette is especially useful for adding fragrance to bouquets of more attractive flowers lacking pleasing odor. Suited only to cool weather, the plants do well in sun or partial shade. They do not transplant well and so should be seeded directly in the garden bed. Seeds germinate in a week, but seedlings take five months to bloom.

MORNING-GLORY. *Ipomoea* spp. (Tender). Two morning-glory species of widely different origins are grown in gardens as rapidly growing vines for covering trellises, shading porches, and hiding fences. The common morning-glory (*I. purpurea*) is native to the American tropics, while the very similar Japanese morning-glory (*I. nil*) comes from the Old World tropics. Both have large, funnel-shaped flowers, from 3 to 5 in. in diameter, which are borne profusely all summer and fall. The delicate, lovely blossoms close by noon on sunny days, but often remain open all day in cloudy weather. Besides the well-loved blue, flower colors may be white, pink, purple, red, blue and white, or red and white. Full sun and only moderate fertility give best blooming. There are varieties with double flowers, and even some bushy, non-vining forms are seen. The large seeds germinate in ten days, especially if nicked to hasten absorption of water, and seedlings bloom in six weeks, continuing to bloom for months. The closely related moonflower (*Calonyction aculeatum*), from the American tropics also, is a similar vine whose large white or pink flowers are very fragrant and open at night, closing again before noon.

NASTURTIUM. *Tropaeolum majus*. South America. (Tender). The single or double fragrant flowers of nasturtiums are borne in profusion for two or three months in spring, providing bright color for edgings, beds, and borders as well as flowers in the home. A riot of flower colors is offered—cream, yellow, orange, salmon, scarlet, mahogany, and various combinations. Both dwarf bushy plants less than 12 in. high and taller plants up to 3 ft. high are available. The old climbing nasturtium makes a good low vine for quick, colorful covering, although it is short-lived. Nasturtiums are very easy to grow, being subject to few pests, and are particularly good for sandy or gravelly soil, but do not tolerate heat. High fertility decreases blossom production. The large seeds germinate in about ten days, and the plants bloom in about two months more. In northern Florida, seeds are planted after danger of frost, but they may be planted in fall or winter in southern Florida.

NICOTIANA. *Nicotiana alata* var. *grandiflora*. South America. (Hardy). In late winter and spring, the flowers of nicotiana, or flowering tobacco, open at evening to exhale a delightful perfume. Usually they close during the next morning, but there are some varieties which remain open all day in bright sun, with a range of flower color from white through rose, yellow, lilac, scarlet, mahogany, and violet. The bushy plants may be dwarf (12 to 18 in.), or tall (18 to 36 in.), and the flowers, like long-tubed petunias, are up to 2 in. across. Not suited to cutting, nicotiana makes colorful and night-fragrant beds and borders. The plants like sun. The tiny seeds take ten days to sprout and another three months to bloom, with two or three months of flowering.

NIEREMBERGIA. *Nierembergia hippomanica* var. *violacea*. Argentina. (Hardy). Known sometimes as dwarf or blue cup-flower, this is another perennial that blossoms the first season from seed and is treated as an annual. The plants form a dense mat, hardly over 6 in. high and up to 12 in. across, which is literally hidden for months by the broadly cup-shaped flowers, about 1 in. in diameter, with lavender-blue or violet-blue petals and yellow eyes. The small leaves, wiry stems, and thickly set blossoms make this an admirable subject for edgings, borders, window boxes, or pots. Suited only to cool weather, nierembergia grows well in sandy soil and in the sun. Seeds sprout in about a week, and blooming follows in three or four months.

PANSY. *Viola tricolor* var. *hortensis.* Europe. (Hardy). For edging and bedding plants in winter and spring, it is hard to excel the pansy. Low, branching plants, not much over 6 in. high, bear large flowers, from 2 to 4 in. in diameter, with plain or ruffled petals of lovely velvety texture. The color range is enormous—apricot, blue, orchid, purple, rose, maroon, yellow, and combinations of these. No species better demonstrates the effect on continued blooming of removal of spent flowers than does pansy. It thrives in a fairly rich, well-drained soil in full sun. Seeds germinate poorly in warm weather, and so it is best to buy small plants from your garden center. Seeds planted in fall will germinate in about ten days. Seedlings transplant well, and gaps in the edging left by weak or dead plants may be filled from the seed bed readily. Blooming takes three or four months from seed. Pansies cannot tolerate Florida summers but endure light frost.

PETUNIA. *Petunia hybrida.* Argentina. (Hardy). The range of color and form in petunias, together with their wide adaptability to soil conditions, makes them basic items in the Florida winter garden. Plants may be tall and rangy (18 to 24 in.) or dwarf and bushy (8 to 16 in.). Flowers may be single, either small or large and with plain or ruffled petals, or double, fringed or ruffled. In size the flowers range from small singles, 1½ in. across, to giant ruffled blossoms 5 in. wide. Color range is great—shades of white, pink, blue, red, and purple, either solid color or with the throat of contrasting color. The huge fringed and ruffled types are almost bizarre in their grotesqueness, and attract much attention. The small single varieties are easily grown from seed, but the fancy double types often germinate poorly and make weak plants unless they are carefully coddled. The giant ruffled petunias are less hardy to cold, also, and need protection from frost. The double-flowered varieties may be propagated by cuttings. The very small seeds, beloved of ants, germinate in about a week, and three months more are needed for flowering. Single-flowered types respond to removal of old flowers by blooming many months.

PHLOX. *Phlox drummondi.* Texas. (Hardy). The dainty flowers of annual phlox in gay colors, borne profusely over several months in winter and spring, and the easy culture of the plants make it one of the most popular species for ribbon edgings or for quick covering of a bare, sunny spot. The flowers are single only, from 1 to 1½ in. across, in varied colors of white, pink, yellow, lilac, and scarlet, self-colored or with contrasting eye. Plants may be dwarf (6 in.) or tall (12 to 20 in.). Seeds are best sown in place in the garden, where they require ten days for germination. Seedlings often volunteer from last year's plants. It takes about three months for seedlings to bloom. Phlox succeeds in any well-drained soil, even rather poor sands, except in summer.

POPPY. *Papaver rhoeas.* Eurasia. (Hardy). The annual poppy cultivated in gardens today is usually the Shirley type, with fragile, fine-textured flowers in pastel shades of rose, salmon, and scarlet, as well as white. These flowers are single or double, tulip-shaped, with large fluted petals self-colored or two-toned, and a white center. Plants are bushy, 1 to 2 ft. high, enduring frost but not summer heat. Seeds should be sown in place in autumn and will germinate in three weeks. It takes two months more for blooming, and then the bloom period lasts only two or three weeks, so that a succession of plantings should be made for continuous spring flowering. Ants are fond of poppy seeds. The growing of opium poppies is now forbidden by law, but volunteer plants may still be seen in Florida gardens, where they were formerly very popular.

PORTULACA. *Portulaca grandiflora.* Brazil. (Tender). Portulaca, or rose-moss, is hard to excel for summer use in beach gardens, as edgings, or in window boxes. The plants form rounded cushions, hardly 6 in. high, with the narrow, fleshy leaves almost concealed by the abundant flowers that open only on sunny days. These are either single or double, the latter resembling little floribunda roses, 1 to 2 in. across, in many colors —white, yellow, orange, rose, salmon, lavender, and scarlet, either solid-color or striped. Portulaca succeeds on any well-drained soil, even light sands, and endures heat and drought. The very fine seeds germinate in five days and should be planted after frost danger is past, with care not to give too moist conditions for germination. Plants bloom in six or eight weeks from seed, but remain in bloom for only a few weeks, so that monthly sowings should be made until mid-summer for continuous blossoming. Seedlings volunteer freely but are not likely to have large, double flowers in attractive shades.

RUDBECKIA. *Rudbeckia serotina*. Eastern United States. (Tender). Known also as black-eyed Susan and coneflower, the annual rudbeckia bears daisy-type flowers about 4 in. across with golden-yellow petals, a dark brown center, and a mahogany zone at the base of the petals around the dark eye. Usually the flowers are single, but semidouble and double forms have been developed, and all are fine for cutting. The plants grow from 2 to 3 ft. tall, and thrive in full sun on any soil of reasonable fertility. The seeds require about ten days to germinate, and the seedlings need three months more to bloom. In southern Florida, seeds may be started in early fall; but in the northern area it is better to wait until January, as the seedlings cannot endure frost. If the weather is not too hot and humid, the blooming period may last many weeks. Rudbeckia may volunteer from seeds dropped from mature plants.

SALPIGLOSSIS. *Salpiglossis sinuata*. Chile. (Hardy). The gold-veined flowers of salpiglossis, or painted-tongue, are 2 to 3 in. across, shaped like petunias, with petal colors white, yellow, pink, red, lavender, or purple. Both low and tall types of plants are offered. Thriving only in cool weather, salpiglossis seeds germinate in about a week, but seedlings need about five months to bloom. Hardy to our winter cold, the plants are very subject to crown rot on the light sandy soils of the peninsula. The flowers are valued for cutting and for borders. A dry, sunny location is desired.

SALVIA. *Salvia splendens.* Brazil. (Tender). Scarlet sage now comes in named varieties with salmon, old rose, and purple colors as well as the familiar flaming red. Plants may be drawf (6-12 in.), medium (15-18 in.), or tall (24-30 in.). There is also blue sage (*S. farinacea*), a Texas native, with both blue and white varieties, all tall (30-36 in.). Seeds of salvia germinate in a week, and seedlings bloom in 3 or 4 months, remaining in bloom for several months. In spite of sometimes being used too freely, salvia is one of our most reliable annuals for colorful bloom.

SCABIOSA. *Scabiosa atropurpurea.* Southern Europe. (Hardy). Sometimes called sweet scabious or pin-cushion-flower, the globular flower heads of scabiosa are 2 in. across and are borne on long stalks. The range of flower color is very great—white, yellow, pink, red, blue, or purplish-black. Varieties with the nearly black flowers give rise to the name "mourning-bride" for this species. Of easy culture, scabiosa may be had with semi-dwarf (12 to 28 in.) or tall (24 to 36 in.) plants. Seed should be sown in place and will germinate in three weeks. It takes five to seven months from seed to bloom, but flowers are borne for many weeks if the old heads are not allowed to seed. Scabiosa is excellent for cutting, as the cut flowers are long-lived.

SCHIZANTHUS. *Schizanthus pinnatus.* Chile. (Tender). Sometimes called butterfly-flower or poor-mans-orchid, schizanthus bears spikes of flowers resembling sprays of orchids. Individual flowers are from 1 to 2 in. across, in white, yellow, buff, pink, mauve, red, or purple, with irregular markings of darker color. The bushy plants have finely cut foliage. Highly esteemed for cut flowers, schizanthus is usually a greenhouse or pot plant and is difficult to grow in the garden. It tolerates neither cold nor heat, and can be grown in northern Florida only for late spring bloom. Seeds should be sown in place and will germinate in ten days. From seed to bloom takes three to four months outdoors.

SNAPDRAGON. *Antirrhinum majus.* Mediterranean area.

(Hardy). Perennial in its native haunts, the snapdragon is known in gardens only as an annual, and in Florida is grown successfully only during the cool season. Long popular for cutting and borders because of the spikes of showy flowers, in recent years plant hybridizers have created larger and more gorgeous types than before, sometimes with spikes 24 in. long. Flowers are from 1 to 1½ in. across, either single or double, and colored white, yellow, copper, pink, bronze, crimson, lavender, or two-toned in some of these colors. The gardener may have dwarf (4 to 6 in.), semidwarf (12 to 18 in.), or tall (24 to 36 in.) plants. In order to assure straight spikes it may be necessary to stake each plant and tie the stems every 6 in. The tiny seeds germinate in about one week, and the plants bloom in another three months or so. Seedlings transplant readily, and culture is not at all difficult in a sunny, well-drained, fertile soil free of disease. Snapdragons are very subject to attack by nematodes and by crown-rot fungus. Strains resistant to rust disease of the leaves make this no longer a problem. The blooming period may last several weeks.

STATICE. *Limonium* spp. Eurasia. (Hardy). Thriving in both cool and hot weather and of very easy culture, three annual species of statice are widely grown in Florida gardens for cut flowers, either fresh or dried, and for borders. *L. sinuatum* and its hybrids are most widely grown, with white, rose, lavender, deep blue, and pastel colors of flowers, borne in loose branching spikes on plants from 2 to 3 ft. high. *L. bonduelli* is similar in habit but has yellow flowers. *L. suworowi* has dense spikes of lavender-pink. All these statice species have basal rosettes of leaves and stiff, strawy flowers of graceful habit. They are most popular for winter bouquets, being treated like helichrysum flowers and retaining color well. Seeds need a week to germinate, and it is another three months to blooming, which continues for many weeks.

STOCK. *Matthiola incana* var. *annua*. Europe. (Hardy). This old garden favorite is another example of how plant breeders have modified and glorified the original garden flowers. The fragrant flowers are now offered fully double in a choice of white, pink, red, yellow, blue, or purple. Plants may be branching for borders or single-stemmed for cutting, and either dwarf (under 18 in.) or tall (over 2 ft.). Culture of stock is easy if care is taken to avoid soil-borne diseases, but the plants thrive only in cool weather and do not develop flower buds in warm weather. There may be no blossoms in a warm winter. Seeds sprout in about two weeks, and blooms may be produced in eight or ten weeks more, the bloom period lasting several weeks. Stocks need rich soil.

SUNFLOWER. *Helianthus annuus.* Northern United States. (Tender). The well-known sunflower is obtainable in a great variety of height, habit, and size of blossoms, not all in the familiar yellow. Besides their value for cutting, sunflowers serve as screens and boundaries if successive sowings of seed are made at monthly intervals. A summer bloomer in the northern part of the state, sunflowers are chiefly grown for winter and spring flowers in southern Florida. The large seeds require two weeks to sprout, and it is two months more until flowers are borne. Both single and double flowers may be had, some like chrysanthemums, in yellow or red and up to 8 in. across. Only full sun is suitable.

SWEET-PEA. *Lathyrus odoratus.* Italy. (Hardy). Sweet-peas have long been esteemed highly for cut flowers because of their wonderful variety of pastel colors and their delightful fragrance. They are satisfactory only when grown in full sun in very rich soil, so that the vines grow rankly. It is usually best to dig a trench 12 in. deep and equally wide, and to fill this with a mixture of equal parts of top soil and of either well-rotted manure, compost, or peat humus. If humus is used, it should be fortified with a little garden fertilizer. Sweet-peas need a trellis about 4 to 8 ft. high to support the vines. This may be poultry netting stretched between two posts, or may be made of heavy wires between the posts at top and bottom, with cotton twine laced back and forth between them. Soil should be close to neutral or slightly alkaline. On sandy soils this means sprinkling with enough lime to whiten the surface of the bed. Since sweet-peas are subject to attack by several soil-borne diseases, use a soil fumigant before planting. Staggering the seeds in a double row makes it easy to have the trellis between the rows of seedlings. Seeds germinate in ten days, and first flowers come two or three months later. If the old flowers are picked regularly, the flowering season should last for months.

TITHONIA. *Tithonia rotundifolia.* Mexico. (Tender). Sometimes called Mexican-sunflower, the single daisy-type flowers of tithonia are 3 to 4 in. across, orange-scarlet in color, and borne profusely for months. The plants are branching and bushy, and

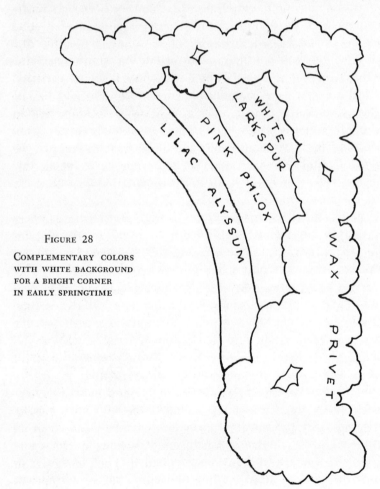

FIGURE 28

COMPLEMENTARY COLORS
WITH WHITE BACKGROUND
FOR A BRIGHT CORNER
IN EARLY SPRINGTIME

may be had in tall form (6 to 8 ft.) or in dwarf types (3 to 4 ft.). The long flower stems make cutting easy. Culture is easy in any well-drained soil in full sun, and spider mites are about the only pests. The large seeds germinate in two weeks, and the first flowers are borne in about two months more. In northern Florida, tithonia is grown for summer and early fall bloom; in southern Florida it is most satisfactory for fall, winter, and spring bloom.

TORENIA. *Torenia fournieri.* Southeastern Asia. (Tender). A profusion of small, snapdragon-like flowers borne on bushy plants about 1 ft. high makes torenia, or wish-bone-flower, a fine edging or rock garden subject for the summer months. The usual flower color is light blue, with yellow throat and dark blue blotches on the flower face. There are white-flowered varieties, too. The peculiar arrangement of stamens gives rise to the name "wish-bone-flower." Torenia prefers moist soil and does well in either full sun or partial shade. The spreading branches often root where they lie on the soil, and those rooted tips may be used to supply new plantings. Seeds germinate in about one week, and first flowering is about three months from seed. In southern Florida torenia may be planted for winter, spring, and summer bloom, but it is at its best in summer; it is satisfactory for planting only after the last frost in northern Florida, for summer bloom. The plants continue flowering for several months.

VERBENA. *Verbena hybrida.* Tropical America. (Hardy). Known only as an annual in northern gardens, verbena is commonly grown in Florida as a perennial; but since it flowers the first season from seed, it is also widely planted as an annual. It is described fully in Chapter Nine. Seeds germinate in about a week; seedlings bloom in about three or four months.

VIOLA. *Viola cornuta.* Spain. (Hardy). Known also as tufted-pansies, violas are just as effective as the better known pansies for edgings, rock gardens, and flower beds. Flowers are about an inch across, in bright clear colors of white, yellow, apricot, crimson, blue, or violet, and even some two-toned. The plants vary in height from 4 to 10 in. according to variety, but are all upright in habit and bloom over many weeks if old flowers are kept picked. Like pansies, violas are perennials that do not tolerate summer heat in Florida. In the northern area, seeds may be planted in early fall, germinating in ten days, to produce flowers during the winter, or plants may be bought in November at your garden center. Culture is easy in a sunny location on well-drained soil.

ZINNIA. *Zinnia elegans.* Mexico. (Tender). One of the most valuable annuals for summer gardens in Florida is the zinnia, now offered in a remarkable variety of flower forms and colors, thanks to the work of plant breeders. Almost every color is available—white, yellow, orange, salmon, rose, crimson, scarlet, blue, purple, and even "peppermint-stick" with pink and white stripes. The fully double flowers range in size from the flat California giants and the rounded dahlia-flowered types, both up to 6 in. across, through the shaggy, fantasy types of half that size, down to the little pompons of the lilliput types, hardly an inch across. Dwarf bushy plants of lilliputs and cupids are only 1 ft. high and wider spreading than tall, while the giant-flowered kinds may be 3 ft. tall. All kinds grow thriftily even in poor soil if planted in a sunny location and given plenty of water and fertilizer, and bloom continuously for many weeks. Seeds germinate in half a week, and seedlings bloom in about two months. Succession plantings at two-month intervals will assure blooming from May to October. Zinnias provide excellent cut flowers as well as color in the garden borders, and the small types do well as edgings. Two other species are good garden plants. Z. *linearis* has single flowers an inch across, orange with a yellow stripe on each ray, borne on low, bushy plants, 10 in. high and twice as broad. Z. *angustifolia,* the Mexicana or miniature zinnia, bears small double or semidouble flowers, a little over an inch across, in shades of yellow, red, and brown, on dwarf plants. Zinnias are subject to attack by powdery mildew, which gives leaves the appearance of a frost coating.

Chart of Annual Flowers for Florida

Kind of Flower	Frost Resistance	Days to Germinate*	Months to Bloom	Northern Florida Plant	Northern Florida Bloom	Southern Florida Plant	Southern Florida Bloom
Ageratum	Tender	4	3	Feb-Apr	May-Aug	Sept-Mar	Dec-Sept
Alyssum, Sweet	Hardy	4	2	Sept-May	All year	Sept-May	All year
Arctotis	Hardy	10	3½	Oct-Jan	Mar-Jun	Aug-Jan	Jan-July
Aster, China-	Tender	7	3½	Feb-Apr	Jul-Aug	Sept-May	Jan-July
Bachelors-button	Hardy	4	3	Oct-Jan	Dec-Jun	Sept-Jan†	Dec-May†
Balsam	Tender	5	1½	Mar-Jun	Apr-Nov	Sept-Apr	Nov-Aug
Begonia	Tender	10	3½	Sept-Dec	Mar-Jun	Sept-Mar	Jan-May‡
Bellis	Hardy	7	5	Sept-Nov	Mar-May	(Not satisfactory)	
Blue lace-flower	Tender	7	3½	Feb-Apr	Jul-Aug	Sept-Jan	Dec-May
Brachycome	Hardy	7	4	Sept-Nov	Jan-Apr	Sept-Dec	Jan-May
Browallia	Hardy	10	3½	Sept-Dec	Dec-May	Sept-Dec	Dec-Jul
Calendula	Hardy	5	3	Sept-Jan	Dec-Jun	Sept-Jan	Dec-Jun
California-poppy	Hardy	7	3	Sept-Jan	Mar-Jun	(Not satisfactory)	
Calliopsis	Hardy	10	4	Oct-Dec	Feb-Jun	Sept-Dec	Jan-Jun
Candytuft, Globe	Hardy	7	4	Oct-Jan	Mar-Jun	Sept-Nov	Jan-May
Candytuft, Rocket	Hardy	7	3	Oct-Jan	Feb-Jun	Oct-Jan	Jan-Jun
Carnation	Hardy	5	4	Sept-Jan§	Feb-Jun	Nov-Jan	Feb-Jul
Celosia	Tender	5	2½	Feb-May	Mar-Sept	Aug-Feb	Nov-Jun
Chinese forget-me-not	Hardy	7	3½	Dec-Feb	Apr-Jul	Nov-Jan	Jan-Jun
Chrysanthemum	Tender	7	4½	Dec-Mar	May-Jul	(Not satisfactory)	
Clarkia	Hardy	7	6	Sept-Jan	Apr-Jun	(Not satisfactory)	
Cleome	Tender	10	6	Sept-Dec	Apr-Aug	(Not satisfactory)	
Cosmos, Early	Tender	7	2½	Feb-Apr	May-Aug	(Not satisfactory)	
Cosmos, Late	Tender	7	2½	Mar-Aug	Oct-Dec	Apr-Oct	Oct-May
Cypress-vine	Tender	7	2	Mar-May	Jun-Nov	Feb-Sept	Apr-Feb
Dahlia	Tender	6	2½	Mar-May	Jun-Sept	Sept-Feb	Dec-Jul
Delphinium	Hardy	10-20	5	Oct-Nov	Mar-May	Aug-Dec§	Feb-Jun

CHART OF ANNUAL FLOWERS FOR FLORIDA (*continued*)

KIND OF FLOWER	FROST RESIST- ANCE	DAYS TO GERMINATE*	MONTHS TO BLOOM	NORTHERN FLORIDA		SOUTHERN FLORIDA	
				PLANT	BLOOM	PLANT	BLOOM
DIANTHUS (PINK)	Hardy	7	3½	Sept-Feb	Jan-Jul	Sept-Jan	Jan-Jun
DIMORPHOTHECA	Hardy	5	4½	Sept-Feb	Mar-Jul	Sept-Dec	Jan-May
GAILLARDIA	Hardy	8	3	All year	All year	All year	All year
GILIA	Hardy	10	4	Sept-Dec	Mar-Jun	Sept-Nov	Jan-May
GLOBE-AMARANTH	Tender	6	2½	Mar-May	May-Jul	Sept-May	Nov-Jun
GODETIA	Hardy	7	4½	Oct-Jan	Apr-Jun	Sept-Nov	Feb-May
GYPSOPHILA	Hardy	6	2½	Sept-Feb	Dec-Jun	Oct-Dec	Jan-May
HELICHRYSUM	Tender	8	3	Feb-Apr	May-Aug	Sept-Dec	Nov-Jun
HOLLYHOCK	Hardy	7	5½	Oct-Dec	Mar-Jun	All year	All year
HUNNEMANNIA	Hardy	10	5	Oct-Dec	Apr-Jun	Aug-Nov	Feb-Jun
LARKSPUR	Hardy	10-20	3½	Oct-Jan	Mar-May	Oct-Dec§	Feb-May
LINARIA	Hardy	5	3	Sept-Feb	Dec-May	Sept-Jan	Dec-May
LINUM	Hardy	10	5	Sept-Dec	Mar-Jun	Aug-Oct	Feb-May
LOBELIA	Tender	10	4½	Sept-Jan	Feb-May	Aug-Nov	Jan-Apr
LUPINE	Hardy	4	3	Aug-Dec	Mar-Jun	Sept-Nov	Feb-Mar
MARIGOLD, AFRICAN	Tender	3	2	Feb-May	Apr-Nov	Apr-Dec	Jun-May
MARIGOLD, FRENCH	Tender	3	2	Feb-May	Apr-Nov	Sept-May	Dec-Sept
MIGNONETTE	Hardy	7	5	Sept-Dec	Mar-May	(Not satisfactory)	
MORNING-GLORY	Tender	10	2	Mar-Jun	May-Nov	All year	All year
NASTURTIUM	Tender	10	2½	{ Sept-Oct / Feb-Mar	Nov-Dec / Apr-Jun	Sept-Jan	Dec-May
NICOTIANA	Hardy	10	4	Sept-Jan	Feb-Jul	Aug-Dec	Dec-Jun
NIEREMBERGIA	Hardy	7	3½	Sept-Dec	Feb-Jun	Oct-Jan	Feb-May
PANSY	Hardy	10	3	Oct-Jan	Feb-May	Oct-Dec	Jan-Mar
PETUNIA	Hardy	7	3½	Aug-Jan	Jan-Jul	Aug-Jan	Dec-Jun
PHLOX	Hardy	10	3	Sept-Mar	Jan-Jul	Aug-Jan	Dec-Jun
POPPY	Hardy	20	2½	Oct-Feb	Jan-May	Sept-Feb	Dec-May

Chart of Annual Flowers for Florida (continued)

Kind of Flower	Frost Resistance	Days to Germinate*	Months to Bloom	Northern Florida Plant	Northern Florida Bloom	Southern Florida Plant	Southern Florida Bloom
Portulaca	Tender	5	2	Mar-Jul	May-Oct	Sept-Mar†	Nov-Jun†
Rudbeckia	Tender	10	3½	Feb-Apr	Apr-Jul	Aug-Jan	Dec-Aug
Salpiglossis	Hardy	7	5	Sept-Jan	Jan-May	Aug-Nov	Jan-May
Salvia	Tender	7	3½	Mar-May	Jun-Nov	Aug-Dec	Dec-Jul
Scabiosa	Hardy	20	6	Sept-Jan	Mar-Jun	Aug-Oct†	Feb-Jun†
Schizanthus	Tender	10	3	Jan-Mar	Apr-Jun	Sept-Jan†	Dec-May†
Snapdragon	Hardy	7	4	Oct-Dec	Feb-Jun	Sept-Nov	Jan-May
Statice	Hardy	10	4	Oct-Dec	Jan-Jun	Sept-Nov	Jan-May
Stock	Hardy	15	3	Sept-Dec	Jan-May	(Not satisfactory)	
Sunflower	Tender	15	2½	Mar-May	May-Aug	Sept-Feb	Dec-Jan
Sweet-pea	Hardy	10	3½	Oct-Jan	Jan-Apr	Nov-Dec	Jan-Apr
Tithonia	Tender	15	2½	Mar-Jun	Jun-Oct	Jun-Dec	Sept-Jun
Torenia	Tender	8	3	Mar-May	Apr-Sept	All year	All year
Verbena	Hardy	7	3½	Sept-Mar	Feb-Jul	Aug-Nov	Dec-Jun
Viola	Hardy	10	3	Sept-Dec	Jan-May	(Not satisfactory)	
Zinnia	Tender	4	2	Mar-Aug	Jun-Oct	Feb-Jul	May-Oct

* Germination time is for outdoors in warm weather, indoors in cool weather.
† Not very satisfactory for southern Florida.
‡ Blooms until July if in shade.
§ Seeds should be chilled a month for early plantings.

11

Bulbs

THE TERM "BULBOUS PLANTS" includes species belonging to many different families having in common the fact that they possess a swollen underground storage organ from which flowering shoots arise during the growing season. As the term is commonly used, it overlaps somewhat the term "herbaceous perennial," since all bulbous plants are herbaceous perennials. For convenience, however, we separate as bulbous plants those herbaceous perennials that are quite seasonal in flowering and that are easily lifted and stored during the dormant season. Many bulbous plants have true bulbs as the perennial portion of the plant. Some have underground stems that are corms, some have tubers, and still others have thickened rhizomes. In a few cases a swollen root like a sweet potato is the perennial organ. The lily, amaryllis, iris, and arum families include nearly all of the bulbous types.

The Florida climate is favorable for the growth and flowering of many "bulbs" that are unusual and beautiful. It is true that unprocessed tulips, bearded irises, and hardy lilies will not succeed here, and the same is true of all the spring-flowering bulbs of northern latitudes; but many bulbs from the tropics and subtropics, known only as potted plants in the North, thrive in the gardens of our warm humid climate.

Bulbs are effective in the landscape when they are planted in groups for color effect. As with other herbaceous flowering plants, a good location is found in bays of shrubbery borders. For cut flowers, they are best grown in a separate cutting bed or garden. The same careful preparation of the planting bed, to eliminate competing roots of shrubs or trees and to incorporate organic matter, is needed for bulbs as for annual and perennial herbaceous flowers.

Most bulbous plants have similar requirements for culture. Usually a porous soil with high content of organic matter is best, and only a few swamp dwellers tolerate poor drainage. Most bulbs like plenty of sunlight, with light, shifting shade only. Most of them also require plenty of water during their growing season. An organic mulch to conserve soil moisture, discourage weeds, and reduce summer soil temperatures is helpful in growing all bulbous plants. In general they have a wide range of tolerance regarding soil acidity, but there are exceptions. Fertilizer should be applied before planting, using 2 to 3 pts. per 100 sq. ft. of a good garden fertilizer mixture, such as a 6-6-6 analysis, and placing it below the bulb, covered by a thin layer of soil to avoid direct contact. During the growing season apply the same amount and analysis two or three times on the surface and wash it in with the hose.

Propagation of bulbous plants is chiefly by separation in the case of bulbs and corms, and by division of tubers, rhizomes, and tuberous roots. Sometimes a mother bulb forms two or three large daughter bulbs, often called "slabs" or "offsets." Sometimes very small bulbs, called bulblets, develop from the base of the mother bulb. These must be grown for two or three seasons before they are large enough to bloom. Corms similarly produce tiny cormels in addition to the one or two large daughter corms. Many fanciers keep these for increase of rare varieties.

True bulbs may also be propagated by cuttage, in cases where it is desired to multiply a rare specimen more rapidly than Nature normally does it. Mature bulbs may be cut vertically into wedge-shaped pieces like orange segments, each having a portion of true stem tissue at the lower end. These segments are placed in flats or pots containing a mixture of equal parts of sand and peat, and are treated like softwood cuttings. Small bulblets begin to form in a few weeks from buds at the bases of bulb scales, and by the end of the season should be large enough to pot separately. An alternative method is to make similar cuts upward from the basal end of the bulb, but leaving the segments united for the upper third. The multilated bulb is placed with the cut basal end down in a rooting medium and treated as just described. These types of bulb multiplication should be started when the bulbs are just ready to start growth for the season.

Some bulbous plants can be left in place for several years before they need to be lifted and separated. Those few that are evergreen are usually left alone until they show evidence of crowding. In the case of the species with discontinuous growth, there is considerable variation between kinds as to whether they need to be dug and stored. When such treatment is indicated, digging should be done when the foliage begins to yellow. After the bulbs are carefully dug and lifted, they should be spread out in a dry, shaded location for a few days; then after the tops and roots are cut off, the storage organ should be stored in a dry, well-ventilated place.

BULBOUS PLANTS RECOMMENDED FOR FLORIDA

Achimenes spp. ACHIMENES. Tropical America. (N,C,S). Window-box and porch plants par excellence, achimenes have been favorites with homeowners for centuries. Of complex hybrid origin, downy little pot plants bear in summer little trumpet-shaped flowers of various sizes and lobings in tones of red and violet. Divide rhizomes for increase.

Agapanthus africanus. AFRICAN-LILY. South Africa. (N,C, S). Clusters of large, blue, funnel-shaped flowers are borne atop tall scapes during summer and early fall. Strap-shaped leaves a yard long arise from the rhizome in spring. The rhizome is planted in autumn or winter, and the plants are left undisturbed for several years until a clump is formed. Old matted clumps may be lifted and divided into several plants. In northern Florida the plants may be killed to the ground, but will recover if they are well mulched before cold weather. The name "lily-of-the-Nile" is given in error, as they are native to the other end of Africa.

Aloe vera. ALOE. Mediterranean. (S). This plant has thick, fleshy leaves with heavy marginal spines, borne on a very short stem. The leaves are filled with a soft jelly which is used to treat sunburn and X-ray burns. A spike of small, tubular, red or yellow flowers is produced. Propagation is by suckers.

Alstroemeria spp. ALSTROEMERIA. South America. (N,C). Several species of alstroemeria are occasionally grown by experienced gardeners for their unusual spotted flowers. Suitable only for shaded, northern exposures, they are difficult subjects for amateurs. Some kinds will grow in place for several years, but more often the tuberous roots are lifted and stored during the dormant period in dry sand or peat.

Amaryllis vittata. AMARYLLIS. Peru. (N,C,S). This species, formerly and better known as *Hippeastrum vittatum,* is the source of nearly all the common hybrid amaryllis types grown in Florida. The strap-shaped leaves that arise from the bulb are an inch or more broad and some 2 ft. long, and usually they are evergreen or nearly so. The large, trumpet-shaped flowers are borne in clusters of two to five in spring on a stout scape, 12 to 18 in. high. Many named varieties in the beautiful Dutch strains are grown along with Mead hybrids in the gardens of advanced fanciers, and many gardeners like the vigorous progeny that result from crossing the two strains. Flower colors range from white to dark red in solid colors and in striped colors. Seedlings are easily grown, requiring several years for flowering, but are quite variable in color and vigor. Amaryllis thrive best in the pH range from 6.0 to 8.0, where most garden plants succeed, and do better in partial shade. Usually the bulbs are left to multiply in place for several years, but some growers lift and separate them every fall, or store them until early winter. Planting stored bulbs at biweekly intervals from November to February gives a succession of spring bloom.

Caladium bicolor. FANCY-LEAVED CALADIUM. Tropical America. (N,C,S). The beautiful, arrow-shaped leaves arising from the tubers show a variety of bright colors—red, green, yellow, purplish, and even white. The tubers are planted in late winter, and the showy foliage remains attractive until late fall, when the leaves die down. In the southern and central areas the tubers may be left in the ground, but in northern Florida it is safer to dig and store them in dry peat to avoid cold injury. Large tubers may be cut into pieces like potatoes, making sure each piece has one good bud. There are dozens of named varieties which grow well in moist, rich soil and tolerate shade.

Crinum spp. CRINUM. Old and New World Tropics. (N,C,S). No bulbous flowers are better adapted to Florida than the crinums, one species of which (*C. americanum*) is native to this state. Crinum bulbs are among the largest true bulbs, some weighing over 40 lbs. Most species are evergreen, and although the principal flowering period is spring and summer, blossoms may appear at other times of year if there is a long period of warm weather. In northern Florida tops are killed to the ground by cold; however, they are replaced quickly. The broadly strap-shaped leaves are often over 4 ft. long, and the flowering scapes may rise to the same height, bearing great clusters of fragrant flowers. Some species have solid colors, white, pink, or rose, but others are striped white and carmine—the so-called milk-and-wine-lilies. Names are often much confused in crinums, and although many seedlings have been named as varieties, it is not easy to be sure of what is grown under a given name without seeing the plants in bloom. *C. amabile* and *C. asiaticum* both form huge plants with very large flower clusters. In the former the flowers are pink; in the latter species, which blooms nearly all year long in southern Florida, they are white. Both have leaves 3 to 4 in. broad.   Being large plants which form clumps, since they are rarely disturbed, crinums should have plenty of space given them. Winter is the best time to make new plantings, lifting a clump and separating some of the offshoot bulbs, but this may be done at any time of year.

Dahlia pinnata. DAHLIA. Mexico. (N,C). Native to the mountains of Mexico, dahlias thrive better on the heavy clay soils of northwestern Florida than on the sandy soils of the peninsula. Being subject to soil pests, it is well to sterilize the soil before planting and keep plants heavily mulched. As dahlias are easily hurt by cold, the tuberous roots are planted in December or January in central Florida and in February or March in northern Florida. They bloom from June to October. Each root must have a piece of stem tissue with a bud, and at planting the root is laid horizontally at a depth of 6 in. with the bud next to a sturdy stake some 6 ft. high. This is to support the stem, which may be tied to it every 8 in. or so. Plants are spaced 2 to 3 ft. apart, depending on their vigor of growth, and thrive in full sun. Usually dahlias die down in November, and the cluster of tuberous roots is carefully lifted and stored in dry sand or peat. At planting time, the roots are carefully cut apart, with a piece of stem attached to each. It is possible to have dahlias blooming in late autumn if roots are held in cold storage by northern dealers until August and are planted out in September. In northwestern Florida dahlia roots are often left in the ground for several years, but in peninsular Florida they should be lifted each year.

Eucharis grandiflora. AMAZON-LILY. Colombia. (S). Rarely grown in the open garden, this is a popular pot plant everywhere. The large, dark green leaves are like those of aspidistra. During the winter, clusters of four or five waxy white flowers like large narcissus blossoms are borne on tall scapes. The name Amazon-lily is a curious error, since the species is not native within a thousand miles of that great river. Being a tender winter bloomer, the plants can be grown outdoors only in extreme southern Florida, and even there they bloom better in pots because a crowded condition is thought to encourage bloom. Old clumps in the open may bloom well, however. The bulbs are planted in spring in soil high in organic matter. Intolerant of sun, the plants should be grown in fairly deep shade.

Freesia spp. FREESIA. South Africa. (N,C). Hybrid freesias have fragrant flowers of white, yellow, pink, orange, red, mauve, or blue, borne in racemes of six to eight trumpet-shaped blossoms. The rachis of each raceme is bent at right angles so that the flowers stand like birds on a perch. Corms are planted from September through February, and take about three months to bloom. In the light sandy soils on which they thrive, they are very subject to root-knot. Plant the corms about 2 in. deep and 2 in. apart in sterilized soil. When the foliage turns yellow, dig the corms and store like gladiolus. However, bacterial diseases often attack the corms and make them unfit for future planting. Freesias are very popular pot plants.

Gladiolus spp. GLADIOLUS. South Africa. (N,C,S). In addition to being important in Florida's cut-flower industry, "glads" are justly popular garden flowers everywhere in our state. They are grown in cutting gardens for cut flowers, or in drifts in shrubbery bays for garden color. The modern gladiolus is the result of hybridization over many years, involving at least four species, so that no cultivated variety can be referred to any true species, except as fanciers may grow unimproved wild forms. Incidentally, the scientific name of this genus is pronounced *Gladi'-olus,* but the commonly accepted pronunciation as a common name is *gladio'-lus,* with the plural the same as the singular. Flowers come in a bewildering array of colors, from white through all shades of yellow and pink to deep red and purple. Only clear blue is missing. Mostly the flowers are solid colors, but some are white or yellow with red throat blotches, or the throat may be light while the rest of the petals are colored. Sword-shaped leaves arise from corms and flowers are borne in tall spikes rising well above the foliage. If flower stalks are cut when the lowest flowers of the spike are just opening, all the flowers will open in turn over a period of several days, making "glads" among the most desirable cut flowers.

In southern Florida it is possible to have gladiolus in bloom every month of the year if the corms are held for a month or so in the refrigerator before planting, but flower quality is very poor in summer and fall unless great pains are taken. Consequently it is better to make plantings from September through February. In northern Florida the planting period is from January 15 to March 1 for garden production, the danger of frost injury making earlier plantings unwise. It requires about three months from planting to blooming.

The usual practice in planting corms is to open a furrow or narrow trench to a depth of about 6 in., and to scatter along the bottom of this depression about 2 or 3 qts. of good garden fertilizer of 6-6-6 analysis per 100 ft. of row, or a cupful to each 10 ft. This fertilizer should be covered with an inch of soil, and the corms then set at intervals of 6 in. (center to center), taking care to have the bud side up, and covered with soil to fill the trench. Dip corms before planting in Morsodren (2 tsp. in 1 qt.) for 15 minutes to control surface fungus infections. All corms more than an inch in diameter will usually bloom, but the larger sizes will generally produce larger spikes than the smaller ones. For exhibition purposes, jumbo corms may be used and spaced 8 or 10 in. apart. Plantings for garden color are not set in rows usually, and individual holes are made for the corms, spaced about 4 in. apart each way. These holes are dug 6 in. deep, a tablespoon of fertilizer placed in the bottom, an inch of soil added to cover, and the corm set in place and covered over. Planting deeply helps maintain proper soil moisture conditions for corm growth, and also helps to keep the plant erect when the weight of foliage and flowers tends to cause it to lean. A second application of fertilizer should be made about 45 days after planting along both sides of the row. This may be the same material as used previously, applied at the same rate, or may be a soluble nitrogenous material only, such as sulfate of ammonia or nitrate of soda, applied at one-fourth the rate of the mixed fertilizer. For mass plantings in shrubbery bays, estimate 30 plants as equal to 10 ft. of row. On very light soils, a third application of mixed fertilizer may be needed after harvesting the flowers, to assure good development of corms wanted for next year. Gladiolus do best in full sun, but tolerate some high, broken shade. Water is a critical factor in flower spike development.

Many gardeners prefer to buy new planting stock each year from northern specialists, and do not try to save their corms. This avoids considerable trouble for storage and the deterioration of varieties because of pests. If corms are to be stored, flower spikes must be cut carefully to avoid injury to the leaves. When the foliage becomes yellowed, the plants should be dug and the leaves cut off close to the corms, which are laid in rows

in a dry, airy place to cure. In about ten days the shriveled old
corm can be pulled away from the bottom of the new corm,
which can then be stored in a well-ventilated place screened
from rodents. The small cormels can be used for multiplication,
but are seldom worth the bother to the home gardener. Corms
should be dusted with 5% DDT dust to eradicate thrips, a major
pest of gladiolus. Elimination of those in the corm sheaths helps
get the plants off to a good start, but flowers maturing in May
and June are sure to be streaked by thrips unless spraying is
done weekly for control.

Gloriosa rothschildiana. GLORY-LILY. Tropical Africa.
(N,C,S). Climbing by tendrils at the tips of the leaves to a
height of 6 ft., the glory-lily needs a trellis of string or netting
to give its weak stem support. The large, showy flowers are crimson, except for the basal part of each petal being yellow, and are
borne at right angles to the pedicels, making them somewhat
difficult to arrange. From two to eight flowers may be produced
on an unbranched vine, in the axils of the upper leaves, or a
very vigorous vine may have several branches with 20 to 30
flowers in all. The aerial stem arises from a V-shaped tuber,
which may be divided at its apex to make two new plants. Thriving in full sun, glory-lily may also be grown under light shade.
It does not tolerate poor drainage, yet needs plenty of soil
moisture during growth. Usually the tubers are left in the ground
for several years to make a large clump of vines. New plantings
may be made at any season, setting the tubers 4 or 5 in. deep,
but usually are made from January to April, with the principal
flowering occurring from April to June. Blossoms may appear
in summer or fall, however, as the old tops die down, and
following a resting period new growth may appear. Heavy fertilizing of this new growth, whenever it starts, makes for vigorous vines with many blossoms. The flowers last for several
days, gradually darkening in red color. Other species with flowers
in various colors are infrequently seen in gardens of advanced
fanciers.

Habranthus robustus. See *Zephyranthes.*

Haemanthus multiflorus. BLOOD-LILY. Tropical Africa.

(N,C,S). The showy, bright red inflorescence of this unusual bulb consists of many dozen slender flowers forming a sphere about 6 in. in diameter at the top of a stout stalk a foot high. From the large amaryllis-like bulb that produces this inflorescence there rises independently a green stem, spotted with dark red, bearing three or four broad leaves about a foot long. Blooming occurs in May or June, and the tops die down in winter. Bulbs are expensive because the species is rather rare in cultivation, but it succeeds under the same conditions as its relative, the amaryllis, and is similarly propagated. It is usually grown as a pot plant.

Hyacinthus orientalis var. *albulus*. ROMAN HYACINTH. Southern France. (N,C,S). These small hyacinths with white, blue, or pink flowers are sometimes grown as garden plants in Florida. Bulbs planted from October to December will bloom from February to April, and often persist for several years if well cared for. The bulbs may be also dug after the foliage dies down, as for narcissus. Roman hyacinths should be planted about 6 in. deep in a sunny spot, and each bulb will produce several slender spikes of flowers.

Hymenocallis keyensis. SPIDER-LILY. Florida and West Indies. (N,C,S). The curious, fragrant, white flowers are borne in clusters on a stout scape much as amaryllis flowers are. Each flower has a 6-in. tube, with six slender petals about 5 in. long and a 3-in. cup formed by the stamens. The bulbs and leaves are also similar to those of amaryllis. Blooming occurs in summer over a long period. Culture of this bulb is very easy. It tolerates poorly drained soil better than most bulbous plants, being native to swamps, and thrives in either full sun or light shade. The leaves are evergreen and endure considerable cold. Propagation and culture are the same as for amaryllis. Several other evergreen species from the American tropics may be grown but are rarely seen in Florida. The Peruvian basket-flower (*H. calathina*), often listed as *Ismene calathina,* is popular as a pot plant in the North but does not thrive in Florida under garden conditions. It is deciduous and is occasionally grown in pots here.

Iris spp. IRIS. (N,C). Few of the dozens of species of iris are suited to Florida, and in particular the showy German and Japanese irises that adorn northern gardens in numberless varieties are generally not satisfactory here. Only in the hills of northwestern Florida do bearded irises succeed at all. Yet there are some species, not the most gorgeous but still lovely flowers, that can be grown in Florida. They include the bulbous irises from southwestern Europe and the native irises of the southeastern United States, especially Florida and Louisiana.

Dutch iris (*I. xiphium*) and its hybrids, including the Wedgwood type, are probably the best adapted of the bulbous kinds. They rarely last more than one season, but are not expensive and make a brave show of color—white, yellow, blue, mauve, and bronze. Planted from late October through November, these bulbs bloom in January and February. For landscape effect the colors should be massed separately, planting the bulbs 4 in. deep and 3 in. apart. For cutting they are spaced similarly in 2-ft. rows. Foliage turns yellow in late spring and the bulbs may be lifted for storage over the summer, but all too frequently many bulbs show some rot and must be discarded. A sunny location in good, well-drained soil is best.

Native irises are evergreen and need moist soil, although swamp conditions are not necessary. They arise from rhizomes and have flowers colored white, pink, yellow, red, blue, or purple. Their culture is not common in Florida, and they deserve wider trial. Rhizomes may be cut into pieces 6 in. long, either in the fall or after the bloom period, and the pieces planted an inch deep and 8 or 10 in. apart. A partly shaded location is best, and soil should be very high in organic matter. During the fall, winter, and spring, the bed should be constantly moist, but may be left to itself in summer. A constantly dripping faucet can keep a small bed moist. The blooming season is from March until May. *Iris hexagona* has been cultivated in Florida for many years, and such other native Florida species as *I. tripetala* and *I. savannarum* have beautiful flowers, too. Species native to southern Louisiana are also favorites.

Leucojum aestivum. SNOWFLAKE. Southern Europe. (N,C). Much like dwarf narcissus in foliage, snowflake bears from four to eight nodding, bell-shaped flowers on a slender scape 8 to 12 in. tall. The petals are white with green tips. The small bulbs are planted in fall and bloom in early spring. Foliage dies down in June, but the bulbs are usually left in place for several years until crowded conditions necessitate digging and separation. In well-drained soil with annual fertilization in spring and a sunny location, snowflake thrives with a minimum of attention. It is the nearest approach we can make in Florida to the popular lily-of-the-valley of northern gardens.

Lilium longiflorum var. *eximium.* EASTER LILY. Japan. (N,C,S). No other true lily is as well adapted to Florida gardens as this one, whose large white trumpets are such a familiar sight in spring. In Dade County, plantings are left undisturbed for several years and form great beds; but in northern and central Florida it may be desirable to lift the bulbs when the foliage dies down in early summer. Stored in dry peat or sand during the hot, wet summer period, the bulbs are planted 6 in. deep from early September until mid-December. Where bulbs are found not to rot in the ground during the summer, they are better left until fall for lifting and transplanting. Soil-borne diseases may make it unwise to grow lilies two successive years in the same bed. Well-drained, fertile soil in full sun is needed for good growth. Tiny bulblets along the stem above the bulb may be planted separately to grow into blooming bulbs, or scales from the large bulbs may be planted similarly. Easter lilies may bloom any time from February to April, depending on the weather. If they are desired for Easter, plantings should be made at two-week intervals for two months, starting about five months before Easter. Covering plants on cold nights in northern Florida with a glass or glass-substitute sash on a wooden frame (that is, making a cold frame) will decrease the retarding effect of chilly weather. The Madonna lily (*L. candidum*), with flowers very similar to those of the Easter lily, is planted similarly for spring bloom. Formosan lily (*L. formosanum*) is a giant, summer-flowering species bearing greenish or yellowish-white flowers with brownish color on the outside that is very popular in home gardens. Several other summer-blooming lilies are occasionally

planted and blossom well during their first season. Among these
are the Japanese lily (*L. speciosissimum* var. *rubrum*), pinkish-
red flowers with recurved petals; the regal lily (*L. regale*),
white trumpets with purplish midribs outside and yellow throat;
and the gold-banded lily (*L. auratum*), wide-spreading flowers
with white petals lined with gold along the midrib and dotted
with purple.

Lycoris spp. (N,C,S). Two species from eastern Asia are
cultivated in Florida, both blooming while the plants are leafless. The hurricane-lily (*L. aurea*) from China has 3-in. golden-
yellow flowers in late August or early September, while the red
spider-lily (*L. radiata*) has red flowers, 1½ in. long, about a
month later. Both species have clusters of flowers on tall scapes,
and produce strap-shaped leaves after blooming is over. Bulbs
are planted in late spring after the foliage dies down. In the
northern half of the state the bulbs are left undisturbed year
after year until they become crowded, but in the southern half
they may persist only a few years. Acid soil seems to be less
satisfactory for them than soil of neutral reaction, and a little
ground shell or agricultural lime may improve flowering. Because they are dormant all summer, care must be taken not to
hoe up the bulbs when cultivating to control weeds. Half shade
seems to be preferred to full sun. Spacing the bulbs 8 to 10 in.
for the hurricane-lily and 4 to 5 in. for the red spider-lily allows
room for expansion.

Narcissus tazetta. POLYANTHUS NARCISSUS. Eurasia.
(N,C,S). Cultivated in Florida for many years as an important
commercial crop, the narcissus is widely grown as a late winter
flower for bedding and cut flowers. Of the many species of
narcissus or daffodil, including jonquils, only the polyanthus
type succeeds in peninsular Florida. Narcissus of this species
have from four to eight fragrant flowers in a cluster, with small,
light yellow crowns, and have slender, grass-like leaves about a
foot long. Three varieties are common as garden plants in Florida, and for forcing in bowls of pebbles everywhere: Paper-
white has pure white flowers, both petals and crown; Soleil d'Or
has yellow petals with dark gold crown; and Chinese Sacred-lily

has white petals with prominent yellow crown. Bulbs planted in late September bloom in late December for Paper-white, in early January for Chinese Sacred-lily, and in late January for Soleil d'Or. Plantings at intervals until the end of October will give a succession of blooming. Grand Monarque is similar to Chinese Sacred-lily but blooms a month later. Large round bulbs should be selected and planted 4 in. deep, spaced 6 to 8 in. apart in beds or 3 or 4 in. apart in 12-in. rows. Full sun is best, although light broken shade is satisfactory. Blossom scapes are picked when half of the flowers in a cluster have opened. After blossoming, the plants need fertilizer and water to enable them to store food in the bulb and develop flower buds for the next year. When the foliage yellows, the plants are lifted and the bulbs are stored dry. Dust with DDT to discourage mealy-bugs, and screen to keep out rodents. In western Florida, on heavy soils and with colder winters, some of the jonquils such as the Campernelles and yellow trumpet daffodils like King Alfred are successful.

Ornithogalum arabicum. STAR-OF-BETHLEHEM. Mediterranean area. (N,C,S). The fragrant, star-shaped flowers of this bulb are an inch across, white with black pistil, borne in large clusters on a tall scape. The leaves are much like those of amaryllis. Bulbs planted in early fall will bloom in spring over many weeks. Growing conditions, propagation, and summer lifting and storage of bulbs are the same as for narcissus, and use for bedding or cut flowers is the same.

Polianthes tuberosa. TUBEROSE. Mexico. (N,C,S). The most fragrant flower in the garden is the tuberose, whose waxy white blossoms are borne in spikes at the top of a slender, leafy stem from a sparse basal rosette of grass-like foliage. Indeed, the scent is overpowering for many people. Planted in a sunny spot in fertile soil from January to March, the flowers are borne from late April until July, each plant making a succession of bloom stalks. The tuberous roots should be set a couple of inches deep and spaced a foot apart in bays of shrubbery borders or 8 in. apart in 18-in. rows in cutting beds. The foliage dies down after the bloom period is ended, and the "bulbs" are usually lifted and stored dry. Where soil drainage is very good, plants may be left undisturbed. The common name is not *tube-rose* but *tuber-ose*, referring to the tuberous roots. Both single and double types of flower are grown.

Ranunculus asiaticus. RANUNCULUS. Southwestern Asia. (N,C,S). The forcing ranunculus of florists gives good results when planted in Florida in the fall for late winter and early spring bloom. From one to four double flowers, 3 in. across, in all shades of yellow and red, are borne on sturdy stems a foot high from a basal rosette of leaves. They are fine for cutting or for landscape color. The tiny clusters of tuberous roots should be planted, claws downward, about 2 in. deep and 6 in. apart in a lightly shaded location. It is not feasible to carry ranunculus over for a second year, but the "bulbs" are inexpensive.

Sprekelia formosissima. JACOBEAN-LILY. Mexico. (N,C,S). The bright red flowers of this bulb are about 4 in. across and resemble in form an orchid more than the amaryllis to which it is closely related. They are borne singly on a slender scape in spring. Culture should be the same as for amaryllis. The Jacobean-lily is rarely seen in Florida gardens, and is only slightly more common as a pot plant. An evergreen, recurrent-blooming form is preferred by some advanced fanciers.

Tigridia pavonia. TIGER-FLOWER. Mexico. (N,C,S). The garish colors of the triangular flowers of this bulb make them distinctive. The blossoms are 5 to 6 in. across with three large, red petals spotted with yellow and purple. They are rarely seen in Florida, but may be planted in late fall for late spring blooming. Flower buds are borne in a cluster on tall scapes and open in succession over many days. The tiger-flower is better suited to give garden color than for cut flowers.

Tritonia crocata. MONTBRETIA. South Africa. (N,C,S). Resembling miniature gladiolus, the dainty flowers of montbretia are produced in slender spikes. A variety with cinnabar-red flowers is most common in Florida, but hybrids in varied colors are available. Corms are planted and plants cared for exactly as for gladiolus, its close relative. While corms are usually lifted and stored, the red-flowered form is sometimes left to form large clumps.

Tulipa gesneriana. Tulip. Central Asia. (N,C). Tulips are not easy to grow in Florida, but some types may be planted for spring bloom if the bulbs have been properly chilled. This requires a period of 50 to 60 days in cold storage at about 40°F. While this may be done in the household refrigerator, it is less trouble to buy bulbs which have already been chilled at seed stores. In late November or December bulbs should be planted 5 to 6 in. deep, spaced 6 in. apart. Full sun or light shade is satisfactory. Tulips may be had in a great range of clear colors, and the bulbs should be grouped by color for best effect. It is not profitable to try to carry bulbs over to another year.

Watsonia spp. Watsonia. South Africa. (N,C,S). This is another close relative of gladiolus, with very similar foliage and spikes of smaller flowers whose petals are all alike. Several species and hybrid forms are available with colors in several shades of red and lavender, or white. Culture is the same as for gladiolus, but they are planted in early fall for late spring bloom and may be left in the ground for several years if drainage is good.

Zantedeschia aethiopica. White calla. South Africa. (N,C,S). On moist, heavy soil, the callas thrive everywhere in Florida, but they can be grown as perennials only in the southern half of the state. Further north they must be planted annually or grown in pots to avoid cold injury. The "flower" is a large white spathe that encloses the spike of inconspicuous true flowers. The Godfrey variety, with the spathe 6 to 8 in. long and arrow-shaped leaves, is most satisfactory for Florida. Full sun is preferred, but callas do well in light shade also. The soil should be constantly moist but not wet, although well-established plants can endure a few days of flooding. The rhizomes are usually planted in late fall or winter, laid flat, and set only 2 in. deep and a foot or more apart. The blooming season is from March to June, and in summer the foliage yellows and dies. In sandy, well-drained soils in southern Florida, plants left in place will bloom more freely than if they are lifted and stored for the summer. If heavy soil is the growing medium, rhizomes should be dug when leaves turn yellow and stored in boxes of dry sand. Yellow calla (*Z. elliottiana*) is a favorite pot subject because of its

bright golden spathes and white-flecked foliage. The pink calla
(*Z. rehmanni*) produces small, closely rolled pink spathes among
upright, long-lanceolate, taper-pointed leaves.

Zephyranthes spp. ZEPHER-LILY. Eastern North and South
America. (N,C,S). Known sometimes as fairy-lily, this dainty
amaryllid thrives as a garden plant in soil of moderate fertility
and in either full sun or light shade. From the tiny bulbs there
arise slender, grass-like leaves and a taller scape bearing a single
lily-like flower, from 1 to 4 in. long, depending on the species.
There are half a dozen well-adapted species, with flowers white,
yellow, or pink, mostly blooming in spring. Planted in late fall,
the bulbs are usually left in the ground from year to year until
they become too crowded. Three species are native to Florida—
the Atamasco-lily (*Z. atamasco*) of northern or northwestern
Florida, *Z. treatiae* of northeastern and central Florida, and *Z.
simpsoni* of southern Florida—all with 3-in. flowers, white or
rose tinted. These may be brought in from the wild. The best
garden species are *Z. grandiflora,* with large pink flowers; *Z.
rosea,* with small pink blossoms; *Z. insularum,* with white
flowers in spring; *Z. candida,* with white flowers in summer; *Z.
citrina,* with bright yellow blossoms; and *Z. ajax,* a hybrid of
straw color. Closely related genera are *Habranthus* and *Cooperia.
H. robustus* from Argentina has large flowers of lavender-pink
in summer. The rain-lilies (*Cooperia* spp.) from Texas and Mexico are white-flowered, opening their fragrant blooms at night in
spring or early summer, but are otherwise very similar to the
zephyr-lilies and are treated in the same way. All must be
planted in considerable numbers to make a mass landscape effect,
but thrive with a minimum of care—fertilizing in spring and
weeding as needed.

12

Lawn Grasses and Ground Covers

Green covering for the ground is one of the indispensable items in landscaping, and usually this is the first element of the landscape picture to be developed. Tradition, custom, and sheer merit have given grass first place in public favor to supply this covering. A well-kept lawn is unsurpassed as the setting for the house and as the "rug" of the outdoor living room. Fortunately, it is possible in Florida to develop permanent lawns quickly and to keep them attractive at all seasons of the year. There are situations, however, in which it is very difficult to establish and maintain a good greensward, because of shade, drought, steep slope, or competition from tree and shrub roots. In such cases some substitute for grass must be used to give a green carpet, and the many plants available for this use are called ground covers. Seldom can they endure the trampling of feet or provide the low, smooth surface which a grass does, so they are not suited for general lawn use. But for special needs they thrive with a minimum of care and provide attractive appearance.

Before planting a lawn it is necessary to have the ground carefully graded to give a smooth, even surface, as nearly level as possible. It is very hard to correct small hollows and humps after the lawn is established. Facilities for irrigation must be provided. If an underground sprinkler system is too expensive, then hydrants should be so located that every part of the lawn can be

255

reached by a revolving sprinkler on the end of one 50-ft. length of hose. If the soil is light sand, it should be enriched by turning under a 3-in. layer of rotted manure, compost, peat, muck, or woods mold and mixing it well with the top 6 in. of soil before the final leveling. It is well also to broadcast and work into the top soil about 15 or 20 lbs. per 1,000 sq. ft. of fertilizer of 6-6-6 analysis. The beginning of the rainy season is the best time to start a new lawn or renovate an old one; the warm weather, abundant rainfall, and high humidity insure rapid growth. Planting may be done at other seasons, but the grass will grow more slowly and need more watering.

There are several ways of planting grass. Quickest but most expensive is to buy enough sod to cover the ground completely. More feasible for the small home owner is to set sods 6 in. square about a foot apart each way from center to center, requiring one-fourth as much sod as for full coverage, or a foot apart between sod edges, which takes 1 sq. yd. of sod for each 9 sq. yds. of lawn. The most common practice in Florida, however, is the economical one of sprigging, except in the case of grasses for which seed is available. Many grasses form new roots readily from each node of the stem. A line is stretched across the area to be planted and sprigs are dropped every 6 or 8 in. along the line. With a notched stick the basal end of the sprig is thrust into the earth until only a small portion remains above the surface, and with the feet the soil is firmed about the sprig to insure good contact. The line is moved over 8 or 10 in. when the end of the row is reached, and the next row set similarly. Alternatively, a small furrow may be opened down the line with a hand plow, the sprigs dropped into the trench along one side, and the soil firmed and leveled about them. The ground should be moist for planting, but not wet, and as quickly as a suitable area is set with sprigs, the sprinkler should start watering that area. Care must be taken, also, not to allow grass that has been dug for planting to become too dry. If rains do not occur frequently, newly planted lawns should be watered every two or three days for a month or more. A lawn sprigged in June should be well covered with grass by autumn.

Some grasses produce seed readily enough that this method of planting permanent lawns can be used. The ground should be put into good condition, as for planting a flower bed, and grass seed broadcast by a mechanical seeder. It is best to go over the area twice, using half of the seed each time and sowing the second half at right angles to the direction traveled while sowing the first. The area should be raked lightly to cover the seed and the ground kept moist until the grass is well up. Usually about three weeks are needed for germination, and the young grass grows much more slowly than sprigs do.

With either method of planting, some weeding is necessary while the lawn is being started. In lawns set with sprigs, most of the weeding can be done with a scuffle hoe or a garden plow with weeding blade, used between the rows of sprigs, with relatively little hand weeding being necessary. Seeded lawns must be hand weeded, and so particular attention should be given to purity in buying lawn grass seed. Various herbicides are available for weed control in lawns, and recommendations for their use should be obtained from garden centers or seedsmen. Once the grass has grown tall enough to be cut with a mower, weed control can be accomplished by mowing. This practice also encourages rapid growth of runners if the mowing is not too close. Mowers should be set to cut about an inch above the surface runners.

Lawns should be mowed every week or ten days during the growing season, to prevent shading and the development of seed heads. Clippings should never be removed from the lawn unless mowing has been neglected so long that the process resembles cutting hay. Most Florida soils need addition of organic matter frequently, and letting the grass clippings decay in place adds organic matter as well as returning plant nutrients removed by grass roots. The clippings may look a little untidy for a short time, but if the lawn is mowed frequently, the short clippings are hardly noticeable.

Water and fertilizer are as much needed by lawn grasses as by any other plants. Lawns once established will usually need little watering during the summer, but the high temperature of this season makes a dry period far more critical for lawns than a longer dry period in winter. Grasses are relatively shallow rooted at best, but our watering practice can modify this somewhat for better or worse. Frequent light watering tends to develop very shallow rooting, while heavy watering at longer intervals encourages deeper rooting. A good soaking of the lawn once a week is advisable. Usually a complete fertilizer is applied in early spring, and nitrogenous fertilizers only are applied during the growing season. About 15 lbs. of a garden fertilizer analyzing 6-6-6 are broadcast over 1,000 sq. ft. of lawn in February or March, while 3 lbs. of ammonium nitrate or 5 lbs. of sulphate of ammonia are applied to the same area in May, July, and September. Unless fertilizing is done just before a rain falls, the lawn should be watered promptly to prevent injury to the foliage by the fertilizer.

None of the permanent lawn grasses can be counted on to remain green during cold weather in northern Florida. To have bright green lawn color in winter it is necessary to make a temporary planting of Italian rye-grass or other frost-hardy annual species. Seeds of one of these are sown right on top of the permanent lawn in October or November. Germination takes only about two weeks, so that daily watering need not be done so long as for permanent grasses, but the young grass must still be watered twice a week until tall enough to mow. When leaves are 2 in. high, mowing should begin and continue as needed all winter. Weekly watering and monthly application of nitrogenous fertilizer as above will keep the winter grass growing luxuriantly and so keep the lawn beautifully green. In late spring, temporary grasses die and the permanent grass takes over again without having suffered any harm if mowing was properly done.

Ground covers are either herbaceous or woody perennials, and soil preparation, planting, and care should be the same as for other plants of the same type in garden usage. Usually ground covers are selected because of ability to thrive under unfavorable growing conditions and so will need less attention to fertilizing and watering than most plants. Even such hardy species will repay, by improved luxuriance, whatever care they receive. Usually no pruning of ground covers is needed and mowing is usually impossible. Vines planted to stabilize a steep slope may need some training to obtain the quickest coverage.

LAWN GRASSES RECOMMENDED FOR FLORIDA

CENTIPEDE GRASS (*Eremochloa ophiuroides*) is probably more widely used than any other grass in Florida. This tenacious perennial from China is a poor-land species, being more often injured by overfertilization than by neglect. Centipede does not stay green in winter and is not tolerant of salt spray. It thrives on thin, sandy soils in full sun, and makes an attractive lawn there with less water and mowing than any other grass. Mowing every ten days in summer and early fall will prevent the untidy short flower spikes from developing. Centipede grass has surface runners and short, narrow leaves which seldom grow more than 3 in. high. The idea that it is a lazy-man's grass requiring no mowing at all is fallacious, unless a very unkempt lawn is satisfactory. It is propagated chiefly by sprigs, but seed is available. Ground-pearls, insects related to mealy-bugs, cause great losses in centipede turf that has been weakened by environmental factors.

ST. AUGUSTINE GRASS (*Stenotaphrum secundatum*), native to the southeastern United States, is Florida's second most popular lawn grass. When properly managed, the turf produced by this lush, broad-leaved grass is hard to surpass, although it is very coarse in texture. It thrives only on moist soils and needs plenty of fertilizer. Tolerant of either sun or shade and of salt, it endures cold quite well. When grown under trees, this grass must be given more water and fertilizer than when growing in the open, since tree roots compete for water and nutrients with the grass roots. Leaves may reach 10 or 12 in. in height if not mowed, so St. Augustine grass must be mowed regularly each week. It forms surface runners and is propagated only by sprigs. All forms of St. Augustine grass are very subject to attack by chinch-bugs. Gray leaf-spot is a fungus disease which attacks St. Augustine grass during certain seasons.

BERMUDA GRASS (*Cynodon dactylon*) is another important lawn grass in Florida. It is native to Eurasia. Fine-leaved, and forming a beautiful turf when properly grown, it thrives only under conditions of good soil moisture and fertilization. It does not tolerate shade and is less able to crowd out weeds than the previous two grasses. Frequent mowing is needed, and every few years the turf should be aerated by a spiking machine. On the credit side, Bermuda grass is less subject to insect pests and nutritional deficiencies than are its competitors. Both surface and underground runners are formed. Several strains of Bermuda with unusually fine foliage have been selected for lawn use. These grasses are planted by setting sprigs and by broadcasting chaff that results when turf is run through a soil shredder. Rolling and watering are essential to success of this new method of planting lawn Bermudas. Dollar-spot, a serious fungus disease of Bermudas, is controlled by spraying with Tersan at very first signs. Army worms and sod webworms must be controlled in autumn.

ZOYSIA GRASS (*Zoisia* spp.) has been rather widely planted in Florida since mid-century. Several species, varieties, and strains are approved for use here. Slow growing, deep rooted, and fine textured, this grass is capable of making exquisite lawns and putting greens. Thorough compounding and fumigation of the soil in advance of planting, very frequent mowing, and ample fertilization are requisites for success. Dollar-spot attacks not only Bermudas, but some zoysia grasses as well. Mascarene grass (*Z. tenuifolia*), exceedingly fine-leaved, almost thread-like, is planted between flagstones. It is notably tolerant of salt spray.

CARPET GRASS (*Axonopus affinis*) is another native species that does well on moist soils that are shaded by scattered pine trees. It is chiefly used as a pasture grass, but is suitable for large, informal lawns where saving in maintenance is more important than smooth finish. Spring fertilization alone is sufficient for carpet grass on moist soil. Like centipede, it turns brown in winter and grows best on soils low in lime. The branching flower stalks are eliminated by two or three mowings during

Coralline Key Largo limestone is a popular paving material.

Begonia, monstera, and peperomia here create a tropical atmosphere.

Massed tropical foliage forms an unusual living-room planting.

Palms form a perfect background for this naturalistic water garden.

A broad-leaved evergreen tree shades part of a terrace.

Monstera and driftwood bring in the outdoors.

Palms are sometimes used directly in foundation plantings.

Tropical foliage embellishes a Florida-room pool.

Framing is an important function of landscape trees.

Monstera and philodendron combine attractively.

Native sea-grape casts a light pattern of shade in this Florida patio.

Manila palm bears cherry-red fruit during the winter season.

Strap vandas have assumed a place of prominence with Florida orchid fanciers.

Hybrid moth orchids are very popular with Florida home owners.

White cattleyas are beloved of all.

Florida's native *Epidendrum tampense* is to be found in most orchid collections.

the summer. Carpet grass is usually seeded, but produces surface runners and may be set by sprigs and sods also.

BAHIA GRASS (*Paspalum notatum*), native to the American
tropics, is widely planted in Florida pastures. Although they are
coarser than the Bermudas and zoysias, several Bahia grasses—
Argentine, Paraguay, and Pensacola—have met with favor for
planting lawns because of their ability to thrive in sandy soil,
their endurance of traffic, and their marked resistance to insects
and diseases. Like carpet grass, Bahias send up branched flower
stalks during warm months, so that frequent mowing with a
rotary mower is required to keep a good appearance. The Bahia grasses are usually established by seeding during warm
months. After thorough preparation of the lawn area, spread
about 5 lbs. of scarified seed evenly over each 1,000 sq. ft.

ITALIAN RYE-GRASS (*Lolium multiflorum*), native to Eurasia, is used only as a temporary winter grass in Florida. The
leaves are very slender but grow rapidly in cool weather and so
require frequent watering and mowing. Seeds should be sown at
the rate of 10 lbs. per 1,000 sq. ft. Several native grasses are
similarly used for green winter lawns, especially Kentucky blue-
grass (*Poa pratensis*) at 2 lbs. and bent-grasses (*Agrostis* spp.)
at 1 lb. of seed per 1,000 sq. ft.

GROUND COVERS RECOMMENDED FOR FLORIDA

Asystasia gangetica. COROMANDEL. Old World Tropics. (S).
A vigorous herb that may climb bushes if allowed, this plant is
one of the few ground covers that can be mowed like a grass.
If allowed to grow with only occasional shearing to keep it under
control, it blooms all fall, winter, and spring, having spikes of
purplish flowers. It is most effective in partly shaded locations
and thrives in a variety of soils. It is propagated by division
and by softwood cuttings or layers.

Carpobrotus edulis. HOTTENTOT-FIG. South Africa. (C,S).
This exotic succulent is a valuable ground cover for seaside
gardens, as it endures heat, drought, and salt spray, and thrives
in alkaline or acid soil. Propagation is by cuttings in summer.

Dichondra carolinensis. DICHONDRA. Southeastern United States. (N,C,S). This creeping native herb rarely exceeds 2 in. in height and can be used for a lawn, but it does not endure tramping well. In most parts of Florida, its small, bright green leaves are likely to appear in lawns on moist soil, where they are considered a troublesome weed. It suffers from a serious fungus blight, the control of which is not yet understood. It is propagated by seeds, cuttings, or sods.

Euonymus fortunei. WINTER-CREEPER. China and Japan. (N) On heavy soils in northwestern Florida this low evergreen shrub is excellent as a ground cover under trees or for use on banks and slopes. Trailing stems root in the ground at the nodes, but they will climb shrubs and trees if not kept in bounds. Propagation is by layering usually, but seeds and softwood cuttings may be used.

Gelsemium sempervirens. CAROLINA YELLOW-JASMINE. Southeastern United States. (N,C). Prized chiefly as a flowering vine, this hardy native is an excellent ground cover for slopes and banks too steep for mowing. It is not tolerant of much shade or of droughty soil conditions. It is propagated by seeds, layers, or cuttings.

Hedera canariensis. ALGERIAN IVY. Northwestern Africa. (N). This subtropical relative of English ivy is a shade-lover, and is an excellent ground cover under evergreen trees and large shrubs where a blanket of green is wanted to hold leaf mulch in place. Ivies offer little competition, and they, in turn, tolerate roots from other plants. Moderate moisture is the main requirement. In this species, and closely related English ivy (*H. helix*), there are many leaf forms. Propagation is by cuttings or natural layers.

Ipomoea pes-caprae. BEACH MORNING-GLORY. Tropical and subtropical coasts. (C,S). Native to the coastal beaches of Florida, this rampant vine is adapted to landscape use as the most satisfactory ground cover for the porous sands of saltwater beaches. It is a succulent herb with trailing stems up to 50 ft. or more, and large, thick leaves. Pink flowers appear in summer. It is propagated by seed.

Juniperus conferta. SHORE JUNIPER. Japan. (N,C). Somewhat slow to get established and cover an area, the shore juniper makes a very satisfactory covering for an open sunny stretch of the poorest sand. The prostrate stem sends up erect branches that rise to 12 or 15 in. only and need no shearing. Shade is not tolerated, nor tramping. The compact branches bear tiny, blue-green leaves. Propagation is by firmwood cuttings in late summer.

Kalanchoë fedtschenkoi. KALANCHOË. Madagascar. (S). Much in demand as a ground cover for sunny exposures in frostless locations, this succulent—improperly called "gray-sedum"—is seen frequently in residential, industrial, and highway plantings. In summer, simply set unrooted cuttings thickly where the earth is to be hidden.

Lantana montevidensis. WEEPING LANTANA. South America. (C,S). Used often in central Florida as a low hedge or in window boxes, this sprawling shrub is a good ground cover for sunny locations. All summer long it is covered with tiny, lavender flowers. It grows well in rather infertile soil and tolerates salt spray. Killed to the ground in northern Florida, it rallies quickly in spring. Principal pest is a caterpillar which chews round holes in the leaves. Propagation is by layers or softwood cuttings.

Liriope spp. LILYTURF. China and Japan. (N,C,S). Lilyturfs have long, grass-like leaves from underground stems, and are adapted to shaded locations. They are remarkably tolerant of a wide range of soil conditions, enduring drought, low fertility, and salt spray, but not full sun. Most commonly grown in the peninsula is *L. muscari* var. *exiliflora,* which has long been popular for edging but covers ground slowly and has leaves up to a foot high. In western Florida, *L. spicata* and various other types are planted. Propagation is by division of the creeping rhizomes or by seed.

Mitchella repens. PARTRIDGE-BERRY. Eastern United States. (N,C). This native evergreen herb forms dense mats in damp woods under deep shade. Well-drained soils with heavy leaf mulch are suited to it, and the shade and mulch under live or laurel oaks form very satisfactory conditions for use of partridge-berry as ground cover. Growth is slow, and it is not feasible to try to cover large areas. No mowing or shearing is needed. Propagation is by transplanting sods from hammock areas or by striking softwood cuttings.

Ophiopogon japonicum. DWARF LILYTURF. Japan and Korea. (N,C,S). This small brother of the lilyturf has even more slender and darker green leaves from similar creeping rootstocks. The adaptability and uses of the two genera are identical, and maintenance and propagation are the same. Growth is very slow and is considerably expedited by supplying water and nutrients, but the main usefulness of the lilyturfs is where heat, drought, and shade are combined.

Pilea microphylla. ARTILLERY-PLANT. Tropical America. (S). This is a succulent herb with fern-like fronds of foliage that stand from 6 to 12 in. high. It thrives in sun or shade and grows rapidly, making a ground cover quickly. Between driveway ribbons, as an edging for walks, or between stepping stones, artillery-plant serves well. Propagation is by softwood cuttings that root very easily in place.

Saxifraga sarmentosa. STRAWBERRY-GERANIUM. Eastern Asia. (N). Popular for use in window boxes and hanging baskets, this perennial herb is also a good ground cover for rocky soils, especially in limited areas. Only heavy soils are suited to it, and partial shade is needed, at least in summer. The common name is given because the plant forms long, slender runners like the strawberry, and has leaves the size and shape of geranium leaves. This stoloniferous habit enables it to form a covering rather quickly. Propagation is usually by division of old plants or transplanting runner plants.

Selaginella spp. SELAGINELLA. (N,C,S). Selaginellas are fern relatives that look like large, much-branched mosses. Many species are known in both the Old World and the New World. Two species from southeastern Asia, *S. caulescens* and *S. uncinata,* are particularly satisfactory anywhere in Florida as ground covers. The former species needs at least half shade, and thrives only in soil of good organic matter and moisture content. The latter species is very vigorous but low growing, and tolerates either sun or shade, so that it can be used on large, rocky areas or on slopes as a ground cover. Propagation is by division usually or by cuttings.

Setcreasea spp. SETCREASEA. Mexico. (C,S). The most widely planted member of this group is Purple Queen (*S. purpurea*), a vigorous, running perennial that covers the earth with a mass of glowing purple. All-green *S. pallida* and striped *S. striata* (properly, *Callisia elegans*) are less vigorous, less dramatic, and so less used in landscaping. Propagation is by cuttings; often unrooted stem pieces are simply stuck in the ground where the ground cover is wanted.

Trachelospermum jasminoides. CONFEDERATE-JASMINE. China. (N,C,S). This evergreen vine is grown more often for its fragrant, white flowers, but is also an excellent ground cover for steep slopes or large open areas. It should not be planted near trees or shrubs, as it will quickly climb them. Either full sun or partial shade is satisfactory, and soil fertility seems to be unimportant. Propagation by air-layering is most satisfactory for amateur gardeners.

Vinca minor. RUNNING-MYRTLE. Europe. (N). This trailing evergreen herb is the common periwinkle of northern gardens and has proved very satisfactory in northwestern Florida as a ground cover on fertile, shaded, well-drained soils of good moisture. The plants branch to make a covering about 6 in. high. Under trees, as an edging for walks, and on rocky or sandy slopes, it serves well. Blue flowers about ¾ in. across are borne in spring and early summer. The big-leaf periwinkle, *V. major,* with flowers twice as large, is equally satisfactory for the same area and uses. The Madagascar periwinkle, *V. rosea,* is a common herbaceous perennial grown for its flowers, but may sometimes double as a ground cover for large, sunny areas in southern Florida. The periwinkles are propagated by softwood cuttings or by division.

Wedelia trilobata. WEDELIA. Tropical America. (C,S). This trailing perennial herb roots along its running stems and bears small, yellow flowers in summer and fall. It thrives equally in sun and shade and is indifferent to soil type if given plenty of water and fertilizer. Even along the seashore it grows well. Rather rapid growing, it makes a cover about 8 in. high that requires no mowing, although it tolerates mowing and tramping quite well. For use under trees, in parkways, or on steep slopes, wedelia is very satisfactory. It is propagated readily by cuttings.

Zebrina pendula. WANDERING JEW. Mexico. (S). The colorful foliage of this succulent, creeping herb, purple below and green or white striped above, puts it in the foliage-plant group of ground covers. Suited only to shady locations and moist soil, wandering Jew grows vigorously and makes a quick cover. Usually it does not exceed 6 in. in height. Under trees and shrubs and in shaded rock gardens, it is hard to surpass as an attractive and dependable cover. Propagation by softwood cuttings is exceedingly easy.

Chart of Lawn Grasses for Florida

Grass	Relative Fertility Requirement	Insect Pests	Diseases	Texture	Winter Color	Shade† Tolerance	Salt Tolerance	Wear Resistance	Mowing Height	Rate of Establishment	Method of Establishment
Improved Bermuda Varieties	High	Mod. serious Armyworms Sod webworms Scale insects Nematodes	Serious at times	Finest	Green*	Very poor	Fair	Very good	½ to 1"	Very rapid	Vegetative
St. Augustine	Moderate	Very serious Chinch bug Armyworms Sod webworms Nematodes	Serious at times	Very coarse	Green*	Good	Good	Poor	2"	Moderately rapid	Vegetative
Zoysia	Moderate	Not serious (Nematodes)	None major	Medium fine	Green*	Very good	Very good	Very good	½ to 1"	Slow	Vegetative
Centipede	Low	Ground pearls Nematodes	None major	Intermediate	Brown	Fair	Poor	Very poor	1½"	Moderate	Seed or vegetative
Carpet	Low	Not serious	None major	Coarse	Brown	Fair	Poor	Intermediate	2"	Moderate	Seed or vegetative
Bahia	Low	Not serious	Serious at times	Intermediate	Green	Fair	Poor	Good	2"	Moderate	Seed or vegetative

* Under proper management, these grasses can be maintained green during most of the year.
† Most of these grasses will grow fairly well under a high canopy of shade as under pine trees. Above ratings refer to dense shade.

13

Orchids and Bromeliads

GROWING ORCHIDS AND BROMELIADS is a hobby with many Florida gardeners, who have learned that these plants are not really difficult to grow but only require different cultural methods from those used with other garden or house plants.

ORCHIDS

Several species of orchids grow wild in the hammocks and the cypress swamps of southern Florida, and this fact has encouraged the growing of exotic, as well as native, species in yard trees where temperatures permit. In northern Florida a greenhouse is desirable for orchid growing, but it need only be a small lean-to type, or even a miniature greenhouse (Wardian case) inside a well-lighted room. However, some orchids can be grown in the house if put in a well-lighted spot and given special provision for high humidity. A slat house can be used if it is covered tightly with a plastic sheet during the cold months. In southern Florida, greenhouses are necessary only to assure top quality of flowers, since shade houses afford sufficient protection.

CLASSES OF ORCHIDS

Orchids are grouped into two classes based on growth habit —*sympodial and monopodial.* The sympodial types have a creep-

268

ing stem, or rhizome, from which arise many aerial branches. In the monopodial types there is a single erect stem which does not share a supporting base with any other aerial stem. A single genus may have some sympodial and some monopodial species, as does *Epidendrum,* but usually all species of a genus are in the same class.

Orchids may also be classed according to where they grow naturally as either *terrestrial,* growing in the soil, or *epiphytic,* growing on trees or shrubs. Both sympodial and monopodial orchids are found in each group. Terrestrial orchids may be grown in garden beds in the southern half of the state, where epiphytic types can be grown in trees. In the northern half of Florida, tropical species of both types must be grown in pots or baskets, but a few native terrestrials thrive in rich earth.

The stems of monopodial orchids are much like those of ginger-lily, with leaves borne at each node, but sympodial types are quite different. Their aerial stems are called "pseudobulbs" because they are greatly thickened and in some species are short and rounded like lily or onion bulbs. They do not have true bulb structure at all, thus the term pseudobulbs, or false bulbs. In many cases they do not look the least bit like bulbs, being more than a foot high and less than an inch thick, or even 3 ft. long and ¼ in. thick, but in most cases the aerial stem is conspicuously modified by thickening and serves largely as a storage organ.

Leaves of orchids vary as greatly in size, shape, and texture as do the leaves of trees. Most commonly they are rather leathery in epiphytic types and each pseudobulb bears only one or two leaves at its tip, although elongated pseudobulbs often have leaves at several nodes. Monopodial species may have a great many leaves and terrestrial orchids of sympodial types usually have several leaves. In most genera the leaves are evergreen, but two popular genera in Florida (*Calanthe* and *Cyrtopodium*) are deciduous part of the year, and *Dendrobium* is represented by both evergreen and deciduous species. Orchid plants not in bloom may be drab and unattractive.

Roots of terrestrial orchids are fibrous and much like those of

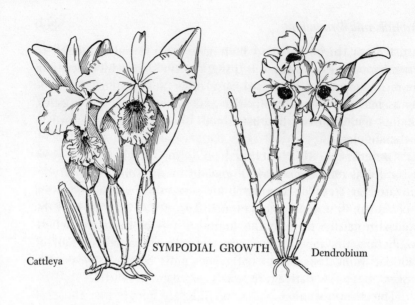

SYMPODIAL GROWTH

Cattleya

Dendrobium

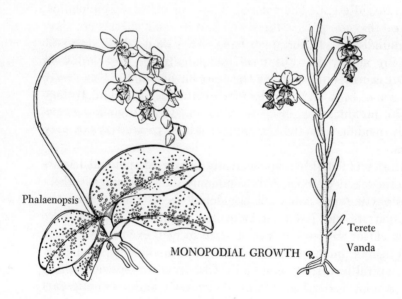

Phalaenopsis

MONOPODIAL GROWTH

Terete
Vanda

FIGURE 29
GROWTH HABITS OF ORCHIDS

garden annuals, but roots of epiphytic kinds are quite unusual, being greatly modified for absorption of water and nutrients from the air. Epiphytes are not parasites; that is, they do not derive any nourishment from host plants, yet it makes a big difference whether the host tree is living or dead. In large part this is related to the shading effect of the tree leaves, but it is also related to the nutrients derived by orchid roots from the decaying bark of the tree and from the dust and moisture caught in bark crevices and used by orchids. It is sometimes asserted that orchids need only sunshine, water, and air, but this is not true, for they need mineral nutrients as much as any other plants do. In their natural habitat they obtain these, as indicated above, from decaying bark and from dust. That is why trees with rough, fissured bark are far more satisfactory on which to grow orchids than trees with smooth, intact bark.

PROPAGATION

All orchids may be grown from seed, but a rather elaborate technique of aseptic culture on agar is required, like that used for culturing fungi and bacteria. Furthermore it takes many years for a seedling orchid to reach blooming size. The average amateur prefers to buy small seedlings or to use vegetative means of propagation, although raising orchids from seed is not very difficult to do.

Most orchids grown by amateurs belong to sympodial types and are readily propagated by division. As each pseudobulb grows up, it forms a bud at its base on the side away from the older part of the plant, and further growth results from development of this bud. When it starts growth eventually, it first pushes out a continuation of the creeping rhizome, and then turns up to form the pseudobulb. Usually a new pseudobulb is formed each year, and a series of pseudobulbs in a continuous line represents several years of growth. Pseudobulbs over three or four years old lose their leaves; they are then called "backbulbs" because they are at the back end of the rhizome, farthest from the growing point. The newest one is called the "lead."

In dividing such orchids for multiplication, it is usually considered necessary to cut off the three or four newest pseudobulbs by severing the rhizome between them and the backbulbs. The multiplication comes from the fact that a latent bud on the leading backbulb, which would otherwise remain dormant, may be stimulated thus to start growth and form a new lead. In a few years another blooming-sized plant has developed. Sometimes the lead develops two basal buds instead of one, making a forked rhizome. When each fork has three or four pseudobulbs, two separate plants can be made by severing the rhizome at its fork, and the usual new growth can be developed from the backbulbs. While four pseudobulbs are very desirable for good bloom in most kinds of orchids, division into single pseudobulbs is standard procedure with *Calanthe. Phaius* may be divided down to two growths if these are large with good foliage.

Cuttage is used for propagation of cane-type species in *Dendrobium* and of *Phaius.* The cane of *Dendrobium* or the lower half of the flower stalk of *Phaius* is laid horizontally on moist sand. From the buds at the nodes tiny plantlets arise in due time. After a few months, when these are some 2 in. high, the stem is cut close on each side of each of the new plants and they are potted up in small pots. *Vanilla* is also produced from stem cuttings, a small piece of stem with buds and leaves being potted at the start and a new plant developing from it in time.

Offsets are often produced by cane-type *Dendrobium* and *Epidendrum* species. These appear near the upper ends of the pseudobulbs and are much like the plants just described from stem cuttings except that they develop without special treatment of the stem. When they are large enough to handle, perhaps 2 in. high, they are carefully removed from the parent stem and potted.

Marcottage, or air-layering, is the method commonly used with *Vanda.* A cut is made one-third the way through the stem several inches below the tip and the cut area surrounded with a handful of sphagnum moss or of loose osmundine, held firmly in place by waxed string or copper wire. When good root development is evident, the rooted tip is cut off, while an axillary bud on the remaining stem near the cut will start into growth to make a new top. The rooting medium must be kept constantly moist until the tip can be cut off and potted up.

POTTING ORCHIDS

The potting medium is of far greater concern with orchids than with almost any other plants, and must be quite different from that in which most other plants thrive, at least in dealing with sympodial epiphytes. The problem is one of insufficient oxygen supply for the roots in ordinary media. Terrestrial orchids (*Calanthe, Phaius, Vanilla*) are sometimes grown in ordinary good potting soil or in gardens, but even they are more certain to be vigorous in a special potting mixture such as one containing equal parts of shredded osmundine, well-rotted manure, peat moss, and sandy loam.

For epiphytic orchids osmundine, the dried mass of aerial roots formed by the *Osmunda* fern, has long been the standard potting material. It is still unexcelled, but it is difficult to use, and it is in very short supply. There is increasing use of chipped barks of certain coniferous forest trees. Although these chipped barks are cheap and very easy to use, orchids must be secured in them and regular fertilization is a necessary adjunct. Chipped barks under liquid fertilization break down more quickly than does unfertilized osmundine, and they usually will not carry plants for two years. Potting with bark involves only dumping the product around the plant roots, but potting in osmundine requires a special technique.

First soak the large chunks of osmundine as they come from the bale in water until the fibers are soft and pliable. Then remove, and when water no longer drains freely, cut the osmundine into blocks about 2½ in. high. A pot should be selected which is wide enough that the division being potted extends two-thirds the way across its top. Too large a pot size is undesirable. Only sound, uncracked, new pots should be used, and if they are not specially designed for orchids, with drainage slots around the bottom, the central hole should be carefully chipped out to twice its diameter to assure good drainage. Fill the pot one-third full of potsherds (broken pieces of clay pot), and you are ready to start potting.

Select for repotting those plants whose leads have reached the sides of their pots or those whose old potting medium has rotted. Remove the plants from the old pots by carefully prying them out with a screwdriver or the pointed end of a file. This is done more easily if the potted plant has been soaking in a bucket of water. Then divide the rhizome behind the fourth pseudo-bulb. Trim away the old, dead roots and remove as much of the old potting material as possible without injuring the live roots; however, it is well to leave a small piece of osmundine under the lead, if possible.

The next step is to remove all of the brown membrane that surrounds the lead pseudobulb so that any scale insects will be exposed. Then dip the leaves and pseudobulbs, holding the plant by the rhizome, into a deep container of an insecticide, such as 2 oz. of 50% wettable DDT powder dissolved in 7 gal. of water, with a teaspoon of any detergent as spreader. There will not be another opportunity as favorable as this for ridding plants of pests until the next repotting.

Hold the division in one hand so that the oldest pseudobulb is against the rim of the pot nearest you, and pack blocks of osmundine all around it until the pot is tightly filled. Then with a pointed stick or screwdriver, force still more osmundine between the wall of the pot and the blocks already in place. A considerable amount of force is needed to do a good job, so that at last the osmundine is packed tightly in a firm mass standing about ¾ in. below the pot rim. An orchid properly potted in osmundine can be shaken upside down without dislodging it. Finally, trim the uneven surface of the osmundine with shears to a smooth, even contour.

The plants must now be provided with support to hold them upright. Cut a piece of No. 9 galvanized wire slightly shorter than the height of the plant and force it into the osmundine just behind the second pseudobulb. With green linen florist's thread, tie each pseudobulb to this stake at the base of the leaves.

Of course, other materials may be used as ties, but nothing else looks as good as this thread.

GROWING CONDITIONS

Like most other plants, orchids thrive within a certain range of temperature, humidity, and exposure to light, and the grower must learn just what the best level of each of these conditions is for each kind of orchid. Temperature must be controlled by the grower. In general, orchids do best when night temperatures are somewhere between 50° and 60°F., although the thermometer must go above 110° to be injurious. Daytime maxima are controlled by shading and by opening ventilators to let hot air escape. Greenhouses in Florida will need to have shading material put on the glass every spring. Orchids with greatest light tolerance should be hung nearest the glass.

Light intensity is a matter of much concern in orchid culture both on account of the heating effect of sunshine on glass, and for the actual light requirement of each genus. *Vanda* and *Cyrtopodium* thrive in full sun like zinnias, while *Phalaenopsis* is quite intolerant of bright light and must be given much shade like African-violets. Most other orchids lie between these extremes, growing best in light shade at all times or in protection from noonday heat but with no shade before 11 or after 2 o'clock. The color of orchid leaves is an indicator of the adequacy of light intensity. Dark green color usually means that not enough light is being received for good food manufacture and blooming; yellowed leaves or yellow areas on green leaves indicate that light intensity is too great; yellowish-green leaves usually show that light exposure is good.

Atmospheric humidity should be high for orchids, especially the epiphytic ones. On sunny days when relative humidity is low, the air can be kept moist by using a misty spray on orchid foliage and by wetting down walks and walls in an orchid house. On dull, cloudy days, relative humidity is already high, and water sprayed on foliage may stand for many hours, which is not good.

Watering of orchid plants themselves is regulated by the

state of growth of the plant. Some kinds, such as *Phaius, Phal-aenopsis, Vanda,* and the evergreen species of *Epidendrum* and *Dendrobium,* never need a resting period and are always in active growth. When temperatures are high, they grow faster and need more water; in winter they grow slowly, and once a week will be often enough to water the pots. Other evergreen orchids, like *Cattleya, Laelia,* and *Oncidium,* and all deciduous kinds need a period of rest before blooming, and this is assured by allowing the plants to become rather dry. However, they should never be allowed to get so dry that the pseudobulbs begin to shrivel.

Fertilizer application is not necessary in growing epiphytic orchids in osmundine or tree-fern chunks, since they obtain nutrients from slow decomposition of these potting media. Orchids potted in shredded tree bark should be watered once during each warm month with a soluble, high-analysis fertilizer formulated especially for orchids. Manufacturer's directions should always be followed exactly.

The above discussion has been written with greenhouses chiefly in mind. When orchids are grown inside the house, they may be placed in a southern or eastern window where they will not be exposed to noonday sun. Maintaining atmospheric humidity is the most difficult problem, and may be solved by use of glass-enclosed cases or by standing the pots above a pan of wet gravel. The water level in the pan must always be kept below the pot itself to assure free drainage. In summer the plants may be put out in the garden or patio in light shade.

Orchids in trees should be given light shade, not dense shade. Plants are usually removed carefully from the pots and fastened in place by large roofing nails, two on each side, driven into the tree, with wire running across the rhizome and roots from side to side. Before the roots expand into the bark crevices, applications of a special orchid fertilizer each month will be beneficial. All epiphytic orchids can be grown on trees in southern Florida. Pest control at potting time and by monthly applications of DDT and malathion, alternated, should keep orchid plants clean.

ORCHIDS RECOMMENDED FOR FLORIDA GARDENERS

Cattleya. This is the genus, native to tropical America, from which most of today's hobby orchids are derived. Without doubt, hybrid cattleyas are the most popular with Florida growers. Some hobbyists grow species, but most are content only with the robust, floriferous hybrid forms that are available in endless variety from orchid nurseries in our state. Osmundine and chipped tree bark are the usual growing media, but tree-fern planks and shredded tree fern are popular. Hybrid cattleyas in heated greenhouses can be maintained at temperatures above 50°F.; those on trees can be protected by hoods of cloth under which are inserted light bulbs on extension cords.

Calanthe. Several deciduous and one evergreen species of *Calanthe* are grown in Florida, since they are terrestrial orchids with large leaves and as easy to grow as most pot plants. Tall spikes of small flowers of exceptional lasting quality are borne in winter from leafless pseudobulbs in the usual deciduous forms, and vegetative growth is made in spring and summer. A minimum temperature of 65°F. is desirable.

Coelogyne. This genus of spray orchids has evergreen leaves which are unusual in being rather attractive when the plant is not in bloom. The blossoms are small but are produced abundantly in winter and early spring, and make a very good show when the plants are grown in large clumps in baskets or on chunks of tree fern. A fair amount of shade is needed. C. *pandurata* and C. *massangeana* are recommended.

Cyrtopodium. A single species, C. *punctatum,* is native to Florida and is called cowhorn orchid from the shape of the pseudobulbs. It produces long clusters of small flowers in early spring, after the corn-like leaves have fallen. Naturally it grows high up in bald-cypress trees, with full sun in winter and feathery shade in summer. Culture is very easy.

Dendrobium. This is a large genus of orchids from the Eastern Hemisphere, with both evergreen and deciduous species which produce large, showy sprays of small flowers, usually lasting many weeks. Recommended for beginners are deciduous

D. nobile, which does well with a 50°F. night temperature during its winter rest, and evergreen *D. phalaenopsis,* which prefers a minimum of 65°F. Both bloom in spring.

Epidendrum. Several Florida indigenes represent this large American genus. There are so many attractive "epis," both species and hybrids, that listing would be incomplete at best. The epiphytic forms grow well on trees in protected locations and in pots or on tree-fern planks in greenhouses. Reed epidendrums, in many attractive colors, grow in full sun in enriched earth in parts of the peninsula that are not subject to heavy frosts,

Oncidium. Another American genus with Florida species, these orchids can usually endure lower temperatures than most other epiphytes. Sprays of small yellow flowers are borne by the species usually grown in Florida. Besides our native *O. luridum,* blooming from late February to early May, these include three from Latin America: *O. ampliatum,* blooming in February and March; *O. flexuosum,* with flowers from December to March; and *O. tigrinum,* blossoming from March to May. Many other species may be grown here, and all like much light.

Phaius. These terrestrial orchids are of easy culture if treated like amaryllis. In the southern half of the state they thrive in open garden soil with light summer shade and some protection on freezing nights. The veiled-nun orchid, *P. grandifolius,* is most often seen and produces tall spikes of starry brown and silver flowers in profusion in late winter and early spring. Dilute liquid fertilizer is recommended when flower spikes first appear at ground level. The large, plaited, lanceolate leaves resemble those of young palm seedlings.

Phalaenopsis. The moth orchid from the tropics of the other hemisphere grows well in Florida. Popular now with hobbyists are hybrids of complex lineage rather than species. Hybrids produce graceful sprays of large pink, yellow, or white flowers that may last several weeks during cool weather. *Phalaenopsis* normally flower from January to May, and each vigorous plant may be encouraged to rebloom if sprays are cut so as to leave the basal parts of scapes on the plants. The foliage is subject to sunburn, and so half shade or more is recommended. Since moth orchids have no pseudobulbs, an abundant, constant supply of moisture is needed. The large net-veined leaves and silvery roots are very decorative and are certain to evoke comment.

Vanda. Of the two types of these Asiatic orchids, the hybrids with strap-shaped leaves now rank with hybrid moth orchids as topflight hobby plants in Florida. Hybrids are many, and full, circular flowers with delicate color blendings in shades of buff, tan, and pink are greatly admired. 'Nellie Morley' is a progenitor of this race of prize-winning strap vandas. *Vanda caerulea* has given us gorgeous blue orchids. Strap vandas are grown in charcoal or feather-rock in full sun with liquid fertilization during warm weather. Protection on cold nights is essential. Vandas with cylindrical leaves, typified by the variety 'Miss Joachim' of *V. teres,* are widely grown in enriched earth in full sun. These terete vandas produce quantities of flowers during the warm months.

Vanilla. This terrestrial genus is interesting because *V. fragrans,* native to Florida, is the source of natural vanilla flavoring. Vanilla is very easy to grow but rarely blooms while confined in little greenhouses. When vines can run, and blossoms do appear, hand pollination is required for fruiting. Vanilla is increased by simply planting pieces of stem that are several nodes in length.

Obtaining plants

It is strongly recommended that beginning orchidists obtain their first plants in flower from orchid firms that specialize in supplying plants for amateurs. In this way, beginners will not be disappointed as they might be if they order by catalog description only. Flowering plants from reputable dealers should be well established in adequate pots of suitable medium that will serve for a year or more before shifting is needed. Later, as novice growers become proficient in orchid growing, they will want to buy unflowered seedlings of fashionable crosses, and bring them into blossom in their own back yards. Then, exchanging plants with other fanciers is one of the real pleasures of orchid growing.

Native Florida epiphytic orchids are protected by state law

which prohibits the buying or selling of orchids collected on public land or on private land without written consent of the owner, under penalty. Permission to collect will usually be granted by landowners to qualified botanists or hobbyists who can properly care for orchids after they are collected from the wilds.

BROMELIADS

Bromeliads include plants varying widely in size and habitat, all native to the Americas. They range in size from 2 to 36 in. in height, and they may live on the ground (often on rocks) or in trees as epiphytes. The majority of them have rather showy inflorescences, of which the brightly colored bracts are usually more important than the flowers they subtend. Some have only highly colorful leaves to make a show, and many have striking leaves in addition to showy bracts. Nearly all have spines on the leaf margins. Each shoot can flower only once, as the terminal growing point finally forms the flower spike, but offsets or suckers are formed at the base of the stem and in turn become shoots with flowers. In recent years bromeliads have increased greatly in popularity in Florida gardens, in large part because of recognition of their ease of culture. Like their distant relatives, the orchids, they are grown mostly in containers in patios or inside houses, but are also suited for growing on branches of trees or even in garden beds.

CULTURE

Light, shifting shade is generally the best exposure for bromeliads, although a few need full sun, and some thrive in considerable shade. Sunlight is less intense in winter than in summer, and so less shade is needed in winter for a given species; or, in winter this species may be placed nearer a window than in summer.

Most bromeliads of horticultural interest are sensitive to cold and will suffer injury at or below 32°F. They thrive with day temperatures of 70°-80°F., and night temperatures around 50°F. are favorable for most species.

Watering needs vary widely in this family, but of the genera commonly grown in Florida, only *Bromelia* is xerophytic. The others thrive under conditions of rather high humidity, and most of them are "tank" bromeliads, holding much water in the deep cup formed by the upright, sheathing leaves. Keeping this receptacle full of water is a desirable practice usually. The potting medium should be kept moist, but should drain freely so that water does not stand around the roots. If the city water is high in lime, it is desirable to catch rain water to use for watering. Almost all bromeliads grow better if they are put out in the rain occasionally in summer.

Generally plants may be grown in a special potting mixture in planter boxes, pots, urns, or tubs, in beds of leafmold under oak trees, or attached to tree limbs. If grown in containers, the "soil" should be somewhat acid and very well drained. A mixture of equal parts (by weight) of coarse, sharp silica sand and either German peatmoss or Florida osmundine is a satisfactory potting medium for all genera here discussed except *Bromelia* and *Vriesia*. New suckers are aided in getting established by tying them to a stiff wire inserted in the medium to hold them upright until they develop roots. Several types of soluble, complete fertilizers are available which can be applied in dilute concentration, either by spraying the whole plant or by pouring from a sprinkling can. Applications may be made monthly during the growing season. When bromeliads are grown as epiphytes, they should be fastened to limbs of rough-barked trees with aluminum or copper wire. The roots from the base of the plants will obtain plant nutrients from decaying matter in the bark crevices.

Most bromeliads produce suckers or offsets from buds on the lower part of the stem, and these offer a convenient means of propagation. Often there will be formed a succession of suckers if each is removed as soon as it reaches a suitable size. If they are borne on lateral creeping stems (stolons), they can easily be broken off by hand; if they grow directly from a leafy stem, a knife may be needed to sever them from the parent plant.

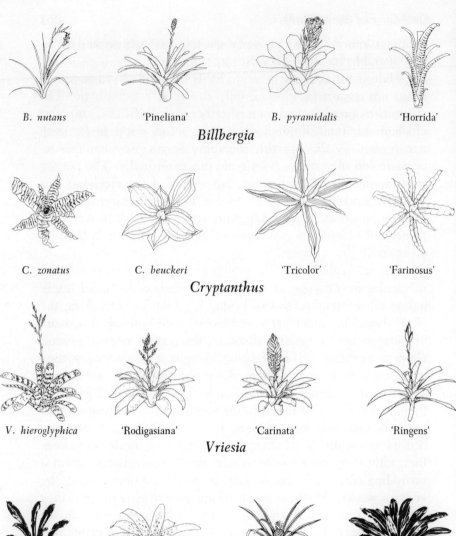

B. nutans   'Pineliana'   B. pyramidalis   'Horrida'

Billbergia

C. zonatus   C. beuckeri   'Tricolor'   'Farinosus'

Cryptanthus

V. hieroglyphica   'Rodigasiana'   'Carinata'   'Ringens'

Vriesia

Aechmea   *Nidularium*   *Pineapple*   *Neoregelia*

FIGURE 30
GROWTH HABITS OF BROMELIADS

Seedlings can be raised of many species, but culture is usually difficult and the seedlings take much longer to bloom than offsets. Hybrid forms must be reproduced vegetatively, since seeds would not come true.

Pests of bromeliads are chiefly limited to a few scale insects, which greatly weaken the plants. Oil sprays are not well tolerated usually, but malathion provides an easy method of control without harm to the plants. The grower may find that mosquitoes breed in the "tanks" and annoy him. If so, he can control the larvae by dissolving 1 tsp. of 25% DDT emulsion in 1 qt. of water and putting 1 tsp. of this dilution in each "tank."

BROMELIADS RECOMMENDED FOR FLORIDA

Aechmea. This genus offers a wide range of colors, with flowers lasting only a few weeks, but the bracts of the medium-tall inflorescence spikes, followed by colored berries, give a show of bright color for several months. The rather upright leaves forming the "tank" are often barred or splotched with color, too. Most of the commonly grown species are epiphytes in Nature, but are easily cultured in containers. Especially recommended are *A. bracteata, A. miniata* var. *discolor,* and *A. orlandiana,* but there are many species and varieties which do well in Florida. The usual conditions of light and culture for bromeliads suit this group, but *Aechmea* leaves retain bright colors better in poorly lighted rooms than most other genera. They are suitable for the customary bromeliad usages, and are propagated by offsets or seeds.

Billbergia. The best known of all bromeliads is probably the *Billbergia nutans,* which is unusually tolerant of neglect and cold. While the genus is mostly epiphytic in the wild, the plants occur near the ground, not high up in trees. The massive flower spikes with pink or red bracts remain showy only a few weeks. These typical "tank" bromeliads thrive in more light than most genera do, but otherwise respond to the usual culture and are suited to the usual variety of uses. Propagation is by seeds or offsets. Besides the common *B. nutans,* the species *B. amoena* var. *viridis, B. horrida, B. pyramidalis,* and *B. zonata* are popular.

Bromelia. Only one of the many species of this genus is common in Florida, the pinguin, *Bromelia pinguin.* This is a large terrestrial species with very narrow, spiny leaves from 2 to 4 ft. long, looking much like those of its close relative, the pineapple. In many parts of tropical America pinguins are planted closely as defensive hedges. Flowers and fruits are not very ornamental, but when the flower spike is about to begin development, the newest half-dozen leaves become brilliant scarlet and remain so for many weeks. Pinguin is suitable only for garden beds in full sun, and prefers sand or sand-peat mixture as soil. Being a xerophyte, little attention to watering is necessary, and fertilizer is applied two or three times a year. There are no varieties, and propagation can be by seeds or suckers. Very similar in culture and ornamental uses are forms of pineapple with variegated leaves, but in this case a very desirable fruit is produced. Either suckers or slips can be used for reproduction.

Cryptanthus. This genus consists of tiny plants, only a few inches high, with low, flat rosettes of fleshy leaves which are usually showy because of bars or stripes in varied colors. There is no central tube to hold water. Flower spikes are inconspicuous, usually too short to be seen above the leaves, and the latter provide the only coloring. While the genus is almost wholly terrestrial in Nature, the plants can be grown on trees. They are more effective, however, in dish gardens and small planters or as a ground cover. The usual conditions of light and culture are satisfactory, except that lack of "tanks" may make it necessary to water more often. Only offsets are available for propagation. Recommended especially are *C. bivittatus, C. lacerdae,* and *C. zonatus,* but there are many attractive hybrids to choose among.

Neoregelia. In this genus of (mostly) epiphytes, the coarse, heavy leaves form a shorter central tube than in most "tank" bromeliads, and the extreme tips are usually bright red, leading to the common name of "painted fingernails." Flower spikes rarely rise above the tube, and as in the pinguin, the main color effect is produced by the youngest leaves becoming brightly scarlet just before blooming and continuing thus for months. While the usual cultural conditions are satisfactory, *Neoregelia* tolerates more light than most bromeliads. Plants have the usual uses and are grown from either offsets or seeds. Popular species are *N. marmorata* and *N. spectabilis,* both of which endure neglect and dry atmosphere amazingly well, and in addition there are many satisfactory hybrids.

Nidularium. Like *Billbergia,* this genus occurs naturally in trees close to the ground, for the most part, but does well in media. It is similar to *Neoregelia* in having center leaves as the showy feature, and it thrives under similar conditions except for less tolerance of light. The garden uses are those usual for bromeliads, but seeds are not often produced, so that offsets are the usual means of propagation. Species recommended include *N. regelioides* and *N. fulgens.*

Vriesia. These "tank" bromeliads are distinguished by their thin, glossy leaves without marginal spines. The species usually grown are epiphytic in Nature and thrive better in osmundine alone, like orchids, than in the usual potting mixture. The colored bracts of the tall, flattened flower spikes remain showy for months. Light, culture, garden uses, and propagation are as for most bromeliads. Recommended especially are *V. carinata* and its hybrid variety 'Marie,' called "Painted Feather," *V. hieroglyphica,* *V. rodigasiana,* and the "Flaming Sword," *V. splendens.*

14

Beach and Retirement Gardening

Florida's coastline, one of the longest of any of the contiguous 48 states, is a favored location for vacation homes. In some areas on the east coast, the entire strip of palmetto and pine barren between the ocean and the tidewater lagoon is residential property. Unusual gardens, distinctively subtropical in atmosphere and strongly characteristic of the section, are a part of these seaside homes.

Three types of beach conditions are to be distinguished, since gardening will be determined by them. These are the Atlantic Ocean beaches, those on the Gulf of Mexico, and the waterfronts of the tidewater lagoons known locally as Biscayne Bay, Indian River, Lake Worth, and others.

Gardening on the oceanfront in Florida is about as difficult as gardening can be anywhere. The exposure of the beach to the full force of Atlantic wind, the salt spray carried inland, the alkaline reaction of the ever present shell and its harmful effect on availability of certain mineral elements, the thin sand devoid of humus content—these are not conditions to the liking of many garden plants. Fortunately there are some plants suitable for garden usage that tolerate these severe conditions, and these form the first line of defense. In the shelter of casuarina, seagrape, yucca, button-bush, and agave may be grown pittosporum, ochrosia, carissa, and red-cedar.

Atlantic beach cottages are built on the crests of the foredunes or just behind them. The additional protection against wind and salt spray furnished by the house or the dune enables a wide variety of both woody and herbaceous plants to be grown. While every conceivable type of building may be seen, most contemporary beach homes are low, rambling cottages, well adapted to the locale.

Gardens for beach cottages should be simple and restrained in style. Plantings around the house may consist only of a few agaves and yuccas for accent and atmosphere, two or three palms for background and framing, and succulents such as sansevieria, kalanchoë, aloe, and euphorbia for filling in under windows. To these may be added a greensward of grass or ground cover, some annuals for highlights and cutting, and shrubbery walls for privacy. The private area is usually not developed in detail, as the water scene is considered most desirable, and the complete enclosure customary in landscaping home grounds in towns is not at all common. Axial lines are usually ignored except in the most carefully designed gardens. Some beach dwellers are even content to have wild front yards sparsely inhabited by native littoral plants such as sea-oats (*Uniola paniculata*), beach morning-glory, and beach sunflower, but most gardeners want a continuous green ground covering to reduce wind erosion and rest the eyes.

On the Atlantic shore it is almost always necessary to have some sort of seawall, behind which the front yard may be gently sloping or nearly level. To have a lawn, enough peat or muck must be hauled in to cover the ground 4 or 5 in. deep, and this must be well mixed in the top 8 in. of thin beach sand. St. Augustine grass is the most popular for oceanfront lawns, but selected types of Bermuda grass are popular, and Manila grass is sometimes seen. Italian rye-grass is as well adapted near the shore as it is inland to provide a green winter lawn. Ground covers other than grasses are widely used also, especially those that tolerate bright sunlight, and interesting effects are achieved with Hottentot-fig, kalanchoë, wedelia, and cissus.

For introduced trees and shrubs, planting holes must be made with extra care in most cases. Oversized holes should be

dug and filled with a mixture of equal parts of the beach sand
with leafmold from hammocks, peat, compost, sludge, or manure.
A sprinkling of a minor element mixture is long-term insurance
against shortages of some of these elements. Deficiencies of iron,
zinc, copper, manganese, boron, and magnesium are not common with most garden plants in inland gardens, but in beach
gardens they often occur. Choice palms, vines, shrubs, or annuals frequently exhibit in beach sand the chlorotic foliage,
stunted growth, and dead tips that are manifestations of mineral
deficiencies. Plants growing in their native soils will thrive without supplements of minor elements, so this extra precaution is
advocated for use only on those plants which are not native to
beach areas.

Palms are so much a part of tropical seascapes that waterfront homes are incomplete without several of them. On the
lower east coast the coconut palm is universally planted. It stands
more salt spray and wind than any other palm, but grows well
back from the beach also. Northward from Palm Beach the
coconut palm gradually gives way to the cabbage palmetto for
beach planting, and this hardy native palm carries on into the
Carolinas.

Gulf dunes are lower, and the line of demarcation between
the shingle and the ridge of sand is often undefined, especially
along the shore of the peninsula. Houses are often built directly
on Gulf beaches, although in the Panama City area the dunes
are developed more like those of the Atlantic coast. Winds off
the Gulf of Mexico are neither so strong nor so laden with salt
as are those off the Atlantic Ocean, and consequently there is
little distinction between the plants that need the protection of
the house and those that grow between the house and the water's
edge. From Naples to St. Petersburg the royal palm graces the
beach gardens, and with a little protection, Manila, caryota, and
date palms may be grown. Tampa waterfront homes are graced
by the queen palm. Northward from Tampa the native cabbage
palm becomes the principal palm in beach plantings. Pindo
palms also grace large lawns along the coastal areas of western Florida.

Intermediate in many ways between Atlantic and Gulf beaches are the shores of the intracoastal waterways of the east coast. Gardeners along the Indian River or Lake Worth experience less wind and salt spray than do those on the oceanfront, but still have more wind-borne salt than is encountered on the Gulf coast. Hard water, shell sand, lack of soil humus, and high water table are common to all Florida beach gardens. Along the shores of Biscayne Bay the royal palm flourishes. North of Hobe Sound it is replaced by the queen palm, which in turn yields to the cabbage palmetto north of St. Augustine.

Palms provide atmospheric charm but are not very satisfactory for shade. On Atlantic beaches, casuarina, pigeon-plum, and sea-grape are front-line trees, but in the lee of them may be grown sapodilla, bucida, and gumbo-limbo in the warmer areas, and loquat, red-cedar, and live oak on the northern half of the coast. For Gulf and lagoon waterfronts, all of these are satisfactory, and in addition tamarind, cajeput, and rubber-trees will succeed where temperatures are favorable. Even orange and grapefruit thrive where salt spray is absent.

The list of shrubs and vines which may be grown in beach gardens protected from wind and salt is too long to give. Annual flowers, too, may be grown with good protection in beach gardens almost as they can in inland gardens. As with exotic shrubs, however, their successful culture requires much more careful preparation of soil than is needed inland. Plant beds should be dug out to a depth of a foot and the beach sand replaced by a fertile, organic soil that is further fortified with minor elements, as described above for shrub planting. Such annuals as gaillardia, periwinkle, and petunia have escaped from cultivation to form large colonies along the shore in some places.

Accessories for the beach garden must be harmonious with the environment. Objects which reflect the nautical, tropical, beachcomber, or driftwood theme are desirable. Cottage furnishings should be colorful and of rather coarse texture, in keeping with the spirit of beach homes. If not designed especially for this usage, furniture should be chosen which is comfortable, of rugged construction, and resistant to salt spray and intense light.

Species for Beach Planting of Great Tolerance for Salt Spray[*]

Trees and Palms

Casuarina equisetifolia
Coccoloba floridana
Coccoloba uvifera
Cocos nucifera
Conocarpus erectus

Acacia farnesiana
Bursera simaruba
Butia capitata
Callitris robusta
Coccothrinax argentata
Juniperus barbadensis
Phoenix reclinata
Pinus spp.
Sabal palmetto
Thrinax parviflora

Herbaceous Plants

Cynodon dactylon
Helianthus debilis
Hymenocallis keyensis
Ipomoea pes-caprae
Kalanchoë spp.
Liriope spp.
Sansevieria spp.
Stenotaphrum secundatum
Uniola paniculata
Zoisia tenuifolia

Hemerocallis spp.
Hylocereus undatus
Wedelia trilobata

Shrubs

Agave spp.
Aloe spp.
Euphorbia spp.
Furcraea gigantea
Yucca spp.

Ardisia escallonioides
Carissa spp.
Chrysobalanus icaco
Genipa clusiaefolia
Myrica cerifera
Ochrosia elliptica
Pittosporum tobira
Raphiolepis spp.
Serenoa repens
Zamia floridana

Callistemon rigidus
Cleyera japonica
Cryptostegia spp.
Elaeagnus pungens
Eugenia axillaris
Eugenia myrtoides
Hydrangea spp.
Ilex vomitoria
Lantana camara
Ligustrum japonicum
Nerium oleander
Pandanus spp.
Severinia buxifolia
Vitex spp.

[*] The groups are listed in order of salt tolerance, those most able to endure salt spray being listed first. Within each group the order is alphabetical only.

RETIREMENT GARDENING

Perhaps you are among the tens of thousands of Americans who have dreamed of retirement in Florida where you could spend a part of each day in the sunshine working in a small plot of earth. All books and articles on retirement list gardening as a leading hobby, one in which the rewards are great both in physical and mental terms.

Keynote for retirement gardens is simplicity. Horticultural enterprises must be small, uncluttered, and easy to maintain. It is important that their care be a happy experience, anticipated with pleasure. Never should retirement gardens become burdensome. Ambitious persons may envision extensive emerald-green lawns surrounded by gay flower beds, rare shrubs, and exotic fruits and palms. More realistic for most of us is a modest greensward enclosed by easy-to-maintain, broad-leaved, evergreen shrubs, with a few drifts of herbaceous perennials, bulbs, and annuals for seasonal color. There will be some days when you will want to pursue other hobbies and times when you will want to be away from home. Here in Florida it's just too hot and muggy for active gardening on many midsummer days.

First step in planning a Florida garden should be an engineered irrigation system: a permanent, underground complex of pipes and nozzles operated in independent sections by two or three valves. One retiree of mechanical bent has fitted his irrigation system with a time clock so that every part of his small, neat yard is wetted for a predetermined period each week. The clock remains plugged in during dry months; it is disconnected for the rainy season.

A fruit garden might appeal to many retirees. Hardy fruit trees can form the background of the outdoor living area, and when they are in flower or fruit they serve also as strong centers of interest. In caring for fruit trees the owner will have to do a minimum amount of bending and stooping, yet there will be work overhead and from steps of a low ladder to prune, thin, and harvest.

Pest control, always a major consideration, should be placed in the capable hands of a reputable pest-control firm. In most Florida cities such enterprises, operating under the supervision of graduate entomologists, are licensed and insured to cover all phases of house and garden pest control.

In warm sections of Florida, hardy orchids and bromeliads can be affixed to large main branches of trees. These epiphytes require nothing from their owner, yet their flowers are very much worth having. Shade-tolerant perennials can be massed as ground covers around the trunks of fruit trees, inside the drip line, the area that is often kept as a circle of sand.

One problem in fruit gardening is that an enthusiastic owner might plant too many trees with the result that there would be no sunny area for grass, flowers, and hobby shrubs. The basic list of fruit trees would have to be compiled with thought, after consultation with your garden center manager and your county agricultural agent. Later expansion of this carefully composed list might lead to overcrowding, to the detriment of all trees in your yard.

Strawberry barrels or jars are convenient, tiny gardens that might be the choice of some retirees. At your garden center buy a jar designed for this purpose. It has lipped openings all around. If you prefer, obtain a wooden barrel and drill 1½-in. holes at staggered, 14-in. intervals all around. Fill your chosen container with rich compost after you have placed a few inches of coarse gravel in the bottom to assure good drainage. Set a strawberry plant into each hole, water carefully, and fog the planted vessel with a light mist from the hose every day that there is no rain, until flower buds form. Place your strawberry barrel on a sunny terrace where it can be protected from birds and squirrels. A strawberry barrel can yield good dividends for the little effort expended, and the vessel would be good for many years of service.

Tomato cages are suggested for persons who want to garden in a very restricted way. Buy about 15 ft. of concrete reinforcing wire at your building-supply house. It comes in 6 x 6 mesh and is 5 ft. wide. Make a cylinder of the wire in a sunny place, and fill the lower 3 ft. or so with waste plant material, peat, muck, sludge, or manure, just as though you were making compost (see pp. 40-41). Around the periphery set tomato plants from your garden center at 2-ft. intervals (you will need seven or eight). As the plants grow, carefully tie them to the wire mesh with Twist-Ems or soft cloth. Pinch out vegetative buds as they appear in the leaf axils, but be very careful not to remove flower buds when *they* appear. Please read page 319, and be reminded that weekly spraying is requisite to success with tomatoes.

Window boxes may be the only garden plots available to some people, yet these can be wholly satisfying little gardens because they are easily managed to yield quantities of colorful flowers, gay foliage, lacy ferns, or even salad greens. Window boxes serve as points of interest for unbroken wall expanses, and they are valuable adjuncts to jalousie windows and to glass walls of Florida rooms. Long, low, wooden planters with annual flowers may brighten sunny terraces. Proper construction of plant boxes is essential to long, useful life. Please refer to pages 27-28 and 35.

Growing media for planters are discussed on pages 29 and 35-37, so please be guided by those suggestions before you fill new containers.

Plants for window-box gardens are limitless. Annuals, foliage plants, ferns, succulents, and miniature vegetables all have possibilities, and they can be planted in infinite combination.

Many retirees look forward to spending leisure hours in small greenhouses. For persons who enjoy routine and daily operations, greenhouse gardening can be pleasurable. Thousands of orchid hobbyists have found it so. Some, on the other hand, want more freedom of movement than greenhouse gardening allows. Manipulation of ventilators, syringing, watering, and care of heating systems during cold weather cannot be neglected, even for a single day. During absences from home landscape plantings will survive with natural rainfall, but collections of greenhouse plants cannot. Styles and types of backyard greenhouses and equipment for them are almost limitless, so that one may have an establishment as elaborate as one chooses.

For persons with strong interests in applied chemistry and mechanics, the production of vegetables and flowers without soil can be real fun. Hydroponics, as this soil-less culture is sometimes called, requires as strict adherence to precise techniques as does greenhouse gardening. There is no relief from daily care, yet for many, the end product is well worth the effort expended.

Vegetative propagation has long been popular with back-yard horticulturists, and now that the constant-mist method has been so widely accepted, every homeowner can become a successful plant propagator. Through a hole in the bottom of a half-drum or old wash tub, run a half-inch water line. At rim level install a mist fitting; then fill the receptacle with sawdust from a lumber yard or turkey grit from your seed store. During warm months, your little constant-mist propagator will induce roots to form on leafy cuttings in a few weeks.

To hold your new plants after you pot them (see p. 63), have a sturdy table or rough bench nearby. A tall standpipe with irrigation fitting should be at hand to fog the young plants until their roots become well established. Such a plant propagation enterprise can operate while the owner is away from home. In this, as in all aspects of retirement gardening, preference should be given to plants that will grow well without day-to-day attention.

15

Fruits in the Garden

A FEW FRUIT TREES and shrubs have already been discussed for their usefulness as ornamental plants in the landscape picture. These and many others are well worth giving garden space primarily for their fruit production, but may often not lend themselves readily to landscape treatment. In a distinct fruit garden, they may be cultivated without worry over their landscape value.

All fruit trees are most productive when grown in full sun. Little can be expected from deciduous fruit trees shaded overhead, but evergreen fruit trees are partially fruitful even in some shade. For good fruit production, trees should be spaced far enough apart that they will not shade each other, or else should be pruned to prevent crowding. Pest control is much more of a problem with fruit than with shade trees.

Evergreen fruit trees are usually fertilized three times a year —in late winter, early summer, and early fall. Deciduous trees are usually fertilized only in early spring on heavy soils, but twice each growing season on light sandy soils, in early spring and early summer. A 4-7-5 or 6-6-6 analysis may be used satisfactorily for all fruits except pineapple. As a rule of thumb, one may apply as many pounds of 4-7-5 as the age of the tree in years—that is, 1 lb. the first year, 2 lbs. the second, and so forth—at each application for the first few years. Thereafter the rate of application increases more slowly than the age does.

Fertilizers should be spread uniformly over the ground beneath the canopy of the tree and a little beyond that diameter. A thick mulch of leaves is beneficial to all fruit trees.

The number of fruits which can be grown increases rapidly as one goes south from the Georgia line, until it reaches a figure near one hundred in the near-tropical areas of the state. Northern Florida is too warm for most of the temperate zone fruits and too cold for many subtropical ones. In central Florida, location has much to do with success or failure, since in places unusually well protected from cold (such as the slopes of the southern Ridge sand hills with their effective air drainage) it may be possible to grow fruits normally recommended only for the southern section. In southern Florida it is only the coastal strip with the moderating effect of sea and gulf which can be used for growing tropical fruits. The following lists give the most common fruits generally suitable for each of the three sections of the state. Each species is then described in some detail as to varieties and cultural needs.

NORTHERN FLORIDA. Satsuma, orange, calamondin, kumquat, peach, pear, plum, Oriental persimmon, fig, grapefruit, grape, blueberry, strawberry, blackberry, pecan.

CENTRAL FLORIDA. Orange, grapefruit, lemon, tangelo, kumquat, avocado, lychee, Oriental persimmon, pitanga, Cattley guava, grape, jaboticaba, blackberry.

SOUTHERN FLORIDA. Orange, grapefruit, lime, tangelo, kumquat, avocado, mango, lychee, papaya, pineapple, pitanga, guava, jaboticaba, sapodilla, banana, peach, carambola.

FRUIT VARIETIES

Avocado. The varieties Lula, Booth 8, Booth 7, Tonnage, and Taylor are recommended for all areas where avocado growing is feasible, being fairly cold-resistant as well as productive. Lula and Taylor are in the A pollinating group, while the others are in the B group. It is desirable to plant at least one tree from each of these groups for good setting of fruit. The normal harvesting periods for these varieties are: Lula, Booth 8, and Tonnage, October-November; Booth 7, November-December; Taylor, December-January. In southern Florida the following varieties greatly extend the season: Ruehle (B), July-August; Waldin (A), September-October; Linda (B), January-February; Itzamna (B), March-April.

Avocados require certain regular applications of spray mixtures to control fruit diseases, but for most varieties only two sprayings are necessary. Lula requires more spraying than any other variety but is also unusually productive.

Banana. Even in northern Florida banana plants occasionally mature a bunch of fruit, and in the southern area they are fairly regular bearers. The low-growing variety Cavendish and the tall variety Ladyfinger are the ones most commonly grown in all sections. Cavendish has large bunches with large fruits, comparable to those commonly seen in grocery stores; its short stature makes it easier to protect it from wind than any other. Ladyfinger bears small bunches of small bananas, very thin-skinned and delicious in flavor. Bananas need abundant supplies of water, but good soil drainage. A common mistake is to allow too many suckers to develop in a thick clump, which decreases the ability of any one plant to produce a good bunch of fruit. Succession of fruiting can be assured by allowing new suckers to develop only at intervals of three or four months. Banana bunches should be cut before the fruits turn yellow, and ripened in a cool, dark place.

Blackberry. Suited only to a very sunny location, a dozen blackberry bushes can supply quite a bit of fruit in late spring. Canes which have fruited should be cut to the ground after harvest, to encourage new canes which fruit the next year. Thin out these canes and head them back halfway to induce branching. Flordagrand variety has very large, rather tart berries, and needs interplanting with Oklawaha (similar in all respects) as a pollinator variety. Brazos has fruit not quite so large and is self-fruitful.

Blueberry. The Rabbiteye blueberry is the only species thriving in Florida. New varieties are being selected with improved size and color over the ones formerly available. Currently recommended are Callaway, Tifblue, and Homebell. Blueberry bushes need acid soil (pH 5.0 to 5.5) and a combination of good drainage with good retention of soil moisture. Blueberries can be left on the bush longer than other bush fruits after reaching maturity, and can be kept in the refrigerator for weeks in fresh condition. The fruiting season is June.

Calamondin. This citrus fruit of uncertain ancestry is essentially a hardy lime with orange-red skin and reddish juice. No named varieties are grown, since the seedlings are so uniform in character. Fruits are available all fall and winter.

Carambola. Highly decorative fruits, waxy, five-ribbed, fleshy, and often pleasant to eat, are produced in abundance by this evergreen tropical tree; they are usually borne on the trunk or large limbs. Fruits vary considerably in tartness, and both sweet and sour forms are available.

Cattley guava. A handsome shrubby tree with small glossy leaves, this species bears little resemblance to the common guava. Fruits are about an inch in diameter, juicy and pleasantly flavored, maturing chiefly in late summer. There are two types, with red or yellow skin color, and these come true from seed. The fruit is excellent for jelly and enjoyable for eating fresh except for the many small hard seeds.

Fig. The types of fig grown in Florida require no pollination for setting fruit. The most satisfactory varieties are Celeste, a small fig with pinkish-violet or bronzed skin, and Brown Turkey, a fig of medium size with greenish-brown skin. Both varieties mature in July and August. One of the big problems in fig-growing on sandy soils is the root-knot nematode. Planting the trees alongside a garage or barn, or maintaining a heavy mulch of hay or straw, helps in keeping this pest under control.

Grape. Two distinct kinds of grape are grown in Florida, the bunch grapes and the muscadine grapes. No really satisfactory bunch grape has been available for this state until very recently, but now two are available which are very well adapted and long-lived. Blue Lake has purplish-blue grapes, and those of Emerald Lake are greenish-yellow. Both mature in July and are recommended for home gardens rather than for commercial planting.

Bunch grapes are usually grown on T-shaped trellises or peaked arbors, and need regular spraying to control fruit pests.

Muscadine grapes are native to the South and so are better adapted to our climate, but they bear small bunches of fruits inferior in flavor to the better bunch varieties. Some of the varieties, such as Willard (white) and Tarheel (black), are self-pollinating and also serve to pollinate the older varieties which produce no pollen. For one or two vines only, the above should be planted. Where there is room for several vines, Scuppernong (white), Hunt (black), and Yuga (red) are excellent varieties to add. Muscadine grapes are popular for arbors or are grown on fence-like trellises, and usually get along well without spraying. The ripening season is late summer.

Grapefruit. This citrus fruit may be had in seedy or seedless form, with either white or pink-to-red flesh. Duncan, the standard seedy, white variety, is unsurpassed in flavor. Marsh is the corresponding seedless variety. Thompson is a pink-fleshed seedless form, and Ruby is seedless with red flesh which gives a pink blush to the rind in places. All these varieties mature in late winter and spring. Triumph and Royal are white seedy varieties maturing before Christmas and excellent for home gardens although not for commercial planting. Grapefruit trees need careful, regular spraying to control insects and diseases.

Guava. In addition to its well-known usage as a prime jelly fruit, the guava can be canned like the peach or even eaten out of hand. Most varieties mature the main crop in summer, but there are also winter-fruiting forms. Red Indian and Ruby are red-fleshed varieties of good dessert quality, while Supreme has white flesh. Redland is a winter-fruiting variety with very little of the characteristic guava odor, which many people dislike. Guavas can be trained to tree form, but when frozen to the ground they recover as many-stemmed bushes unless given careful pruning. Some spraying must be done to maintain trees in healthy condition.

Jaboticaba. This Brazilian fruit deserves wider growing in home gardens, since the quality is good for eating fresh and for making jelly. Several crops a year are borne on the trunk and older branches, individual fruits being about an inch in diameter, with tough black skin and juicy flesh. The shrubby trees are somewhat slow growing, but this is their only handicap. No named varieties are propagated yet, although there is some variation among seedlings.

Kumquat. Hardiest to cold of all citrus fruits, kumquat thrives throughout the state. Nagami, the large oval kumquat, is most commonly grown, but the large round variety, Meiwa, is just as satisfactory. Trees are dwarf, taking little space, and are highly ornamental in addition to bearing useful fruit. The season of maturity is all winter and spring. Scale insects are troublesome pests.

Lemon. Three types of lemon are of interest for the home garden. Villafranca is the true lemon variety best suited to Florida. Ponderosa is a hybrid lemon of rather inferior quality, distinguished for its huge size and thus a show specimen. Meyer is another hybrid lemon of good quality, distinctive for its orange-colored skin and flesh and for its unusual hardiness to cold. The Villafranca tree is about as large as an orange tree, but the other two are much smaller. All lemons have some fruit maturing at almost any season, but the main crop matures in autumn. Being used fresh, Villafranca never has the "lemon" color of the cured fruit in the stores.

Lime. Only two types of lime are grown in Florida, the seedless Tahiti or Persian and the seedy Key or Mexican. The latter is satisfactory only on the coastal islands, so that peninsular gardens chiefly have the Tahiti. The large lemon-like fruits are harvested and used while the skin is dark green, although at full maturity they would turn yellow. Fruit matures at all seasons, with the main crop in summer. Lime trees are small and may be spaced much closer than orange trees. No named varieties have been segregated within the Tahiti type.

Lychee. Suited to much the same growing conditions as the orange, except for being a little less hardy to cold, the lychee is a popular fruit in Florida. The fruits are bright red, about an inch in diameter, with a thin, brittle rind enclosing a white, juicy pulp of delicious flavor around a large brown seed. The crop matures in June. Most lychee trees in Florida are of the Chen (Brewster) variety. Newly planted trees need more than average protection from wind and sun for the first year, but culture is easy thereafter and pests are few. Especially notable is resistance of lychee to burrowing nematode.

Mango. Not so satisfactory in the southern Ridge section as avocados and limes, the mango thrives in the coastal areas of the southern section as far north as Cocoa. Trees are large and need plenty of room. A sequence of varieties can be planted to supply fruit from May to September. For home use, the fruit can be allowed to color fully on the tree or to drop on the ground if it is well mulched. The chief problem is selection among the many fine varieties available, although the trees require regular spraying for pest control. Zill, Irwin or Kent, and Keitt give a sequence of varieties with handsome color and fine flavor. Some varieties of very good flavor lack brillant color. Edward and Carrie are midseason examples worthy of garden space. Cambodiana and Cecil are varieties without red color which also lack the richness of flavor of Indian mangos but have delicious taste in a subacid flavor. They mature with Zill. Borsha and Paheri are old varieties unsurpassed in flavor for the Indian types, but they do not bear regularly enough for commercial culture. Fruit setting of mango seems to be favored by presence of bees at blooming.

Orange. There is not a great deal of difference in hardiness to cold among orange varieties, but not all are equally satisfactory for the colder areas. Late varieties like Valencia are not ready to harvest until after all winter cold is past, and so run maximum risk of crop loss. Temple oranges, which are hybrids and not true oranges, are more tender to cold than are oranges. Earliest to mature is a new hybrid, the Page, which peels easily like the Temple and has few seeds. It can be picked in late October. Few-seeded Hamlin and seedy Parson Brown are ready in early November usually. Midseason varieties are represented by Pineapple (seedy) and Jaffa (few-seeded), and by the seedy Temple, which has a distinctive flavor. Valencia is the principal late variety, maturing in spring and summer. Oranges have no ripening period but gradually reach an acceptable stage of maturity which changes very slowly to overmaturity over several months. Consequently, one tree each of Hamlin, Pineapple, and Valencia may furnish fresh fruit continually from November to August. In northern Florida the Washington navel orange is very satisfactory as an early variety, and it is occasionally grown in central Florida. The only satisfactory criterion of maturity of oranges for home use is the taste, as rind color does not necessarily indicate palatability. Orange trees require regular spraying for the control of insect and disease pests.

Oriental persimmon. Among the attractive and tasty autumn fruits, the kaki, or Oriental persimmon, takes a prominent place in northern Florida gardens, and to a less extent in central Florida. The chief handicap is the relatively short life of the trees, for reasons not yet fully understood. The variety Tanenashi is most commonly grown, as it requires no pollination and is always seedless. Fuyugaki also fruits well by itself and is seedless if unpollinated. It has the distinction of being the only variety which can be eaten while still firm; all others contain astringent tannins until fully soft-ripe. Okame is a variety of superior flavor but requires a pollinating variety (Gailey) to assure a set of fruit in some seasons. Being deciduous all winter, persimmons are fully hardy anywhere in the state.

Papaya. In the warmest parts of the state it may be possible to have a ripe papaya almost any morning in the year from a few plants. One may grow either unisexual plants, some of which bear fruit, while others only provide necessary pollen, or bisexual plants, all of which bear fruit and most of which also produce pollen. If the unisexual type is grown, only one male plant need be left in a small patch of a dozen fruiting plants. Blue Solo (bisexual) is one of the most satisfactory varieties, but it is difficult to find reliable sources of seeds or seedlings of any named varieties. Sanitation—burying infected or infested fruits —is an important means of pest control with papayas. Only occasional spraying is necessary as unusual need arises, but bagging young fruits prevents fruitfly infestation. Virus diseases, for which there is no cure, are serious handicaps.

Peach. Varieties popular in more northern states are not

satisfactory in Florida because of inadequate winter chilling, and even varieties suitable for northern Florida are not satisfactory in southern Florida for the same reason. Red Ceylon and Okinawa are suitable for the southern area, maturing in early June. Flordawon in late April and Jewel in late May are adapted to central Florida. In the north-central area, Flordahome in late May and Tejon in early May are satisfactory. In the Panhandle region, adapted varieties include Earligold in early May, Maygold in late May, Flordaqueen in early June, and Suwanee in mid-June. Tejon, Earligold, and Maygold are clingstone. The serious pest, root-knot nematodes, can be avoided by having trees budded on Okinawa stocks. Larvae of plum curculio make wormy peaches if timely spraying is not done. Borers often attack and kill young trees, but are easily controlled by spraying trunk bases in late summer with Thiodan. Life of peach trees is rather short but they begin bearing very early, often yielding a good crop the second year.

Pear. As is true with peaches, northern varieties of pear are not suited to Florida; the reason is partly winter chilling but even more largely due to fire blight disease. This attacks all the good dessert varieties of pear in Florida, and most of the resistant varieties are of low quality except for canning. Pineapple is blight-resistant and well adapted, and bears fruits of good canning quality, but is inedible as fresh fruit. Hood is a pear of fair quality which grows here fairly well, but fruits break down readily on the inside unless they are picked before ripe and softened at 65° to 70°. Le Conte and Baldwin are also fair in quality and fairly resistant to blight. It is better not to fertilize pears very heavily.

Pecan. These trees require considerable room, comparable to that for laurel oaks, but provide tasty nuts in addition to summer shade and require minimum maintenance. Curtis, Desirable, and Elliott are good varieties for home planting.

Pineapple. On the acid sandy soils of the east coast and the southern Ridge, the varieties Abakka, Smooth Cayenne, Natal Queen, and Red Spanish can all be grown successfully where temperatures are not too low. On the calcareous soils of the lower east coast, the variety Pernambuco (Eleuthera) is more satisfactory. Fertilizer for pineapples should be very low in phosphorus, such as 4-1-4 or 8-2-10 analyses. Slips or crowns planted in the fall will have mature fruit the second summer after planting, but large suckers set out in the spring may fruit in a little over a year. The normal fruiting season is June to August, but by treatment with calcium carbide or certain plant hormones it is possible to bring plants into bearing out of season. Mealybugs and red spider mites are serious pests and hard to control. If possible, buy slips which have been dipped in demeton. Infestations on established plants may be sprayed with malathion to which wettable sulfur has been added.

Pitanga. Widely grown for its ornamental value, this shrub bears attractive and tasty red or black fruits which are enjoyed both fresh and in jellies.

Plum. This is another temperate zone fruit, for the best varieties of which Florida is too warm in winter. Certain hybrids of native plums with imported kinds have given us the Excelsior variety, most commonly grown in northern Florida. Another hybrid, the Methley, is of better quality and seems well adapted to the same area. The plum curculio causes wormy fruit and must be controlled by timely spraying. The ripening season is May and June.

Sapodilla. In the warmest section of the state this tropical fruit is seen in home-ground plantings. Large-fruited types, such as Modello and Russell, are available at nurseries. The tree is handsome and has few pests. Sapodillas do not change color at ripening, which is recognized by the softening of the fruit.

Satsuma. Belonging to a different species than the sweet orange, the satsuma is one of the Mandarin group. The tree is dwarfed on the usual rootstock, and is more hardy to cold than the orange, so that it can be grown in the northern part of the state with fair success. Owari, the variety usually grown in Florida, is mature from late October to Christmas. Culture is the same as for oranges.

Strawberry. In Florida the strawberry blooms and fruits in winter and spring, and few varieties are adapted. Florida 90 is best known, but Torrey is as good in quality and heavier in yield, and both Daybreak and Fresno are superior in both quality and yield. Plants are set out in rows in early October usually, and begin to bear in December or January, continuing for several months. A new planting should be made each fall, to reduce pest problems. In the northern half of the state it is usually necessary to cover plants with pine straw or newspaper during temperatures below freezing to avoid injury to flowers and fruits.

Tangelo. This is a group of hybrids between tangerine and grapefruit. Minneola is the best variety, looking like a very large Dancy tangerine and maturing in February and March. Orlando matures in November, and Seminole in December. Tangelos are generally very juicy with distinctive flavors. Culture is the same as for oranges.

Tangerine. Adapted to the same conditions as oranges, tangerines are in the Mandarin group. Dancy is the variety best known, with dark red rind color, and matures in winter. Earliest maturing is a hybrid tangerine, Robinson, also red in color, which can be picked in late October. Ponkan, with larger fruits of yellow-orange hue, is edible in November.

16

Vegetables in the Garden

To A PAST GENERATION the word "garden" usually connoted first of all the area in which vegetables were grown. Today, for suburban gardeners at least, this is likely to be a secondary meaning; but for many Floridians there is still much interest in growing vegetables for home use. One important reason is that home-grown vegetables may be harvested at the peak of their eating quality instead of gathering them enough earlier to get them to market in firm condition. Such freshly harvested vegetables of superior quality not only taste better, but they are more nutritious and healthful, especially in vitamin content. Apart from this aspect of vegetable gardening are the sheer enjoyment which many people obtain from growing vegetables and the pride in production of fine specimens. Nor is the healthful and pleasant exercise offered by a vegetable garden to be overlooked.

To obtain the above benefits from a vegetable garden, certain fundamental principles must be observed. Planting too large a vegetable area should be avoided, as a sure means of destroying pleasure and inducing discouragement. An area 10 ft. square may supply sufficient leafy greens for a family of four or five, while an area 60 x 30 ft. may provide all the vegetables such a family can eat except potatoes, if properly planned and tended. Only good soil should be planted in vegetables—well-drained, of good tilth, and of good organic matter content. Provision for watering the plants is an absolute necessity. The varieties planted must be adapted to the section and the season. Finally, the garden will produce satisfactory crops only if it receives constant, almost daily, care to provide cultivation, fertilization, irrigation, and pest control as needed. But then, if such activities are burdensome, you should not try to garden anyhow.

The garden location should be near the kitchen if possible, but there are more important considerations. It is difficult to use satisfactorily a piece of ground with much slope. If the area is not fairly level, then rows should run at right angles to the slope to decrease erosion. On fairly level ground, rows running north and south get the best use of the sun. It is not worthwhile trying to grow vegetables under the shade of trees. They need at least a full half day of sun, and all day is better. Root competition from trees and large shrubs growing nearby can seriously stunt the growth of vegetables. If the planting must be close to big woody plants, then all roots from them should be cut to a depth of 16 in. along the side of the garden nearest them. This will have to be repeated annually. Rabbits are likely to be very troublesome unless a fence of chicken wire 24 in. high surrounds the garden.

Not all vegetables are equally worth the time and care of the gardener, except for the enjoyment he may take in producing them. Potatoes, sweet potatoes, and watermelons require fairly large areas to produce significant quantities and so are not well suited for the small home garden. These vegetables, as well as cabbages, celery, and onions, are available all year on the local market in very good quality, since they are not harvested less mature for commercial shipment than for home use. It is the vegetables which deteriorate in quality rapidly after being picked, or which are shipped before they are fully ready to eat, which are most satisfactorily grown in the home garden.

Some of these, in turn, require too much space for small gardens. No vegetable is more appreciated fresh from the home garden, as compared to what can be bought, than peas or sweet corn, both of which deteriorate rapidly in quality unless put at once in the refrigerator after harvesting in the cool of the morning. But it is not worth while planting less than 20 ft. of each, and 40 ft. every ten days is needed for adequately supplying a small family. Melons (cantaloupes) and squash spread out small garden. On the other hand, a single 10-ft. row will supply widely and require space out of proportion to their yield in the radishes or pot greens for several months, and will do the same for peppers, eggplants, or okra, while two such rows of tomatoes will give a fair supply for a month or more.

Some vegetables listed hereafter require a choice among two or three kinds of which only one need be grown in any one garden. Thus chard, collards, and spinach serve exactly the same role at the same time of year. For Florida, spinach is probably the least satisfactory of these. Cabbage and Chinese cabbage are too similar for both to be desirable in the same garden. Endive and leaf lettuce are similarly used, and escarole is a type of endive. Since some families will prefer one and some the other of these duplicating types, directions are given for growing all of them; those vegetables which the family likes best should be grown.

Almost any garden soil can be used for vegetables if it is well drained, but not all will give equally good results. Loams, especially silt loams and fine sandy loams, are the best, but are scarce in Florida. Sandy soils are usually well drained—too well, often—but are lacking in mineral nutrients. Liberal incorporation of organic matter improves both water-holding and nutrient-supplying properties of sands. Most garden vegetables thrive on loams near neutrality or even of slight alkalinity on the heavier soils, but sandy soils should be slightly acid, pH 6 being best.

In a suburban or farm home grounds, it may be feasible to change the location of the garden each year, but on the usual city lot there will be no choice in this matter. After vegetables have been planted for a few years on the same ground, there is usually built up a large population of soil pests which greatly reduce plant vigor. For the city garden, at least, the only practicable solution of this problem is to fumigate the garden soil every two or three years. Either the whole area may be fumigated at once, choosing the time when there is the least use being made of the ground, or each row may be treated at the same time as fertilizer is applied. The former method is preferred but makes a big chore when it must be done. (See p. 340 for discussion of materials and methods.)

One important factor in vegetable gardening, as in the very similar culture of annual flowers, is planning for most efficient utilization of the available space. Unlike shrubs or herbaceous perennials which occupy a given area permanently, a vegetable crop needs space for only part of the year. A sequence of plantings should be planned, both to give successive harvesting of any single vegetable over as long a time as possible, and to assure the maximum use of the garden space as seasons change by following one kind of crop by another.

Two points need emphasis here. One is the desirability of setting aside a block of space for successive plantings of a single kind of vegetable. If four plantings are to be made of snap beans, each 20 ft. long, in rows 18 in. apart, then a block 20 x 6 ft. (or 40 x 3 ft.) should be allotted to snap beans. The other point is that it is undesirable to replant a given crop on the same ground. Almost any other crop may follow except one closely related. If possible, do not plant in succession carrots, beets, and turnips, members of the cabbage family (broccoli, cabbage, Chinese cabbage, collards, turnip), tomato relatives (pepper and eggplant), or beans (snap, lima, pole, and cowpea). Sometimes a related crop cannot be avoided, but an effort should be made to plan for avoiding it.

Some vegetables thrive in cool weather, whereas others need considerable warmth for good growth. Summer is the season when vegetable growing is most difficult in Florida, although some kinds may be grown then. In the northern part of the state, the spring season is the principal one for vegetables, with a secondary period in autumn. In southern Florida, the vegetable season runs from September to May or later, and all kinds are grown together, both warm season and cool season. The letter C or W after each crop name in the following discussion indicates cool or warm season adaptation.

Seeds are planted in shallow furrows, preferably made along a stretched cord to assure straight rows. The depth of the furrow

Timing, Quantities, and Spacing of Vegetables in the Home Garden

	Interval Between Plantings	Quantities for Each Planting				Inches at Planting		
		Feet of Row	*Amount of Seed*	*Plants or Sets*	*Cups of Fertilizer*	*Between Seeds or Plants*	*Between Rows*	*Depth of Seed*
Beans, Snap	2 weeks	20	3 tbsp.	——	4	2½	18	1½
Beans, Pole	5 weeks	20	3 tbsp.	——	6	*	42	1½
Beans, Lima	4 weeks	15	1 tsp.	——	4½	4	24	1½
Beets	4 weeks	10	¼ tsp.	——	1	2	12	¾
Broccoli	4 weeks	10	1/12 tsp.	——	3	2	24	½
Broccoli (plants)	4 weeks	10	——	6	3	17	24	——
Cabbage	4 weeks	10	1/12 tsp.	——	3	2	24	½
Cabbage (plants)	4 weeks	10	——	6	3	17	24	——
Cabbage, Chinese	4 weeks	10	1/12 tsp.	——	3	2	18	½
Carrot	4 weeks	10	¼ tsp.	——	1	¼	12	½
Chard	3 months	10	½ tsp.	——	1	2	18	¾
Collards	3 months	10	1/12 tsp.	——	2	2	24	½
Collards (plants)	3 months	10	——	7	2	15	24	——
Corn, Sweet	10 days	40	2 tbsp.	——	8	*	36	1
Cowpeas	4 weeks	20	2 tsp.	——	2	6	24	1½
Eggplant	3 months	10	——	4	2	30	(36)	——
Endive	2 weeks	10	⅛ tsp.	——	1½	½	12	½
Lettuce	2 weeks	15	⅛ tsp.	——	2	¾	12	½
Melon	2 weeks	20	¼ tsp.	——	4	*	72	¾
Okra	2 months	10	½ tsp.	——	1	1½	36	1½
Onions, Green	4 weeks	10	——	½ cup	2	2	12	1½
Peas	2 weeks	40	⅓ cup	——	4	2	9-24	1½
Pepper	(once)	6	——	4	⅓	18	(24)	——
Radish	2 weeks	4	¼ tsp.	——	½	¾	12	¾
Spinach	2 weeks	10	¼ tsp.	——	2	2	18	¾
Spinach, New Zealand	(once)	25	1 tbsp.	——	5	(6)	(24)	1
Squash	4 weeks	10	1 tsp.	——	3	*	48	1
Tomato	4 weeks	15	——	10	3	18	36	——
Turnip	4 weeks	10	¼ tsp.	——	1	1	12	½

tsp. = teaspoon   tbsp. = tablespoon   *See Cultural Suggestions varies with kind of seed, type of soil, and season. The smaller the seed, the shallower it must be placed; the lighter the soil (i.e., the sandier), the deeper the planting; and in dry weather plant a little deeper than in rainy seasons. The depth suggested for each seed is an average value for Florida sandy soils. After scattering the seed or spacing it carefully in the bottom of the furrow, cover it with a slight mounding and press the surface level. Try to keep the soil moist but not wet until seedlings appear.

Transplanting of those crops not planted in the field as seed should be done on a cloudy day or late in the afternoon on a sunny day. Shade the transplants for a few days by a shingle pushed into the ground on the south side of the plant, or by a newspaper tent along the row, the edges covered with soil. A transplanting solution often helps plants get started into growth sooner. Use a commercial preparation such as Hyponex at recommended dilution, and pour 1 cup of this solution around each transplant after firming it in place.

The sandy soil of Florida gardens needs complete fertilizers for growing succulent vegetables, for quality is poor if growth is stunted by low fertility. The best general recommendation is to apply fertilizer along the row about ten days before planting seed or setting transplants, in a band about a foot wide. Spread it as evenly as possible, and then hoe it into the soil so that it is well mixed with the top 6 in. In discussing each kind of vegetable the amount of fertilizer of the usual 4-7-5 analysis for the stated feet of row is given in measuring cup units. For a 6-6-6 analysis, use two-thirds as much. Mixing liberal amounts of well-decomposed organic matter into the garden soil is a most desirable preliminary to planting and should be done a month in advance. Spread the compost, manure, or leaf mold to a depth of 4 in., and mix it thoroughly into the top foot of soil. Crops grown on sandy soils for several months need supplemental applications of fertilizer as side-dressings. Usually these are of nitrogen alone but sometimes of complete mixtures. After heavy rains, which leach nitrogen from sandy soils, side-dressings of nitrogen are helpful in keeping plants vigorous.

CULTURAL SUGGESTIONS FOR EACH VEGETABLE

The vegetables discussed and our planting directions are for small home gardens where space is limited and the work will be done by hand. Wider spacing of rows would be needed for machine cultivation.

The table on page 310 presents needed information about how much to plant at what interval of time in order to have a continuous supply of each vegetable, during the part of the year when it can be grown, in quantity adequate for an average family of four. It is not expected that every one will wish to have a continuous supply of even a few vegetables, let alone that any one will try to grow all of the kinds listed, but the information is given for those who may want it. The period from planting to first harvest is average; it will be a few days longer in the cooler part of the season of each crop and a few days shorter in the warmer part of that season. The charts at the end of this chapter indicate when to plant each crop in different areas of the state, and when harvesting can be expected. The dashes (---) indicate the length of the period for planting, and S, B, and T indicate most desirable planting times for a sequence; s indicates a possible, but hazardous, very early planting.

Beans, Snap or Bush (W). These grow readily in almost any well-drained garden soil and should give several pickings from each planting. One-half pound of seed makes five of the plantings suggested. Do not let pods get too mature, and do not pick them when vines are wet. Picking should be done every three days. Recommended varieties are Contender (45 days), Extender (46 days), and Wade (48 days).

Beans, Pole (W). Pole beans take longer to reach bearing age than bush beans, but yield more heavily and longer. They need stakes to support the vines. Use stakes (1½ x 1½ pine) or bamboo poles 8 ft. long, set 1½ ft. in the ground. Plant the seeds in hills 18 in. apart, placing six seeds 2 in. deep in each hill, and when the plants are 6 in. high, thin to the best two plants per hill. Set a stake midway between each two hills and train a vine from each hill around it. Pole beans should be planted on the north edge of the garden if the rows run east and west, and may be trained on a fence there. One-half pound of seed makes five plantings. For long continued production it is necessary that no pods be allowed to reach maturity. Pick them every three days. Recommended varieties are Florigreen and Dade, both maturing in 65 days.

Beans, Lima (W). Lima beans are even slower to bear than pole beans, but like them they continue bearing for several weeks. More sensitive to cold, they must be started later in the spring. Setting of pods is poor when temperatures are over 90°F., and pod rot is common in warm, rainy weather. Thin plants to stand about a foot apart when they are 4 in. high. Pick as indicated for pole beans. Large-seeded limas will need 3 tbsp. of seeds and small-seeded ones only 1 tbsp. for each planting. Recommended varieties are Fordhook 242 (large seed, 72 days) and Henderson (small seed, 65 days).

Beets (C). Beets are grown chiefly for the fleshy roots, but the tender tops are often enjoyed as greens. The "seeds" are actually fruits with several seeds in each. Germination will be hastened if the "seeds" are soaked for 24 hours in water before planting. Thin the seedlings when 4 in. high to stand 4 in. apart. Do not let the roots become old enough to be woody. Recommended varieties are Early Wonder (56 days) and Detroit Dark Red (68 days).

Broccoli (C). Broccoli is easy to grow and is high in vitamin value. Follow the cultural directions for cabbage, of which it is just a form. Recommended varieties are Early Green Sprouting (70 days), Atlantic (65 days), and Waltham 29 (60 days). Each of these is available in seasonal strains. Medium season strains are fairly satisfactory everywhere in Florida, but early strains are a little better in the northern area and late strains in the southern area.

Cabbage (C). Cabbage seed is usually sown in flats or seedbeds and transplanted to the garden when the plants are 4 or 5 in. high. In Florida this is recommended for fall and winter plantings, but from July to October seeds may be sown directly in garden rows. When seedlings are 4 in. high, thin them to 18 in. apart. Cabbages need a high level of fertilizing for rapid growth to make succulent leaves. When plants are two months old, side-dress with nitrate of soda, applying 1 tbsp. along each side of the 10 ft. of row. Repeat this a month later. Seedlings for transplanting are available in season at seed stores and garden centers. Recommended varieties are Marion Market and Badger Market for green leaves, and Red Acre for red leaves. All of these require about 110 days from seed or 75 days from transplants.

Cabbage, Chinese (C). This Oriental cabbage relative, sometimes called celery cabbage, matures more quickly than cabbage and makes tall, cylindrical heads. Its culture is very similar to that of cabbage. Thin the seedlings when 4 in. high to stand 8 in. apart. Only a single side-dressing will be needed. Michihli (70 days) is the only recommended variety.

Carrot (C). Carrots are notably high in vitamin A. Seed is sown rather thickly and the seedlings thinned when 2 in. high to stand 3 in. apart. Harvest the largest roots when they are an inch or so in diameter at the top, and let the others come on for later use. Recommended varieties are Red Core Chantenay and Nantes, both maturing in about 70 days, and Imperator, 75 days.

Chard (C). Chard, often called Swiss chard, is just a variety of beet which develops a great mass of leaves with no fleshy root. However, it thrives in hot weather better than beets, and so can be grown as a pot-herb over a very long period, like collards. Chard is used for the same purpose as spinach or collards, but is more tasty to many people than either of these. Soak the "seed" as for beets, and when seedlings are 4 in. high, thin them to 1 ft. apart. Two months after planting side-dress as for cabbage, and repeat a month later. Pick the outer leaves frequently as they reach full size. Recommended variety is Fordhook Giant (68 days).

Collards (C). This non-heading cabbage is a reliable source of greens over much of the year as it endures both heat and cold, although growing better in cool weather than warm. Thin seedlings to 16 in. apart when they are 4 in. high. Culture is like cabbage; harvest like chard. A single packet of seed will make five plantings. Recommended varieties are Georgia or its improved strain Georgia 912, both maturing in about 50 days from transplants or 80 days from seed.

Corn, Sweet (W). To assure good pollination it is best to plant at least two rows together. Thus 40 ft. of row should be planted as two rows of 20 ft., or even better as four rows of 10 ft. in a solid block. Make hills 1 ft. apart in the row and plant three seeds in each hill. When seedlings are 6 in. high, thin to leave only the strongest one in each hill. When plants are a foot high, side-dress with 1 tbsp. of nitrate of soda along each side of each 10 ft. row. Five plantings can be made from ¼ lb. of seed. Corn earworm is the major pest and is controlled by dusting DDT on the silks as soon as they emerge. A few days after the silks turn brown the ears will be ready to pick. Kernels should be well filled and full size, but should still spurt milk when punctured by the thumb nail. Pick corn in the cool of the morning and put the ears at once in the refrigerator. They will remain in good eating condition thus for two or three days. Recommended varieties are yellow Golden Cross Bantam, Golden Security, and white Silver Queen, all maturing in about 75 days.

Cowpeas (W). Cowpeas are really beans rather than peas. The forms used as human food are often called "conch-peas" and "black-eyed-peas," and recently "Southern-peas." They are among the few vegetables which thrive in Florida summers. When seedlings are 4 in. high, thin them to about 9 in. apart. Harvest the pods as soon as the green color begins to change to yellow (or purple in some varieties); only the seeds are eaten, not the pods. Pick every other day. Recommended varieties are Blackeye, Producer, Topset, and Dixie Lee, all maturing in about 70 days.

Eggplant (W). Since four plants will supply enough fruit, the smallest quantity of seed you can buy will be far more than can be used in a year—hence the preference for buying plants rather than growing them. If it seems unlikely that plants will be available, sow 20 seeds ½ in. deep and ½ in. apart in a 6-in. flower pot about two months before the first transplanting date.

Keep the pot in a warm room in a window, well watered, and when seedlings are 3 in. high, thin them to the best six plants. This will give four to use and two for replacement. Transplant when 6 to 8 in. high. Side-dress with ½ cup per plant of 4-7-5 when the first fruits are half-grown. The recommended variety is Florida Market, maturing 75 days from transplanting.

Endive (Escarole) (C). This lettuce relative is a popular salad green also. It was formerly the custom to blanch the center leaves, which reduced both the nutritive value and the bitterness of the leaves, but in tossed salads the green leaves are satisfactory. Thin the plants to 10 in. apart when they are 3 in. high. For blanching, tie the outer leaves together when the center ones are well developed. It will take about two weeks for them to blanch to creamy white. Recommended varieties are Deep Heart Fringed and Full Heart Batavian, both maturing in about 70 days.

Lettuce (C). Both head and leaf lettuce can be grown in home gardens, but the leaf type is recommended for beginners. It is easier to grow, matures sooner, is more flavorful, and has a higher vitamin content than head lettuce. When plants are 3 in. high, thin them to 6 in. for leaf types or 12 in. for head types. For early fall planting, seeds will sprout better if placed between folds of wet cloth in a tight container placed in the refrigerator for four or five days before planting. Lettuce must grow rapidly to be tender, and if growth is slow, a tablespoon of nitrate of soda may be used as side-dressing on each side of the 15-ft. row. Recommended variety is Salad Bowl (45 days) as a leafy type or Great Lakes 118 (85 days) for head lettuce.

Melons (W). Muskmelons or canteloupes are suitable only in rather large gardens. Space hills 4 ft. apart, planting six seeds in each hill, spaced 3 in. apart around a circle 6 in. in diameter. When the seedlings have four leaves, thin to the strongest two in each hill. When they are a month old, side-dress with ½ cup of 4-7-5 per hill, spread thinly in a circle about a foot from the plants. Harvest when the melons have developed some yellow color and a noticeable aroma. At this stage a crack begins to form where stem joins fruit, so that it "slips" easily. Check fruits every two or three days for maturity. Sometimes melons exposed to the sun are injured by the heat; this can be avoided by placing a handful of grass or pine straw across the fruit as it matures. Recommended variety is Smith's Perfect or Florisun, both about 90 days.

Okra (W). Okra plants thrive in summer heat and bear continuously for two or three months if pods are never allowed to mature. Soak seeds for 24 hours just before planting and discard any which do not swell. When plants are 3 in. high, thin them to stand 2 ft. apart. As plants begin to bloom, side-dress monthly with 1 tbsp. of nitrate of soda on each side of the 10 ft. of row. Pods are ready to harvest about six days after bloom, and should be picked every two or three days to assure tenderness. Recommended varieties are Clemson Spineless or Perkins Long Green, both about 54 days.

Onion (C). Mature onions are in your supermarket all year so only green onions are worth space in small gardens. Onion sets are much preferred to seed, as they produce edible onions much faster and are quite inexpensive. A pint of sets will suffice for a whole season usually. Onion rows must be kept very clear of weeds. Recommended varieties are Excel (yellow) and Texas Grano (white), although variety is a less important matter for green onions than for mature bulbs. The first edible green onions can be pulled in about 35 days.

Peas (C). Sometimes called English peas, this popular vegetable is available in frozen packages of good quality all year; nevertheless, the fresh product can be superior to frozen peas. It is better to plant two rows, 20 ft. long and 9 in. apart, than to plant 40 ft. in one row, because plants in the double row support each other. Allow 24 in. between double rows. Keep pods from becoming too mature by picking them every three days at least. If peas are not to be cooked at once, they should be stored in the refrigerator in the pods. Recommended variety is Little Marvel (52 days) or Emerald (54 days).

Pepper (W). A single planting of pepper usually suffices for a whole season, except in the southern area. If transplants are not available, seedlings may be grown as explained for eggplant.

Sidedress the plants with 1 tsp. per plant of 4-7-5 a month after setting them out, and repeat twice at monthly intervals. Green peppers are picked when fully sized but before any red color develops. Recommended varieties are Yolo Wonder and World Beater, both maturing in about 70 days from transplanting.

Radish (C). Radishes mature more quickly than any other vegetable. An ounce of seed will make continuous plantings for all season. When seedlings are 2 in. high, thin them to 1½ in. apart. They must grow rapidly to be succulent. Recommended varieties are Early Scarlet Globe and Cherry Belle, both ready in three weeks.

Spinach (C). Rarely hurt by Florida cold except when the plants are very small, spinach is sensitive to soil acidity and needs a pH of at least 6.5 for success. It was promoted once for its high iron content, but research has shown that the iron is not very readily available. In sandy soils it is hard to free spinach leaves from grit, so that chard or collards may be more satisfactory. An ounce of seed will suffice for all season. When plants are 3 in. high, thin them to 4 in. apart. Spinach needs lots of nitrogen and may benefit from side-dressing with a tablespoon of nitrate of soda when the plants are 6 in. high. The whole plant is harvested at once. Recommended varieties are Virginia Savoy, Dixie Market, and Hybrid 7, all maturing in about 38 days.

Spinach, New Zealand (W). This plant is not even remotely related to spinach but is so called because its leaves are used similarly. It has quite a different growth habit, spreading widely with many side shoots. These are cut off when they are a few inches long, and are followed by more, so that a plant remains productive for months. A packet of seed contains about 1 tbsp. These "seeds" (actually fruits as in beets) should be soaked in warm water for 24 hours just before planting. Plant three "seeds" close together every 18 in., and when seedlings are 3 in. high, thin to leave the best of the three. After plants are two months old, side-dress once a month with 1 tbsp. of nitrate of soda for each 10 ft. of row. Rows of other plants should be at least 2 ft. away. It takes about two months for plants to reach the first cutting stage. There are no varieties.

Squash (W). Only summer squash, technically a pumpkin, is considered here. Running squash vines take up entirely too much space for any but large gardens, but one may grow in small gardens either the small yellow squash, the long green marrows, or the round white pattypans as bush types. Make hills 2 ft. apart in the row and plant four seeds in each hill, spaced as discussed under melons. When seedlings are 3 in. high, thin them to two plants per hill. A packet of seed will make three plantings, and an ounce will make nine. Apply preplanting fertilizer at the rate of ½ cup per hill, spread over a circle of 2-ft. radius. Fruits should be picked regularly before they become too mature. Recommended varieties are Early Prolific Straightneck (42 days) for yellows, Cocozelle or Zucchini (45 days) for marrows, and White Bush Scallop (48 days) for pattypans. A semi-bush type of Table Queen (60 days) makes this popular acorn squash suitable.

Tomato (W). Every home gardener will want a few tomato vines, preferably staked and pruned to make best use of space. Set treated stakes of 1 x 1 pine about 5 ft. long a foot in the ground beside each plant when plants are 8 in. high. As they grow, pinch off any lateral branches and tie leaders loosely to the stakes with soft, thick twine every 6 in. Side-dress at monthly intervals with ⅔ cup of 4-7-5 for each 10 ft. If tomato plants are not available, as they almost always are, plant seed about five weeks before the first transplanting date, using sterilized soil. In ¼ tsp. are about 100 seeds. Sow 25 seeds in each of two 6-in. pots and thin them to ten seedlings per pot when they are 2 in. high. Transplant the best ten when they are 6 in. high. Tomato plants must be sprayed every week for control of diseases and insects. Fruits should be definitely pink before picking, but production will hold up longer if they are not left until eating ripe. Setting of fruit is poor when temperatures are above 85°F., so production is low in summer in Florida. A heavy organic mulch on the ground is especially good for tomatoes. The recommended varieties are Homestead 24 and Indian River (70 days) and Manalucie (80 days), times being from transplanting. Never use volunteer seedlings.

Turnip (C). Turnips may be grown over a long period for either roots or tops. Thin plants to 4 in. apart when they are 3 in. high. A packet of seed will make ten plantings. Recommended varieties are Purple-top White Globe for roots and Shogoin for green, both maturing in about 50 days.

PLANTING AND HARVESTING CHART FOR HOME VEGETABLE GARDENS IN NORTHERN FLORIDA

Vegetable Crop		Aug.	Sept.	Oct.	Nov.	Dec.	Jan.	Feb.	Mar.	April	May	June	July
Beans, Snap	*	S-	S-S						s-S-	S-S			
					xxxx	xx					xxxx	xxxx	
Beans, Pole	*								s-S-	S			
											xx	xxxx	xxxx
Beans, Lima	*								s-	S---			
												xxx	xxxx
Beets	*		S-	--S-	--S-	--S-	--S-	--S-	--S				
					xx	xxxx	xxxx	xxxx	xxxx	xxxx	xxxx		
Broccoli	*		S---	S---		T---	T---	T---	T-				
					xx	xxxx	xxxx	xxxx	xxxx	xxxx	xx		
Cabbage	‡		S---	S---		T---	T---	T---	T-				
					xx	xxxx	xxxx	xxxx	xxxx	xxxx	xxxx	xx	
Cabbage, Chinese	*			S---	S---	S---	S---	S-					
						xx	xxxx	xxxx	xxxx	xxxx	xx		
Carrot	*		S-	--S-	--S-	--S-	--S-	--S-	--S				
					xxxx	xxxx	xxxx	xxxx	xxxx	xxxx	xx		
Chard	*		S-	----	----	--S-	----	----	--S-				
					xx	xxxx	xxxx	xxxx	xxxx	xxxx	xxxx	xxxx	xxxx
Collards	*		S-	----	----	--S-	----	----	--S-				
					xxxx	xxxx	xxxx	xxxx	xxxx	xxxx	xxxx	xx	
Corn, Sweet	†								SSS	SS			
											xx	xxxx	xx
Cowpeas	*								S---	S---	S---		
											xxx	xxxx	xxxx
Eggplant	‡*									-T-			
		xx										xxxx	xxxx
Endive	*		-	S-S-					S-S-				
						xxxx	xx				xxxx	xx	
Lettuce	*		-	S-S-	S-S-				S-S-	S			
						xx	xxxx	xxxx			xx	xxxx	xx
Melon	†								S-S-	S			
												xxxx	xx
Okra	*								--S-	----	----	S	
		xxxx	xxxx								xxx	xxxx	xxxx
Onions, Green	*			B-	--B-	--B-	--B-	--B-	--B-	--B-	--B-		
					xx	xxxx	xxxx	xxxx	xxxx	xxxx	xxxx	xx	
Peas	†					S-S-	S-S-	S					
								x	xxxx	xxxx	xx		
Pepper	‡*								T---	-			
		xx									xx	xxxx	xxxx
Radish	*			S-S-	S-S-	S-S-	S-S-	S-S-	S-S-				
					x	xxxx	xxxx	xxxx	xxxx	xxxx			
Spinach				S-S-	S-S-	S-S-	S-S-	S-S-					
						xx	xxxx	xxxx	xxxx	xxxx	xx		
Spinach, New Zealand	*								-S-				
		xxxx									xx	xxxx	xxxx
Squash			S-							-S-	--S-		
					xxxx						xxxx	xxxx	
Tomato	‡*		T-						T---	T			
					xx	xx						xx	xxxx
Turnip	*		S-	--S-	--S-	--S		S---	S---	S---	S---		
					xxxx	xxxx	xxxx	xxx	xx	xxxx	xxxx	xxxx	xx

S=plant seeds   x=harvesting   T=set transplants   B=plant sets
* Recommended for small gardens.
† Recommended only for large gardens.   ‡ Transplants preferred to seeds.

Planting and Harvesting Chart for Home Vegetable Gardens in Central Florida

Vegetable Crop	Aug.	Sept.	Oct.	Nov.	Dec.	Jan.	Feb.	Mar.	April	May	June	July
Beans, Snap	*						--S-	S-S-	xxxx	xxxx		
Beans, Pole	*						S-	----	S-- xx	xxxx	xxxx	xx
Beans, Lima	*	xx					S---	----	S---	xx	xxxx	xxxx
Beets	*		S--- xxxx	S--- xxxx	S--- xxxx	S--- xxxx	S-- xxxx	S--- xxx				
Broccoli	*	S---	S---	xx	T--- xxxx	T--- xxxx	T--- xxxx	T--- xxxx	xxxx	xx		
Cabbage	‡	S---	S---	xx	T--- xxxx	T--- xxxx	T--- xxxx	T--- xxxx	xxxx	xx		
Cabbage, Chinese	*		S-	--S- xxxx	--S- xxxx	--S- xxxx	--S- xxxx	xxxx				
Carrot	*		S---	S--- xx	S--- xxxx	S-- xxxx	S--- xxxx	S xxxx	xxxx			
Chard	*		S--- xxxx	---- xxxx	---- xxxx	S--- xxxx	---- xxxx	---- xxxx	S-- xxxx	xxxx	xxxx	xxxx
Collards	*	S--- xx	---- xxxx	--S- xxxx	---- xxxx	---- xxxx	S--- xxxx	xxxx	xx			
Corn, Sweet	†						SSS	SSS	xx	xxxx	xx	
Cowpeas	*						S---	S---	S--- xxxx	xxxx	xxxx	
Eggplant	†‡*	xx					-T--			xx	xxxx	xxxx
Endive	*		S-S- xxxx	S-S- xxxx	S-S- xxxx	S-S- xxxx	S-S- xxxx	S xxx				
Lettuce	*		S-S- xx	S-S- xxxx	S-S- xxxx	S-S- xxxx	S-S- xxxx	S-S- xxxx	xxx			
Melon	†						S-S-	S-S-	x	xxxx	xxxx	
Okra	*	S- xxxx	xxxx	xxxx	xxxx			S---	---- x	--S- xxxx	---- xxxx	---- xxxx
Onions, Green	*	B- xx	--B- xxxx	-B- xxxx	--B- xxxx	--B- xxxx	--B- xxxx	--B- xxxx	-B- xxxx	xx		
Peas	†		S-	S-S- xxx	S-S- xxxx	S-S- xxxx	S-S- xxxx	S-S- xxxx	xxxx			
Pepper	†‡*						-T---		xx	xxxx	xxxx	xxxx
Radish	*		S-	S-S- xxx	S-S- xxxx	S-S- xxxx	S-S- xxxx	S xxxx	xx			
Spinach			S-	S-S- xxxx	S-S- xxxx	S-S- xxxx	S-- xxxx					
Spinach, New Zealand	*	xx					--S-		xx	xxxx	xxxx	xxxx
Squash	*	S- xxxx	--S- xxxx				--S-	--S-	xxxx	xxxx		
Tomato	†‡*	T---	T--- xx	xxxx			--T-	--T-		xxxx	xxxx	
Turnip	*		S---	S--- xx	S--- xxxx	S--- xxxx	S--- xxxx	S--- xxxx	S xxxx	xxxx		

S=plant seeds   x=harvesting   T=set transplants   B=plant sets

* Recommended for home gardens.

† Quality better from home gardens but need more space.

‡ Transplants preferred to seeds.

Planting and Harvesting Chart for Home Vegetable Gardens in Southern Florida

Vegetable Crop		Aug.	Sept.	Oct.	Nov.	Dec.	Jan.	Feb.	Mar.	April	May	June	July
Beans, Snap	*		S-	S-S-	S-S-	S-S-	S-S-	S-S-	S-S-				
					xxxx	xxxx	xxxx	xxxx	xxxx	xxxx	xxxx	xxx	
Beans, Pole	*		-S-				S ---	-- S -	--				
					xx	x			xxxx	xxxx	xxxx		
Beans, Lima	*		S--	----	----	S---	----	-S-	----				
						x	xxxx	xxxx	xxxx	xxxx	xxxx	xxxx	xxxx
Beets	*			S-	-S-	-S-	-S-	-S-					
						xx	xxxx	xxxx	xxxx	xxxx	xx		
Broccoli	*			S---	S---		T---	T---					
						xxxx	xxxx	xxxx	xxxx	xxxx			
Cabbage	‡			S---	S---		T---	T---					
						xxxx	xxxx	xxxx	xxxx	xxxx			
Cabbage, Chinese	*				S---	S---	S-						
							xx	xxxx	xxxx	xxxx			
Carrot	*			--S-	--S-	--S-	--S-	--S-					
						xxxx	xxxx	xxxx	xxxx	xxxx			
Chard	*			-S-	----	----	-S--	----	----	-S--			
						x	xxxx	xxxx	xxxx	xxxx	xxxx	xxxx	xxxx
Collards	*			S-	----	----	--S-	--					
						xxx	xxxx	xxxx	xxxx	xxxx	xxxx		
Corn, Sweet	†			S-				SSS	SSS	S			
						xx				xxxx	xxxx		
Cowpeas	*	xxx						S---	S---	S---	S-		
										xx	xxxx	xxxx	xxxx
Eggplant	‡*			T---	----	----	T---	----	--T-				
						xx	xxxx	xxxx	xxxx	xxxx	xxxx	xxxx	xxxx
Endive	*		----	S-S-	S-S-	S-S-	S-S-	S-S-					
						xxxx	xxxx	xxxx	xxxx	xxxx			
Lettuce	*			S-S-	S-S-	S-S-	S-S-	S-S-	S-S-				
						xx	xxxx	xxxx	xxxx	xxxx	xxxx		
Melon	†							S-S-	S-S-				
												xxxx	xxxx
Okra	*			S---	----	S		S---	----	S---	----	S-	
		xxxx	xxxx	xxxx	xxxx					x	xxxx	xxxx	xxxx
Onions, Green	*			B---	B---	B---	B---	B---	B---	B			
						xxxx	xxxx	xxxx	xxxx	xxxx	xxxx	xxxx	
Peas	†			S-	S-S-	S-S-	S-S-	S-S-	S-S-				
						xxxx	xxxx	xxxx	xxxx	xxxx	xxx		
Pepper	‡*			T---	----	----	T---	----					
						xx	xxxx	xxxx	xxxx	xxxx	xxxx	xxxx	xxxx
Radish	*				S-	S-S-	S-S-	S-S-	S-S-	S			
						xxx	xxxx	xxxx	xxxx	xxxx	xxx		
Spinach						S-S-	S-S-	S-S-					
						xxx	xxxx	xxxx	xx				
Spinach, New Zealand	*	xxx						S---	----	----	S		
										xxxx	xxxx	xxxx	xxxx
Squash				S---	S---	S---	S---	S---	S---	S-			
						xx	xxxx	xxxx	xxxx	xxxx	xxxx	xxxx	xx
Tomato	‡*		T-	--T-	--T-	--T-	--T-	--T-	--T-	--T			
					xxxx	xxxx	xxxx	xxxx	xxxx	xxxx	xxxx	xx	
Turnip	*				S---	S---	S---	S---	S-				
						xx	xxxx	xxxx	xxxx	xxxx	xxx		

S=plant seeds   x=harvesting   T=set transplants   B=plant sets
* Recommended for home gardens.
† Quality better from home gardens but need more space.
‡ Transplants preferred to seeds.

17

Garden Pests

Part of the price that Florida gardeners pay for their subtropical climate is that many garden pests flourish here with little natural check. Some of these pests are animals and some are plants; methods of control differ vastly for these two major divisions of living things.

ANIMAL PESTS OF PLANTS AND THEIR CONTROL

Insects far outnumber all other animals in numbers and diversity, and they naturally constitute the bulk of animal pests of plants. A few rodents are often troublesome in the garden, however, and far below insects in evolution, nematodes cause much garden injury.

Rodents

Moles, gophers, and squirrels are the rodents most often injurious in Florida gardens. They do not have definite host species but injure a wide variety of garden plants.

Moles do not deliberately eat plant parts, but in pushing their way through the soil in search of grubs and worms, they may cut some roots. More often they cause harm to plants by leaving roots exposed to air in their tunnels, or by raising sod unattractively and at the same time causing grass roots to dry out. The excellent tilth of a bed of annuals encourages worms to

324

live there, and moles have fun hunting them, to the detriment of the annuals. The surest control for moles is a good mole trap. Sometimes the family cat helps control this pest.

POCKET GOPHERS, frequently miscalled "salamanders" in Florida, are sometimes troublesome on deep, well-drained, sandy soils. They do not cause much injury by eating plants, but they throw up large, unsightly mounds of sand in the most undesirable places, and their tunnels may cause drying out of roots just as mole runways do. Gopher traps are the most certain control measure, but some gardeners swear by poisoned peanuts.

SQUIRRELS, protected by law and by public sentiment, are occasionally very destructive of camellia buds. Fruits of privet, holly, and firethorn are usually abundant enough so that feeding on these by squirrels does not cause serious objection; but when they eat the swollen flower buds of camellias, most gardeners rise up in righteous indignation. One simple method of protection, if squirrels in your neighborhood have developed this bad habit, is to cover twig tips with little mesh bags. Green, open-mesh cabbage bags, cut into 8-in. squares, can easily be sewn into small bags which can be fastened over twig tips with paper clips. While not decorative, mesh bags are effective and are easily removed when buds show color.

Nematodes

Species causing root-knot are most troublesome to the gardener, although other species cause damage also. Root-knot is due to infestation of plant roots by tiny nematodes or eel-worms of microscopic size. These multiply abundantly in the root tissue and cause abnormal swelling, so that often a root resembles a piece of twine with large knots tied at intervals. These organisms are particularly troublesome in light, sandy soils. Sterilizing garden soil before planting species subject to root-knot gives only temporary freedom from infestation and is more useful for annual beds than for perennials, whether woody or herbaceous. Maintenance of a heavy mulch over the area occupied by the roots of a plant helps to avoid root-knot. Some plants, such as gardenia, hibiscus, and wax privet, can be grafted on nematode-resistant stocks. This extra precaution seems more necessary in the southern part of the state than in the northern section. Drenching soil around infected plants with Nemagon or VC-13 (follow directions carefully) is often very helpful.

Insects and mites

Scientists make careful distinction between insects, which have six legs, and mites, which are related to spiders and have eight legs; but since mites are too small for gardeners to examine easily for leg count, and since they do damage similar to that caused by some insects and are similarly controlled, gardeners think of them as insects.

The hundreds of insect species that injure garden plants can be divided conveniently into two groups for our purposes. One group bites holes in leaves or eats away portions of leaves or stems—the biting and chewing insects. The other group consists of insects that either insert a tiny hypodermic proboscis into leaves and suck out cell sap, or rasp away the epidermis and lap up sap from exposed cells—the piercing, rasping, and sucking insects. The reason for grouping insects thus is that methods of control are somewhat determined by their feeding habits. Biting-chewing insects take pieces of plant tissue into their digestive tracts, and so can be controlled by stomach poisons sprayed or dusted on foliage or fruit. Piercing-rasping insects push through any surface deposit and take in only food from the interior of the leaf, flower, or stem. These must be controlled by contact poisons, which are absorbed through the body wall when in contact with some part of the insect, or by materials that have a smothering effect on the insect or give off a poisonous gas next to the insect.

Biting-chewing insects consist chiefly of the larvae (caterpillars, grubs, "worms") of moths, butterflies, and flies, grasshoppers and crickets, and beetles. Their damage is readily visible as soon as they begin to feed, and if the gardener is alert and observant, they can easily be checked before much damage is done. On the other hand, they can do a great deal of injury in a few days if not detected promptly. Tiny caterpillars that hatch out of eggs laid on leaves of a shrub or tree grow rapidly as they feed, and in a few days they can completely defoliate a large plant. Very often the insects feed at night and are not themselves in evidence when the gardener sees the damage, but it is enough to see that pieces of the plant are being eaten, to know what steps to take for control.

Caterpillars, worms, and beetles that feed on leaves, flowers, and fruits can usually be controlled readily with residual sprays of lead arsenate, DDT, lindane, malathion, or chlordane. Grasshoppers and mole-crickets yield better to chlordane. Cutworms, which cut off small seedlings in the seedbed or soon after they are set out in the garden, may be controlled by spraying the soil around the base of the plants with chlordane at double strength or by poisoned bait. All seed stores carry this material, which is applied at dusk around the seedlings. Cutworms feed at night and hide in the soil by day.

PIERCING-SUCKING INSECTS troublesome to garden plants are largely the scale insects and their kinfolks—aphids, whiteflies, and mealy-bugs—together with the true plant bugs. To these may be added the rasping-sucking thrips and mites, including red spiders. Usually the damage done by these insects is not readily visible until it has progressed to a considerable extent. Unless one examines the undersides of camellia leaves on each bush at monthly intervals, the pernicious tea scale may be widely established before yellow areas on the upper surface of leaves call attention to the presence of this pest.

SCALE INSECTS start as tiny crawlers no larger than a pencil dot, but after wandering around a few days, they settle down permanently to suck juice out of one spot and begin to cover themselves with a protecting scale. Adults may be anywhere from 1/32 to 1/8 in. in diameter, but always can be identified by the fact that slipping a penknife or needle under the edge of the scale allows it to be pried loose, exposing the soft body of the insect beneath. In the brief crawler stage, scale insects are easily killed, but the adult scales are hard to control because of their protective covering. Summer oils have long been depended upon for control, but cannot safely be used in cold weather or when temperatures run above 90°F. Malathion will control some scales, and its use is not limited by temperature. Cygon is even more effective.

APHIDS, or "plant lice," are tiny, soft-bodied insects that feed almost solely on tender, new growth only partly developed. They multiply rapidly and cause permanent stunting and often curling of young leaves. By the time curled leaves are evident, it is too late to remedy that situation, but it can stimulate a search for aphids on other shoots just pushing out from the buds. A wide variety of woody and herbaceous garden plants suffers from the activities of this pest. Aphid control is easy, and prompt action is all that is needed. For a few infested shoot-tips, dipping in soapy dishwater is sufficient. For more extensive or less accessible infestations, spraying with nicotine sulfate, pyrethrum, rotenone, cygon, or malathion gives prompt control.

WHITEFLIES are closely related to scales and look very similar when young. They never develop a scale covering, however, and the adults are conspicuous as the swarms of tiny, white insects, much like flies, which rise from disturbed branches of privet, gardenia, and other shrubs, especially in March, June, and September. The black film on the upper surface of leaves, made by the sooty-mold fungus that grows in the honey-dew secreted by larvae of white-flies, aphids, and soft scales, is often the first indication of need to spray. Control is easy, using summer oil, malathion, or cygon.

TRUE BUGS include such large pests as the big green stink bug or pumpkin bug and the harlequin bug, and such small pests as lace bugs and various mirids like the four-lined plant bug. The large ones can fly away quickly and have heavy body armor, so that they are often very hard to control. Chinch bugs so destructive to St. Augustine grass lawns are very persistent and hard to eradicate. Chlordane and sabadilla dusts control the tougher ones, while nicotine sulphate or rotenone kills the soft-bodied species.

THRIPS are tiny, yellow, winged insects hardly large enough to see without a magnifying glass, which move around rapidly. They cause discoloration of flower petals by their rasping and sucking, being especially troublesome on gladiolus and roses, but also spoiling the attractiveness of many other flowers. Flower thrips are at their worst in late spring and early summer, during warm, dry weather. Gladiolus thrips also cause silvery streaks on foliage, and weaken the corms during storage. Nicotine, rotenone, malathion, cygon, lindane, and dieldrin are all effective in controlling thrips when used frequently.

SPIDER MITES are too small for the naked eye to see easily, the common red spider being about 1/60 in. long. They are primarily pests of foliage, which turns gray or reddish-brown as the result of their feeding on cells of the upper epidermis. In addition to their unattractive appearance, such leaves are greatly reduced in food-making ability. Mites become very numerous in warm, dry weather, but are washed off the leaves by rain or spray from the hose or syringe. Rain or spray must come at least once a week to be effective in control, however, and hosing the foliage every two or three days is safer prevention. Sulfur dust, and sprays of Aramite, Tedion, chlorobenzilate, and Kelthane are effective in killing mites. Azalea, camellia, croton, camphor, rose, snapdragon, and chrysanthemum are especially infested.

ANTS of the leaf-cutting type sometimes cause trouble in citrus nurseries, and home gardeners need to control chiefly those ants that make unsightly nests in lawns. These are killed by sprinkling chlordane dust liberally around the entrance to the nests. Ants also plant and protect colonies of aphids and soft scales on new shoots of many shrubs and trees for the sake of the honeydew secreted by these insects. When ants are seen running up and down the trunks and branches of garden plants, it is well to examine carefully for an infestation of one of these.

PLANT PESTS AND THEIR CONTROL

Most plant diseases are due to the activities of microscopic plants called fungi and bacteria. There are also diseases due to viruses and to unfavorable soil conditions other than living organisms. Not the least troublesome of the plants that make life hard for the gardener are the large ones called weeds.

WEEDS have no special garden plants which they oppress, but are about equally harmful to all of them by competing with them for water, light, and mineral nutrients. Only dodder, rarely seen in gardens but often on roadsides, is actually parasitic. Gardeners pull or hoe weeds as they appear, or discourage them by heavy mulching. In lawns, however, it is possible to combat the non-grass weeds by spraying with herbicides, which must be used carefully according to the directions of the manufacturer. Drift to a neighbor's shrubbery may cause unpleasant relations, so great care is needed. It is better not to use a sprayer which has had weed killers in it for any other spray application, since minute amounts of these potent chemicals may injure plants being sprayed for insects or diseases. It is best to obtain advice from seed stores or garden centers on herbicides.

FUNGI cause a wide variety of plant diseases, attacking leaves, stems, and roots of garden plants, and occasionally flowers also. Most fungi develop wholly within the tissues of the host plant, and control must be based on preventing the spread of the organism to new plants or uninfected parts of plants, rather than on killing established fungi. Fungicides kill germinating spores before the fungus penetrates plant tissue, and must be present ahead of time. Mildews are exceptional in that the fungus growth remains mostly outside the leaf tissue, and therefore mildews are more easily controlled than most other fungi. A few fungi live in the soil, especially those causing damping-off, wilt, and stem rots. These can be controlled by sterilization of the soil with chemicals or steam, and to some extent by treating seeds or by watering seedlings with a solution of such fungicides as Spergon and Tersan. Those fungi causing disease of aerial parts of plants are checked by applying fungicidal sprays of many kinds, some of which are effective for a very wide range of diseases, as is true of Bordeaux mixture, while others are effective for a limited number of pests but control them very effectively with no injury to the host plant. Sulfur sprays for mildew and zineb for azalea petal-blight are examples.

DAMPING-OFF is the collapse of small herbaceous seedlings due to infection by various soil-borne fungi at the soil line.

Keeping soil too wet lowers the ability of plants to resist attack. Often the fungi kill tiny seedlings before they ever get above ground, so that it is hard to tell whether seeds had low germination or the seedlings were killed by damping-off. Shaking seeds in a jar or sack with Arasan is worthwhile and cheap insurance against the pre-emergence damping-off, so that seedlings have a chance to emerge from the soil. Planted in sterilized media, seedlings will grow vigorously, but when seeds are planted in garden rows or in flats of unsterilized soil, seedlings may be attacked. Methods of soil sterilization for seeds were discussed in Chapter Four. Damping-off of well-started seedlings may sometimes be prevented from spreading through a flat or bed in which it appears by drenching the soil with a dispersion of Spergon, Fermate, or equal parts of Fermate and Tersan.

LEAF-SPOTS are small areas of dead tissue on leaves resulting from attack by various fungi. These areas are sharply outlined and bear no relation to location of veins. On shrubs such as hibiscus and pittosporum the spread of this disfiguring disease is checked by spraying with copper or ferbam. Chrysanthemums often suffer severely from leaf-spotting, frequently causing old leaves to die and fall off, leaving only a few healthy leaves next to the blossoms. Hand picking of all spotted leaves as soon as observed helps prevent spread, and may be sufficient remedy if faithfully done. Weekly sprays with a copper compound, ferbam, or zineb will give good control. Many garden shrubs and herbaceous flowers suffer to some extent from leaf-spots, which may be similarly controlled.

BLACK-SPOT of roses, a leaf-spot disease, is the chief handicap to rose culture in Florida. The initial small, black spots rapidly enlarge, and the weakened leaf turns yellow and falls. The disease is active all through the year, but is most serious in the hot, humid weather of summer. Picking and destroying all infected leaves as fast as they appear is helpful, but fungicidal applications are needed also. Spraying every week or ten days with copper, sulfur, or ferbam, or dusting with sulfur will effect control. However, sulfur may cause injury when used during the heat of summer, and both ferbam and the usual copper sprays stain foliage and light-colored flowers unattractively, while non-staining copper sprays are somewhat troublesome to prepare. Phaltan is very effective. There are several good combination sprays and dusts which take care of all rose insect and disease pests at once. Ferbam and sulfur, together with lindane, makes an excellent all-purpose rose spray or dust.

POWDERY MILDEW is easily identified by the grayish-white coating that covers and disfigures foliage. Rose, hibiscus, crape-myrtle, chrysanthemum, marigold, snapdragon, and zinnia are particularly subject to attack. Fortunately powdery mildew is easily controlled by sulfur or copper, although some organic fungicides are not effective. Dusting with sulfur is the quickest procedure, but keep in mind that when temperatures run above 85° in the shade, sulfur may cause marginal injury to rose leaves. Acti-dione PM, used as directed, gives best and safest control.

CROWN ROT occurs at the base of the stem of many garden plants as the result of attack by fungi living in soil, often causing the plants to wilt and fall over. It may be of some permanent value to dig out the dead plants with as much soil from near them as possible, but the causal fungus will still remain in the garden soil. The only practical courses are to plant in that area of the garden only species not subject to crown rot, or to sterilize a small bed with Mylone or Vapam.

SOUTHERN BLIGHT is the most common of these basal stem rots, and all the following species are susceptible to attack if planted in infected soil: ageratum, amaryllis, aster (China-), caladium, calendula, calla, canna, carnation, chrysanthemum, cosmos, dahlia, delphinium, dianthus, gladiolus, hibiscus, holly-hock, hydrangea, larkspur, lupine, marigold, morning-glory, pansy, phlox, rose, rudbeckia, scabiosa, snapdragon, sweet-pea, and zinnia. If a garden becomes so thoroughly infected that none of these can be grown, the beds should be fumigated (see p. 340). Soil fumigants may seriously damage nearby shrubs and trees. Terraclor drenches are fairly effective controls. Fortunately southern blight is not very active in cool weather and is chiefly an affliction of summer gardens.

MUSHROOM ROOT-ROT, caused by a fungus which normally is parasitic on roots of oak and hickory, kills a great many woody plants in Florida gardens. When pieces of these roots remain in the soil when the land is cleared, the fungus may attack cultivated shrubs and trees. It requires several years for it to injure roots enough to be evident above ground, and often the mushrooms may appear on crown roots or trunk base before the top of the plant looks unhealthy. If roots on only one side are infected, as may be ascertained by digging away the soil carefully, dead roots may be cut off and removed, along with any pieces of oak roots, and the exposed crown left open to the air for a few weeks. Drenching the soil with Tersan may be helpful also. Among the plants reported as attacked by this disease are acalypha, Amazon-lily, azalea, casuarina, cherry-laurel, citrus, crape-myrtle, hamelia, hibiscus, holly, ixora, jacaranda, Jerusalem-thorn, jasmine, loquat, oleander, pittosporum, podocarpus, poinsettia, privet, queen palm, rose, turks-cap, viburnum, wax-myrtle, and Washington palm. Fortunately the disease is not very common, although widely spread.

PETAL BLIGHT of azaleas is by far the most serious disease of that shrub from the garden standpoint, although it does no harm to the plant itself. Starting as small white spots on colored petals, or as brown spots on white petals, blight causes petals to hang limp and slimy within a day or two, so that all the flowers on a bush look as if someone had poured boiling water over them. Flowers which fall to the ground carry the causal fungus over winter and start the disease again the next spring. It is rather futile to attempt to gather up all diseased flowers, because a very few that escape collection suffice to start the dread disease next year, and neighboring bushes can easily reinfect your flowers at blooming. Once petal blight appears, only regular application of effective sprays can make beautiful azalea blossoms certain, and the spray programs must be repeated annually. Plants blooming during dry weather may escape infection, but the first good rain will bring the blight. Spraying under high pressure must be done every three days, starting with first color and continuing as long as there are flowers. The most satisfactory fungicides for this disease are Acti-dione, zineb, thiram, and Dithane Z-78. Where there are many azaleas and good community cooperation, it would be more sure and less laborious to hire custom sprayers to treat entire neighborhoods, as mosquito control is now done in many cities.

BACTERIA are much less troublesome in landscape plantings than in commercial fruit and vegetable growing, and only one bacterial disease is common in Florida gardens. This is fire blight, which attacks pears, loquats, and firethorns. New shoots and blossom clusters in spring are infected chiefly, and are killed so quickly that they simply turn brown or black without the leaves falling. Once a twig is infected, the disease progresses down the branch, killing it as it goes, and may eventually kill the whole tree or shrub. Control consists in pruning off infected branches as soon as they are noted, making cuts several inches below any evidence of disease, as shown by dead bark. Final cuts should be made with knife or shears sterilized in denatured alcohol (95%).

VIRUS diseases are caused by substances inside plant cells that may or may not be independent organisms and that cannot live outside of plant cells except in insects. A common symptom of virus infection is a mottled green and yellow pattern of leaf surface, known as a mosaic, but not all viruses cause mosaic. Some merely cause yellowing of foliage, and others cause deformities of some sort, or merely constantly decreasing vigor. Variegated color in tulip flowers and camellia flowers and leaves is usually due to viruses that do not otherwise injure the plants. Yellows of China-aster, chrysanthemum, marigold, and zinnia, and mosaic of delphinium, larkspur, carnation, stock, and petunia are virus diseases seen in Florida gardens which are harmful to their hosts. Easter lilies sometimes suffer from two virus diseases, one a mosaic type and the other causing small flecks of dead tissue in the leaves. Many vegetables, such as squash, pepper, tomato, bean, and cucumber, suffer severe virus infections, and viruses cause several serious citrus diseases. Usually, the virus is transmitted from diseased to healthy plants by insects, chiefly aphids, but in camellias and citrus trees, budding or grafting transmits the virus. No spray is effective in eradicating a virus once it is inside a plant, but insecticides may prevent spread of virus infection by killing sucking insects that transmit it. The chief remedy for virus disease is prompt destruction of infected plants, called roguing. Usually initial infection comes from wild host plants, but Easter lilies may carry the virus in the bulb and chrysanthemum cuttings may carry the stunt disease. In these cases, the source of supply should guarantee freedom from virus. Only bean and petunia mosaic are known to be transmitted by seed.

CHLOROSIS is the condition in plants when healthy green color changes to yellow or white. Many different causes for chlorosis are known, and it is often difficult to know which one is operating in a given case. A deficient intake of nitrogen induces chlorosis, but this may be due to an actual shortage of nitrogen in the soil, to excessive soil moisture making roots unable to take in nitrogen, or to death of roots due to their attack by soil organisms. Deficiency of iron, zinc, magnesium, or manganese can also cause chlorosis. A very common chlorotic condition in Florida is that azaleas, gardenias, and ixoras are unable to obtain sufficient iron because the soil is not acid enough. Spraying foliage with a teaspoon of iron sulfate (copperas) in a gallon of water will give prompt recovery of green color, but this is only a temporary palliative. Use of sulfur dust to acidify soil was discussed in Chapter Three. Certain organic compounds called chelates make metals available in spite of unfavorable soil reaction. Chelated iron is marketed as sequestrene or ferro-green. Municipal water in most of Florida comes from limestone strata, and continued use of it makes soil neutral instead of acid in pots of azaleas and gardenias. These may be repotted in acid soil when they become chlorotic. All potted plants benefit from being placed in the rain so that accumulated salts are leached.

PESTICIDES FOR CONTROL OF INSECTS AND DISEASES

In years past the choice of a pesticide was relatively simple, as there were only a dozen or so from which to choose. Continually there appear on the market new chemical compounds for insect and disease control, and each of these compounds has as many trade names as there are manufacturers who prepare and package it. Not all pesticides are equally useful for the home gardener, although each has unusual potency for control of some special pest. In the following discussion only a few of the most widely useful pesticides are discussed; others not mentioned may be equally good. Ask your garden center or seed store manager for further help in selecting pesticides to use in your garden.

One feature of organic pesticides is worthy of note: they are often highly specific, controlling one pest well but not effective on another similar one. Lead arsenate will kill any kind of insect which eats it; DDT controls boll-worms but not leaf-worms of cotton. Copper is a good material for control of any fungus; ferbam is effective for leaf-spots but not for mildews. It is more important than formerly to know just how a pesticide acts on the particular pest that troubles your plants. Most modern insecticides combine the functions of stomach poison and contact poison. Lead arsenate and cryolite are strictly stomach poisons, and pyrethrum and nicotine are contact poisons, but malathion kills most insects that any of them control and some that they do not.

Insecticides.—Most insecticides are poisonous to humans as well as to insects, and organic ones are often very toxic if breathed or if spray stays on the skin for some time. Directions of the manufacturer as to dilution, dosage, and care in handling should be very carefully followed. Many homeowners prefer to leave control of pests to firms that specialize in this work.

CHLORDANE is one of the most effective materials for control of ants, plant bugs, chinch bugs, grasshoppers, and mole-crickets, and is as effective as anything else for thrips, cutworm, leaf-miners, caterpillars of all kinds, and beetles. It is usually marketed as a 5% dust, or a 50% wettable powder for sprays, used at the rate of 5 tsp. to a gallon of water.

CHLOROBENZILATE is one of the most effective controls for spider mites.

CYGON is especially recommended for control of tea scale of camellias, but it is a good material for general control of scales, aphids, thrips, and mites. Standard dosage is 2 tsp. of the 25% emulsion per gal. for most ornamentals.

DIAZINON controls sod webworms and household pests well.

DDT controls a wide range of garden pests—some beetles, caterpillars, leafhoppers, leaf-miners, thrips, and many others. However, it encourages mites and is often fatal to bees and other desirable wildlife. A 5% dust is often used, and in sprays the 50% wettable powder is used at 2 tbsp. per gal. Care is important that the dust is not breathed and that spray solution on skin is washed off quickly.

DIELDRIN controls chinch bugs, as a 5% dust or as a spray using 2 tbsp. of 15% emulsion per gal. Two gallons of this should be applied per 100 sq. ft. of lawn.

KELTHANE is very effective for spider mites.

LINDANE is the active principle in benzene hexachloride (BHC) and controls aphids, lace bugs, thrips, leaf-miners, and most caterpillars and beetles. It is used as a 1% dust or as a spray containing 1 tbsp. of 25% wettable powder per gal.

MALATHION has a wide range of use, killing scales, aphids, mites, leaf-miners, thrips, cutworms, and most beetles and caterpillars. A 5% dust is made, and for sprays the 25% wettable powder is used at 3 tbsp. per gal., or the 53% emulsifiable concentrate at 2⅓ tsp. per gal.

NICOTINE SULFATE has long been the standard insecticide for aphids, and is sometimes effective for thrips and lace bugs, especially in stronger concentration than usual. It is not effective in cool weather. It is usually marketed as Black Leaf 40, a 40% solution, which is diluted for sprays by using 1 tsp. per gal. To this should be added a detergent as a spreader.

SUMMER OILS give good control of scales and white-flies, aphids and mites. Only white summer oils, typified by Volck, are safe to use on foliage, and they may cause injury if applied in hot weather. Leaves sprayed with oil in early winter are more likely to be hurt by cold than unsprayed ones. Cygon and malathion are free from these objections, and widely used for scale control now, but oil is more effective when a thorough job of wetting is done.

TOXAPHENE is recommended for control of army worms and azalea defoliators.

Fungicides.—Most fungicides are not very toxic to humans, and little or no hazard to health is involved in their use. Formerly fungicides were usually made of some copper compound or of sulfur, either as free sulfur or a sulfide. Now there is a bewildering array of organic compounds.

ACTI-DIONE is a good, non-staining control for azalea petal blight and Acti-dione PM is very effective for powdery mildew of roses when used according to directions on the container. A mixture of Acti-dione and Terraclor, called Acti-dione RZ, is used at 1 tsp. per gal. as both flower spray and soil drench for better control of azalea petal blight.

ARASAN is a fungicide for general use in treating seeds against pre-emergence damping-off, without injury to seedlings. Seeds are simply coated with the dust by shaking in a closed container.

BORDEAUX MIXTURE, the oldest dependable fungicide, is still one of the best in its power to kill fungi. It has a depressing effect on plant growth in many cases, however, and leaves an unsightly residue on foliage, flowers, and fruit, which sometimes encourages increase of scale insects. It is effective in control of all fungus diseases attacking aerial parts of plants, and is usually employed in 6-6-100 formula, meaning 6 lbs. copper sulfate, 6 lbs. hydrated lime, and 100 gal. of water. As it is troublesome to prepare small quantities, home gardeners usually prefer to buy prepared package mixtures.

CAPTAN is widely useful for control of foliage diseases. It does not cause any discoloration of leaves or flowers, and is a good control for black-spot of roses and of mangos. The 50% wettable powder is used at 1 tbsp. per gal., and needs no spreader.

COPPER in fixed or neutral compounds, requiring no lime, is widely used for the same purposes as Bordeaux. Such compounds as Tribasic Copper Sulfate, Copper-A Compound, Cuprocide, and Copper Hydro 40 are well-known examples. They leave much less residue than Bordeaux, but may injure some plants just as it does. Directions of the manufacturer should be followed as to rate to use in mixing sprays. In most cases these copper compounds are used at 2 tbsp. per gal., and the compound should be made up into a paste before finally mixing it with water.

DITHANE D-14 must have some zinc sulfate added if it is to be very effective, so it is usually easier to buy a fungicide already combining these two, called zineb (*q.v.*). The dithane-zinc mixture has a slight advantage over zineb, leaving a little less residue on flower petals. Kits of dithane, zinc, and lime for azalea petal blight have directions for mixing.

FERBAM is the official name of a potent general fungicide known as Fermate or as Karbam Black. It is easy to use, and is effective against a large number of fungi, including leaf-spots and rusts, but not mildews.

KARATHANE controls mildew of rose and crape-myrtle. Wettable powder is stirred in water at ¾ tsp. per gal. Mildex and Iscathane are the same compound.

MORSODREN is an organic mercury compound that stops damping-off (in which roots die away) caused by the fungus *Pythium*.

PHALTAN is unusually effective for control of black-spot of roses and is the only organic fungicide which also controls powdery mildew. Use 1 tsp. of Phaltan 75 per gal.

SPERGON is hardly ever used as a spray or dust on foliage, but is quite effective for treating seeds and seedlings to control damping-off. It is used as a drench at 3 tbsp. of wettable powder per gal.

SULFUR as a fungicide is rather weakly effective against many diseases, but gives good control of powdery mildews and some rusts and leaf-spots. It is particularly useful for applying as a dust, for which purpose only the fine, 325-mesh form should be used, and not the flowers of sulfur used for soil application. Wettable sulfurs are used in sprays, especially for adding to ferbam or zineb sprays. The rate used alone is 4 tbsp. per gal., but half that much is used in mixtures with other fungicides.

TERRACLOR is especially valuable as a soil drench for control of soil-borne fungus diseases, notably Southern blight, camellia flower blight, and damping-off caused by *Rhizoctonia*. Application rate is 2 qts. per sq. ft., using 2 tsp. of the 75% powder in a gallon of water.

TERSAN is the wettable form of thiram, called Arasan in the non-wettable dust form. It is particularly effective for control of the fungi causing brown patch of lawn grasses and for those causing damping-off of seedling annuals in flats or seedbeds. Use 4 tsp. per gal. of water.

ZINEB is the formal name of the dithiocarbamate compound sold as Dithane Z-78 or Parzate. Closely related to ferbam, it has much the same usefulness but leaves only a light stain residue on flowers and leaves. It is one of the most satisfactory controls for azalea petal blight and black-spots.

Fumigants.—Soil fumigants free seed beds, garden beds, and lawn areas from many pests. Some are easily applied by the home gardener but others should be applied by custom pest control operators. Treatment of single rows before planting will protect the plants grown in that row for one season, but the treatment of permanent garden beds should give effective control for several years.

ETHYLENE DIBROMIDE controls nematodes and is easily applied after fertilizer has been mixed in the row. Open a furrow 6 in. deep along the row and pour in the liquid fumigant slowly at the rate recommended by the manufacturer. Then fill the furrow again with soil and firm it. Wait two weeks before planting.

METHYL BROMIDE is very good for nematode control in light doses, and for fungi and weeds also in heavier dosages. It is usually formulated with a small content of tear gas as a warning of leakage, since it is odorless itself. A compressed gas in tanks under pressure, it must be applied under a gas-tight cover of plastic sheeting, and hence is not very satisfactory for use in home gardens although very popular with custom operators. Only a four-day waiting period is needed before planting. Manufacturer's directions must be carefully followed as to dosages. MC-2 and Pestmaster are well-known brands.

MYLONE is effective against nematodes, fungi, and weeds. It is easily applied as a drench from a watering can or sprayer. Mix ½ lb. of the 85% wettable powder or 1 pt. of the liquid formation in 4 gal. of water and distribute this evenly over an area of 100 sq. ft. Run a sprinkler on the drenched area for an hour to seal the soil surface and keep the fumigant in the soil. Apply four days before fertilizer is mixed in the soil, and wait ten days more before planting.

NEMAGON is for nematode control and is of special interest because it can often be used around growing plants with little or no harm to them. It may be applied as a drench or as dry granules; in either case irrigation for an hour should follow application. Dosages will vary with the kind of plant being treated, and should follow manufacturer's recommendations closely. A similar product is called Fumazon.

VAPAM, or VPM, is similar to Mylone in its effectiveness as a soil fumigant, and is applied in the same manner and at the same rate. Usually it is sold in liquid form as Vapam 4S. At 1 qt. per 100 sq. ft. it is reported to kill nutgrass, too.

VC-13, like Nemagon, kills nematodes already infesting living plants. It is also lethal to chinch bugs, treatments remaining effective two to three months.

EQUIPMENT FOR APPLYING PESTICIDES

In general, insecticides and fungicides are applied as sprays or dusts. Both are effective if the job is done throughly, and each has certain advantages. Dusting can be done satisfactorily only if there is no breeze at all, so that the cloud of dust settles slowly over the plant surfaces. Spraying may be done without regard to air movement, although less pleasant and effective in a good breeze. Dusting controls most insects except scales; scale control makes a sprayer necessary and in most gardens will be the deciding factor. Dusting is more rapid, but spraying gives more lasting coverage.

SPRAYERS of several sizes find a place in the home garden. Smallest and least expensive is the *atomizing* sprayer, familiar as the flit-gun type. This is suitable for spot spraying of aphids or for use on a few house plants, but is very tiring to use for any length of time. Such a sprayer with a ½- pt. glass jar is convenient for quick action on a few shoots.

The next larger size of sprayer worth considering is one which holds 2 gal. of spray. This may be had at about the same price either as a *compressed air tank* or as a *bucket pump*. The small compression sprayer can be carried on a strap over the shoulder or held by one hand, either way giving mobility. The disadvantage of this type is that it must be set down at short intervals to be pumped up, and operates thereafter with steadily decreasing pressure. The bucket pump with the trombone-type action is likely to be tipped over easily and is troublesome to pick up and move every few seconds, since both hands are needed to operate the spray pump, but it maintains pressure well. Bucket pumps with pump-handle operation require two people to operate them. For very small gardens in the average city lot, this size will probably suffice.

For larger gardens of less than an acre, *knapsack* sprayers of 4 or 5 gal. capacity are satisfactory. Pressure is easily maintained with relatively little effort by one hand while the other hand directs the spray rod. While 4 gal. of spray are fairly heavy —about 50 lbs. including the sprayer—the knapsack sprayer allows the load to be carried easily on the back, and the more you spray, the lighter the load gets. The type with an agitator paddle is preferred, as this prevents settling of many types of spray out of solution.

Gardens of an acre or more will need a *wheelbarrow* sprayer if there is considerable spraying to do. These hold from 10 to 15 gal. and require two persons, one to do the pumping and one to do the spraying. They give higher pressures than the knapsack type, which means more efficient application, and can be used with 10 to 20 ft. of hose, allowing great mobility. They cost about twice as much as knapsack sprayers and are worth it if there is enough spraying to warrant using their size. An air tank is a very desirable item of equipment for this sprayer, to maintain even spray pressure. Sprayers of this size may be had with gasoline or electric power, more effective and less wearing than manpower.

Whatever the type of sprayer chosen, it should always be well flushed with clean water after use, care being taken to pump water through the spray nozzle for several seconds also. Screens in the nozzles should be removed and cleaned occasionally, too; frequently an uneven spray cone indicates a clogged screen.

DUSTERS come in fewer types than sprayers. Least efficient is the *telescoping tube* duster, sold with a special dust mixture already in it, which has a usefulness about like the atomizing hand sprayer. *Plunger type* dusters, with a capacity of 1 lb. of dust and an extension tube to direct the dust, give fair satisfaction for small gardens and are inexpensive. The dust does not always flow evenly, and if there are many plants to be treated, the arm soon grows tired of pushing the plunger.

Rotary and *bellows* dusters carried by straps over the shoulders give a steady flow of dust at a controlled rate without much effort. They hold 20 lbs. of dust, so that they are considerably lighter than 4-gal. sprayers. For fast coverage of a large number of plants they are very satisfactory.

Dusters require no cleaning after use, and dust can be left in the hopper until it is needed again.

Diagnosing and treating Florida garden ills

A. *Ailments common to many plants*

Plant symptoms	Cause	Control
Leaves on young shoots infested on lower side with tiny green, black, or pink stationary insects; older leaves often curled backwards.	Aphids	Spray or dust with nicotine sulfate, pyrethrum, or malathion.
Leaves with holes eaten in margins or sometimes in middle portion only.	Caterpillars, beetles, and grasshoppers	Spray or dust with DDT, chlordane, lindane, or lead arsenate.
Leaves with white coating like powdered sugar on either or both surfaces.	Powdery mildew	Spray with Karathane, Acti-dione PM, or wettable sulfur.
Leaves become gray, yellowish, or rusty looking.	Red spider mites	Dust with sulfur, or spray with Kelthane, Aramite, or chlorobenzilate.
Leaves covered on upper surface with thin black film.	Sooty-mold fungus	Spray with summer oil or malathion.
Leaves with winding tunnels just under the upper surface.	Leaf-miners	Spray with cygon, lindane, or malathion.
Leaves showing discolored spots later becoming dead areas, increasing in size with age, until whole leaf dies and falls.	Leaf-spot fungi	Spray or dust with Captan, ferbam, zineb, Phaltan, or copper compounds.
Leaves yellowed, with green veins but pale green to white between the lateral veins, or often yellow all over.	Chlorosis, due to lack of iron, zinc, magnesium, or manganese	Usually chlorosis of shrubs is due to soil not acid enough to make iron available in sandy soils, or manganese in marl areas. See discussion in Chapter Three.
Flowers streaked or browned, often not opening from bud; active, tiny, yellow insects working in flower.	Thrips	Spray or dust with malathion, lindane, or dieldrin.
Young seedlings cut off just above the ground but otherwise healthy looking.	Cutworms	Dust or spray soil around base of plants with chlordane, or apply cutworm bait.
Stems of young herbaceous seedlings wilting and collapsing at the base, so that they fall over (Rhizoctonia).	Damping-off fungi	Keep soil surface as dry as possible; drench soil around seedlings with suspension of Terraclor.

PLANT SYMPTOMS	CAUSE	CONTROL
Plants rot at ground, wilt, and fall over. Often white threads cover ground at base of plant with little "clover seeds" scattered among them.	Southern blight or other crown- and stem- rot fungi	Remove infected plant with all soil possible around roots; sterilize bed (see p. 340) before planting this species in this bed again.
Leaves and twigs of woody plants infested with small bodies of pin-head size, red, black, brown, or white in color.	Scale insects	Spray with summer oil, cygon, or malathion.
Whole plant unthrifty and yellow in spite of careful attention to fertilizing and watering. Many roots swollen and distorted.	Root-knot nematode	Fumigate soil before planting.

B. *Ailments of specific plants, not common to many*

PLANT SYMPTOMS	CAUSE	CONTROL

ASTER, CHINA-

plants suddenly wilt, wither, and die.	Fusarium wilt	Plant only seeds of wilt-resistant varieties.
plants develop stiff, yellowish, stunted growth, often with greenish flowers.	Aster-yellows virus	Plants must be grown under screen or cheesecloth, or sprayed or dusted frequently with DDT to control leafhoppers that carry this virus.

AZALEA

flowers develop spots; in a day or two all petals collapse as if boiling water had been poured on them.	Azalea petal blight	Spray three times a week during blooming with zineb, thiram, or Acti-dione.
plants are stripped of terminal leaves.	Azalea defoliator	Spray with Toxaphene, DDT, or malathion.
upper leaf surface gray, blanched or stippled; lower surface covered with dark, varnish-like drops.	Lace bugs	Spray with malathion or summer oil.
young leaves of spring flush are whitened, greatly thickened, and distorted.	Leaf-gall fungus	Pick off and destroy all galls as soon as they are seen.

Plant symptoms	Cause	Control
CALLA		
edges of the spathe—the showy white, yellow, or pink "flower" part —browns.	Thrips	Spray or dust with nicotine sulfate, rotenone, malathion, cygon, lindane, or dieldrin.
leaves droop, die, and rot at base.	**Bacteria or fungi**	Clean rhizomes before planting, cut out any decayed spots, and let dry a day or two. Then soak 1 hour in 2 tsp. Ceresan plus 1 tsp. Dreft in 1 gal. of water.
CAMELLIA		
leaves show yellow areas on top surface, with same areas on lower side covered with fine cottony growth. Badly infested leaves often fall.	Tea scale	Spray with cygon, or summer oil plus malathion, applied to well-matured foliage, being sure to wet lower side of all leaves.
twigs suddenly die while rest of bush is healthy.	Dieback	Prune out dead twigs with sterilized shears.
leaves have areas of bright yellow, but are glossy and healthy with no sign of insect or disease.	Mosaic virus	No remedy is known, but the virus is not readily transmitted except by grafting. Buy only plants with all-green leaves.
leaves fall, buds drop unopened, some twigs may die back.	Poor drainage	Correct the drainage by tile, or raise plants if set too deep.
CENTIPEDE GRASS		
lawns die out in large brown areas.	Brown patch disease or ground-pearls	Sometimes due to a fungus, which can be checked by drenching areas with Tersan. No control for ground-pearls.
lawns brown all over in winter.	Too cold	Sow winter grass on top of centipede.
CHRYSANTHEMUM		
wedge-shaped brown areas between large veins gradually kill leaves from ground upwards.	Leaf nematode	Spray infected plants weekly with malathion.

PLANT SYMPTOMS	CAUSE	CONTROL
DOGWOOD		
trunks have large deep gashes through the bark into the younger wood, especially on newly planted trees.	Dogwood cambium borer	Prevent by wrapping trunks when transplanting. Cut out borer grubs, paint wounds, and give tree good care.
foliage sheds prematurely and twigs die back at tip.	Possibly poor drainage	Correct drainage situation.
twigs show a thick wrapping of felty material and diminish in vigor.	Felt fungus	Prune out small twigs; scrub off coating on large branches with rag soaked in kerosene.
EASTER LILY		
leaves flecked with small irregular spots, plants stunted, flowers small and distorted.	Virus mosaic	Buy only certified bulbs. Discard diseased plants, and prevent spread by spraying for aphid control.
FIRETHORN		
branches turn brown and die back.	Fire blight	Prune out dead branches, making the cut well below any sign of injury, disinfecting shears in alcohol.
leaves speckled with yellow, then brown; undersides show small drops like dark varnish.	Lace bug	Spray with DDT or malathion.
GARDENIA		
small, white, cottony bodies in the axils of the leaves.	Mealy-bug	Spray with summer oil or malathion as for scales.
brown dead areas on stem near ground, first sunken, later swollen with cracked bark.	Gardenia canker or stem gall	Remove and destroy infected plants. Infection usually occurs when cuttings are made, not in garden bed.
GLADIOLUS		
leaves with silvery streaks, later brown and die; flowers deformed, streaked with white.	Thrips	Spray or dust with dieldrin, DDT, or chlordane. Treat corms before storage with DDT dust.

Plant symptoms	Cause	Control
Holly		
young leaves are distorted and discolored, or die and drop; whole small shoots sometimes die.	Adults of spittle-bug	Spray or dust with DDT, lindane, or malathion every ten days during hot weather.
Hydrangea		
flowers pink instead of blue, or vice versa.	Soil acidity	Flowers are blue when soil is acid, pink when soil is slightly alkaline, dirty white in between.
Lilyturf and Dwarf Lilyturf		
leaves yellowed, unthrifty, with many brown dots that can be lifted off.	Scales	Spray with summer oil or malathion in early spring and repeat three months later.
Loquat		
leaves turn brown on one branch which dies, but leaves do not fall. If left alone, whole tree may die back slowly.	Fire blight	Prune out dead branches, making cut 6 in. below visible dead tissue, and sterilize shears in alcohol. Paint large wounds with shellac, followed by paint.
whole tree declines markedly in vigor, eventually dying back, or one side of tree dies while other side is healthy.	Mushroom root-rot	Usually no remedy. Dig out, leaving no big pieces of root or old pieces of oak root, sterilize soil with Terraclor, and replant.
Mango		
fruit disfigured by black spots that enlarge and rot the flesh as the fruit ripens.	Black-spot fungus	Have commercial caretaker spray trees during and after blooming.
Marigold		
plants are stunted with many upright stiff branches, leaves are yellow, flowers distorted, few.	Aster-yellows virus	Control leafhoppers that spread the disease with DDT or malathion. Destroy abnormal plants.
Oleander		
tufts of slender shoots develop where one shoot is expected, and these turn brown.	Witches-broom fungus	Remove and burn all witches-brooms promptly, and after pruning spray plants with ferbam.

Plant symptoms	Cause	Control
plants defoliated.	Oleander caterpillar	Spray at very first signs with DDT, Toxaphene, or malathion and repeat.
twigs unthrifty, pock-marked with many small swellings having holes in center.	Scale	Spray with oil plus malathion.

Palms

fronds develop brown areas, followed by death of pinnae or fronds; web filled with caterpillars seen on low leaves.	Palm leaf skeletonizer	Repeated spraying, every two months throughout the year, may be needed, using DDT, chlordane, or lindane.
large specimens of *Phoenix, Sabal,* or *Washingtonia* palms die back, beginning with the youngest leaves.	Palm weevil in bud	No remedy is known.
specimens of coconut, queen palm, and royal palm die back similarly.	Bud rot or wilt fungus	Remove and burn tips of dead palms. Spray if possible in bud of any adjacent palms of these kinds with neutral copper compounds.
large fungus growth on trunk of queen palm.	Shelf fungus denotes infection within	No remedy is known.

Rose

canes encircled by brown areas, above which shoots die.	Brown canker	Do not buy rose bushes that show cankers; prune canes below cankers and shellac cut surface.

St. Augustine grass

brown areas develop in lawns and increase rapidly in size in spring and summer.	Chinch bug	Irrigate heavily, then spray with Diazinon, Trithion, or VC-13 at concentrations recommended on the labels. Repeat applications during the hot months.

Silverthorn

branches turn brown and die.	Diplodia blight	Prune well below infected region with shears sterilized in alcohol. Shellac cut surfaces.

Plant symptoms	Cause	Control

Snapdragon

corollas of older flowers on spike drop prematurely, leaving few flowers to make a show.	Pollination by bumblebees	Normal in warm weather outdoors. Avoid by enclosing flower spikes in cheesecloth bags.
reddish-brown areas on leaves and stems.	Rust fungus	Hand pick infected leaves, destroy badly infected plants, spray with ferbam, zineb, or copper.

Stock

plants grow well but fail to bloom.	Weather too warm	Cool weather is needed for flower buds to form.

Zoysia grass

small brown spots in lawns, about the size of a silver dollar, becoming yellow.	Dollar-spot	Spray with Tersan or a cadmium fungicide.

PESTICIDE DILUTION TABLE

PESTICIDE	FORMULATION	AMOUNT TO USE IN MAKING		
		1 QT.	1 GAL.	10 GAL.
ARAMITE	15% wettable powder	1¼ tsp.	1½ tbsp.	1 cup
CAPTAN	50% wettable powder	1 tsp.	1⅓ tbsp.	¾ cup
CHLOROBENZILATE	25% wettable powder	¼ tsp.	1 tsp.	3⅓ tbsp.
CHLORDANE	50% wettable powder	1¼ tsp.	5 tsp.	1 cup
COPPER, FIXED	45% copper content	1½ tsp.	2 tbsp.	1¼ cups
CYGON	25% solution	½ tsp.	2 tsp.	½ cup
DDT	50% wettable powder	1½ tsp.	2 tbsp.	1¼ cups
DIAZINON	25% emulsifiable concentrate	1 tsp.	1 tbsp.	¾ cup
DIELDRIN	15% emulsion	1½ tsp.	2 tbsp.	1¼ cups
FERBAM	(Fermate, Karbam Black)	2 tsp.	2⅓ tbsp.	1½ cups
KARATHANE	(also known as Mildex)	¼ tsp.	¾ tbsp.	2½ tbsp.
KELTHANE	18½% emulsifiable concentrate	1 tsp.	1⅓ tbsp.	¾ cup
LINDANE	25% wettable powder	¾ tsp.	1 tbsp.	⅔ cup
LINDANE	20% emulsifiable concentrate	¼ tsp.	1 tsp.	3⅓ tbsp.
MALATHION	25% wettable	4 tsp.	5 tbsp.	3 cups
MALATHION	57% emulsifiable concentrate	½ tsp.	2¼ tsp.	½ cup
MANEE	(Manzate, Dithane M-22)	1 tsp.	1½ tbsp.	¾ cup
MORSODREN*	2.2% solution	3 drops	10 drops	1 tsp.
NICOTINE	40% solution	¼ tsp.	1 tsp.	3⅓ tbsp.
OIL, SUMMER	95 to 98% oil, emsulifiable	4 tsp.	5 tbsp.	3 cups
PHALTAN	75% wettable powder	¾ tsp.	1 tbsp.	⅔ cup
ROTENONE	Variable	See directions on bottle		
SPERGON	Wettable powder	1¾ tsp.	2⅓ tbsp.	1½ cups
SULFUR	Wettable powder	1 tbsp.	4 tbsp.	2½ cups
TERRACLOR*	75% wettable powder	½ tsp.	2 tsp.	½ cup*
TERSAN		1 tsp.	4 tsp.	⅞ cup
TOXAPHENE	40% wettable powder	2 tsp.	3 tbsp.	2 cups
V-C 13	emulsifiable concentrate	2 tsp.	3 tbsp.	2˙ cups
ZINEB	(Dithane Z-78, Parzate)	1 tsp.	1½ tbsp.	¾ cup
DETERGENT	(As spreader and sticker for pesticides)	¼ tsp.	1 tsp.	3⅓ tbsp.

NOTE: All measurements are *level*, not heaping.
* Drench with 2 qts. per square ft. of soil.

18

Your Florida Garden Month by Month

THIS MONTHLY GUIDE of what and when to plant and how to care for gardens throughout Florida will help gardeners achieve maximum beauty and health in Florida gardens with minimum expenditure of time and effort.

SEPTEMBER

NORTHERN FLORIDA

September starts the garden year in Florida. Lift and replant Easter lily bulbs, and, at the same time, prepare enough bed space to accommodate narcissus bulbs. Red spider mites on camellias, and scale insects, too, will need to be checked, particularly by those gardeners who are returning from vacations. Azaleas should be syringed during dry periods to help control mites and thrips. The unremitting campaign against leaf-spotting must be continued in rose and chrysanthemum beds. Tie chrysanthemums to stakes to prevent bent stems.

SEEDS TO PLANT—sweet alyssum, begonia, bellis, brachycome, browallia, calendula, California-poppy, carnation, clarkia, cleome, dianthus, dimorphotheca, gaillardia, gilia, gypsophila, linaria, linum, lobelia, lupine, mignonette, nasturtium, nicotiana, nierembergia, petunia, phlox, salpiglossis, scabiosa, statice, stock, verbena, viola.

BULBS TO PLANT—narcissus, ranunculus.

352

CENTRAL FLORIDA

Hibiscus should be inspected for snow scale and prompt treatment made if the clusters of white flakes are found. Caladiums and callas can be dug if desirable. Shrubs that have grown out of bounds during vacation time should be pruned back into shape. Pansy and viola plants can be ordered for November delivery, and roses can be ordered, too, as it is desirable to order direct from producing nurseries. Christmas cactus must have a last fertilizing, then be subjected to gradual drying off and exposure to bright sunlight to assure good flower bud set. Prune and fertilize vigorous rose bushes for fall blooming.

SEEDS TO PLANT—sweet alyssum, arctotis, bachelors-button, begonia, bellis, brachycome, browllia, calendula, California-poppy, clarkia, cleome, delphinium, dianthus, dimorpho-theca, gaillardia, gilia, gypsophila, hollyhock, hunnemannia, linaria, linum, lobelia, lupine, mignonette, nasturtium, nicotiana, nierembergia, petunia, phlox, salpiglossis, scabiosa, snapdragon, statice, stock, verbena, viola.

BULBS TO PLANT—calla, hyacinth, Easter lily, narcissus, ornithogalum, montbretia, watsonia.

SOUTHERN FLORIDA

Turn under any green-manure crop, or apply peat or compost and dig in for winter annual flower beds. Vigorous rose bushes should be pruned and fertilized for autumn cut flowers. Spraying or dusting must commence as the first new leaves mature, for leaf-spot is continually with us. Gardeners in frost-free sections can fertilize shrubs, trees, and vines for renewed activity. Study notes for central Florida; they apply south, too. Many bulbous species can be potted now for house or patio decoration. Trees, palms, or shrubs that have been partly or wholly uprooted by storms should be replanted as quickly as possible, with the tops headed back in proportion to root injury. Set them erect again and tie to stout stakes.

SEEDS TO PLANT—ageratum, sweet alyssum, arctotis, China-aster, bachelors-button, balsam, begonia, blue lace-flower, brachycome, browallia, calendula, calliopsis, globe candytuft, celosia, late cosmos, cypress-vine, dahlia, delphinium, dianthus, dimorphotheca, gaillardia, gilia, globe-amaranth, godetia, hollyhock, hunnemannia, linaria, linum, lobelia, lupine, African marigold, morning-glory, nasturtium, nicotiana, petunia, phlox, poppy, portulaca, rudbeckia, salpiglossis, salvia, snapdragon, statice, sunflower, tithonia, torenia, verbena.

BULBS TO PLANT—amaryllis, calla, freesia, gladiolus, gloriosa, Easter lily, ornithogalum, montbretia, watsonia, zephyranthes.

OCTOBER

NORTHERN FLORIDA

Caladiums should be dug and tubers stored in dry peat or sand in a frost-free place for the winter. Fertilize cool-weather bulbs and annuals during their first forty days of growth. Lazy gardeners may use volunteer plants of petunia, calliopsis, and linaria, with the understanding, of course, that flowers will be small and colors less than perfect. Watering may be needed during dry periods at this time of the year. Sweet-peas may be given a boost with high-analysis fertilizer in water solution, and a protective spray against aphids may be in order. Seeds of delphinium and larkspur should be chilled in the refrigerator for a week or two before planting. Winter grasses should be sown for a green lawn during cold months. The fall application of fertilizer may be given all broad-leaved evergreen shrubs and trees.

SEEDS TO PLANT—sweet alyssum, arctotis, bachelors-button, begonia, bellis, brachycome, browallia, calendula, California-poppy, calliopsis, candytuft, carnation, clarkia, cleome, delphinium, dianthus, dimorphotheca, gaillardia, gilia, godetia, gypsophila, hollyhock, hunnemannia, larkspur, linaria, linum, lobelia, lupine, mignonette, nasturtium, nicotiana, nierembergia, pansy, petunia, phlox, salpiglossis, scabiosa, statice, stock, sweet-pea, verbena, viola.

BULBS TO PLANT—amaryllis, freesia, iris (Dutch and native), leucojum, Easter lily, lycoris, narcissus, ornithogalum, ranunculus, sprekelia, tigridia.

CENTRAL FLORIDA

Place orders for callas—white, yellow, and rarer sorts as well—if you want to have unusual pot plants for spring. If Shasta daisies are on hand, divide old clumps. Notes above apply in this section as well. Daylilies, and true bulbs, too, that have become crowded may be lifted and set at intervals in newly enriched beds.

During the first week, head in poinsettias to induce compact branching for attractive habit and maximum bloom. Be on the alert for lawn pests, such as sod web-worms and fall army-worms, and apply dust at first signs. Watch for thrips on chrysanthemums. If sweet-peas have not been planted, prepare a trench for them early in this month.

> SEEDS TO PLANT—sweet alyssum, arctotis, bachelors-button, begonia, bellis, brachycome, browallia, calendula, California-poppy, calliopsis, candytuft, carnation, clarkia, cleome, delphinium, dianthus, dimorphotheca, gaillardia, gilia, godetia, gypsophila, hollyhock, hunnemannia, larkspur, linaria, linum, lobelia, lupine, mignonette, nasturtium, nicotiana, nierembergia, pansy, petunia, phlox, salpiglossis, scabiosa, snapdragon, statice, stock, verbena, viola.
>
> BULBS TO PLANT—agapanthus, amaryllis, calla, freesia, hyacinth, hymenocallis, iris (Dutch and native), Easter lily, leucojum, lycoris, montbretia, narcissus, ornithogalum, ranunculus, sprekelia, tigridia, watsonia.

SOUTHERN FLORIDA

Make fall fertilizer applications on avocado, citrus, lychee, mango, hibiscus, and all flowering shrubs. Early this month prune back poinsettias and bougainvilleas for the last time. Unending war on rose leaf-spot must be continued if blooms are expected. Order pansy plants for November delivery, if arrangements have not been made. Plant seed of hardy grass for a bright green winter lawn. Prepare the trench for sweet-peas and get beds ready for fall rose planting. If the weather is dry, be alert for spider mites.

SEEDS TO PLANT—ageratum, sweet alyssum, arctotis, China-aster, bachelors-button, balsam, begonia, blue lace-flower, brachycome, browallia, calendula, calliopsis, candytuft, celosia, late cosmos, dahlia, delphinium, dianthus, dimor-photheca, gaillardia, gilia, globe-amaranth, godetia, gypso-phila, hollyhock, hunnemannia, larkspur, linaria, linum, lobelia, lupine, African marigold, morning-glory, nasturtium, nicotiana, nierembergia, pansy, petunia, phlox, poppy, portu-laca, rudbeckia, salpiglossis, salvia, snapdragon, statice, sun-flower, tithonia, torenia, verbena.

BULBS TO PLANT—agapanthus, amaryllis, calla, freesia, gladi-olus, gloriosa, hymenocallis, leucojum, montbretia, narcissus, ornithogalum, ranunculus, sprekelia, tigridia, watsonia, zephyranthes.

NOVEMBER

NORTHERN FLORIDA

Attacks of sod web-worms may come as late as this. Apply dust at first sign. At this season, too, it is well to dust all ant hills carefully to kill the colonies. Okra pods, magnolia cones, sweet-gum fruits, and other local dried materials should be col-lected and stored for later use in arrangements or for Christmas decorations. If frost threatens, cover plants of calendula, snap-dragon, and double-fringed petunias with generous handfuls of Spanish-moss. This fluffy material can be left on for two or three days until the threat of cold passes. Summer-blooming de-ciduous shrubs, such as crape-myrtle, should be pruned now for appearance. Pansy plants should be set out now.

SEEDS TO PLANT—sweet alyssum, arctotis, bachelors-button, begonia, bellis, brachycome, browallia, calendula, California-poppy, calliopsis, candytuft, carnation, clarkia, cleome, del-phinium, dianthus, dimorphotheca, gaillardia, gilia, godetia, gypsophila, hollyhock, hunnemannia, larkspur, linaria, li-num, lobelia, lupine, mignonette, nicotiana, nierembergia, petunia, phlox, poppy, salpiglossis, scabiosa, statice, stock, sweet-pea, verbena, viola.

BULBS TO PLANT—alstroemeria, amaryllis, freesia, hyacinth, iris (Dutch and native), leucojum, Easter lily, narcissus, ornithogalum, ranunculus, sprekelia, tigridia, tulip, watsonia.

CENTRAL FLORIDA

Notes above apply to this section as well.

Thrips and mirids may be troublesome in chrysanthemums unless frequent spraying is resorted to. Bed-out seedlings of winter annuals. Plants in bands can be bought at garden supply stores. Pansies will arrive this month. Set at the same depth in narrow beds that have been enriched. Protect your investment with cutworm bait during the first two or three nights. Order chilled tulip bulbs, or buy bulbs to chill in the home refrigerator.

> SEEDS TO PLANT—sweet alyssum, arctotis, bachelors-button, begonia, bellis, brachycome, browallia, calendula, California-poppy, calliopsis, candytuft, carnation, clarkia, chrysanthemum, cleome, delphinium, dianthus, dimorphotheca, gilia, gaillardia, godetia, gypsophila, hollyhock, hunnemannia, larkspur, linaria, linum, lobelia, lupine, mignonette, nicotiana, nierembergia, pansy, petunia, phlox, salpiglossis, scabiosa, snapdragon, statice, stock, sweet-pea, verbena, viola.
>
> BULBS TO PLANT—agapanthus, amaryllis, calla, crinum, freesia, gladiolus, gloriosa, hyacinth, hymenocallis, Dutch iris, leucojum, Easter lily, lycoris, montbretia, narcissus, ornithogalum, ranunculus, sprekelia, tigridia, tulip, watsonia.

SOUTHERN FLORIDA

Poinsettias can have the last application of fertilizer early in the month. Plant roses as soon as they are delivered from your mail-order source or buy your needs at your local garden supply store. Plant no deeper than they grew formerly. If winter grass has not yet been seeded, get it in at once. Divide and replant rhizomatous begonias, verbenas, violets, and other flowering perennials. Fertilize annuals that were started last month. Callas, freesias, watsonias, and similar northern-grown bulbs must be ordered by mail or through your local garden supply store. Prepare window and porch boxes for winter annuals. Storm-damaged trees and shrubs should be pruned, staked, and tied.

> SEEDS TO PLANT—ageratum, sweet alyssum, arctotis, China-aster, bachelors-button, balsam, begonia, blue lace-flower,

brachycome, browallia, calendula, calliopsis, candytuft, carnation, celosia, Chinese forget-me-not, dahlia, delphinium, dianthus, dimorphotheca, gaillardia, gilia, globe-amaranth, godetia, gypsophila, hollyhock, hunnemannia, larkspur, linaria, lobelia, lupine, African marigold, morning-glory, nasturtium, nicotiana, nierembergia, pansy, petunia, phlox, poppy, portulaca, rudbeckia, salpiglossis, salvia, snapdragon, statice, sunflower, sweet-pea, tithonia, torenia, verbena.

BULBS TO PLANT—agapanthus, amaryllis, calla, crinum, freesia, gladiolus, gloriosa, hymenocallis, Dutch iris, leucojum, montbretia, narcissus, ornithogalum, ranunculus, sprekelia, tigridia, tuberose, tulip, watsonia, zephyranthes.

DECEMBER

NORTHERN FLORIDA

Fertilize annuals and bulbs that are growing now and be prepared to cover plants with Spanish-moss when the Frost Warning Service forecasts a freeze. Plant chilled tulip bulbs. Set out rose bushes late this month or early in January. Cover camellia buds with mesh bags if squirrels are eating them. Keep camellia bushes well watered in dry periods. Make cuttings of deciduous trees and shrubs, and transplant these species now for best results. Late this month is the best time to spray for scale on deciduous plants. Crape-myrtles should be cut back severely after the leaves have fallen, to assure compact habit and heavy flowering next spring. This suggestion applies below, too.

SEEDS TO PLANT—sweet alyssum, arctotis, bachelors-button, begonia, browallia, calendula, California-poppy, calliopsis, candytuft, carnation, Chinese forget-me-not, chrysanthemum, clarkia, cleome, dianthus, dimorphotheca, gaillardia, gilia, godetia, gypsophila, hollyhock, hunnemannia, larkspur, linaria, linum, lobelia, lupine, mignonette, nicotiana, nierembergia, petunia, phlox, poppy, salpiglossis, scabiosa, statice, stock, sweet-pea, verbena, viola.

BULBS TO PLANT—alstroemeria, amaryllis, crinum, eucharis, freesia, hyacinth, hymenocallis, Dutch iris, leucojum, lilies (other than Easter), montbretia, sprekelia, tulip, watsonia.

CENTRAL FLORIDA

Study notes above. Make hardwood cuttings of leafless, pencil-sized shoots of shrubs and trees. Transplant woody plants, too. Chilled tulip bulbs should be planted this month. Camellias and azaleas must be soaked during dry periods so that foliage will be retained and blossom buds will not be shed. Rose bushes should be planted if they are not already in place. When deciduous plants, such as peach, plum, Oriental magnolia, and mulberry, are bare of leaves, spray for scale.

> SEEDS TO PLANT—arctotis, bachelors-button, browallia, calendula, California-poppy, calliopsis, candytuft, carnation, Chinese forget-me-not, chrysanthemum, clarkia, cleome, dianthus, dimorphotheca, gaillardia, gilia, godetia, gypsophila, hollyhock, hunnemannia, larkspur, linaria, lobelia, lupine, mignonette, nicotiana, nierembergia, pansy, petunia, phlox, poppy, salpiglossis, scabiosa, snapdragon, statice, sweet-pea, verbena.
>
> BULBS TO PLANT—agapanthus, amaryllis, calla, crinum, dahlia, freesia, gladiolus, gloriosa, hyacinth, hymenocallis, Dutch iris, leucojum, lilies (other than Easter), lycoris, montbretia, sprekelia, tigridia, tuberose, tulip, watsonia, zephyranthes.

SOUTHERN FLORIDA

Fertilize all herbaceous garden plants for strong, wintertime growth. Winter grass lawns will need this attention as well as watering and mowing. Notes above on deciduous plants and hardwood cuttings apply here, too. Clip faded blossoms from flowering annuals to extend the blooming period. Protect the plants from chewing insects and spider mites. Select new kinds of bougainvilleas now while they are in bloom. Remove braces that were placed to protect palms and trees from autumn winds. Tender shrubs that are injured by frost should be pruned back to live wood just as soon as possible. There is no advantage in allowing brown twigs to remain.

> SEEDS TO PLANT—ageratum, sweet alyssum, arctotis, China-aster, bachelors-button, balsam, begonia, blue lace-flower,

brachycome, browallia, calendula, calliopsis, carnation, rocket candytuft, celosia, Chinese forget-me-not, dahlia, delphinium, dianthus, dimorphotheca, gaillardia, globe-amaranth, gypsophila, hollyhock, larkspur, linaria, African marigold, morning-glory, nasturtium, nicotiana, nierembergia, pansy, petunia, phlox, poppy, portulaca, rudbeckia, salvia, sunflower, sweet-pea, tithonia, torenia.

BULBS TO PLANT—agapanthus, amaryllis, calla, crinum, dahlia, freesia, gladiolus, gloriosa, hymenocallis, Dutch iris, lilies (Easter and others), montbretia, narcissus, sprekelia, tuberose, tulip, zephyranthes.

JANUARY

NORTHERN FLORIDA

Transplant dormant trees and shrubs. Prepare soil for summer annuals to be sown during the last week; prepare ground for gladiolus corms during last week. Fertilize narcissus bulbs after flowering. Protect calendulas from worms with dusts. Cover recently transplanted annuals when frost is forecast. Root-prune shrubs to help keep them within bounds. Prune deciduous shrubs and trees of non-flowering types, and evergreen species, too, which have grown out of bounds. Prune frost-injured woody plants. Azaleas must be sprayed every third day if flower spot disease is to be controlled, starting when first buds open. Spray deciduous trees and shrubs for scale while they are dormant and leafless.

SEEDS TO PLANT—sweet alyssum, arctotis, bachelors-button, calendula, California-poppy, candytuft, carnation, Chinese forget-me-not, chrysanthemum, clarkia, dianthus, dimorphotheca, gaillardia, godetia, gypsophila, larkspur, linaria, lobelia, nicotiana, pansy, petunia, phlox, poppy, salpiglossis, schizanthus, sweet-pea, verbena.

BULBS TO PLANT—agapanthus, alstroemeria, amaryllis, crinum, freesia, gladiolus, gloriosa, hyacinth, montbretia, ranunculus, sprekelia, tuberose, watsonia.

CENTRAL FLORIDA

Be guided by notes above for New Year garden chores. Almost all jobs listed above will have to be done when yard work is resumed after the holidays. Homeowners in warmest sections of the middle peninsula might be guided by notes below.

SEEDS TO PLANT—ageratum, sweet alyssum, arctotis, China-aster, bachelors-button, begonia, blue lace-flower, calendula, candytuft, carnation, celosia, Chinese forget-me-not, chrysanthemum, clarkia, early cosmos, dianthus, dimorphotheca, gypsophila, hollyhock, larkspur, linaria, nasturtium, nicotiana, petunia, phlox, poppy, scabiosa, schizanthus, sweetpea, verbena.

BULBS TO PLANT—agapanthus, alstroemeria, amaryllis, caladium, calla, crinum, dahlia, eucharis, freesia, gladiolus, gloriosa, hymenocallis, montbretia, tuberose, zephyranthes.

SOUTHERN FLORIDA

Last call for gladiolus to flower for Mother's Day. Freesias, callas, and Dutch irises should be obtained. Blooming annuals must be protected from pests and fertilized twice during the month for vigorous growth and heavy flowering. Faded blooms must be clipped to prevent seeding. Amaryllis will benefit from application of fertilizer and produce larger blossoms on taller stems. Tropical aroids are prepared for vigorous production of large, healthy leaves by late winter fertilizing now. Winter grass lawns need fertilization and mowing to appear neat. Spray roses for black-spot.

SEEDS TO PLANT—ageratum, sweet alyssum, arctotis, China-aster, bachelors-button, balsam, begonia, blue lace-flower, calendula, rocket candytuft, carnation, celosia, Chinese forget-me-not, dahlia, dianthus, gaillardia, globe-amaranth, hollyhock, linaria, French marigold, morning-glory, nasturtium, nierembergia, petunia, phlox, poppy, portulaca, rudbeckia, schizanthus, sunflower, torenia.

BULBS TO PLANT—caladium, calla, crinum, dahlia, eucharis, freesia, gladiolus, gloriosa, Easter lily, montbretia, narcissus, tuberose, zephyranthes.

FEBRUARY

NORTHERN FLORIDA

Continue spraying every third day if control of azalea petal blight is planned. Transplant azaleas, but other field-grown woody species should no longer be moved this spring. Be certain that flowering shrubs do not want for water during periods of drought. Graft camellias, spray camellias for spider mites, and syringe other shrubs occasionally to discourage mites and thrips. Cover annuals on nights when freezing weather is forecast. Aid winter grass to carry well into the late spring by fertilizing and mowing frequently. During the last week, sow seeds of tender summer annuals. Prune all broad-leaved evergreen shrubs for size and shape.

> SEEDS TO PLANT—ageratum, sweet alyssum, China-aster, blue lace-flower, celosia, Chinese forget-me-not, chrysanthemum, early cosmos, dianthus, dimorphotheca, gaillardia, gypsophila, helichrysum, linaria, marigold, nasturtium, phlox, poppy, rudbeckia, schizanthus, verbena.

> BULBS TO PLANT—agapanthus, alstroemeria, amaryllis, calla, crinum, dahlia, freesia, gladiolus, gloriosa, haemanthus, hymenocallis, montbretia, sprekelia, tuberose, watsonia, zephyranthes.

CENTRAL FLORIDA

Gardeners of the middle peninsula can refer to the other paragraphs for suggestions for timely gardening activities.

Nursery plants in containers are moved every day in the year, but field-grown trees and shrubs should have been transplanted before this date, except for azaleas. Fertilize camellias and azaleas and all other shrubs, trees, and palms. Vigorous succulent growths on azaleas should be pinched to encourage good branching and to avoid the two-story effect so often seen.

> SEEDS TO PLANT—ageratum, sweet alyssum, China-aster, balsam, blue lace-flower, celosia, Chinese forget-me-not, chry-

santhemum, early cosmos, cypress-vine, dahlia, dianthus, gaillardia, globe-amaranth, helichrysum, linaria, marigold, morning-glory, nasturtium, phlox, poppy, portulaca, rudbeckia, salvia, schizanthus, sunflower, tithonia, torenia, verbena, zinnia.

BULBS TO PLANT—agapanthus, alstroemeria, amaryllis, caladium, calla, crinum, dahlia, eucharis, gladiolus, haemanthus, hymenocallis, montbretia, tuberose, zephyranthes.

SOUTHERN FLORIDA

Control aphids, mealy-bugs, and caterpillars at first signs on annuals, and continue to clip all fading blossoms to extend the period of flowering. Fertilize amaryllis. Plant gladiolus at intervals for extended flowering. When poinsettias have shed their bracts, cut the stems back to 12-in. stubs and utilize the canes for hardwood cuttings. Winter grass lawns need extra water and nitrogenous fertilizer to carry good green color into next month. This is a good time to take cuttings of all but the most tender garden shrubs, if bottom heat can be provided on cold nights or the cutting box moved indoors.

SEEDS TO PLANT—ageratum, sweet alyssum, China-aster, balsam, begonia, celosia, cypress-vine, dahlia, gaillardia, globe-amaranth, hollyhock, French marigold, morning-glory, poppy, portulaca, sunflower, torenia, zinnia.

BULBS TO PLANT—caladium, crinum, eucharis, gladiolus, gloriosa, haemanthus, montbretia, tuberose, zephyranthes.

MARCH

NORTHERN FLORIDA

Fertilize all trees, palms, shrubs, and lawns. Control pests as they increase their activities. Spider mites can be troublesome during dry periods, and they must be killed as soon as their presence is detected. Amaryllis blossoms will be improved in size by fertilizer applied now. Winter grass lawns, at their best, must have unremitting care lest they become untidy. Cannas, dahlias, and fancy-leaved caladiums are planted now, and after the middle of the month all tender annuals and tropical house plants can be set out of doors. Prune poinsettias heavily if not already cut down by cold.

> SEEDS TO PLANT—ageratum, sweet alyssum, China-aster, balsam, blue lace-flower, celosia, chrysanthemum, cosmos, cypress-vine, dahlia, gaillardia, globe-amaranth, helichrysum, marigold, morning-glory, nasturtium, phlox, portulaca, rudbeckia, salvia, schizanthus, sunflower, tithonia, torenia, verbena, zinnia.
> BULBS TO PLANT—alstroemeria, caladium, calla, dahlia, eucharis, gladiolus, haemanthus, iris (native), montbretia, tuberose, zephyranthes.

CENTRAL FLORIDA

Any chores listed above which were not completed last month should be done before this month is out. While many gardeners are inclined to overwater, few use too much fertilizer over the period of a year; so if the soil is light and sandy, be sure to apply sufficient fertilizer for the needs of your plants. Remember that frequent small applications are always preferred to infrequent ones. Spray gladiolus for thrips and roses for leaf diseases. Annuals of the hardy, winter-flowering group will have to be replaced with heat-tolerant kinds.

> SEEDS TO PLANT—ageratum, sweet alyssum, China-aster, balsam, blue lace-flower, celosia, chrysanthemum, cosmos, cypress-vine, dahlia, dianthus, gaillardia, globe-amaranth, helichrysum, linaria, marigold, morning-glory, nasturtium, phlox, poppy, portulaca, rudbeckia, salvia, schizanthus, sunflower, tithonia, torenia, verbena, zinnia.
> BULBS TO PLANT—caladium, dahlia, eucharis, gloriosa, haemanthus, iris (native), tuberose, zephyranthes.

SOUTHERN FLORIDA

Winter annuals, passing out of the picture, should be replaced with hot-weather varieties. Gladiolus must be sprayed for thrips, roses for leaf-spot, and St. Augustine lawns for chinch bugs if yellow spots are seen during the latter part of this month. As suggested for last month, winter grass lawns begin to go to pieces now, and last-minute fertilizing, watering, and mowing are needed to extend their usefulness as long as possible. Start a compost pile to provide good soil to sow seeds and set plants and bulbs in next autumn. Fertilize all garden plants now, and take cuttings of all but the very tender kinds. Transplant evergreen trees and shrubs not in tender flush. Divide and replant herbaceous perennials that bloom in late summer or fall.

> SEEDS TO PLANT—ageratum, sweet alyssum, China-aster, balsam, begonia, cypress-vine, gaillardia, globe-amaranth, hollyhock, French marigold, morning-glory, portulaca, torenia, zinnia.
>
> BULBS TO PLANT—caladium, gloriosa, haemanthus, montbretia, tuberose, zephyranthes. If dormant bulbs can be obtained, add amaryllis, crinum, and eucharis.

APRIL

NORTHERN FLORIDA

Layering, both in the earth and with enclosed balls of sphagnum moss, can be used to increase shrubs and trees now and for a few months to come. Prune spring-flowering shrubs as soon as bloom has passed. Continue to pinch azalea shoots of rank growth. Watch for spider mites and tea scale on camellias and white-flies on new gardenia leaves toward the end of the month. Spray gladiolus for thrips and roses for black-spot. Set out plants of tender annuals to replace those of the winter group that have stopped blooming.

> SEEDS TO PLANT—ageratum, sweet alyssum, China-aster, balsam, blue lace-flower, celosia, cosmos, cypress-vine, dahlia, gaillardia, globe-amaranth, helichrysum, marigold, morning-glory, portulaca, rudbeckia, salvia, sunflower, tithonia, torenia, zinnia.
>
> BULBS TO PLANT—caladium, eucharis, gloriosa, haemanthus, lycoris.

CENTRAL FLORIDA

Visit daylily plantings to view new kinds that you might like to add to your collection. Order chrysanthemum cuttings. This month may witness a severe drought, so soak shrubs once every ten days, if there is no soaking rain. Fertilize palms, if this chore was not attended to earlier. Prune rank-growing hibiscus bushes, and cut back hydrangeas and other spring-blooming shrubs immediately after flowering. Watch for aphids on all new flushes of growth.

Be guided also by notes above directed to gardeners in northern Florida.

> SEEDS TO PLANT—ageratum, sweet alyssum, China-aster, balsam, celosia, cosmos, cypress-vine, dahlia, gaillardia, globe-amaranth, helichrysum, marigold, morning-glory, portulaca, salvia, sunflower, tithonia, torenia, zinnia.
>
> BULBS TO PLANT—caladium, gloriosa, haemanthus, lycoris, tuberose.

SOUTHERN FLORIDA

Take cuttings of garden favorites. Continue to spray to control thrips on gladiolus and leaf-spot on roses. Set out heat-tolerant annuals—zinnias, marigolds, torenias, and globe-amaranths. Watch for thrips, spider mites, and mealy-bugs on croton foliage, and syringe twice a week with the garden hose as insurance. Graft hibiscus and gardenias on resistant stock. Air-layer crotons, beaumontias, lychees, and guavas. Fertilize amaryllis after flowering for good blooms next year, and divide and replant the bulbs at this time if crowded. Spray gardenias for white-flies.

> SEEDS TO PLANT—sweet alyssum, China-aster, balsam, late cosmos, cypress-vine, gaillardia, globe-amaranth, hollyhock, marigold, morning-glory, torenia, zinnia.
>
> BULBS TO PLANT—caladium, gloriosa, haemanthus, lycoris, zephyranthes.

MAY

Northern Florida

Order chrysanthemum cuttings. Spray camellias and gardenias for mites, scales, and white-flies with summer oil and malathion. Make cuttings of azaleas, hollies, camellias, and other choice shrubs as new growth becomes half-hardened. Layers, too, can be used for increase. Tie dahlias to stout stakes, syringe the plants to control mites, and spray to control thrips. Trim hedges frequently from now until fall. Fertilize spring-flowering sweet-peas for final spring cutting. Dig narcissus bulbs and gladiolus corms when foliage turns brown. Sow cowpeas in garden plots which will be idle during the summer.

> SEEDS TO PLANT—sweet alyssum, balsam, celosia, late cosmos, cypress-vine, dahlia, gaillardia, globe-amaranth, marigold, morning-glory, portulaca, salvia, sunflower, tithonia, torenia, zinnia.
> BULBS TO PLANT—caladium, lycoris.

Central Florida

Cuttings and layers of garden shrubs respond well now. Edge grass plots periodically for a neat garden. Keep lawn grasses well back from specimen trees and shrubs. Control mites, thrips, and mealy-bugs with malathion. Stake and tie tall annuals. Sow seeds of heat-tolerant annuals. Continue to spray for rose leaf-spots and for palm leaf skeletonizer on *Butia* and *Phoenix* palms. Mow winter grass close to aid in its disappearance. Dig bulbs with brown, mature leaves and sow cowpeas. Watch for mildew on crape-myrtle leaves. Trim formal hedges frequently.

> SEEDS TO PLANT—sweet alyssum, balsam, late cosmos, cypress-vine, dahlia, gaillardia, globe-amaranth, marigold, morning-glory, portulaca, salvia, sunflower, tithonia, torenia, zinnia.
> BULBS TO PLANT—caladium, gloriosa, lycoris.

SOUTHERN FLORIDA

Consult list of chores just above. Make cuttings of begonias, torenias, and other flowering favorites. Prune oleanders heavily to keep them in bounds. Spray for control of oleander caterpillar at first signs. Clip fruit clusters from crape-myrtles as soon as blossoms fade and protect foliage from mildew (sulfur dust) and aphids (rotenone or malathion). Cover bare land with a legume for the summer months. Dig bulbs and corms when leaves turn brown. Red spider mites flourish in warm, dry weather. Transplant broad-leaved evergreens not in flush, and also palms. Divide and replant herbaceous perennials that bloom in winter or early spring—daylily, morea, lilyturf, strelitzia, zephyr-lily, maranta, and others.

SEEDS TO PLANT—sweet alyssum, China-aster, late cosmos, cypress-vine, gaillardia, globe-amaranth, hollyhock, marigold, morning-glory, torenia, zinnia.

BULBS TO PLANT—caladium, gloriosa, lycoris, zephyranthes.

JUNE

NORTHERN FLORIDA

Beds can be fertilized and tilled preparatory to setting plants of heat-tolerant annuals for late summer and early fall blooms. Dig bulbs, corms, and tubers when leaves turn brown. Allow glory-lilies to remain in place, however. Fertilize all trees, palms, shrubs, and vines when rains begin. Set out chrysanthemums, and pinch back to insure branching. Watch for aphids and spittle bugs on them. Make cuttings of shrubs and vines, and pinch back vigorous shoots of shrubs for compact habit.

SEEDS TO PLANT—balsam, late cosmos, cypress-vine, gaillardia, morning-glory, portulaca, tithonia, zinnia.

BULBS TO PLANT—dahlia, iris (native).

CENTRAL FLORIDA

Be guided by notes above. Fertilize lawns with sulfate of ammonia after rains start. Trim hedges while tips are succulent and easily clipped, about once each month during growing weather. Transplant palms. Set grass sprigs in new areas to be turfed, or sow seeds if available in wanted varieties. Keep on lookout for chinch bugs in St. Augustine grass and spray, or call your local pest control service at first signs of telltale yellow patches. Divide daylilies.

> SEEDS TO PLANT—late cosmos, cypress-vine, gaillardia, marigold, morning-glory, portulaca, tithonia, torenia, zinnia.
> BULBS TO PLANT—native iris.

SOUTHERN FLORIDA

Study notes in sections above; they apply equally well in southern Florida this month. Plant, from containers, those rare tropical trees and palms you have been planning to add to your outdoor living area. Set out new lawns, or plant ground covers in shady spots where grass will not grow. Set plants of zinnia or marigold from plant bands purchased at your garden center. Keep lawn grasses back from yard specimens of trees. Make summer application of fertilizer to all garden plants, and renew mulch around trees and shrubs. Move iris and ginger-lily.

> SEEDS TO PLANT—late cosmos, cypress-vine, gaillardia, hollyhock, African marigold, morning-glory, tithonia, torenia, zinnia.
> BULBS TO PLANT—dahlia.

JULY

NORTHERN FLORIDA

Fertilize annuals that are being grown for summer cut flowers and spray them at first signs of aphids. Hand picking of brown chrysanthemum leaves is effective in checking the spread of leaf-

spotting diseases in small back-yard plantings. For larger plantings a regular spray program is essential. Rose foliage must be
protected against leaf-spotting diseases as well. Powdery mildew
on crape-myrtles is controlled most easily by dusting with sulfur.
New growth on shrubs should be pinched to insure thick, compact branching. Camellia cuttings may well be made now.
Lawns are growing rapidly and must be mowed regularly for
neat appearance.

SEEDS TO PLANT—late cosmos, gaillardia, portulaca, zinnia.
BULBS TO PLANT—native iris.

CENTRAL FLORIDA

Palm leaf skeletonizer must be controlled on feather-leaved
palms by application of DDT or chlordane with spreader. Yellow
spots in St. Augustine grass may indicate the presence of chinch
bugs, and prompt dusting with chlordane or other insecticide is
needed. Be guided by notes above, which apply equally well to
central Florida.

SEEDS TO PLANT—late cosmos, gaillardia, portulaca, zinnia.
BULBS TO PLANT—native iris.

SOUTHERN FLORIDA

Garden suggestions above can be used also by those who live
near the tip of the peninsula.

SEEDS TO PLANT—late cosmos, cypress-vine, gaillardia, hollyhock, African marigold, morning-glory, tithonia, torenia,
zinnia.
BULBS TO PLANT—dahlia.

AUGUST

NORTHERN FLORIDA

Lawn grass pests must be watched for carefully. Propagate
azaleas and camellias by cuttage. This is the latest that air-layer-

ing is recommended for these shrubs. Daylilies may be divided if this has not been done earlier. Wooden garden stakes should be dipped in preservative before they are stored away. Continue to pick and destroy all disease-spotted leaves of chrysanthemum and rose. Dahlias must be tied to stout stakes and protected against insects. Disbudding must continue if large flowers are wanted.

> SEEDS TO PLANT—late cosmos, gaillardia, lupine, petunia, zinnia.
> BULBS TO PLANT—none.

CENTRAL FLORIDA

Keep as cool as possible.

> SEEDS TO PLANT—late cosmos, gaillardia, petunia, zinnia.
> BULBS TO PLANT—none.

SOUTHERN FLORIDA

Keep as cool as possible.

> SEEDS TO PLANT—arctotis, celosia, late cosmos, cypress-vine, delphinium, gaillardia, hollyhock, hunnemannia, linum, lobelia, African marigold, morning-glory, nicotiana, petunia, phlox, rudbeckia, salpiglossis, salvia, scabiosa, tithonia, verbena.
> BULBS TO PLANT—Easter lily, gloriosa, watsonia.

Index

GLOSSARY

Acid. See Soil Acidity in Index.

Adventitious. Appearing at unexpected places.

Alum. Aluminum sulfate, a soil acidifier.

Annual. Completing a life cycle—from seed to seed—in one season.

Aroid. A member of the family Araceae, like elephant-ear and philodendron.

Axillary. In the leaf axil, the angle where leaf joins stem.

Balled. Dug with a mass of soil intact around the roots.

B & B. Balled-and-burlapped, i.e., the ball of soil enclosed by burlap.

Base. See Soil Acidity in Index.

Bedding plant. Annuals or perennials planted in beds for massed color.

Bract. A leaf-like appendage at the base of a flower or flower cluster.

Calcareous. Containing considerable lime.

Calyx. The sepals collectively; the outermost set of parts in flowers.

Cambium. The thin layer separating bark and wood and adding new cells to each.

Cane. A long, vigorous shoot.

Chelate. An organic compound which holds iron or other heavy metals in a form easily taken in by plants, when it would otherwise become insoluble.

Compound. Of leaves or inflorescences, consisting of several branches which may branch in turn.

Coniferous. Bearing cones, like pine trees.

Corm. An underground stem, swollen with stored food, upright in the soil with a terminal bud at the top.

Corolla. The petals collectively, especially if they are joined together in their lower parts.

Crown. Of stems, the branched canopy on top of the trunk; of roots, the main roots branching from the stem at the ground surface.

Deciduous. Shedding leaves regularly, usually in autumn, and bare of leaves for several months each year.

Digitate. Compound with several branches from a common point.

Dormant. Not growing, inactive, usually because of low temperature.

Edging plants. Annuals or perennials planted at the sides of a walk or at the front edge of a bed.

Epiphyte. A plant which grows upon the trunk or branches of other plants but draws no food from them.

Espalier. A shrub trained in two dimensions—height and breadth—with very little depth.

Evergreen. Covered with leaves at all times, never bare.

Forcing. Stimulating to growth out of a normal season.

Fungicide. A compound which kills fungi.

Glabrous. Smooth, without hairs.

Green manure. Plants grown primarily to be turned under for increasing soil organic matter.

Hammock. A tree-covered area slightly higher than surrounding low, marshy terrain.

Herbaceous. Never developing woody tissues.

HUMUS. The dark brown, slowly decomposable residue from organic matter turned under the soil.

INFLORESCENCE. A flower cluster.

INSECTICIDE. A compound which kills insects.

LATENT. Of buds, one still present on older stems and capable of growth.

LOAM. A mixture of sand, silt, and clay, usually a very desirable soil.

MARL. Finely divided limestone, looking like gray clay.

MUCK. Deposits of plants under water which have been decomposed until no identifiable particles remain; very finely divided.

NEUTRAL. See Soil Acidity in Index.

OFFSET. A basal branch or sucker from a bulbous plant or palm.

PALMATE. With main veins radiating from a common point.

PANICLE. A compound raceme, with main axis and lateral branches.

PEAT. Deposits of plants under water which have been only partially decomposed, with identifiable fragments; coarser than muck.

PERENNIAL. Growing from year to year with no fixed life span.

PETAL. One of the inner set of leaflike flower parts, usually some color other than green.

PETIOLE. The leaf stalk which bears the leaf blade or leaflets.

PINNATE. With leaflets borne on both sides of a common axis.

PISTIL. The female organ of a flower, containing ovules.

PISTILLATE. Having pistils but no stamens in the flower.

PUBESCENT. Covered with hairs; velvety.

RACEME. An unbranched inflorescence with the oldest flowers at the base and newer ones toward the tip as the axis grows, each flower on its own small stalk.

RHIZOME. A horizontal underground stem.

RUGOSE. With wrinkled, washboard-like surface.

SCAPE. A stout, leafless inflorescence stem with one or several flowers at its top.

SCION. A piece of stem with two or more buds, inserted in a stock by grafting; also spelled cion.

SEPAL. One of the outermost set of leaflike organs in a flower, usually green.

SPATHE. A large, often brightly colored, leaflike organ enclosing an inflorescence in aroids and palms.

SPIKE. A raceme with flowers seated directly on the central axis, with no individual flower stalks.

STAMEN. One of the male organs in a flower, producing pollen.

STAMINATE. Having stamens but no pistils in the flower.

STOCK. The rooted stem on which a scion is grafted; a rootstock.

SUBTROPICAL. A climate with mild winters having occasional but brief periods of freezing temperature.

TRANSPIRATION. The loss of water from living plant parts.

TRIFOLIATE. Having three leaflets; correctly but less commonly written trifoliolate.

TUBER. A swollen, underground storage stem borne horizontally at the end of a slender branch.

WHORL. A group of plant parts all arising around an axis at the same level.

Condensed pest control guide

Pest	Suggested Control
Algal leaf-spot	Usually not controlled.
Ants	Chlordane dust.
Aphids	Lindane, malathion, or nicotine sulphate.
Azalea defoliators	DDT, malathion, or toxaphene.
Azalea leaf-miners	Lindane, malathion, or nicotine sulphate.
Azalea petal blight	Zineb or Acti-dione.
Bagworms	DDT or chlordane.
Borers	Wrap trunks of newly transplanted trees.
Caterpillars	DDT, chlordane dust, or toxaphene.
Chlorosis	Correct growing medium, supply minor elements.
Cottony cushion scales	Malathion.
Crickets	Poison bran bait.
Earthworms	DDT as a soil drench.
Fire blight	Deep pruning with sterilized shears.
Florida red scales	White summer oil emulsion
Grasshoppers	Chlordane dust, toxaphene, or BHC.
Lace bugs	Malathion, BHC, toxaphene, or white summer oil
Leaf-miners	DDT, lindane, malathion, or Diazinon.
Leaf-gall fungus	Pick malformed leaves and destroy.
Leaf-spot fungi	Captan, ferbam, Phaltan, or copper compounds.
Mealy-bugs	Malathion.
Mildew	Acti-dione PM, sulfur dust, or Karathane.